Essays in Honour of
John Humphreys Whitfield

JOHN HUMPHREYS WHITFIELD

Essays in Honour of

JOHN HUMPHREYS WHITFIELD

*presented to him
on his retirement from
the Serena Chair of Italian
at the University of Birmingham*

EDITED BY
H. C. DAVIS   D. G. REES
J. M. HATWELL   G. W. SLOWEY

London 1975
ST GEORGE'S PRESS
*for the Department of Italian
University of Birmingham*

*This edition
is limited to 600 copies
of which this is
No 129*

Printed and published with the assistance of
the Modern Humanities Research Association

Published in 1974 by
ST GEORGE'S PRESS
37 Manchester Street, London W.1
for the Department of Italian
University of Birmingham

Designed and produced by John Mitchell
Printed in Great Britain by
W. & J. Mackay Limited, Chatham

CONTENTS

FOREWORD

This volume of essays is intended to mark the esteem and affection widely felt for John Humphreys Whitfield upon his retirement from the Serena Chair of Italian at the University of Birmingham after a tenure of twenty-eight years.

Under his guidance as scholar and teacher the University Department of Italian has steadily expanded until latterly he has been backed up by four full-time members of staff. Over this period he has played a full and active part in fostering Italian studies in Britain: his many books, essays and papers bear ample witness to the precision of his scholarship, his penchant for the unorthodox, his love of humanism and desire to instil it in others, and the depth and range of his interests. These include a wide knowledge of painting and figurative art combined with a sensitive awareness—shared by Joan Whitfield—of the value and beauty of *objets d'art*. The Departmental environment itself has benefited greatly from this.

His energy and enthusiasm in a wider sphere will not quickly be forgotten. For many years he has been an Editor and, more recently, Senior Editor, of the Annual Review of the Society for Italian Studies; conferences and symposia, national and international alike, have been enlivened by his presence and contributions; the Dante Alighieri Society and the Venice in Peril Fund are indebted to him for unfailing efforts to promote their ends; and the award of a *Commenda al merito della Repubblica Italiana* in 1973 was a recognition of such manifold services.

We hope that the variety and quality of the papers in this volume will be a worthy testimony to a distinguished *maestro*: his retirement cannot but evoke a sense of loss in colleagues, pupils and friends; but this emotion is tempered by the thought that he will continue to be near at hand, pursuing things of the mind with undiminished vigour.

The Editors wish to thank hard-pressed contributors for their patience and forbearance; the Secretary of the Italian Department at Birmingham, Mrs Hilda Bruce, for her willing cooperation;

Professor Mario Montuori and the Italian Institute for their generous support and encouragement; the Vatican Library for permission to reproduce a page of the autograph of Speroni's *Canace*; and the Modern Humanities Research Association and the Research Committee of the University of Birmingham for the financial assistance they have provided.

It is deeply regretted that harsh economic facts have made it impossible for the Editors to include an article by Professor Montuori or to accept offers of contributions from a number of other friends and colleagues of Professor Whitfield.

H. C. DAVIS

J. M. HATWELL

D. G. REES

G. W. SLOWEY

J. H. Whitfield

John Humphreys Whitfield was born in Wednesbury in 1906 and educated at Handsworth Grammar School and Magdalen College, Oxford. Fifty years ago, joint or combined degrees were less common in British universities than they are today, and an honours degree usually implied specialization in one subject, at least towards the end of the undergraduate course. To those who have known Professor Whitfield only as an Italianist, it may be surprising to learn that it was with a first-class degree in French that he graduated in 1928. He stayed on for a further First in Italian. The knowledge of French language and literature that he acquired in his school and university courses was reinforced and extended in the seven years that he spent teaching French at King Edward School, Sheffield, and the tastes formed in that time have persisted: his French has remained fluent, and close attention to his publications and conversation will reveal that French culture (particularly of the sixteenth, seventeenth and eighteenth centuries) has been a major influence in his life.

Nevertheless, from his undergraduate days there has been one other period in European culture that has fascinated him even more than the French seventeenth century (and to which, as he himself has from time to time helped to demonstrate, that century is in any case closely related): the Italian Renaissance. To his interest in the literature of this period and in other aspects of the culture of Italy, Whitfield was fortunately able to return professionally in the Autumn of 1936, when he became University Lecturer in Italian at Oxford. This second Oxford period of his life was to last exactly a decade. In 1946 he left to become Serena Professor of Italian Language and Literature in the University of Birmingham, where he has continued to teach until what University regulations refer to as the normal age of retirement. In fairness to Nature, it should be noted that, when she made Whitfield somewhat intolerant of official procedures, she also saw to it that he was congenitally or prenatally equipped to outwit them. His birth on 2 October, 1906, meant that for him the 'normal age of retirement' would be the end of the academic year 1973–4. Had he, with his customary impatience, burst on the scene on 30 September, he would have been banished a year earlier.

When Whitfield went back to Oxford in 1936 the Serena Professor there was still Cesare Foligno, who had occupied the Chair when Whitfield had been an undergraduate and who had been teaching in Oxford since 1909. E. R. Vincent, who had been Whitfield's tutor, had recently left to go to the Chair in Cambridge. The events of 1940 sent Foligno back to Italy; the teachers of the Oxford school of Italian had thus been reduced to two when I arrived there during the war. One of the two, Miss Olga Bickley, was a Fellow of St Hugh's, and her duties were not limited to teaching Italian. The other, J. H. Whitfield, seemed to spend his afternoons in some mysterious work for the Admiralty. Yet lecturing continued over a considerable range of Italian literary and linguistic history, and Whitfield was ready to offer individual tuition to any man who had come to the University to read Italian. In those days boys who wished to read arts subjects and who had come to the end of their normal school career before the age of eighteen usually went up to the University for a year, or part of a year, before leaving for war service. Students in scientific and medical disciplines remained for longer at the University, since their studies were adjudged to be relevant to their eventual role in the war. There were also service cadets on six-month courses (some of them reading Italian), a few men who were unfit for military service or who had been discharged from the forces, and women students. My impression was that both the teachers of Italian were busy enough.

My first meeting with my tutor was entirely unremarkable. He saw me for two minutes at the Taylorian on the first Saturday of term, asked me to write an essay on Foscolo, and arranged that I should take it to his house at eleven on the following Thursday for our first tutorial. I arrived a little early on that day and, before the pupil then with J. H. W. had emerged, was given a cup of coffee and a cheerful welcome by Mrs Whitfield[1]. At ten past eleven F. J. Jones came out, and I went in. I did not know Jones at that time, and I remember thinking that he appeared somewhat incensed, rather as if he had been the teacher and had been dealing with a pupil wilfully reluctant to see the light. I had no time to meditate on this strange occurrence, as I was immediately invited to start reading my essay. Since I had come from the Taylorian, where I had heard a lecturer on French literature mumble, sometimes inaudibly and consistently monotonously, for almost an hour, I was tempted to deliver my piece on Foscolo as if it had been one of my grandfather's sermons, just to show that in places outside Oxford people had discovered that the voice, suitably modulated, could be useful in communication. I realized in time that for that kind of performance I was not suitably placed in relation to my audience: for he was seated at a high desk-chair and had motioned me to squat on a low pouffe. In the posture in which I found myself, even the most ambitious orator would have decided against pulling out most of the stops: if, for instance, after a fortissimo passage, one had attempted to lean forward suitably before the pause and the *vox humana*, one would have been bent double, with one's utterance reduced to a squeak, or fallen off the edge[2]. I chose to sit bolt upright and, after two or three minutes, had just worked up to a brisk pace at moderate volume when my tutor got up and turned sideways, with his hand outstretched towards me, but with his forefinger pointing to the ceiling, where my hurried glance could discern nothing unusual. He then interrupted me with a vehemence which threw me right out of my stride and a statement that made it clear that our conceptions of poetry could have little in common. I started reading again. A couple of minutes later came the second interruption: this consisted of quite a patient and illuminating exposition of the views implied in the first. These seemed to me no less heretical when clarified, and I now replied at some length, exaggerating somewhat by way of illustration and thus laying myself open to some painful ripostes, delivered with diabolical zest. Fierce argument followed. As I walked back to college, I was still smarting from what I saw as the injustice of some of the criticism, as well as reflecting ruefully on the fact that the long and bitter argument had caused me to miss college lunch. But I also wondered that anyone could be so concerned over minor deviations from the reasonable in my views on Foscolo. During the rest of that year the tutorials varied from the stormy to the peaceful. With time, I learned not to make quite so many statements that I could not adequately defend with the evidence available to me. But the concern never diminished; as a seventeen-year-old undergraduate, I found myself contradicted with the same seriousness that I was later to see Whitfield devote to the views of major Italianists. Nor was there only disagreement: there was an occasional word of praise, while the short terminal reports to the college were puzzlingly generous additions to the criticism of the tutorials. Moreover, after the first few weeks, discussion ceased to be confined to my essay, and frequently moved to painting and architecture. Whitfield had discovered that my Welsh education, which had given me an ear tolerably well trained for verse, had left me with eyes trained for no art at all. His tutorials and later the proximity of the Ashmolean (to which he early directed my attention) were here the beginning of opportunity. As a teacher he had, apart from concern and interest, one invaluable gift: either on account of his eccentric modes of expression or one's own injured vanity, it was impossible to forget what he said. I frequently went over the arguments of the tutorials in my mind long after they were over, sometimes imagining myself stating the arguments I should have used instead of those I had.

When I went back to Oxford at the end of the war, I saw another side of Whitfield. At the end of my time in the mines, I had suffered from corneal ulcers, and when I returned to academic life, I found that I was unable to read and write as I had been used to doing. To my intense embarrassment, I was unable to produce an essay for three consecutive tutorials. Then, as antibiotics were adapted for use against infections of the eye, things began to improve. The man who had been so quick to pounce on defects in my first-year essays now showed unsuspected patience and kindness. I was astonished at the end of my first term back, when I appeared before the Provost and Fellows of my college to hear my tutors' reports read, to find that there was no mention of the missing essays, only a vague sentence to the effect that during the gap in my academic career, little or nothing of my Italian seemed to have been lost. Then, just as I felt that I was recovering my strength in tutorials and able to hold my own again, he was gone: in a vacation in 1946 he wrote to his pupils to explain that, since he had been elected to the Serena Chair at Birmingham, he would not be there when they returned.

I think it is fair to say that, while he was at Oxford, Whitfield was not at all widely known in the academic world outside. His first book, *Petrarch and the Renascence*, had appeared in 1943. Although it was a provocative work, it was hardly to be expected that, in time of war, when academic contacts were few and many Italianists in Europe were engaged in a desperate struggle to keep alive, much attention could be spared for a scholar who showed a tendency to militant criticism in dealing with aspects of medieval and early Renaissance literature. Circumstances had changed by 1947, when *Machiavelli*, considerably delayed by post-war shortages, eventually appeared. It, too, had been written in what seems to me now to have been the most polemical time in Whitfield's life, and it was followed by a period of controversy, which was the background to the composition of several of the *Discourses on Machiavelli* which were much later to be collected in a rich volume. I remember the original delivery of one of those discourses very well.

With splendid initiative, the Society for Italian Studies had in 1953 contrived to bring to England the first congress of the *Associazione Internazionale per gli Studi di Lingua e Letteratura Italiana* and to give that august body a good start in life by arranging for it a smoothly organized series of meetings in Cambridge, on which the sun obligingly shone for almost the whole week that the gathering lasted. The congress began on Sunday, 16 August. The papers on the opening days were good and all quietly and politely received by scholars who, in the first large post-war assembly devoted to their discipline, did not know many of the colleagues from other countries who were sitting with them. Whitfield addressed them on the Tuesday after dinner. I remember the occasion because I was sitting immediately behind Professor Fredi Chiappelli, and I saw his neck turn red when the speaker made, near the beginning of his lecture, what Chiappelli considered an unjust remark on his recent book on Machiavelli's language. As soon as the lecture ended, Chiappelli got up and made a vigorous reply. So did others, some with a polemical note until then absent from the congress. When the chairman properly brought the meeting to a close after the usual time for discussion, the majority of us moved to a nearby public house to continue the argument less formally but no less seriously. The congress had caught fire. I date my friendship with Fredi Chiappelli from that evening, when I found myself on his side for a part of the argument and thus earned for myself a number of boutades that showed that J.H.W. had lost nothing of his agility in the years since our first tutorial. I think it is true to say of Whitfield that it was from that congress that he emerged as a figure well known to the major Italianists in Europe, some of whom have marked their friendship for him by contributing to the present volume.

It was hardly likely that they would forget him after the congress, for he was by this time in full spate. Although, in the years following the publication of *Machiavelli*, he was frequently engaged in controversy over the author who has probably been the predominant preoccupation of his academic life, he had not by any means limited his scholarly activity to the sixteenth century. A slim volume on *Dante and Virgil* (1949) was followed by a much fuller one on *Giacomo Leopardi* (1954). Judging by my experience in tutorials over the last twenty years, I think this is the work by Whitfield which has been of greatest assistance to undergraduates, largely because of the help given them to appreciate the consistency of Leopardi's thought in the chapter 'Leopardi's system in the pages of the *Zibaldone*'. Whitfield's taste for Leopardi's verse also led to the publication of his English verse translation of the *Canti* (1960) and an edition of them for the Manchester University Press (1967), as well as to the delivery of a commemorative address at Recanati. By the end of the fifties he had also written the book which was to be the best known of his works outside the universities, the general survey which first appeared as the Pelican *Short History of Italian Literature* in 1960 and was later published in a hard-cover edition by Cassell, as well as his *Barlow Lectures on Dante*, also printed in 1960. To those of us who remember the interests of the early Whitfield, it is not surprising that in more recent times he should have returned to Machiavelli and to Valla (on whom there was so enthusiastic a chapter in his first book, *Petrarch and the Renascence*).

This output should be considered in relation to the demands made on Whitfield's time by his other duties. When he first went to Birmingham, he went to a department that consisted only of himself. In 1948 he was joined by an ex-pupil from Oxford, D. G. Rees. For several years these two laboured without any other permanent colleague to lay the foundations of the large and respected department that Birmingham has today: then came a period of more rapid expansion in staff as well as students. But the fifties and sixties also saw Whitfield play an ever larger role in Italian studies outside his own department. He had been a member of the committee of the Society for Italian Studies since the war. In 1949 he became one of the editors of *Italian Studies* and, after the death of Professor Roberto Weiss in 1969, its Senior Editor. Moreover, from the retirement of Professor E. R. Vincent in 1962 until he himself retired from its executive committee in January 1974, he was Chairman of the Society. He has also been in wide demand as an examiner and as an adviser to other universities in connection with new developments in Italian and senior appointments arising from them. And few British Italianists, if any, can have accepted more invitations to lecture without fee to University departments and societies: as one whose students have benefited from this aspect of his industriousness, I must record that I have never known him to refuse. In all of these activites, he has shown himself willing to go beyond what is asked of him. A glance at the bibliography, for instance, will show that, apart from his editorial duties, he has contributed a great deal to *Italian Studies* in the form of articles and reviews. He also reviewed very widely in other journals.

Nobody who knows him imagines that Professor Whitfield's retirement from the Serena Chair at Birmingham will mark the end of his devotion to Italian literature. Indeed, we trust that it merely means that he will now have more time to give to those aspects of his work which he has found most inspiring. If we ask him to pause at this stage in his career to receive a tribute, it is merely because we consider this an appropriate point at which to express the respect and affection we feel for a colleague, who, by teaching and writing, by organizing and examining, and by censuring and provoking and encouraging, has made a notable contribution to Italian studies. This he will no doubt continue to do, and with more vigour than most of us, for, if I may steal a characteristic phrase from one of his books, Life is where Life is.

University of Manchester   T. GWYNFOR GRIFFITH

NOTES

1. Like other undergraduates, I was to find that the unfailing kindness of Mrs Whitfield made my occasional brief periods of waiting as pleasant as her devotion to the visual arts made them interesting. To anyone who knew them in those days, it is not surprising that the two young Whitfields who were always with her should have acquired the tastes and knowledge that have shaped their later careers.

2. I had not yet realized that some at least of my English contemporaries might take a very different view of the techniques which I regarded as necessary: see Donald Davie's poem 'The Evangelist' (in *Brides of Reason*).

A Bibliography of
the Published Writings of
Professor J. H. Whitfield

Apart from two review articles mentioned in the list, this bibliography excludes reviews, which have appeared in the following publications: *Oxford Magazine; Modern Language Review; Medium Aevum; Notes and Queries; Spectator; Journal of Ecclesiastical History; Italian Studies; French Studies; Comparative Literature; Renaissance News; European Studies Review; Times Literary Supplement; Birmingham Post; English Renaissance Quarterly*

1936

1. 'Approach to Ariosto', *Scrutiny*

1938

2. 'A newly discovered Dürer drawing for the Ashmolean', *Old Master Drawings*
3. 'A second edition of Capecelatro's *Storia di Napoli* prepared by the author', *Italian Studies*, ii, pp73–76
4. 'Boccaccio and Fiammetta in the *Teseide*', *Modern Language Review*, xxxiii, pp22–30

1943

5. *Petrarch and the Renascence.* Oxford, Blackwell, 173pp (Republ. New York, 1966, and in Italian, Bari, 1949.)
6. 'The anatomy of Virtue', *Modern Language Review*, xxxviii, pp222–225

1944

7. 'New views upon the Borgias', *History*

1946

8. 'The doctrine of *virtú*, *Italian Studies*, iii, pp28–33

1947

9. *Machiavelli.* Oxford, Blackwell, vii, 167pp (Republ. New York, 1966)
10. 'Poetry and patriotism in Giacomo Leopardi', *Modern Language Review*, xlii

1948

11. 'Gli studi italiani in Inghilterra dopo il 1939', *Lo Spettatore Italiano*, June, pp86–88

1949

12. *Dante and Virgil*. Oxford, Blackwell, v, 103pp
13. 'Savonarola and the purpose of the *Prince*', *Modern Language Review*, xliv, pp44–59
14. *Petrarca nel Rinascimento*. Bari (Italian edition of no. 5)

1950

15. 'Ariosto', 'Manzoni', 'Pascoli', 'Petrarch', 'Tasso', *Chambers' Encyclopedia*
16. 'Italian Literature', *Hutchinson's Encyclopedia*

1951

17. Review of *Discourses of Niccolò Machiavelli; trans. L. J. Walker, Italian Studies*, vi, pp100–106

1953

18. 'Machiavelli and Castruccio', *Italian Studies*, viii, pp1–28

1954

19. *Giacomo Leopardi*. Oxford, Blackwell, vii, 261pp (Republ. in Italian, Naples, 1964)

1955

20. 'On Machiavelli's use of *ordini*', *Italian Studies*, x, pp19–30
21. 'The politics of Machiavelli', *Modern Language Review*, l, pp433–443

1957

22. 'From Matchavel to Machiavelli', *Comparative Literature*
23. 'Machiavelli secondo i piú recenti studi', *Problemi della Pedagogia*, iii, 6, pp295–310

1958

24. 'Machiavelli e il problema del Principe', *Problemi della Pedagogia*, iv, i, pp61–78
25. 'Machiavelli e la via di mezzo', *Problemi della Pedagogia*, iv, 2, pp254–271
26. 'Discourses on Machiavelli VII: Gilbert, Hexter and Baron', *Italian Studies*, xiii, pp21–46

27.   'Pirandello and T. S. Eliot: an essay in counterpoint', *English Miscellany*, ix (Published in Italian, *Le Parole e le Idee*, iv, 1–2, 1962)

1959

28.   *Studi sul Machiavelli*. Cambridge, 50pp (Items 23, 24, 25 of the bibliography)
29.   'Il caso Machiavelli', *Le Parole e le Idee*, i, 2–3, pp80–94
30.   'Il caso Guicciardini', *Le Parole e le Idee*, i, 4, pp185–192

1960

31.   *A short history of Italian literature*. Pelican, 302pp (Hardcover edition, Cassell, 1962: 2nd Pelican edition, 1970)
32.   *Barlow Lectures on Dante, 1959: Essays in the Like and the Unlike*. Published as a supplement to *Italian Studies*, xv, 48pp
I. The changing face of Dante. II. Dante in Boccaccio. III. Dante and Leopardi.
33.   'T. S. Eliot's "Four Quartets" and their Italian version', *English Miscellany*, xi, pp211–222
34.   'Thoughts on the state of Universities', *Hibbert Journal*, lix, pp118–124

1961

35.   'Prefazione al Leopardi', *Le Parole e le Idee*, iii, pp150–154
36.   'Aeneas Sylvius Piccolomini', *Life of the Spirit*

1962

37.   *Giacomo Leopardi, Canti; translated into English verse*. Napoli, Scalabrini, 268pp
38.   *A short history of Italian literature*. Cassell (Hardcover edition of no. 31)
39.   'Dante e Leopardi', *Atti del I Congresso Nazionale di Studi Danteschi, 1961* Florence
40.   'Mr Eustace and Lady Morgan', *Italian Studies presented to E. R. Vincent* pp166–189

1963

41.   'La Belle Charite: the Italian pastoral and the French seventeenth century', *Italian Studies*, xviii, pp33–53
42.   'A note on Molière and M.lle de Scudéry', *Le Parole e le Idee*, v, 1–2, pp175–187

1964

43.   *Giacomo Leopardi*. Naples (Italian edition of no. 19)
44.   'In margine alla legge Tobler-Mussafia: la proclisi della negativa', *Le Parole e le Idee*, vi, 1–2, pp61–72
45.   'Sir Richard Fanshawe and the Faithfull Shepherd', *Italian Studies*, xix, pp64–82

1965

46. 'Dante e Virgilio', *Le Parole e le Idee*, vii, 1, pp3–16 (Spanish translation in *Dante en su centenario*, Madrid, 1965)
47. 'Dante's Virgil', *Books Abroad*, May, pp136–140
48. 'Poesia italiana e gusto neoclassico', *Problemi di lingua e letteratura italiana del settecento*, Wiesbaden, pp70–83

1966

49. *Machiavelli.* (New York edition of no. 9)
50. *Petrarch and the Renascence.* (New York edition of no. 5)
51. 'Leon Battista Alberti, Ariosto and Dosso Dossi', *Italian Studies*, xxi, pp16–30
52. 'Vitalità di Giacomo Leopardi', Il Casanostra, lxxxiii, pp5–16

1967

53. *Giacomo Leopardi, Canti.* Edited with introduction and notes, Manchester U. P., viii, 215pp
54. 'Postilla per la poesia di Michelangelo', *Le Parole e le Idee*, ix, pp206–209
55. 'Humanism v. scientific humanism', *Arts v. Science*, ed A. S. C. Ross, Methuen
56. 'La Metamorfosi della Novella', *Atti del Congresso Internazionale di Studi Pirandelliani*, Florence
57. 'The Charlecote manuscript of Machiavelli's *Prince*', *Italian Studies*, xxii, pp6–26

1969

58. *Discourses on Machiavelli.* Cambridge, Heffer, viii, 243pp
59. Introductory essay to facsimile reprint of the Charlecote Manuscript, *Il Principe*, Wakefield, ppv–xxix
60. 'Presentazione del volume *Pagine Italiane* del Prof. Aldo Ferrabino, 30 giugno, 1969', *Il Veltro*, xiii
61. 'La Belle Charite II: Racine, Molière and the *Pastor Fido*', *Italian Studies*, xxiv, pp76–92

1970

62. *A short history of Italian literature.* (Second Pelican edition of no. 31)
63. 'Chinese Armorial at Lotherton Hall', *Burlington Magazine*, June, p661

1971

64. 'Machiavelli's use of Livy', *Livy*, ed T. A. Dorey, Routledge & Kegan Paul, pp73–96
65. 'Momus and the nature of humanism', *Classical influences on European culture*, ed R. R. Bolgar, pp177–181

66.   'The poetry of Michelangelo', *Collected essays on Italian language and literature presented to Kathleen Speight*, pp101–121

1972

67.   'Considerazioni pratiche sui *Discorsi*', *Studies on Machiavelli*, ed M. P. Gilmore, pp361–369
68.   Review of Penguin version of L. J. Walker's translation of the *Discourses of Niccolò Machiavelli*, *European Studies Review* (Subtitle: 'Father Walker rides again')

1973

69.   'Machiavelli, Guicciardini, Montaigne', *Italian Studies*, xxviii, pp31–47

1974

70.   'Chaucer fra Dante e Boccaccio', *Atti del Congresso di Studi sul Boccaccio in Inghilterra*, Olschki, Florence
71.   'Castiglione and the culture of Europe', introductory essay to *The Courtier*, Dent
72.   'Petrarch', 'Pirandello', *Encyclopaedia Britannica*.

University of Birmingham   G. W. SLOWEY

Dante's Vision of God:
an Exposition of Paradiso XXXIII

We read in the third chapter of the Book of Exodus that when Moses tended Jethro's sheep, he led them to the westside of the desert, and there, by the mountain of God, he saw a preview of the Incarnation —a thornbush ablaze with fire, which yet was not consumed. And Moses said: 'I will now turn aside, and see this great sight, why the bush is not burnt'. But God called to him out of the midst of the bush and said: 'Moses, Moses!'. And he replied: 'Here am I'. And God said: 'Draw not nigh hither; put off thy shoes from off thy feet, for the place whereon thou standest is holy ground'.

If there is any patch of holy ground in Italian literature it is surely the final Canto of Dante's *poema sacro*, for its subject is no longer the vision of Man, of Nature, or of created things, but the Vision of God Himself, than which no greater theme for prose or poetry can be conceived. All the preceding ninety-nine Cantos have led up to this climax, which, more than anything else that has gone before, earns for the Comedy the name Divine. The Vision of God is not only the end of the poem but also the end of all human existence. Like Moses, we too have turned aside to see this great sight, and (metaphorically at least) we stand unshod on the threshold of the Beatific Vision of the Essence of God Himself.

Dante is in the Tenth Heaven, the Empyrean. In the thirtieth Canto of *Paradiso* he has begun to gaze upon the Celestial Rose, whose petals are God's Elect of both the Old and New Covenants. This lovely and effective image of the Church Triumphant fills with its fragrance the intervening Cantos XXXI and XXXII, which might be described as the unfolding of the Rose. Already before the end of Canto XXX Beatrice has pointed out, in that immense amphitheatre of rapture whose centre is a sea of light, the empty seat which awaits Henry of Luxembourg, the Holy Roman Emperor; but when, in the first half of Canto XXXI, Dante turns to her for her familiar guidance, he discovers that she is no longer by his side. Instead, he sees beside him 'an old man, dressed like the glorified'— that is, the Saints. His last guide is revealed as St Bernard of

Clairvaux, whom Dante-the-poet has chosen to usher Dante-the-character into the presence of God.

The prime reason for the choice of this twelfth-century contemplative mystic to complete what Virgil and Beatrice had begun is that Bernard was reputed to have seen God in Essence during his lifetime. But almost equally cogent for Dante was the fact that in the divine mediatorial economy of Grace, the feudalism of Heaven, St Bernard stood in the same relationship to the Blessed Virgin Mary that she stood to God: he had her ear, as she had Christ's. Legend even had it that he had been mystically suckled by her milk. Certainly in all the past millennium of Catholic piety, no one has done more to promote the cult of Mary than St Bernard, and in Dante's day no one was held to have such access to the Virgin as he. Do you seek Divine Grace in the crisis of your life? Let Bernard pray to Mary, and she will pray to God.

Little wonder, then, that in the last three tercets of Canto XXXII Bernard has told Dante that in order to sustain the Vision of God without dismay, Grace must be won by prayer, *grazia da quella che puote aiutarti* (line 148). Then the Canto closes with the words: 'E cominciò questa santa orazione'. And so the final Canto opens with the prayer addressed by St Bernard to the Virgin Mary. Like most prayers, it falls into two distinct parts: first, praise (lines 1–21), and, secondly, petition (lines 22–39); but, unlike many prayers, it is clothed in language so limpid and so warm, so direct and so moving, that it might soothe the scruples of an Orangeman. In St Bernard's mouth it has an authentic ring, for many of its concepts and images are culled from his writings. Much (but not all) of its charm was captured for fourteenth-century England by Chaucer's adaptation of it in *The Prologe of the Seconde Nonnes Tale*, beginning: 'Thow Mayde and Mooder, doghter of thy Sone . . .'.

Here is Mariolatry at its bewitching best, and I use the word 'Mariolatry' advisedly, for the cult of Mary in this prayer transcends *hyperdulia*. Here, too, is the poetry of Courtly Love in apotheosis, and we remember that Bernard of Clairvaux was a Frenchman who lived from 1091 to 1153, hence a younger contemporary of the first of the troubadours whose poetry is known to us, Guillaume, Count of Poitiers, who died in 1127 at the age of 56. Purged of the erotic overtones so often heard in his devotional writings, the language of his prayer is the fine flower of *fino amor*; yet Blessed Mary excels every other lady sung by the poets of Provence or Sicily, for she is Maid, Mother and Spouse in one. Eleanor of Aquitaine may be Queen of France and England, but Mary of Nazareth is Queen of Heaven, and in Feudal Paradise her attributes appear divine: 'Regina, che puoi / ciò che tu vuoli' (lines 34–35). Did not Albertus Magnus call her 'the Great Goddess'?

Vergine Madre: at once we are plunged into the poetry of paradox. Indeed, the opening tercet of the Canto expresses a triple paradox, reflecting the quintessential conundrum of Christianity, whose symbol is the Cross which bears a contradiction at its heart. For a Maid to be a Mother, and a Mother remain a Maid, is not strictly a practical impossibility, because of the known if rare phenomenon of parthenogenesis; but it is so contrary to normal human experience that the juxtaposition of the two conditions captivates the imagination, and from the Canto's outset prepares us for the stupendous paradox of the Incarnation glimpsed at the Canto's climax. Mary has the radiant purity of a virgin (who knew not a man, as she tells the angel Gabriel) and yet the tender compassion of a mother; and she possesses them in one and the same act, at one and the same time.

Figlia del tuo figlio: the second paradox is still more striking, for it has the ring of formal impossibility that the Virgin-Mother should be the daughter of her Son. Like a round square, dark light, or living death, there is a logical contradiction here whose epigrammatic pithiness hits us between the eyes and drives home the factual mystery of God's Incarnation. Christ begets Mary by creation, Mary begets Christ by generation, Christ re-begets Mary by regeneration . . . *figlio della figlia, figlia del figlio, figlio della figlia* . . . the images begin to spin, and the mind reels in breathless adoration. (I note in passing that there is no stress on 'figlio' here: the focus is wholly on Mary as the vehicle of Incarnation.)

The third paradox beacons compellingly from the second line. It is true that in the language of Courtly Love *umiltà* has a particular and non-scriptural meaning which has been defined as the radiant power to confer Grace, to be benign; but here the context of seeming contradiction, controlled by that poignant picture of Mary's *umiltà* in the tenth Canto of *Purgatorio*, demands that we hear the echo less from the Dolce Stil Novo than from the *Magnificat*: 'Deposuit potentes de sede, et exaltavit humiles'. The Mother of Jesus is lowly, yet exalted more than any other creature. Nor is this only a time-sequence of rags-to-riches, Cinderella, or King Cophetua and the beggar maid: not just that Mary was once a village-girl from Nazareth, and is now Queen of Heaven (although this pregnant line contains that meaning also): but rather—like Luther's description of the believer, *Simul justus et peccator*—Mary is both lowly and exalted at one and the same time, just as she is Maid and Mother not in series but in parallel, to filch a term from Physics. *Umile e alta più che creatura* was as true yesterday in Bethlehem as it is today in the Empyrean, because it is what characterises her morally and makes her attractive to God, although sovereignly chosen before time was (line 3). This moral attractiveness to God is seen also in Beatrice, who takes character from Mary, for Dante claims in the third Canzone of his *Vita Nuova* 'ché luce de la sua umilitate / passò li cieli con tanta vertute, / che fé maravigliar l'etterno sire'.

Now *umiltà* and *altezza* are cardinal concepts in Scripture. Satan was *alto*, but had the wrong kind of *altezza*—he would go higher and usurp the place of God: hence he is cast down in enforced *umiltà*, crawling upon his belly as a serpent, the lowest of the low. By contrast Christ is shown as *alto, altissimo*, existing in the form of God, yet empties Himself in voluntary *umiltà*, becoming obedient unto death, and that the death of the Cross: wherefore God has highly exalted Him (Philippians ii 5–11).

This is the true nobility of human nature, of creatureliness, to be lowly yet exalted. Mary, full of Grace, has it intrinsically, and to such a degree that the Creator of the human species—*il suo fattore* (line 5)—did not disdain *di farsi sua fattura*, to be made the product of that species, to be found in fashion as a Man, to become the Son of Man, the Son of Mary.

Did I say that the first tercet contained three paradoxes?—I should have said three-and-a-half, for that a point in time should be the subject of eternal counsel, that Mary should be 'termine fisso d'etterno consiglio', is half paradoxical in itself. In Scripture the eternal counsel means the deliberation of the Triune Godhead before the foundation of the world to effect the salvation of Man and the formation of the Bride of Christ, prefigured in Eve. This counsel centred in the Incarnation of the Son, and logically entailed its means, the Virgin's womb. St Paul expounds this cosmic theme in his Epistles, but the Roman liturgy also appropriated the words of Proverbs viii (which properly refer to Christ as the Divine Wisdom, *la somma sapienza* of *Inferno* III 6) and applied them to Mary: 'The Lord possessed me in the beginning of His way, before His works of old. I was set up from everlasting, from the beginning, or ever the earth was'.

And so late in time the Virgin's womb became the vehicle of the Incarnation of God (line 7), the warm bed in which the Holy Spirit planted the divine seed of rekindling Love—and Dante here alludes to Gabriel's promise to Mary that 'the Holy Ghost shall come upon thee', Love being the distinguishing attribute of the Spirit— the Love which, in the eternal peace of the Empyrean (though Chaucer understood *l'etterna pace* to refer to Mary's womb), flowered in the Celestial Rose, the 'fiore' of line 9. The poet is echoing St Ambrose: 'In Virginis utero...lilii floris gratia germinabat'.

God is Love, and what was conceived in the Virgin's womb was Incarnate Love, the Son of God, in the heat of whose passion was

born the Church of God. But, as so often happens in Dante's art,
the role of Christ is assumed by *das Ewig-Weibliche* that *zieht uns
hinan*: it is the Mother, rather than the Son, who 'beacons from the
abode where the Eternal are'. Indeed, three merging images of
Mary fill the third and fourth tercets (lines 7–12): she is the seed-bed
of Love in the history of time, the noonday torch of Charity 'qui' in
Heaven, 'a noi' = to the Blessed of the Celestial Rose, and the living
spring of Hope down there on earth, 'giuso' (line 11). The melting
metaphors coalesce: the spark of Love rekindled in her womb becomes the meridian blaze in highest Heaven, the fountain of Hope
for men on earth—*mortali*—who have yet to pass through death.

The following three tercets (lines 13–21) are less image-packed,
less complex with concepts, and describe the greatness of Mary in
the pure but plain poetry of praise. Our Lady is the puissant chate-
laine of God's Castle, usurping the function of Christ while He is on
Crusade. All the heavenly qualities of Jesus that gleam from the
Gospels are here transferred to Mary: the *grazia*, the *benignità*, the
misericordia, the *pietate*, the *magnificenza*, the *bontate*: only in Mary
they are joined in *creatura*, in Christ in *creatore*. Who would be so
fond and foolish as to seek favour with God and not repair to this
Mighty Mistress of His Treasury of Grace?—his desire would plum-
met to earth (line 15) like Icarus in the heat of the sun. Mary not
only comes to the aid of those who express their need in prayer, but
often freely anticipates their supplication—and Dante had experience of this in the first two Cantos of *Inferno*. This paean of
praise reaches its full volume in lines 19–21: what a living compendium of virtues both human and divine is Mary! Thus in her in-
trinsic worth did she *nobilitare sì l'umana natura* (line 4) that God the
Father chose her to be the Mother of His Son—and that mother's
heart of compassion is open to all her children in need.

The second half of St Bernard's prayer begins with line 22, when
he turns from praise to petition. His requests on Dante's behalf are
four: first, that he may see God; secondly, that he may so transcend
his mortal condition that he may enjoy the Vision; thirdly, that he
may be preserved from pride or folly after so great a sight; and
fourthly, that he may henceforth be characterised by the virgin
affections of Mary herself.

Now this man, says Bernard, is nearing the end of an immense
journey, and begs you for the Grace and power to complete it. He
has come from one end of the Universe to the other, from the sump
and sink-hole of the Pit to this highest pinnacle of Heaven, and in the
course of this journey he has seen 'le vite spirituali ad una ad una'
(line 24), all those saints and sinners, demons and angels—Francesca,
Farinata, Ulysses, Cato, Manfred, Bonagiunta, Matelda, Piccarda,

Cacciaguida, Adam, Virgil, Statius, Beatrice—which remain in our minds after reading the preceding ninety-nine Cantos, and this has all been part of his *salute*, his salvation. We recall Virgil's words to Dante in *Inferno* I: 'A te convien tenere altro viaggio', followed by the outline of the three realms through which he must pass, and the sights that he must see: but his journey will not be complete until he sees the uncreated and Eternal Spirit, God Himself, and this will be his *ultima salute*, his final salvation. (Bernard here is Dante's spokesman and advocate; it is Dante who supplicates, Bernard who voices his supplication.)

In the following tercet (lines 28–30) we find one of the hall-marks of heroic sanctity: Bernard longs more for the good of another than for his own. We are reminded of Moses being willing to be blotted out of God's book rather than that his people should perish; of St Paul, wishing himself to be accursed for Israel's sake; but supremely of our Lord Jesus Christ Himself, 'the Man for Others' (as Bonnhoeffer called Him), who, though He knew no sin, was made sin, in order that we might become the righteousness of God in Him. Bernard in his lifetime had so yearned to see God that his yearning had been satisfied in the Beatific Vision; but now in glory he burns with even more ardent desire that Dante should share that sight. He prays that Mary may pray that the last vestiges of original sin may be dispersed from his soul, so that the *Sommo Piacer* may be revealed to him in the Vision of God (line 33). The echo is Virgilian, and comes from the second book of the *Aeneid*, where Venus promises to dispel from the sight of her son Aeneas the clouds which prevent him from seeing the gods who are helping the Greeks to overthrow Troy.

St Thomas taught that the loss of original righteousness (*justitia*) in the fall of Adam inflicted four wounds on human nature: *ignorantia in intellectu, malitia in voluntate, infirmitas in irascibili, et concupiscentia in concupiscibili*. Such are the 'nubi di sua mortalità' that Bernard prays Mary to disperse by her intercession; for just as these clouds gathered from the disobedience of Eve, so they can only be dispelled by the obedience of Mary—it was a charming scholastic conceit that the AVE of Gabriel's annunciation reversed the EVA of Satan's seduction.

Nothing in all this incomparable Canto appeals to me as more spiritual than Bernard's third request that after so great a vision Dante's affections might be kept pure (lines 34–36); for this concern with after-care, so often neglected by the evangelist, is proof positive of the authentic pastor. We notice here that the Saint prays nothing doubting (the secret of effective prayer is faith), for he says *dopo tanto veder* when he is begging for the Grace for Dante to see (line 36).

Bernard's protégé is to have an experience that few other men have had: will it unbalance his mind and heart? Will he be lifted up in pride? Or will he sink back into the spiritual fornication of *la selva oscura*, and dally once more with *pargolette*? May Queen Mary, who *can* do what she *will*, keep his affections whole, and may her Virgin *aegis* protect and canalise his human impulses. Then with a sweep of his uplifted arms, Bernard calls Mary's attention to Beatrice (it is the last glimpse and mention of her in the poem) and *quanti beati* of the Celestial Rose whose hands are clasped in the heavenly fellowship of silent supplication: the greatest prayer-meeting on record, and all for one man, Dante. So ends Bernard's *santa orazione*.

Mary's eyes, beloved by God the Father and reverenced by God the Son, are fixed on Bernard as he prayed, and make plain to us how welcome, how well-received, how dear to her are all such prayers which come from the heart. The Virgin does not smile, as Beatrice has so often smiled, and as Bernard will smile in line 49; she utters no word with her lips, but speaks volumes with her eyes, which grant the Grace which Bernard sought in prayer. (If it were not too banal in such a context, one might say that they flash the Green Light for Dante to go ahead to his ultimate goal.) Then, like Beatrice before her, the Virgin directs her gaze once more to the *etterno lume*, in which we must believe that it can penetrate deeper and more clearly than any other creature's.

Is Mary, who stands at the apex of a pyramid of ladies in this poem which contains Francesca, Matelda, Pia and Beatrice, a poetically realised figure here? Or is she the conventional Donna of the Courtly Love lyric, the blue and gilded plaster Madonna above the altar in the side-chapel, starry-eyed, encircled by lighted tapers? We must confess that in *Paradiso* she is both more and less than human; Dante depicts her at this climax of his Comedy with such restraint—for nothing must detract from the Vision of God—that she appears little more than a stucco goddess. If we seek her human personality, we must search the cameos of *Purgatorio*.

Dante is now drawing near to the 'end of all desires' (line 46), is crossing the threshold of the Beatific Vision, that *ultimus finis humanae vitae*, as St Thomas called it; but line 48 surely cannot mean, as one version suggests, that at this moment of all moments Dante 'ended the ardour of his craving': *finii* means rather 'I brought to its very point of culmination' that desire which was so thrillingly close to its satisfaction.

With a gesture of his hand and an encouraging smile, Bernard invites Dante to raise his eyes on high and gaze on God, but the poet is now so attuned to the Saint that the invitation is superfluous, for Dante's sight, becoming pure, is already entering upon the

Vision of the 'lofty light which in itself is true'—that intellectual consummation which will engage him to the poem's end. *Exeunt* Bernard, Mary, all Angels and every other creature: henceforth Dante is conscious only of God.

We come now to the second and greater part of the Canto, which describes what Dante saw as he gazed into the Eternal Light. His Vision of God is articulated in five phases: first, he sees nothing but the light itself (lines 52–84); secondly, he discerns in that light the consummation of the Universe (lines 85–105); thirdly, he describes in one Substance the three Persons of the Trinity (lines 106–126); fourthly, he views within the Second Person the image of the Incarnation (lines 127–132); fifthly and finally, by supernatural revelation he glimpses the why and wherefore of it all in the Love that moves the sun and the other stars (lines 133–145). Five phases: but the Vision is not a kaleidoscope, for all five phases cohere and coexist—opening out from one another like the sections of a telescope —and together make up the total Vision of God.

The four tercets which contain lines 55–66 hang together, and stress the ineffability of Dante's experience. Gazing upon the Ultimate Reality, his vision transcends his power of speech, for Dante-the-character sees more than Dante-the-poet can express. Following Petrocchi's reading *mostra* in place of the traditional *nostro* in line 56, we understand the poet to confess that from the moment his eyes began to feast upon that Beatific Vision his power to see was greater than speech can show or is capable of representing, for in view of such a vision human utterance fails, gives up the ghost, admits itself vanquished—just as human memory is incapable of coping with 'tanto oltraggio' (line 57).

Oltraggio: the basic meaning of this suggestive word is 'excess', 'a going beyond a given limit', whether by way of outrage, transcendence or abuse. The sight of God is an *oltraggio* to the human eye, and the remembrance of that sight is an *oltraggio* to the human memory. God tells Moses in the thirty-third chapter of Exodus: 'You cannot see My Face, for man shall not see Me and live'. The life of God is in *oltraggio* of human means, and only divine Grace can fit us to bear its vibrant superabundance.

Dante hammers the point home with one of his compelling similes: 'Qual è colui che somniando vede'—or, as Petrocchi here prefers (line 58): 'Qual è colui che sognando vede, / che dopo 'l sogno la passione impressa / rimane, e l'altro a la mente non riede, / cotal son io [...]'. Poetry, said Wordsworth, takes its origin from emotion recollected in tranquillity, and practically all that Dante recollects from this transcendental experience is the emotion: but what poetry springs from that emotion! We dream: we see, and, as we see in

sleep, we feel; we wake: the image fades, but the feeling roused
remains. This is a common enough experience: we have an en-
chanting dream, and two hours later we sing blithely in the bath,
though for the life of us we could not explain why; we have a hideous
nightmare, and come down to breakfast apprehensive and de-
pressed, though quite what it was we saw escapes us. The content
of the vision is beyond our reach, and hence incommunicable, but
la passione impressa rimane.

What remains with Dante always, a comfort and confirmation
for the rest of his natural life, is the emotion of joy which abides
within him, the sweetness of ecstasy distilled within his heart from
that supreme experience (lines 61–63). 'O joy! that in our embers /
Is something that doth live, / That Nature yet remembers / What was
so fugitive.' The Vision leaves its residue of *dolcezza* within Dante
because it assures him of final salvation, of *ultima salute*, but it does
so primarily because it was divinely beautiful in itself. The artist in
him, as well as the philosopher and the pilgrim, is satisfied to all
satiety. (Fascinating in this poem is the relationship between the
mind and heart: where the prayer to the Virgin is all heart, the
re-evocation of the Vision is all mind; the only time in the whole
Canto that Dante mentions his heart is in this line 63.)

The Vision vanishes like a dream, and 'a la mente non riede';
but I apprehend that the point of the double simile in the following
tercet (lines 64–66) is one of communication. Each snowflake falling
from the hand of God is stamped with an intricate and unique
geometrical pattern, reminiscent of what Dante will see in the
Blessed Trinity, yet in the heat of the day it turns to formless slush.
But this is not all the poet's meaning: not just that snow melts in the
sun—that would be somewhat trite—but rather that in the sun
the snow 'si disigilla', that is to say, loses its distinctive message, the
imprint of animal hoof or human foot. Likewise the oracular pro-
nouncement—*la sentenza*—of the Cumaean Sibyl (described by Virgil
in the third book of his *Aeneid*) was irretrievably lost when the wind
rustled through her cave and scattered the tree-leaves on which it
was written. Snow and leaves bore intelligible seals which sun and
wind unsealed.

And therefore Dante invokes the Supreme Light, so far above
our utmost conceiving, to give back to his mind a little (and the
'poco' of line 69 is echoed in lines 74 and 123) of what that Light
appeared to him in his Vision, and to empower his tongue to be-
queath but a spark of its glory to future generations; for if that
Vision may in some degree be recaptured by his memory and enshrined in his poem, his readers will have a better idea of God's
victory: and I take the *vittoria* of line 75 to hark back to the Prologue

of St John's Gospel, in which the Incarnation of the Word is seen as
the triumph of Light over Darkness, and to the words of Jesus Himself: *Ego vici mundum* (St John xvi 33).

Here Dante prays to God as God—there is no more recourse to
Apollo or the Muses; and from his prayer we learn the dual purpose
for which he writes his Comedy: first, the greater glory of God (line
71), and, secondly, the salvation of Man. Nor are his words addressed
to his contemporaries only, but constitute an inheritance *a la futura
gente*: we too are included in his audience and embraced in his
purpose, for the didactic scope of his poem is as universal as its
theme.

The second half of the Canto is intended to contain God's answer
to this prayer. The following two tercets (lines 76–81) remind us of
that cardinal Pauline exhortation to work out our own salvation with
fear and trembling, for it is God who works in us both to will and to
do His good pleasure (Philippians ii 12–13). He who hesitates is lost,
smarrito (line 77), and if Dante had but averted his eyes as he had
done hitherto in the growing light of Heaven, had he but blinked in
the face of this incandescence, he would have been dazzled by it. He
who endures to the end will be saved, said Christ, and Dante per-
severes until he attains the fulness of the *ultima salute* promised in line
27, until he reaches with his gaze the Infinite Goodness, *il valore
infinito* of line 81. But, like St Paul, and with an instinctive Christian
reflex, having said that he was *ardito a sostener* (as though it were all
his doing), in the next breath he attributes it all to the Grace of
God.

Oh abbondante grazia!—that a mere man in flesh and blood should
dare to gaze on God was not of nature but of Grace, for in his
natural state no man can or shall see God. That it was *abounding*
Grace echoes the great Pauline affirmation that where sin abounded,
there did Grace superabound. The divine sovereignty and compassion have taken up Dante, a blind sinner lost in the labyrinth of
sin—the *selva oscura* of the poem's first tercet—and have directed his
opened eyes upon the Eternal Light: and in that sustained and
rapturous vision his sight is spent. Line 84 does not mean, as Lord
Vernon supposed, that 'I exhausted all there was to be seen in it',
but the exact opposite: 'I was all exhausted in the seeing of it'.

The next three tercets describe the second phase of Dante's Vision,
in which he sees the consummation of the Universe in God. Being a
clerk and a scholar, it is natural that he should use a bookish image:
what I saw in the depths of that Eternal Light, he tells us, was like a
volume in which are bound together all the pages which are scattered through the Universe (the obverse of the Sibyl's leaves in lines
65–66)—a stupendous *Summa Cosmologica* whose binding is Love.

Legato con amore in un volume: one summer I was taken a tour of the restoration laboratories of the National Library in Florence, where scores of skilled workers repair the ravages of the flood of 1966; I saw the damaged leaves, floating free in a hundred tanks, being brought together with devoted care in a binding more durable yet flexible than ever before: *con amore*. Dante, too, had passed by the bookbinder's *bottega* in Florence and seen half a thousand loose manuscript sheets—hung, strewn and festooned around the workshop—brought together and bound with loving care in one great volume, perhaps the *Summa* of Albertus or Aquinas. But here 'con amore' means so much more than with loving care: it is Love itself that by its very nature binds the Universe together in one, Love that was born in Bethlehem, that held Jesus to the Cross, that moves the sun and the other stars. God is Light, says St John the Divine, and God is Love: in the Light of God Dante discovers His Love.

Of course the elements of cosmic reality bound together in God are not pages of a book, but are analysed in terms of Aristotelian physics as substances, accidents, and their relationship (*costume*). Dante sees them as if fused together (*conflati insieme*) in such a way as to form a simple—that is, single and unadulterated—light. Line 90, however, is patient of another (but, in my judgement, weaker) interpretation, which refers 'lume' to the poet's description, and understands him to say that all that he can offer is a poor ray of light compared with what he saw.

The following tercet describes something very like a conditioned reflex (lines 91–93). Pavlov's dogs salivated at the sound of a gong: Dante's pulse quickens, his joy expands at the mere sound of his own description. As we have seen, the content of his Vision *quasi tutta cessa*, but the concomitant emotion remains, and from the strength of this emotion he infers the magnitude of what he must have seen. He believes he saw—the 'credo' of line 92 is more assertive than 'I think'—*la forma universal di questo nodo*. In the first Canto of *Paradiso*, Beatrice explained to him: 'Le cose tutte quante / hanno ordine tra loro, e questo è forma / che l'universo a Dio fa simigliante.' We are, of course, viewing the Universe with scholastic eyes and describing it in scholastic terms. What Dante saw was the Platonic idea or form of the Universe itself, the conflation of substance, accident, and their metaphysical relationship (here pictured as 'questo nodo') which entails the very principle of causality, of what causes a cause to cause: the imponderable Bradleian relation between the noumenon and the phenomenon. Dante sees the Universe in God. Peering into the Mind of the Creator he beholds the inter-relationship of all created things. 'Though earth and man were gone, / And suns and universes ceased to be, / And Thou wert left alone, / Every existence would exist in Thee.' For in that *mens creatrix* is sustained the totality of all that is.

The most famous crux of the whole Canto is contained in the following three lines (94–96). What does Dante mean by 'Un punto solo m'è maggior letargo'? Where leading commentators have not agreed, I can offer only my own approach to a solution. I find the clue to his meaning in those two words 'impresa' and 'ammirare'. Jason's voyage in the dawn of history to obtain the Golden Fleece was a pioneering enterprise, the first time man had ever crossed the sea by ship—an event from which the Ancient World dated its calendar; as such it was a pale forerunner of Dante's journey, in the consummation of history, to obtain the Beatific Vision, a still more pioneering enterprise, in which for the first time man had crossed outer space to reach the Empyrean and gaze into the light of God. They were both 'imprese', and both evoked wonder: the voyage of the *Argo* in Neptune, the Vision of God in Dante (lines 97–99, where the verb 'mirare' is repeated): but Jason's enterprise is better remembered two thousand five hundred years after the event than was Dante's Beatific Vision one moment after it took place. What Neptune wondering saw is remembered to this day: it was the shadow of the *Argo*. What Dante wondering saw he could not have told you five minutes afterwards. In either case, the wonder endures —*la passione impressa rimane*: but in Dante's case, the content of the Vision is lost in oblivion, *letargo*.

The good ship *Argo* is not chosen fortuitously here, dictated by the rhyme, as sometimes happens in the Comedy. There is an obvious sense in which Christopher Columbus and Neil Armstrong are linked in history: the first man to set foot on the New World, having crossed the Atlantic, and the first man to set foot on the Moon, having crossed intervening space. Similarly, what the *Argo* was to the element of water, Dante's journey is to the dimension of space. They are both objects of wonder; indeed, the voyage of the Argonauts, with all its attendant circumstances, was a fount of wonder even to themselves, as we learn from the second Canto of *Paradiso*. But the point here is that what Neptune *saw* when the strange shadow passed over him that day is better remembered twenty-five centuries later than what Dante *saw* in the Beatific Vision *un punto solo* after he had seen it.

Line 96 here is incongruous, but stupendous. Incongruous, in that a supreme Christian poet, at the most sacred moment of his religious experience, when we might suppose that the pure gold of his Christianity would glitter unalloyed, should drag our eyes from the very Face of God down to the depths of the sea, and weary our minds with some pensioned-off pagan divinity. Stupendous, on the other hand, in its imagination: we see old Neptune down there, lolling complacently on his throne in post-prandial stupor on the bed of the Aegean Sea, trident abandoned on his lap, when suddenly he starts up amazed and dumbfounded as a strange, long shadow passes over him and, in passing, cuts off the meridian sun. A magic moment of purest poetry.

The more Dante rapt and wondering gazes into the Light, the more his mind is enflamed to gaze, for it is impossible that one who fixes his eyes on God should ever avert them to another sight (lines 97–102). For God is not only the *ben dell'intelletto*, as Virgil describes the Vision of Absolute Truth in the third Canto of *Inferno*, but also the *ben del volere*, or rather, the good which is the object of the will is all gathered and concentrated in that Eternal Light of God, and outside of that Light all that is perfect within it is imperfect (lines 103–105).

With line 106 begins the third phase of Dante's Vision, and it begins with a still more abject confession of his incapacity to describe in words what his eyes saw in the Light of God, *pur a quel ch'io ricordo*—even of what he remembers. Compared with the magnitude of his Vision, from now on his power of speech will prove less than a suckling's. For him that Vision progresses from phase to phase, yet there is no change or variation or fluctuation in God, who from eternity to eternity is the same, nor does His *vivo lume* pass through successive phases. The change, the transformation, is all in Dante himself, as his sight gains strength with seeing. 'In Thy Light', sang the Psalmist, 'we shall see light'; therefore line 114 is a fitting commentary on the whole of *Paradiso*: 'mutandom' io, a me si travagliava' the one sole appearance of the Beatific Vision. Just as Beatrice has explained to him in Canto IV that the souls of the Saints in Heaven are not in reality deployed through space as they appear to him throughout the Cantica, so for the glorified the Vision of God is immediate and entire. But Dante is still in flesh and blood, and has not passed through death; hence for him the whole experience of Paradise is phased to suit his finite apprehension, as God tempers the wind to the shorn lamb.

The Christian doctrine of the Trinity teaches us that God is one *substantia* yet three *personae*, and as Dante's sight is strengthened to see (lines 115–117), he descries in that uncreated Coherence of the Essence of God (which is both deep and clear) three circles distinguished by three colours and yet of identical dimension. How this can be is a mind-defeating mystery, and Dante intended it to be, for Virgil had warned him in Ante-Purgatory: 'Matto è chi spera che nostra ragione / possa trascorrer la infinita via / che tiene una sustanza in tre persone'.

I have no doubt that Dante's prime source here, and for much of this final Canto, is the first chapter of *Ezekiel* (which he cites in *Purgatorio* XXIX), for the prophet's great Vision of God before the Incarnation is there described in terms of light, colours and wheels. 'The heavens were opened'—Ezekiel affirms—'and I saw visions of God...a fire infolding itself, and a brightness was about it, and out of its midst as the colour of amber...The appearance of the wheels ...was like unto the colour of a beryl: and they four had one likeness...as it were a wheel within a wheel.' And behind Ezekiel is the repeated Mosaic prohibition of *Deuteronomy* IV: 'When the Lord spake to you out of the fire, ye saw no similitude, therefore make no similitude'.

Dante depicts the Trinity in terms of *giri* because the circle or sphere is the perfect figure, flawless and uniform from every point of view. There is a formal and impersonalised beauty about his image which reminds us of a geometrical pattern, for it is studiously unanthropomorphic. But *giri* also suggest motion, the wheels that turn, and (perhaps to us at least) the wheels within wheels of clockwork with its harmony, cooperation, precision and balance. The social life of the Trinity is not static, but active with the activity of Love, and the heavenly spheres take character from the life of God: they wheel around us in *giri*—the Moon a sphere, the Planets spheres, the Sun a dazzling sphere.

This active life of the Trinity is seen in the next tercet (lines 118–120), for within the Triune Godhead one of the *giri* appeared to Dante to derive from another by reflection, as a second rainbow was thought to derive from the first. This spawning of one rainbow by another—'nascendo di quel d'entro quel di fori'—has already been described in *Paradiso* XII, and in view of that earlier description it is clear that Dante is here alluding to the Eternal Generation of the Son by the Father. *L'uno* of line 118 is the Father, *l'altro* is the Son, whilst *il terzo* of the following line is the Holy Spirit, a circle of fire which is breathed forth equally from the Father and the Son; so that in this tercet we find imagined not only the Alexandrian doctrine of Generation, but also the Western doctrine of Procession: for Scripture teaches that the Spirit proceeds from the Father, but the Catholic Church added 'and from the Son'—and we may recall that the addition of *Filioque* to the Creed was the final straw which ruptured East and West in the Great Schism of 1054.

Once more the poet's visionary flight is punctuated by a confession of inadequacy, in which his tongue bewails its incapacity to match his eye, and where the 'poco' of line 123 harks back to the 'poco' of lines 69 and 74. But here he is not so much blaming himself as the limitations of human language.

The fourth phase of Dante's Vision is enshrined in this Canto's third articulated prayer, contained in the next three tercets (lines 124–132). 'O luce etterna che sola in te sidi, / sola t'intendi, e da te intelletta / e intendente te, ami e arridi!' Nowhere in the whole poem do we find lines more tellingly packed with subtle meaning than this outburst of pure adoration as Dante's being responds to the light of the Trinity, like a flower opening to the sun. Throughout the Comedy, but especially in *Paradiso*, Dante is transforming the theologian's concept into the poet's image, and for him the theologian *par excellence* is St Thomas. The warp and woof of his thinking here is Thomist in this apotheosis of scholasticism: the *intendente* is the Father, the *intelletta* the Son, and *chi ama e arride* is the Holy Spirit. The Blessed Trinity is complete in itself, and (in the best sense) complacent in its mutual understanding and reciprocal Love. The Eternal Light of God is its own source and its own satisfaction. Eternity is consummated in the inner life of the Trinity, for the secret of perpetual motion is there, and the secret of unending rest. Where God abides in all the majesty of underived existence, there the Mind and Heart of Love are one.

That circle which, thus conceived in the Eternal Generation, appeared in the Trinity as reflected light, is revealed and identified as the Son. When Dante's eyes had stared at Him for a while, that second circle 'dentro da sè, del suo colore stesso, / mi parve pinta de la nostra effige' (lines 130–131) – seemed to me etched with *our* likeness, in fashion as a Man: Man in God – humanity in the Trinity – yet all divine: *del suo colore stesso*. Not only Dante's eyes, but his very face is absorbed in the marvel of its mystery.

This glimpse of the humanity of Christ revealed in the Triune Godhead of the Trinity is the climax of the Divine Comedy. Line 131 undoubtedly refers to the Incarnation, yet even a pious Jew might expect the Ultimate Reality of God to bear 'la nostra effige', for we read in the beginning of the Law that 'God created Man in His own image, in the image of God created He him'. Ezekiel sees in God 'the likeness of a man'; and in the Book of Daniel, when Nebuchadnezzar cast Shadrach, Meshach and Abednego into the midst of the burning fiery furnace, he asked his counsellors: 'Did not we cast three men bound into the midst of the fire?' They answered and said: 'True, O King'. Then said he: 'Lo, I see four men loose, walking in the midst of the fire, and they have no hurt; and the form of the fourth is like the Son of God.' (Daniel iii 24–25).

Pinta de la nostra effige: it is Jesus whom Dante sees, the incarnate Son of the Father, conceived of the Holy Ghost in the womb of the Virgin Mary, born in Bethlehem under Caesar Augustus, suffered under Pontius Pilate. 'He is the image of the invisible God,' –

declares St Paul – 'the first-born of all creation; for in Him all things were created, in heaven and on earth, visible and invisible, whether thrones or dominions or principalities or authorities—all things were created through Him and for Him. He is before all things, and in Him all things hold together...For in Him all the fulness of God was pleased to dwell...' (Colossians i 15–17, 19).

The wonder of the Incarnation is the crowning marvel of the Vision, the central miracle of time and space: 'Our God contracted to a span, / Incomprehensibly made Man'—yet neither does His humanity detract from His divinity, nor does His divinity quench His humanity. It is the great sight which Moses turned aside to see: the thorn-bush is ablaze with fire, yet is it not consumed.

Cur Deus Homo?—we ask with Anselm—and *cur Homo Deus?* It is the problem of all problems that engages Dante's intellect in the next two tercets (lines 133–138) and baffles his highest powers. Like the geometer who gives his mind wholly—*tutto s'affige*—to the problem loosely defined as 'squaring the circle', which was propounded by the Greeks of Antiquity and shown to be insoluble in the nineteenth century, so Dante's mind is wholly absorbed *a quella vista nova* (line 136)—at that strange, that extraordinary sight. 'Veder voleva (and let me call attention to this verb, for it links with the *voglia* of line 141 and the *velle* of line 143) come si convenne / l'imago al cerchio e come vi s'indova'—'I wanted to see *how* the image of humanity—*la nostra effige*—was fitted to the circle of divinity—*quella circulazion* of line 127 above—and *how* it has its place there'—but Dante's intellect is incapable of taking it in, for just as the circle cannot be measured in terms of the square, in the same way God is irreducible to human terms. The wings of the poet's understanding had been insufficient for such flight had not his mind been struck by a lightning flash of divine illumination (the fifth and final phase of his Vision) *in che sua voglia venne* (line 141)—in which his wish, his desire to see—back to line 137—to understand the mystery of the Incarnation was satisfied by the intuition of Divine Love.

But at this point, when Dante's gaze had penetrated to the heart of the Beatific Vision, his magisterial power to imagine and conceive failed him. The final intuition of Love is inexpressible in image or concept, neither may the memory follow the intellect in the consummation of desire—for, as we learn from the opening lines of *Paradiso*: 'perché appressando sé al suo disire, / nostro intelletto si profonda tanto, / che dietro la memoria non può ire'. But Dante is at peace, for at last his desire and will, so sadly at variance at the beginning of his journey, are brought into harmony with the Will of God, and, like a wheel that spins with even motion, are revolved by the Love that moves the sun and the other stars.

And so the great poem ends, as it began, *in medias res*. It began without prologue, it ends without epilogue. It began with an image, it ends with an image: the bark of Dante's genius comes home to haven in full sail. The hundredth Canto ends, as all human activities sooner or later must end, including this exposition: but to the Vision of God there is no end, only a glorious beginning.

University of Birmingham   PHILIP MCNAIR

Il Ludo Dantesco dei Barattieri

'Baratteria' significava, in antico, genericamente, 'insidia truffaldina', specie al livello popolaresco: per es., il piccolo imbroglio giocato nelle piazze, nei mercati, ai danni degli ingenui. Ma significava anche la colpa di coloro che, ricoprendo cariche pubbliche, concedevano dietro pagamento, o per ottenere altri vantaggi personali, uffici, privilegi, assoluzioni o condanne, eccetera. Non è mancato chi (M. Principato, lettura del c.XXI dell'*Inferno*, Roma, Signorelli, 1951) ha sostenuto, con ingegnosa erudizione, che i peccatori puniti nella 5ª bolgia dantesca siano generici truffatori; ma i testi danteschi non consentono di accettare questa tesi: non solo i personaggi introdotti son tutti barattieri per così dire pubblici, che ricoprono 'uffici' (XXII 81; anche in *Parad*. XVI 56–57 colui che 'per barattar ha l'occhio aguzzo' è un uomo politico); ma di Lucca, cioè d'una città che secondo Dante è zeppa di barattieri, è detto che 'del no per li denar vi si fa ita', cioè per denaro si approva quel che si dovrebbe respingere, o comunque si cambia parere: il che evidentemente si riferisce a organi di governo, assemblee, tribunali e simili.

Tuttavia, bisogna osservare che il contrapasso, l'unico che sia indicato dal poeta e che del resto è il solo ravvisabile, allude genericamente all'astuzia. A un barattiere di fresco scaraventato nella pece i diavoli dicono (XXI 53–54): 'coverto conven che qui balli, / sì che, se puoi, nascosamente accaffi', cioè arraffi denari agendo copertamente: un contrapasso che si addice a qualunque imbroglione e non specificamente a magistrati corrotti. Coerentemente, di uno dei dannati della bolgia 5ª, frate Gomita, è detto, a caratterizzarne la colpa, che era stato in vita 'vasel d'ogni froda' (XXII 82). In conclusione, sebbene i barattieri pubblici possano, a rigore, anche non esser furbi e agire sfacciatamente, il poeta, secondo il significato generico di 'baratteria', attribuisce loro come carattere essenziale la furberia, la 'malizia', i 'lacciuoli' di cui il personaggio principale della bolgia, Ciampolo, ha 'gran divizia'. Tutto l'episodio è intessuto appunto sul tema della furberia, fortunata e sfortunata.

Esso comprende i canti XXI e XXII, buona parte del XXIII, e

ha il suo epilogo alla fine di quest'ultimo canto: questa ampia
sequenza ha, travalicando la misura dei canti, una compatta unità
narrativa e tonale. Assistiamo qui a una grande 'rappresentazione
sacra', che segue l'altra svoltasi dinnanzi alle mura della città di
Dite e anticipa l'altra di *Purg.* VIII 19 ss.: in tutte e tre sono in
primo piano i diavoli; ma mentre nel dramma dei canti VIII–IX
dell'*Inferno* spira vento di tragica violenza e di sortilegio, e la
rappresentazione del *Purgatorio* si risolve in un solenne rito liturgico,
in questa commedia la violenza e la crudeltà dei diavoli son viste in
tutt'altra luce.

La scena della commedia è un nero fiume di pece bollente: all'inizio
non si scorgono che le bolle e il 'gonfiar tutta' e 'riseder compressa'
della 'pegola spessa': i dannati e i diavoli non si vedono: gli uni se
ne stanno sommersi, gli altri acquattati sotto il ponte che sovrasta la
bolgia; la scena si popolerà e si animerà in un secondo momento.
I diavoli della palude Stigia erano una minacciosa anonima
moltitudine: 'più di mille.....da ciel piovuti' (*Inf.* VIII 82–83);
anche questi dei barattieri sono numerosi, dal momento che essi
dilaniano un dannato 'con più di cento raffi' (XXI 52) ma il poeta
ha cura di personalizzarne alcuni, esattamente tredici: il primo che
appare è anonimo, ma ben individuato nella persona e nell'animo;
gli altri dodici hanno ciascuno il suo nome, alludente per lo più
a caratteristiche fisiche o della sua indole; e ciascuno con una sua
propria parte o particina nella commedia. Accanto a dannati e
diavoli, Virgilio e Dante: qui l'uno e l'altro, come non mai, 'personaggi'. Nella commedia il dialogo ha parte naturalmente rilevante:
dei diavoli coi dannati, con Virgilio, tra loro; di Virgilio con Dante,
di Ciampolo con i diavoli e con Virgilio; né mancano le didascalie,
cioè le descrizioni degli atteggiamenti e dei gesti che accompagnano
il dialogare.

Come il dramma sullo Stige, anche questa commedia può essere
distinta in 'atti'. Primo (XXI 22–57): un diavolo arriva in Inferno,
da Lucca, nel momento stesso della visita di Dante, e butta giù nella
pece un anonimo dannato, un magistrato, un 'anziano' di Lucca,
che per essere tornato alla superficie, è subito dilaniato e dileggiato
dai diavoli. Secondo atto (XXI 58–fine; XXII 1–15): Dante,
incuriosito ma non atterrito testimone delle precedenti scene, per
consiglio di Virgilio si nasconde dietro una sporgenza del ponte;
il maestro scende sull'argine che divide la 5ª dalla 6ª bolgia, e ferma
con autorità i diavoli che gli si erano fatti incontro minacciosi:
parlamenta con un loro emissario, Malacoda, mettendo come di
consueto innanzi la volontà del cielo. Sicché l' 'orgoglio' del diavolo
cade; Virgilio è ormai sicuro d'aver vinto quest'altra battaglia
diabolica e chiama a sé il discepolo; questi accorre, ma non ha

deposto la paura e si stringe al maestro. Malacoda spiega che il
ponte che partendo da quel punto avrebbe dovuto scavalcare la
bolgia seguente è stato spezzato dal terremoto seguito alla morte di
Cristo: procedano i due sull'argine e ne troveranno uno intatto:
darà loro come scorta una 'decina' di diavoli, che sceglie a uno a uno,
nominandoli; loro capo sarà Barbariccia. Ma la scorta è sospetta a
Dante; Virgilio lo rassicura; la decina si muove così lungo l'argine,
e i poeti con essa: Dante, tuttora non persuaso, si è tuttavia rassegnato
alla brutta e pericolosa compagnia: 'nella chiesa / coi santi e in
taverna coi ghiottoni'.

Terzo atto (XXII 16-fine): uno dei dannati, Ciampolo, che si è
come gli altri sollevato un po' sul pelo della pece per avere un po'
di sollievo, non fa in tempo a ritrarsi all'apparire dei diavoli; è
uncinato e deposto sull'argine. Dice chi egli è; pure tra i diavoli
avidi di esercitar crudelmente le loro unghie e uncini, può, con la
protezione di Barbariccia, continuare il discorso, nominare due dei
suoi compagni di pena, due sardi, dir delle loro baratterie. Intanto
ha pensato una 'malizia': propone ai diavoli di appartarsi in modo
da non esser visti dai dannati: questi, rassicurati da un fischio
convenzionale di lui, verranno a galla, e i diavoli potranno farne
strazio. Egli specula sull'ingordigia di crudeltà dei diavoli, e sul loro
gusto per l'inganno. Essi abboccano, Ciampolo spicca un salto e
dilegua sotto la pece; il diavolo Alichino, che aveva persuaso gli
altri a seguire il consiglio di Ciampolo, si slancia subito ma non può
raggiungerlo; un altro diavolo, Calcabrina, si azzuffa, irato con lui;
e tutti e due finiscono col cadere nella pece, dalla quale a fatica son
tratti dai compagni.

L'inganno e la beffa scompaiono nel quarto atto (XXIII 1-57).
Dante e Virgilio procedono sull'argine soli e silenziosi, dopo tanto
movimento e trambusto; Dante teme che i diavoli irritati anche per
essere stati 'scherniti con danno e con beffa' possano tornare
all'assalto; e questa volta Virgilio partecipa alla paura; cerca un
punto meno ripido per scendere nella 6ª bolgia; ma all'apparire dei
diavoli, senza più porre tempo in mezzo, afferra il discepolo e con
lui si cala giù, 'supino', sino al fondo della nuova bolgia. I due poeti
sono ormai al sicuro perchè ai diavoli è vietato lasciare la bolgia alla
quale sono addetti.

Nell'epilogo (XXIII 127-148) il sorriso riappare: Virgilio
domanda a uno dei dannati della nuova bolgia la via per uscirne, e
viene a sapere che non solo un ponte, ma tutti i ponti sulla bolgia
degli ipocriti son rotti; il discorso di Malacoda era stato dunque una
bugia beffatrice (tale esso probabilmente è, più che un inganno):
solo adesso Virgilio se ne rende conto. E l'ipocrita sottolinea
ironicamente l'ingenuità di lui.

Come sono presentati i personaggi? Cominciamo da quelli solitamente così solenni, Virgilio e Dante. Si è detto che il primo non sospetti la bugia di Malacoda per l'altezza dell'animo suo per la quale una menzogna così smaccata, volgare e inutile è inconcepibile; ma se fosse così, questa altezza bisognerebbe negarla a Dante, che invece diffida. Comunque, Virgilio crede ingenuamente, in pieno, nella remissività di Malacoda dopo il suo ammonimento; non dubita minimamente, poi, dell'esattezza delle notizie e dell'utilità dei consigli e degli aiuti datigli da quel diavolo. Il Parodi osservò che 'se da Malacoda è ingannato Virgilio, non è meno ingannato il lettore, il quale fino agli ultimi versi del canto XXIII non sospetta nulla del diabolico tradimento' e che quindi l'episodio può essere capito appieno solo a una rilettura o a un ripensamento a lettura finita. Sarebbe un errore di costruzione, inconcepibile in Dante. È chiaro che se l'inganno di Malacoda fosse stato più esplicito, il discorso di lui meno suadente, tutto il racconto sarebbe caduto; d'altra parte il lettore si accorge bene della bugia e dei propositi dei diavoli attraverso tante vie: la profferta dell'inutile scorta (necessaria è invece quella offerta da Chirone nel cerchio dei violenti, *Inf.* XII 97 ss.: lì il centauro Nesso deve servire a far guadare a Dante il fiume di sangue): l'atteggiamento e le parole di Dante che il pericolo ha intuito; il digrignare i denti e i minacciosi occhi dei diavoli; i cenni furbeschi d'intesa che essi fanno al loro 'duca': essi infatti sanno che tutti i ponti sulla bolgia sono rotti. Il Parodi pensa anche, forse con ragione, che nell'espressione di Malacoda 'costor fien salvi infino a l'altro scheggio' si celi una perfidia verbale, che i diavoli coglierebbero, ma non Virgilio; egli assicura la salvezza solo sino all'altro scoglio; poi i diavoli saranno liberi di far quello che vorranno. Comunque, il fatto che la beffa sia avvertita da Dante e dal lettore fa che la luce del racconto sia proiettata sull'ingenuità di Virgilio, e sottolineata anche dalla sicurezza impervia di lui sino all'ultimo: 'e per nulla offension che mi sia fatta / non temer tu, ch'i'ho le cose conte' (XXI 61–62): egli conosce bene come vanno e andranno le cose! Ingenuità, dicevamo, commentata alla fine dell'episodio dall'ipocrita Catalano che con ironica gravità gli svela una verità così difficile a conquistare, che lui ha dovuto impararla all'università di Bologna: nientemeno che il diavolo è 'bugiardo e padre di menzogne', che poi è nient'altro che una traduzione del Vangelo di Giovanni (VIII 44). Lo stesso Virgilio accusa il colpo, rimanendo mortificato ad ascoltare la spiegazione, 'a testa china', mostrandosi poi 'turbato un poco d'ira', e per la concitazione di questa allontanandosi 'a gran passi': tutt'altro, dunque, che imperturbabile come egli è di solito nel poema e come sono sempre i grandi spiriti danteschi. A dar risalto a questo momento della

figurazione di Virgilio è l'immagine del 'savio gentil che tutto seppe'
(*Inf.* VII 3) quale ci è apparsa sin qui e ci apparirà.

Allo stesso modo, si direbbe che qui Dante sorrida nel disegnare
un sé stesso assai diverso dal fiero indomabile Dante che conosciamo:
un Dante che è desideroso, sì, di guardare il diavolo sopravveniente,
ma non senza che le forze gli vengan meno per la paura (XXI 25–
27); che poi se ne sta 'quatto quatto' dietro una roccia; che resta
pauroso e diffidente anche quando sembra che la battaglia coi
diavoli sia vinta: se lascia il nascondiglio, corre subito, 'ratto', a
rifugiarsi presso il maestro, stringendosi a lui con tutta la persona;
e anche allora non riesce a distogliere lo sguardo dai brutti ceffi dei
diavoli ('e non torceva li occhi / da la sembianza lor ch'era non bona').
Le linee di questo disegno di paura sono volutamente caricate. Non
si tratta di discutere, come è stato fatto, se questa paura sia o no
giustificata dall'eccezionalità della situazione; sta di fatto che in
altre circostanze non meno eccezionalmente paurose il personaggio
Dante non ha paura; e se l'ha, essa è rappresentata come un sentimento terribilmente serio, non con la lievemente scherzosa esagera-
zione di questi versi. La scena è strutturalmente simile a quella
dinnanzi alla città di Dite: anche lì Virgilio, per andare a parla-
mentare coi demoni, lascia il discepolo solo; anche lì questo è
impaurito e incerto; ma è una pusillanimità su cui il poeta narratore
non scherza. E si pensi anche a Dante che diviene 'gelato e fioco',
al suo rimanere tra vita e morte alla vista di Lucifero (*Inf.* XXXIV
20–27): ma questi era 'imperador del doloroso regno', mentre i
diavoli dei barattieri del regno infernale non sono neppure degni
cortigiani: sono sguatteri (XXI 55–57). Ciò appunto conferisce alla
paura di Dante una patina scherzosa: questi diavoli, vorrei dire
questi poveri diavoli, son troppo umani e, nella loro crudeltà, troppo
deboli per ispirare una paura da rappresentare con tono sostenuto e
'tragico'. Già il primo diavolo, quello che porta l'anziano di Lucca,
è, sì, nero, ha aspetto feroce, atteggiamento crudele, come ogni
diavolo che si rispetti; ma il lettore non ne trae certo un'immagine di
spavento, perché nella sua figura prevale fantasticamente l'agilità
dei movimenti, la rapidità, il suo affaccendarsi, anche la sua arguzia.
È uno di quei diavoli della tradizione, che abitano la terra, si
mescolano alla vita quotidiana; diavoli mezzi uomini, insomma (per
altri diavoli di questo genere si veda anche *Inf.*XXVII 116–117,
*Inf.*XXXIII 124 ss., *Purg.* V 103 ss.). E gli altri hanno nomi più
strani e bizzarri che spaventosi, coniati con allusioni, per lo più,
alle loro caratteristiche, ma anche identici o simili a nomi e sopran-
nomi del tempo: il che non ci autorizza a fare precise identificazioni
con persone storiche; ma certo quei nomi dovevan avere per i
lettori immediati del poema un suono familiare, dovevano avvicinare

i loro titolari alla comune umanità, alla vita d'ogni giorno. Diavoli che cercano d'ingannare i dannati con il non certo diabolico espediente di stare nascosti sotto un ponte; e basta che un uomo sia a sua volta acquattato dietro una roccia perché non lo vedano; che poi si faranno clamorosamente ingannare da Ciampolo, nonostante l'avvertimento di uno di essi, così come Virgilio si fa ingannare da Malacoda nonostante i replicati avvertimenti di Dante: una vicenda di scambievoli furberie e ingenuità, tutte mediocri. Combattono dunque con gli uomini, dannati o no, pari contro pari; giocano con loro come il gatto col topo ('tra male gatte era venuto il sorco', XXII 57); ben diversi da quei dignitosi ministri che sono i Centauri di *Inf.*XII, i quali pure hanno ufficio dal loro non dissimile. Si ingiuriano e si dileggiano tra loro ('fatti 'n costà, malvagio uccello!', XXII 96), addirittura si accapigliano: Calcabrina giunge a desiderare che Ciampolo sfugga pur di 'aver la zuffa' con Alichino. Ma prima tutta la 'decina' era stata compatta con furbesca complicità, ma con militaresca disciplina, agli ordini sia di Malacoda sia di Barbariccia: una pattuglia, però, che si muove al segnale d'un peto, e che ha pronte le lingue tra i denti, per produrre un rumore analogo, che s'immagina facilmente segnerà il ritmo della marcia: accompagnamento, si deve credere, abituale, dal momento che tutti nell'accingersi a muoversi si preparano a emettere quel suono, senza intesa preventiva. Basta questo finale del c. XXI, su cui così a lungo s'insiste nell'inizio del XXII, a dirci su quale registro tutta la scena vada letta. No, non sono davvero diavoli da averne troppa paura.

Il c. XXI si chiude su una parola crudissima; ma qui essa non ha l'ufficio che hanno consimili parole nel canto precedente degli indovini, dove segnavano la miseria attuale dei dannati in contrasto con l'audacia della loro pretesa di dominare il futuro; è invece uno scherzo volutamente grossolano, ribadito poi in ben 12 versi, con cui il poeta segue la volgarità di questi suoi allegri e crudeli diavoli di second'ordine. Si noti anche in questo episodio, come in quello degli usurai (si tratta sempre di gente per cui il danaro è tutto), il ritornare frequente di paragoni animaleschi, per diavoli e dannati: mastino che insegue un ladro, cani addosso a un mendicante, delfini, ranocchi, rana, lontra, porco, gatti e sorci, malvagio uccello, cagnazzo che come bestia leva 'il muso', anitra e falcone, Calcabrina con artigli, sparviero, la favola delle rane e del topo, ancora cane che afferra una lepre (XXI 44–45, 67 ss.; XXII 19 ss., 25 ss., 32–33, 36, 56, 58, 96, 106, 130–132, 137, 139; XXIII 4 ss., 18). Orrendo lo stare immersi nella pece bollente, ma il poeta non solo non ne è scosso, ma schernisce, 'convien che qui si balli' (XXI 53); i diavoli sono simili a sguatteri che coi forchettoni fanno sì che la carne messa

a cuocere non galleggi (XXI 55 ss.), e parla ancora di dannati
'lessi dolenti' (XXI 135), di diavoli 'cotti' (XXII 150). Anche in
*Inf.*XII 101 si parla di 'bolliti' per l'analoga pena dei violenti contro
il prossimo: ma si rilegga quel canto per individuare la natura di
questo: nel XII nessuna gara di furberia: i violenti se ne stanno
immersi nel sangue ciascuno quel tanto che gli è destinato, e non
cercano affatto d'ingannare i Centauri, che del resto non sono esseri
che si possano burlare; né i Centauri sono cupidi di saettare i
dannati. Il poeta si sofferma sulla sofferenza di questi: 'la divina
giustizia...punge...in etterno munge / le lagrime, che col bollor
diserra' (XII 133-136). Qui invece alla sofferenza dei dannati
si accenna in un sol verso, che ci mostra Ciampolo indugiare a
guardarsi la ferita infertagli (XXII 77); ma in generale pena e
ferite son guardate con scherno, con ironiche attenuazioni: graffi,
toccare sul groppone, render ragione 'in questo caldo', sdrucire,
grattare la tigna (XXI 50, 100-101; XXII 54, 57, 93; per simili
attenuazioni, ma in contesto 'serio', cfr. *Inf.* VII 24, VIII 53, XXXII
60, 117). Il dannato tirato su per i capelli sembra al poeta una
lontra, viscido nero e inerte com'è; due diavoli si azzuffano, si
ghermiscono l'un l'altro, ma il caldo immediatamente li induce a
lasciar la presa: 'lo caldo sghermitor subito fue' (XXII 142): si noti
l'efficacia sorridente del neologismo, che attribuisce al caldo della
pece la funzione e quasi l'intenzione di far da paciere. Spira per
tutto l'episodio un'aria di scherno e di beffa.

Soprattutto su questi canti dei barattieri s'accentrano le discussioni
se ci sia o no un Dante comico: comico, s'intende, nel senso moderno
della parola (se ne ha uno solo); giacché nel senso che le dà Dante,
coi suoi contemporanei, non c'è ovviamente luogo ad alcuna di-
scussione. Cominciò il De Sanctis (*Storia della letter. ital.*) a negare in
Dante il comico, che sarebbe immediatamente soffocato dalla collera,
dall'indignazione, dall'orrore: si avrebbe in lui solo un comico
plebeo e rozzo, ovvero il sarcasmo, 'la porta per la quale volgiamo le
spalle al comico e rientriamo nella grande poesia'. Il romantico De
Sanctis non poteva districarsi da quello che a noi ora sembra un
pregiudizio: la superiorità della poesia 'impegnata' sulla 'comica' che
sembrava non contenesse alcun messaggio, che fosse puro divertimento. Da questo pregiudizio nasce il convincimento che il Dante
'vero', da ammirare, sarebbe unicamente quello su cui soffia il vento
delle passioni magnanime. Eppure lo stesso grande critico mise in
luce un Dante assai diverso, e non meno 'vero' e ammirabile, nel
Purgatorio. Né sembra legittimo, una volta determinato un carattere
prevalente d'un poeta, rifiutare tutto ciò che non rientra in esso: la

vita e la poesia non si volgono in direzione unica, chiudendosi al resto.

Sulla base di questo convincimento, molti si affannano a negare la 'comicità' dell'episodio dei barattieri, insistendo sulle atrocità oggettive che vi sono descritte, ma trascurando il modo con cui queste sono presentate; c'è persino chi vi avverte una 'sensazione di orrore e di sbigottimento' che investirebbe la coscienza cristiana di Dante narratore. Come se fosse in dubbio la condanna dei barattieri come di tutti gli altri peccatori, e non piuttosto si cercasse se, in questo caso specifico, nella concretezza della pagina, non prevalgano sulla condanna altri interessi artistici. Qualcuno, ed è uno dei maggiori scrittori italiani di oggi, Riccardo Bacchelli, per giustificare la 'farsa' che anche a lui sembra abnorme, ne dà un'inammissibile interpretazione allegorica. C'è anche chi, acutamente, ammette che l'episodio 'deve essere sentito nell'ambito d'un gusto teatrale e novellistico, tipicamente medievale e popolare', ma si affretta ad aggiungere che 'la rappresentazione non sarebbe così compatta se non ci fosse l'iniziale attitudine polemica verso il costume contemporaneo e particolarmente comunale' (Sapegno). Polemica anch'essa indubitata, ma determina veramente questo episodio? È dubbio quel che sostiene quel critico, rammodernando il De Sanctis alla luce dell'odierna predilezione per i moventi teologici e strutturali, che l'anima di Dante non consenta 'nessun abbandono ad un libero estro comico'.

Sempre in coerenza con quel convincimento, molti altri si muovono in direzione autobiografica. Dante fu condannato per 'baractarie, lucra illicita'; la stessa opposizione al papa è presentata nella sentenza come effetto di desiderio di guadagni personali. Non è mancato nel passato persino chi ha preteso d'identificare in questo o quel diavolo questa o quella persona; o nel loro complesso i nemici in genere, a cui Dante riuscirebbe a sfuggire. Rozza tesi positivistica ormai abbandonata (non ci stupiremmo però, con l'aria che tira, che ritornasse); ma resiste sempre quella secondo cui bisogna leggere nell'episodio una più o meno allegra vendetta di Dante contro chi lo aveva calunniato. Del disprezzo contro i calunniatori sarebbe tutto impregnato— secondo un lettore d'eccezione del XXI canto, Luigi Pirandello— il riso dei versi che stiamo considerando; il quale perciò sarebbe 'grottesco e laido e sconcio'; un disprezzo, dice un altro lettore di altissimo livello, il Parodi, 'così gigantesco e schiacciante da diventare buffonescamente allegro'. Anche qui, che Dante disprezzasse i Neri che lo avevano bandito, non è dubbio; ma è dubbio che potesse essere particolarmente indignato per la specifica accusa di baratteria. Sostenere che un uomo politico abbia agito non già per conseguire quello che in buona fede ritiene il bene pubblico, ma per interessi

privati, è espediente di rozza polemica che ancora oggi è tutt'altro
che sparito; ma allora, nel rapido rovesciarsi delle situazioni politiche,
era il pretesto giuridico consueto con cui gli uni eliminavano i loro
avversari, e che questi, se le cose volgevano in loro favore, ritorcevano
contro i primi. Dante non poteva far caso drammatico di una formula;
tanto meno poteva sentire il bisogno di difendersi da un'accusa che
tutti, gli avversari per primi, sapevano infondata. E infatti, in tutta
l'opera sua non se ne difende: il torto che i suoi concittadini gli
hanno fatto è di natura politica, si basa sull'ingratitudine: hanno
ricompensato con l'esilio il 'ben far' cui egli aveva posto l'ingegno.
Non accetta mai di considerare colpa la sua azione; respinge sdegnoso
la condanna, non la motivazione di essa, che era formula valevole
contro tutti. E infatti nella sentenza l'accusa è rivolta non solo a lui,
ma a tutto un gruppo di Bianchi. Dell'accusa poteva tutt'al più
ridere, sia pure amaramente: ma in verità nell'episodio dei barattieri
non c'è neppure amarezza. Anzi, si direbbe che egli abbia voluto
deliberatamente eliminare ogni allusione che potesse sembrare
autobiografica o apologetica: di barattieri fiorentini, Neri o no,
aveva certo abbondanza (e uno, in tutt'altro contesto, lo designa
come tale nel già citato passo di *Par.*XVI 56–57); e invece tra i
dannati di questi canti ci sono lucchesi, un navarrese, due sardi:
nessun fiorentino. Infierisce invece contro Lucca; e certo al momento
del viaggio ultraterreno questa città era governata dai Neri; anzi,
forse proprio mentre scriveva questo canto, Dante era stato per così
dire bandito anche da Lucca, il cui governo, il 31 marzo 1309, aveva
proibito il soggiorno nella città e nel suo territorio agli esuli fiorentini.
Ma in sostanza contro Lucca non c'è nulla di più di quel che Dante
dice contro tante altre città e regioni, toscane o no: per non andar
troppo lontano, contro la vicina e nemica di Lucca, Pisa, verso la
quale non aveva alcuna ragione di risentimento personale (*Inf.*
XXXIII 79 ss.; e cfr., in quello stesso canto, l'invettiva contro i
Genovesi, 151 ss.).

    È dunque, questo dei barattieri, un episodio 'comico'? chi
oserebbe affermarlo o negarlo, dal momento che, per sforzi che nei
secoli si siano fatti, non si è mai giunti a una definizione del concetto
di 'comico'? Vano sembra anche appellarsi all'ugualmente astratta
categoria d'un comico 'medievale', che sarebbe più grossolano,
meno raffinato del comico 'moderno'; come se di raffinatezze
variamente comiche non abbondasse il Medioevo, e il Rinascimento
e i giorni nostri non ci offrissero tanti testi che attingono la loro
comicità dallo sconcio e dal plebeo volutamente perseguiti. D'altra
parte, con tutto il rispetto e la gratitudine che dobbiamo al De
Sanctis e al Parodi, è difficile ammettere 'un comico più di situazione
che di espressione e di carattere, pel quale basta l'attenta osservazione

della realtà esterna': un comico dunque che s'identificherebbe col realismo, 'il fresco e sano realismo delle parole e del gesto'. È difficile ammettere ciò, perché non pare esista un realismo che sia 'fuori dello spirito dell'autore'; comunque, 'comico' (comunque lo si voglia intendere) e 'realismo' non sono intercambiabili fra loro, potendoci essere, evidentemente, un realismo non comico, e una comicità non realistica.

Anche nel corpo di questo solo episodio è dato ravvisare molte gradazioni di comico: anzitutto il vivacissimo movimento scenico, in un poeta che ama tanto le figure isolate e magari le statuarie; la rappresentazione d'un mondo di gente comune, di piccole furberie in gara: i beffati non tardano a beffare a loro volta, scambiandosi le parti in commedia: e si tratta, badiamo, d'una gara che non si limita ai fatti singoli cui assistiamo, ma che il poeta rappresenta come perenne (i diavoli stanno sempre acquattati per ingannare i dannati, questi zufolano, mettono in opera speciali tecniche per ingannare i loro aguzzini); l'attenzione al gioco dell'intelligenza sia pure degradata ad astuzia, che la vince sulla forza anche demoniaca (Ciampolo). E poi: l'acre divertimento visivo che dà una figura (il dannato che sembra una lontra); la blanda canzonatura (i due sardi che anche nell'Inferno non parlano d'altro che della loro isola; la paura di Dante; lo scherno ('qui si nuota altrimenti che nel Serchio'); l'ironia ('ogn'uomo v'è barattier fuor che Bonturo'); l'eroicomico (la disciplina militare dei diavoli); il grottesco (i nomi e gli atteggiamenti dei diavoli); il plebeo (il segnale di Barbariccia). Si potrebbe continuare nell'analisi delle varie gradazioni; e i riferimenti al testo non sono che esemplificativi.

Comico o non comico che tutto ciò si voglia definire, non par dubbio che ci troviamo di fronte a un episodio nello scrivere il quale —all'opposto di quel che avviene, per es., nella bolgia dei Simoniaci —il risentimento morale e civile di Dante si è allentato. Il poeta mantiene per tutto l'episodio un tono disteso, che per la sua estensione e articolazione è isolato nel poema. Il fatto è che ci sono peccatori, come i barattieri, i ladri, i falsari, contro i quali un risentimento religioso e politico ad alto livello sarebbe sproporzionato alla mediocrità delle colpe, e anche inutile ai fini ammaestrativi perché si tratta di colpe sotto gli occhi di tutti e da tutti condannate (ma senza acredine, specie quella dei truffatori: è un'esperienza che si fa quotidianamente): si ricordi che anche i barattieri son visti come piccoli imbroglioni. 'Plebeo è lo spettacolo, e Dante ride, non come plebe che si affiati con plebe, bensì sempre come lui Dante che getta lo sguardo su quell'aspetto dell'umanità, di un'umanità che è quasi naturalità e non permette la seria indignazione' (Croce). Sicché il poeta può distendersi, come in questa commedia dei diavoli, o come in alcune delle scenette e dei dialoghi nei canti dei falsari (*Inf.* XXIX, XXX); ovvero impegnandosi in direzione diversa dalla solita, e facendo passare in secondo piano (non eliminando, ben s'intende!) il suo sdegno e le sue alte passioni, come nei canti dei ladri (*Inf.* XXIV, XXV), dove egli s'impegna in un'ardua impresa letteraria, l'emulazione con i classici, con Lucano e Ovidio, nell'arte delle metamorfosi poetiche.

Anche qui il poeta si cimenta in un'impresa letteraria difficile: costruire con alta e raffinata sapienza una rappresentazione popolaresca: è una strada che sarà percorsa poi dal Boccaccio e, largamente, dagli uomini del Rinascimento. Tutto nell'episodio dei barattieri ci riporta al gusto popolare: i diavoli ci appaiono neri, con le ali, probabilmente di pipistrello, l'omero 'aguto', come erano rappresentati nella tradizione figurativa che era alle spalle di Dante, e come apparivano nelle feste del popolo minuto (G. Villani, *Cron.*, VIII 70, ci ha trasmesso il ricordo di una di queste feste, consuete a Firenze, e proprio 'con uomini contraffatti a demoni orribili a vedere'). Del resto, che Dante volesse dar luogo a una scena di teatro popolare, lo dice lui stesso: 'o tu che leggi, udirai nuovo ludo' (XXII 118); e *ludus* già in latino classico valeva appunto 'rappresentazione teatrale', e al tempo del poeta era nome tecnico della rappresentazione scenica.

I diavoli del popolo sono alla mano, si può venire a patti con essi, non sono grandiosi né terrificanti, tentano d'ingannarci e possono essere ingannati e scornati. L'immaginazione popolare godeva appunto di vedere sconfitti i diavoli tentatori e bugiardi, e tanto più quanto più essi erano crudeli. Anche il nostro poeta toglie loro ogni dignità, anche quella che nella loro protervia conservavano gli angeli del male a guardia della città di Dite; li chiama 'ghiottoni', cioè mascalzoncelli. Tanto può in lui il gusto popolaresco, che in fondo egli sta dalla parte di Ciampolo e non dei diavoli: eppure questi sono obiettivamente ministri della giustizia divina. Questo va osservato per ribadire quanto abbiano torto coloro—e sono oggi tanti—che vedono nella *Commedia* unicamente un trattato di teologia morale.

Rome   UMBERTO BOSCO

An Uncharted Phase in
Dante's Political Thought†

To try to map the details of the evolution of Dante's political thought is an ungrateful task; indeed, Ercole's celebrated title 'Le tre fasi del pensiero politico di Dante', with Nardi's equally famous rejoinder, should serve as a powerful deterrent to us all.[1] Yet it is no less an authority than Dante who tells us that the Florentine poet held two radically opposed views during his lifetime: first, the Guelf idea that the Roman empire was based on violence alone, followed by his realization that the Ghibellines were right in claiming that the Empire was willed by God and founded on justice. Dante's confession occurs at the beginning of the Second Book of the *Monarchia*, and it is worth quoting at least in part:

> Sicut ad faciem cause non pertingentes novum effectum comuniter admiramur, sic, cum causam cognoscimus, eos qui sunt in admiratione restantes quadam derisione despicimus. Admirabar equidem aliquando romanum populum in orbe terrarum sine ulla resistentia fuisse prefectum, cum, tantum superficialiter intuens, illum nullo iure sed armorum tantummodo violentia obtinuisse arbitrabar. Sed postquam medullitus oculos mentis infixi et per efficacissima signa divinam providentiam hoc efficisse cognovi, admiratione cedente, derisiva quedam supervenit despectio...[2]

It is therefore hardly surprising to find oneself wondering when the conversion took place, and whether it occurred as a complete volte-face or developed through various stages. Two things seem reasonably certain: that the Guelf outlook corresponded to Dante's upbringing and involvement in Florentine politics, and that this first phase had been completely eradicated by 1307, when he wrote the fourth and fifth chapters of *Convivio IV*. It is of course important

† I should like to express my gratitude to Professor Whitfield for having encouraged me in my study of Dante. I must also thank the Leverhulme Foundation for its generosity in granting me a Research Fellowship, which enabled me to turn my thoughts and reading to the problem dealt with in this study.

to remember that, as far as we know. Dante never accepted the views of the extremists on either side, while we would do well to heed a historian's warning that 'A concept as vague as "guelfism", which was current in Italian politics for at least a century and a half, can have no meaning at all except in the context of a particular political situation.'[3] The 'white' Guelfs of Florence did their best to resist Boniface VIII's political ambitions, and one of the most interesting records of Dante's actions tells us of his opposition to the pope's request for troops from Florence.[4] Nevertheless, we have Dante's word for it that his attitude towards the Empire was a negative one, typically Guelf, which wrote off the imperial power as having been acquired 'nullo iure sed armorum tantummodo violentia'. And a reading of *Inferno* X still shows us Dante the pilgrim, depicted as he was in the year 1300, encountering the Ghibelline pride of Farinata degli Uberti, the heroic opponent of the Alighieri family: as I have tried to show elsewhere, Dante in 1300 was still overmuch involved in the partisan feelings and politics of Florence and had not yet risen to the universal vision that inspired the *Comedy*.[5]

What evidence we have therefore points the same way as common sense: that the conversion was a result of Dante's exile from Guelf Florence. His wanderings through Italy brought home to him the tragic discord and lack of unity, so vividly depicted in *Purgatorio* VI. Two things are certain about Dante's exile: that his 'first refuge' was in Verona and that he cut himself off from his fellow-exiles, condemning them for their 'bestiality'.[6] The break with the White Guelfs is generally supposed to have taken place in 1304, presumably after Dante wrote the Epistle to Cardinal Niccolò da Prato (March–June) and about the time of the Lastra failure (July 20), when Dante is thought to have disassociated himself from the exiles' attempt to return to Florence by force. The poet's conversion to the imperial cause is even more likely to have occurred at this moment, as a result of his stay in the fiercely Ghibelline city of Verona, from May–June 1303 to March 1304.[7]

What internal evidence, if any, can be gleaned from Dante's works?—Fortunately, Barbi's chronology is generally accepted for this period. This ascribes two works to the years 1304–1307: the *Convivio* and the *De Vulgari Eloquentia*.[8] From *Conv.* I.v.10, it seems likely that the First Book was begun in 1304, while the second part of the Fourth Book must have been written after March 1306 and before 27 November 1308. The first three books are almost void of political allusions. Nevertheless, the whole orientation is in harmony with the 'Ghibelline' tradition set up by Frederick II. In his encyclical of 1232, Dante's great emperor had preceded the author of the *Convivio* in his belief that learning brings true freedom to man; and, like Dante's ideal audience, Frederick had tried to overcome the handicaps of the active life:

> Post regni vero nostri curas assumptas, quanquam operosa frequenter negociorum turba nos distrahat, et civilis sibi ratio vendicet solicitudinis nostre partes, quidquid tamen temporis de rerum familiarium occupatione decerpimus, transire non patimur ociosum; sed totum in lectionis exercitatione gratuite libenter expendimus, *ut anime clarius vigeat instrumentum in acquisitione scientie, sine qua mortalium vita non regitur liberaliter.*[9]

And, like Dante in *Convivio* IV, the emperor insists that the sharing of knowledge in no way decreases it, but on the contrary augments it and is of the greatest benefit to all:

> scientiarum generosa possessio in plures dispersa non deperit...sed eo diuturnius perpetuata senescit, *quo publicata fecundius se diffundit*...nec estimavimus nos eadem retinere jucundum, *nisi tanti boni nobiscum alios participes faceremus.*[10]

Eight years earlier, in a letter announcing the foundation of the University of Naples, Frederick had spoken of his intention to nourish those who were starved of intellectual food and help them to overcome the material difficulties placed in their way—while, even more significantly, he had underlined the idea of intellectual nobility acquired through knowledge. This is the language and spirit of the *Convivio*.[11]

In fine, it was Frederick's active interest in and promotion of Latin translations of Greek and Arab philosophers that made possible the great Aristotelian debates of the thirteenth century. In particular, Michael Scot's translations of Averroes were to have portentous results; and Vittorio Russo rightly comments on Frederick's activity: 'Quale che fosse la coscienza che Federico II avesse della portata rivoluzionaria e moderna della sua azione per i destini della cultura, sta di fatto che le conseguenze dell'attività culturale della corte sveva furono di enorme portata storica per la formazione delle strutture ideali della cultura laica. Le nuove forze storiche della civiltà comunale ne ricevettero in eredità la coscienza di poter elaborare una cultura indipendente e autonoma dall'autorità della cultura della Chiesa.'[12] There was a clear connexion between the Ghibelline spirit and Latin Averroism; and the latter element in the *Convivio* has been stressed by Bruno Nardi.[13] Certainly, in this work, Dante wished to make a break with the closed shop of scholasticism and to destroy the cultural monopoly exercised by churchmen and lawyers:

Ché la bontà de l'animo, la quale questo servigio attende, è in coloro che per malvagia disusanza del mondo hanno lasciata la litteratura a coloro che l'hanno fatta di donna meretrice; e questi nobili sono principi, baroni, cavalieri, e molt'altra nobile gente, non solamente maschi ma femmine, che sono molti e molte in questa lingua, volgari e non litterati (*Conv.* I. ix. 5)

This cultural revolution had its origin in the work of Frederick II.[14]

The *Convivio* has at least one more thing to tell us concerning the development of Dante's political thought. It is in the Fourth Book that we find for the first time the idea of the providential mission of Rome and her empire. I believe this conviction came to Dante especially through a re-reading of the *Aeneid*.[15] Virgil's poem exalted Rome's imperial destiny, and nowhere more clearly than in the Sixth Book, which contains both the description of Aeneas' descent to the underworld and his vision of the glory that was to come (cf. *Inf.* II. 13–27). In the *Convivio*, Dante establishes a providential synchronization between Aeneas' arrival in Italy and the birth of Christ's ancestor, David: 'Per che assai è manifesto la divina elezione del romano imperio per lo nascimento de la santa cittade che fu contemporaneo a la radice de la progenie di Maria.'[16] The Roman poet is moreover quoted on a par with Holy Scripture, to prove that the Empire of Rome was destined to last for all time: 'Onde non da forza fu principalmente preso [the office of empire] per la romana gente, ma da divina provedenza, che è sopra ogni ragione. E in ciò s'accorda Virgilio nel primo de lo Eneida, quando dice, *in persona di Dio parlando*: "A costoro—cioè a li Romani—né termine di cose né di tempo pongo; a loro ho dato imperio sanza fine"' (*Conv.* IV. iv.11; italics mine). This passage was most probably written *c.* 1307. From this time on, the rôle of Rome and her Empire remained preeminent in Dante's work and thought.[17] It was no doubt this discovery that helped to change Dante's attitude towards the pagan poets and poetry in general, from *Convivio* II, where the writer seems bent on devaluing the literal sense of his own poems, to Books III and IV, where historical truth is contained in Ovid, Lucan, and Virgil.[18]

But there is nothing of all this before *Convivio* IV. Indeed, what evidence we have is in the *De Vulgari Eloquentia*; and that evidence is entirely negative.

As is well known, Dante begins his 'hunt' for Italy's illustrious vernacular by examining the credentials of Roman speech in *DVE* I.xi.1–2. He justifies this order of choice by referring to the Romans' claim to priority 'over all others' and ironically deciding to deal with them first: 'Sicut ergo Romani se cunctis preponendos existimant, in hac eradicatione sive discerptione *non inmerito eos aliis preponamus, protestantes eosdem in nulla vulgaris eloquentie ratione fore tangendos*' (italics mine). They are thus excluded from all further consideration, their speech condemned as 'potius tristiloquium, ytalorum vulgarium omnium...turpissimum.' Not content with this linguistic judgment, however, Dante goes on to attack them for the general turpitude of their lives: 'cum etiam morum habituumque deformitate pre cunctis videantur fetere.' Linguistic proof? They say: '*Messure, quinto dici?*'

And that is all. There is not one word about the true mission of the Roman people or of the city of Rome; no hint of the contrast between the poet's later vision of Rome and the sordid reality of Roman jargon and customs. Of course, such observations can easily be denigrated as *argumenta ex silentio*. But is such silence conceivable after the exaltation of Rome's imperial mission in *Convivio* IV? There, the fact that Dante must attack the definition of nobility attributed to Frederick II leads him to make a long digression in which he goes to extraordinary lengths to remove any possible misconception about the scope of his argument. In so doing, he makes a nice distinction between the emperor's authority *qua* emperor and Frederick's competence in the independent realm of philosophy. A. P. d'Entrèves regards this as 'una casuale digressione' and sees in it 'un aspetto stranamente negativo.'[19] In fact, I think quite the opposite is true. Dante takes great pains to define the emperor's authority, so that this philosophical debate should not be interpreted as in any way undermining that authority; but he also uses up a great deal of space in an additional attempt to prove that the pagans of ancient Rome were frequently guided by God, that the empire belongs to Rome and that 'spezial nascimento e spezial processo, da Dio pensato e ordinato, fosse quello de la santa cittade' (*Conv.* IV.v.20). It would be useful if critics were to point out that most of this digression is hardly relevant, in any strict sense, to the problem of Frederick's authority as emperor. The whole chapter is in fact a paean to Rome, where the name of the Eternal City returns obsessively in the course of a few lines: 'la gloriosa Roma...nacque Roma...la cittade romana...essaltata non con umani cittadini, ma con divini, ne li quali non amore umano, ma divino era inspirato in amare lei...liberare Roma...per amore di Roma...liberare Roma...la franchigia di Roma...la santa cittade.' Is it likely that such a vision, if it already existed, should have been completely hidden in the *De Vulgari Eloquentia*, where the claims of Rome as *caput mundi* are derided in order to dismiss her utterly and ignominiously? I do not wish in any way to suggest that, after *Convivio* IV, Dante's condemnation of the speech of fourteenth-century

Romans would have been any less harsh; what I do suggest is that he would most probably have accompanied it with some hint of the contrast between the baseness of Roman speech and manners on the one hand and the ideal destiny of Rome on the other; between her degenerate citizens and the 'cittadini...divini' of *Conv.* IV.v.12. An attitude not unlike the poet's condemnation of contemporary popes, which is heightened by his reverence for the papal office and by the contrast with Peter of old.[20] Is it possible to imagine Dante writing the eleventh chapter of *DVE I* as it now stands, after the final sentence of the fifth chapter in *Convivio IV*? Let there be no mistake: the whole chapter is an exaltation of Rome's pagan past, ending with the heartfelt cry, 'Certo di ferma sono oppinione che le pietre che ne le mura sue stanno siano degne di reverenzia, e lo suolo dov'ella siede sia degno *oltre quello che per li uomini è predicato e approvato*.'[21]

It is surely noteworthy that, in *DVE* I.xviii.5, Dante speaks of an ideal *curia* in Italy, which, while not physically united and located 'ut curia regis Alamannie', has its 'membra...gratioso lumine rationis unita.' There is again no mention of the essential rôle of Rome, despite the recognition that a political vacuum exists 'cum curia careamus'. But another court is predominant in the *De Vulgari Eloquentia*: it is the Sicilian court of Frederick II and his son, Manfred. Its memory remains 'in obproprium ytalorum principum ...qui non heroico more sed plebeio secuntur superbiam.' Attracted by the noble example of the Hohenstaufen rulers, the noblest and most gifted Italians of their time strove to be near them: 'ita ut eorum tempore quicquid excellentes animi Latinorum enitebantur primitus in tantorum coronatorum aula prodibat' (I.xii.4). Here, any doubts aroused by the previous chapter's attack on Roman speech must surely vanish. The whole tone of this episode goes far beyond the factual recognition of the 'Sicilian' poets as the first to have written lyric poetry in an Italian vernacular; as P. Renucci has pointed out, it forms 'un tributo di ammirazione che va molto al di là di quanto richiedesse l'argomento'.[22] The exaltation of Frederick II, *stupor mundi*, is accompanied by an even more polemical reference to Manfred. Not only is Frederick's son seen as the emperor's ideal successor, but, in the teeth of Guelf persecution and insistence on his illegitimacy, he is hailed as *benegenitus* (cf. Dante's reference to Giuseppe, Alberto della Scala's bastard, 'che mal nacque', *Purg.* XVIII.125): 'Siquidem illustres heroes, Fredericus Cesar et benegenitus eius Manfredus, nobilitatem ac rectitudinem sue forme pandentes, donec fortuna permisit, humana secuti sunt, brutalia dedignantes. Propter quod corde nobiles atque gratiarum dotati inherere tantorum principum maiestati conati sunt...'[23] There can be no doubt about Dante's vigorously Ghibelline, anti-Guelf attitude when he wrote this passage.

The *De Vulgari Eloquentia* therefore confirms the hypothesis that Dante was converted to the Ghibelline cause *c.* 1304; especially since the reference to Giovanni, Marquis of Monferrato, in I.xii.5 shows that this chapter was written before February 1305.

We may, perhaps, glean a little more information. In *DVE* I.xii.2, the author mentions the Sicilian vernacular's claim to the illustrious prize: 'nam videtur sicilianum vulgare sibi famam pre aliis asciscere, eo quod *quicquid poetantur Ytali sicilianum vocatur*'— where the present tense of the last two verbs is not always noticed. The reason for this terminological inexactitude is given in I.xii.4: 'et quia regale solium erat Sicilia, factum est ut quicquid nostri predecessores vulgariter protulerunt, sicilianum vocetur: quod quidem retinemus et nos, nec posteri nostri permutare valebunt.' *Quia regale solium*: the message seems clear—'because Sicily was the seat of royal power', it was also the cultural centre of Italy and gave its name to that culture. It is only when one begins to reflect that in 1304 Sicily was still a kingdom, ruled by the 'tuba novissimi Frederici',[24] but without any cultural leadership, that one or two doubts set in— which may give a further dimension to that short phrase 'quia regale solium erat Sicilia.' Among other things, it is interesting to note that *regale* is a *hapax* in Dante, while *solium* appears in only one other context, the pregnant phrase 'solio Augustali vacante totus orbis exorbitat' (*Ep.* VI.12). Moreover, *regale solium* is found only once in Latin poetry, where it refers to the supreme throne of Jupiter: 'Iuppiter ad solium superis regale vocatis.'[25] Both the context and the wording would therefore suggest that Dante is pointing to a unique set of historical circumstances, when Sicily was the centre of the universal empire under Frederick II and then retained for a short while her pre-eminent rôle and cultural prestige under Frederick's heroic successor, Manfred.[26] Under both rulers, in Dante's view, Sicily was the centre of political power and royal authority; so that its name was used to describe 'quicquid excellentes animi Latinorum enitebantur.'

The *De Vulgari Eloquentia*, when considered by students of Dante's political thought, has been seen as representing an intermediate stage between *civitas* and *imperium*, at a time when Dante's exile made him aware of Italian spiritual and linguistic unity.[27] However, I would argue that the evidence points not to the *regnum italicum* but to a totally Ghibelline phase, when Dante had just been converted to the imperial thesis. What is especially significant about this moment is the silence regarding Rome's destiny and her imperial mission. The centre of imperial power under Frederick II had been in Sicily—and Dante makes no mention that it should have been otherwise. This was in the best medieval tradition, according to which the imperial court followed the emperor, just as the papal curia was wherever the pope might be. I would suggest that such an attitude is incompatible with the discovery Dante soon made and expressed in *Convivio* IV. Here, the exaltation of Rome in the fifth chapter finds its *raison d'être* in the vision of the Eternal City as the centre of empire—not just an abstract idea, but a physical city, whose very walls are worthy of reverence 'oltre quello che per li uomini è predicato e approvato.' This is the vision expressed in *Purgatorio VI*, with its denunciation of *Alberto tedesco* and its bitter cry:

> Vieni a veder la tua Roma che piagne
> vedova e sola, e dì e notte chiama:
> 'Cesare mio, perché non m'accompagne?' (vv. 112–4)

It is the message repeated in *Purg.* XVI.106–14, with the tragic consequences of opposition to Frederick's imperial authority (v. 117). It is still to be found in Dante's letter of 1314 to the Italian Cardinals, in the nightmarish picture of 'Romam urbem, *nunc utroque lumine destitutam*, nunc Hannibali nedum alii miserandam, *solam sedentem et viduam* ["vedova e sola"]...illustrium Scipionum patriae...'[28]

The description of *Fredericus Cesar* and *benegenitus eius Manfredus* as *illustres heroes* reveals an aggressively Ghibelline outlook; the lack of any reference to Rome as the unique seat of empire in Dante's condemnation of Roman speech, in his exaltation of the *Magna Curia* in Sicily, and in his observation that the Italians are without a court comparable to the 'curia regis Alamannie'—all the evidence points the same way. It shows that the *De Vulgari Eloquentia* and the years 1304–5 represent the high-water mark of Dante's Ghibellinism, a moment when the neophyte's political convictions had not yet been tempered by the discovery of the imperial mission of Rome.[29] That discovery—and the poet's teleological view of history—is first apparent in 1307, when he came to write the Fourth Book of the *Convivio*.

University of Reading   JOHN A. SCOTT

NOTES

1.   F. Ercole, 'Le tre fasi del pensiero politico di Dante', *Il pensiero politico di Dante*, Vol. II, Milan, 1928, pp. 271–407; B. Nardi, 'Tre pretese fasi del pensiero politico di Dante', *Saggi di filosofia*

dantesca, Florence, 1967², pp. 276–310. Another well-known attempt to plot the development of Dante's political thought is found in A. P. d'Entrèves' study, *Dante as a Political Thinker*, Oxford, 1952, reprinted in *Dante politico e altri saggi*, Turin, 1955; I shall quote from the later, Italian edition.

2. *Mon.* II.i.2–3. The Guelf argument is mentioned in *Conv.* IV. iv.8 and violently attacked in IV.v.9.

3. P. Partner, 'Florence and the Papacy: 1300–1375', in *Europe in the Late Middle Ages*, ed. J. Hale *et al.*, London, 1970, p. 76. The extreme enthusiasm aroused by Henry VII's descent into Italy and Dante's anger at Florentine opposition (*Epistles* V-VII) must be seen in context and balanced by *Par.* XVII.68–9 and VI.97–108.

4. On 19 June 1301, in the Council of Florence, 'Dante Alagherii consuluit quod de servitio faciendo d. pape nichil fiat' (R. Piattoli, *Codice diplomatico dantesco*, Florence, 1940, p. 95).

5. J. A. Scott, 'Politics and *Inferno X*', *Italian Studies*, XIX (1964), pp. 1–13. The ascent from *civitas* to the universality of Dante's empire is evident in *Inf.* VI–*Purg.* VI–*Par.* VI.

6. Both pieces of information are contained in *Par.* XVII. 61–75. Cf. *Inf.* XV.70–78.

7. The most recent and authoritative reconstruction of this period in Dante's life is G. Petrocchi's 'La vicenda biografica di Dante nel Veneto', *Itinerari danteschi*, Bari, 1969, pp. 119–141.

8. See Barbi's introduction to D. A., *Il Convivio*, ed. G. Busnelli– G. Vandelli, Vol. I, Florence, 1968², pp. xvi–xix.

9. J. L. Huillard-Bréholles, *Historia diplomatica Friderici II*, Vol. IV (I), Paris, 1854, p. 384 (italics mine). Cf. *Conv.* I.i.13.

10. Huillard-Bréholles, *op. cit.*, pp. 384–5. In *Conv.* IV. x–xiii, Dante insists on the contrast between riches and knowledge: only the latter is increased by its distribution. The ardent desire to share his knowledge with his fellow-men is of course one of the driving forces of the *Convivio*.

11. The letter begins with the emperor's intention 'ut jejuni et famelici doctrinarum in ipso regno inveniant unde ipsorum aviditati satisfiat . . .' Later, we find the important declaration: 'Bonum autem hoc rei nostre publice profecturum intendimus, cum subjectorum commoda speciali quadam affectionis gratia providemus, quos sicut convenit eruditos pulcherrima poterit spes fovere, et bona plurima promptis animis expectare; *cum sterilis esse non possit accessio, quam nobilitas sequitur*' (Huillard-Bréholles, *op. cit.*, II (I), Paris, 1852, pp. 450–1. (On the foundation of the University of Naples) see: E. Kantorowicz, *Frederick The Second*, London, 1931, pp. 132–5, and T. C. Van Cleve, *The Emperor Frederick II of Hohenstaufen*, Oxford, 1972, pp. 155–7.

12. V. Russo, *Esperienze e/di letture dantesche*, Naples, 1971, p. 123. Which translations are definitely to be attributed to Michael Scot is still a controversial question: see, e.g., F. Van Steenberghen, *Aristotle in the West*, Louvain, 1955, pp. 90ff.; Vol. III of the *Enciclopedia Dantesca*, Rome, 1971, pp. 950–1; Kantorowicz, *op. cit.*, pp. 339–40.

13. For Nardi's (slightly exaggerated) emphasis on the Averroistic element in the *Convivio*, see: B. Nardi, *Dante e la cultura medievale*, Bari, 1942, pp. 176–209; *Nel mondo di Dante*, Rome, 1944, pp. 41–90; *Dal 'Convivio' alla 'Commedia'*, Rome, 1960, pp. 37–83; *Saggi di filosofia dantesca*, Florence, 1967², pp. 341–80. As is well known, the

leading representative of 'Latin Averroism', Siger of Brabant, is mentioned in *Par.* X.133–8, where his formidable opponent, Thomas Aquinas, is made to acknowledge the *invidiosi veri* propounded by Siger. The most satisfying analysis of this episode is still the one offered by E. Gilson, *Dante et la philosophie*, Paris, 1972³, pp. 256–79, with the conclusion that 'Siger y est introduit comme représentant, non le contenu de l'averroïsme, mais le séparatisme de la philosophie et de la théologie qu'impliquait l'averroïsme latin . . . son propre séparatisme philosophique ne fut, dans la pensée de Dante, qu'un corollaire de la séparation entre le temporel et le spirituel, entre l'Église et l'Empire, à laquelle il aspirait' (p. 273).

14. Cf. Kantorowicz, *op. cit.*, pp. 293–365 ('this intellectual court of his reared a new human species in whom philosophy was no kingly caprice, but a begetter of life'); A. Vallone, 'La componente federiciana della cultura dantesca', in *Dante e Roma*, Florence, 1965, pp. 347–69; G. Tarugi, 'Federico II e il suo umanesimo', in *Dante e la cultura sveva*, Florence, 1970, pp. 207–230; Van Cleve, *op. cit.*, pp. 299–346. Manfred proved himself yet again to be Frederick's true heir when he claimed that 'Nulla scientiarum est similis scientie philosophie, que clarificat animam et facit eam delectari in hoc seculo in perfectione et rectitudine, quod est principium bene esse sui' (quoted by A. Vallone, *op. cit.*, p. 364).

15. Cf. U. Leo's interesting study, 'The Unfinished *Convivio* and Dante's Rereading of the *Aeneid*', *Sehen und Wirklichkeit bei Dante*, Frankfurt-am-Main, 1957, pp. 71–104, and B. Nardi, *Dal 'Convivio'* . . . , ed. *cit.*, pp. 101–2.

16. *Conv.* IV.v.6. The significance of this passage has been well grasped by G. Padoan in his article on 'Enea' in Vol. II of the *Enciclopedia Dantesca* (Rome, 1970, pp. 677–9): 'Ritenendo il racconto virgiliano verità storica narrata in stile poetico, D. "scopre" il disegno provvidenziale che ha voluto l'Impero romano, e che dunque, proprio come affermava il poeta latino, aveva guidato anche il viaggio *di quel giusto/figliuol d'Anchise che venne di Troia (Inf.* I. 73–74) in precisa contemporaneità con ciò che in Palestina veniva preparandosi per l'avvento del Messia . . . rapporto di contemporaneità tutt'altro che pacifico e indiscusso secondo le stesse cronografie medievali, ma che per D. costituisce un'illuminazione decisiva, e che egli pertanto dichiara con quella baldanzosa sicurezza, che non ammette repliche, con la quale suole proclamare le verità che più gli stanno a cuore.' As I have shown in an article to be published in *Studi danteschi*, Dante found this 'rapporto di contemporaneità' in Brunetto Latini's *Tresor* I.xxxiv and invested it with a new significance.

17. For an excellent study of the importance of Rome in Dante's works, see C. T. Davis, *Dante and the Idea of Rome*, Oxford, 1957. That Rome's imperial mission remained a constant factor in Dante's world plan may be seen, e.g., in *Par.* XXVII.61–3, where the reference to Scipio's providential action is placed in the mouth of St Peter, the archetypal pope.

18. *Conv.* III.iii.7–8 and IV.xxvi.9. For a fuller discussion of this evolution and Dante's conception of the literal and allegorical senses in poetry, the reader may wish to consult my article, 'Dante's Allegory', *Romance Philology*, XXVI (1973), esp. pp. 571–91.

19. A. P. d'Entrèves, *op. cit.*, pp. 65–6.

20. I have tried to illustrate the antithetical presence of Simon Peter in the canto devoted to the followers of Simon Magus, in 'The Rock of Peter and *Inferno XIX*', *Romance Philology*, XXIII (1970), pp. 462–79.

21. The words placed in italics offer further proof, if more were needed, that Dante was thinking of pagan Rome: the glory of Christian Rome had been sufficiently 'predica*ta*.' For Dante's exaltation of the Roman heroes, see C. T. Davis, *op. cit.*, esp. pp. 43ff. and 83–4.

22. P. Renucci, 'Dante e gli Svevi', in *Dante e l'Italia meridionale*, Florence, 1966, p. 131.

23. *DVE* I.xii.4. The expression *brutalia dedignantes* calls to mind Ulysses' famous exhortation to his companions, 'fatti non foste a viver come bruti' (with—possibly—a last backward glance at Circe), and the impassioned tones of the *Convivio*: esp. IV.vii, 'coloro dirizzare intendo ne' quali alcuno lumetto di ragione per buona loro natura vive ancora, ché de li altri tanto è da curare quanto di bruti animali ... manifesto è che vivere ne li animali è sentire—animali, dico, bruti—, vivere ne l'uomo è ragione usare ... così levando l'ultima potenza de l'anima, cioè la ragione, non rimane piú uomo, ma cosa con anima sensitiva solamente, cioè animale bruto.'

24. For a recent summary of Dante's attitude towards Frederick III of Aragon, see: P. Palumbo, 'Il "novissimo" Federico nel giudizio dantesco', in *Atti del convegno di studi su Dante e la Magna Curia*, Palermo, 1967, pp. 226–35. Cf. D. Mack Smith's surprising announcement that Frederick 'became Dante's favourite because he defied the political intrusions of five Popes' (*A History of Sicily: Medieval Sicily, 800–1713*, London, 1968, pp. 81–2). See also E. Moore, 'Dante and Sicily', *Studies in Dante: II*, Oxford, 1899, pp. 269–302. Despite other criticisms, Dante did not hesitate to refer to Frederick as King of Sicily in *Conv.* IV.vi.20.

25. Ovid, *Fasti*, VI.353. The phrase *solium Iovis* occurs in Horace, *Ep.* I.xvii.34, and Suetonius, *De Vita Caesarum*, IV.lvii.3.

26. As Kantorowicz points out. 'It is by no means accidental that Frederick's first really close approximation to the Caesars occurred in Sicily' (*op. cit.*, p. 223; cf. R. Folz, *The Concept of Empire in Western Europe*, London, 1969, pp. 111–2). The Emperor referred to Sicily as the 'apple of his eye' and intended it to be *invidia principum et norma regnorum*. Manfred was crowned King of Sicily and Apulia in 1258. Of course, he never became emperor, though the Ghibelline victory at Montaperti in 1260 seemed to open the way to the highest power. He solicited the imperial title from the people of Rome in his Manifesto of 24 May 1265. See: R. Morghen, *Il tramonto della potenza sveva in Italia (1250–1266)*, Rome, 1936.

27. This awareness led Ercole (*op. cit.*, Vol. I) to claim that Dante at this time pinned his hopes on national unity embodied in the *regnum italicum*. Ercole's arguments won favour with Barbi (*Problemi fondamentali per un nuovo commento della D.C.*, Florence, 1956, pp. 69–89), but were subjected to detailed criticism by B. Sumner in 'Dante and the "Regnum Italicum"', *Medium Aevum*, I (1932), pp. 2–23. Cf. P. G. Ricci, 'Dante e l'impero di Roma', in *Dante e Roma, ed. cit.*, pp. 137–49. Nevertheless, the idea of an intermediate stage (represented by an Italian kingdom or national unity)

lingers on. See the inaccuracies contained in A. Marigo's introduction to his edition of the *De Vulgari Eloquentia* (Florence, 1957³, pp. lxxxii-iv).

28.   *Ep.* VIII.107–28 (italics mine; pp. 137–41 of Toynbee's edition, *Dantis Alagherii Epistolae*, Oxford, 1966²). In the chapter entitled 'Ecclesia', d'Entrèves uses this letter to prove that 'la Chiesa e non lo Stato è divenuta ora la maggiore preoccupazione di Dante' (*op. cit.*, p. 86). But the letter was written to the cardinals in conclave at Carpentras. It is therefore hardly surprising that the emphasis is mainly on Rome as the seat of church and papal power —quite simply, the cardinals were not there to elect an emperor or to be reminded of imperial rights in Rome. They were to act 'ut Vasconum opprobrium, qui tam dira cupidine conflagrantes Latinorum gloriam sibi usurpare contendunt, per saecula cuncta futura sit posteris in exemplum' (140–2).

29.   I do not wish to imply that Dante was unaware of, or that he rejected, the traditional—and largely rhetorical—link between Rome and the Empire; but, whatever his views on the subject, they were very different from his later convictions, and an ideological abyss separates his references to Rome in the *DVE* from his exaltation of the Eternal City in the *Convivio*. Frederick II, indeed, had striven to turn the prestige of Rome into a political reality: see Kantorowicz, *op. cit.*, pp. 444–56, and Folz, *op. cit.*, pp. 90–97, 112–3, 203–4. If Dante was aware of this attempted *renovatio*, his silence is all the more striking—cf. the emphasis deliberately placed on Rome in *Mon.* III.x.1, where he attacks the idea that the Donation of Constantine had transferred to the popes not the Empire but 'Imperii sedem, scilicet Romaii . . . cum multis alms Imperii dignitatibus.'

Il Mito e il Concetto
dell'Eroe nel Boccaccio

Il concetto e il mito dell'eroe si evolvono nell'autunno del Medioevo in senso decisivo soprattutto per opera del Boccaccio. Sono avviati da lui risolutamente a una impostazione non tanto rinascimentale quanto fondamentalmente moderna: perché con ardita novità e con sensibilità umana pluralistica egli vi fa successivamente intervenire la classe borghese mercantesca, il mondo femminile, il poeta considerato vate.

Come hanno mostrato i classici studi di Joseph Campbell e di Sydney Hook, la forza in senso antropologico e in senso storico è al centro di quel mito. E in un folgorante saggio Simone Weil ne ha rivelato nell'*Iliade* l'espressione poetica insuperata, perché aperta alla patetica simpatia per la distruzione della forza stessa e quindi per il vinto. La possanza è l'anima e il segno dell'eroe: eroe nella guerra o nell'amore o nel reggere i popoli o nel redimerli vincendo la morte. Persino l'eroe-santo più emblematico—cioè il martire o l'asceta—vince fisicamente con la sua forza quella dei persecutori o dei demoni: è infatti per antonomasia 'il santo atleta'.

La civiltà feudale, al di là dell'epopea di potenza di Carlo e di Orlando, tenta con Tristano e Lancillotto di innestare sull'elemento della prestanza fisica quello dell'amore. Ma l'amore rimane soprattutto una meta ideale: un punto di arrivo al di là delle azioni e delle rappresentazioni, ancora sempre prevalentemente dirette ad avventure di violenza e di guerra.

Tutte le prime opere del Boccaccio riflettono questa incertezza, questo bilicarsi tra forza e amore della letteratura cavalleresca quando vuole delineare i suoi eroi. Sono del resto opere scritte nell'atmosfera di cultura francese caratteristica della Napoli angioina, dove, com'è noto, il Boccaccio visse il suo tirocinio letterario tra il 1327 e il 1340.

Troiolo, il protagonista del primo poemetto, il *Filostrato* (1335?), ci riporta proprio per le sue gesta guerresche e per il suo amore infelice nell'ambiente omerico di Troia assediata dai greci. È il più possente dei troiani dopo Ettore, è terrore di guerra per i greci. Ma quella sua Troia è una 'città grande e dilettosa' che 'in triegua' svolge una vita tranquilla e operosa, da grande comune medievale; quei guerrieri—si chiamino Troiolo o Diomede, Pandaro o Ulisse, Ettore o Achille—non sono eroi da mito ma cavalieri da corte, personaggi non da epopea ma da romanzo. Il racconto infatti, nonostante la profluvie di eroi presentati, mira (rifacendosi a Benoit de St Maure) non a creare modelli umani ma a oggettivare esemplarmente una vicenda amorosa lasciandola sospesa fra la lirica e la narrativa. Il Boccaccio opera positivamente soprattutto in quel processo che, attraverso Chaucer, imporrà i contrastanti profili di Troiolo e di Criseida (il primo dei maliosi ritratti femminili del Boccaccio) come una suprema emblematizzazione tutta amorosa— della passione e della civetteria—nel dramma di Shakespeare.

Dal poema cavalleresco al romanzo, cioè dal *Filostrato* al *Filocolo* (1336–38?), il gioco si inverte ma i risultati sono simili. L'ambiente è ancora fittiziamente classico, della tarda romanità, ma in realtà comunale e cortigiano. Florio, figlio del re di Marmorina (cioè Verona), conduce una *quête* tutta amorosa per ritrovare la sua rapita Biancofiore: ma la conduce secondo i moduli e i *topoi* più consueti e caratteristici dell'eroe tradizionale. Impone il suo vigore in battaglie, in tornei, e persino contro potenze mostruose; conquista l'amata espugnando un castello munitissimo, fonda città e domina e pacifica popoli; diventa campione della fede e converte popolazioni intere. La sua figura rimane per questo incerta fra abbandonati e sentimentaleggianti sospiri d'amore e tipiche espressioni di possanza, da campione della corazza e della spada. E anche per questo il *Filocolo* resta un centone composito.

Neppure il *Teseida* (1339–41?), nonostante i suoi generosi scenari dell'Ellade mitica, riesce a superare queste ambiguità e a proporre un chiaro modello di eroe. Eppure è un poema decisamente epico: anzi il Boccaccio, rispondendo idealmente a un lamento levato da Dante nel suo *De vulgari eloquentia* (II 2, 10), afferma di essere finalmente il 'primo a cantare di Marte Nel volgar lazio' (XII 84). Ma Teseo resta una figura astratta, una convenzionale *silhouette* di guerriero e di reggitore di popoli. I protagonisti sono invece Arcita e Palemone, i due giovani tebani che si contendono l'amore della pisanellesca amazzone Emilia: e nel guerreggiare, nel torneare, nel duellare sono due tipici cavalieri di corte arturiana, con pesanti scadimenti borghesi. La stessa dolente pietà che accompagna la fine di Arcita non è di sublime origine omerica, ma come è stato recentemente dimostrato, è un puntuale calco tristaniano.

Il Boccaccio cioè, lungo tutto il suo tirocinio letterario a Napoli, non giunge a superare gli schemi della letteratura romanzesco-cavalleresca. Non riesce a proporre un nuovo o almeno un chiaro modello di eroe: gli stessi protagonisti delle sue opere sono il risultato ambiguo e composito di suggerimenti delle contrastanti tradizioni letterarie precedenti.

Il trasferimento, fra il 1340 e il '41, nella Firenze comunale e mercantile, in una cultura prevalentemente allegorico-didattica e moralistica, determina una svolta decisiva nella sua visione del mondo e della vita e nelle sue scelte artistiche. A narrazioni incertamente oscillanti fra amori, avventure, armi, si sostituisce un grande e grandioso tema che si impone sempre più risolutamente dalla *Comedia delle Ninfe* al *Decameron* e poi alle opere morale-storico-erudite della maturità. È la rappresentazione – continuamente variata ma sempre più chiara e sistematica—della misura che delle sue capacità di bene e di male dà l'uomo al confronto con le grandi forze, che, quali strumenti della Provvidenza, dominano il mondo: la Potenza, la Ricchezza, la Fortuna, l'Amore, l'Ingegno. È questa la grande 'commedia umana' che deve idealmente integrare la 'commedia divina' così entusiasticamente ammirata dal Boccaccio. È il tema che emerge dalle varie e faticate esperienze vissute dal Boccaccio nella raffinata e cosmopolita corte angioina, nell'avventuroso e spregiudicato ambiente mercantesco della sua famiglia, nella vita galante e *dorée* della gioventù napoletana, nei miraggi letterari ed eruditi delle sue ostinate e dure ore di studio, nelle procellose vicende del comune fiorentino stretto fra la potenza economica dei suoi grandi banchieri dominanti l'Europa e la cupidigia della politica angioina e papale. Giorno per giorno il Boccaccio—attraverso i racconti del padre e le proprie dirette esperienze di giovane commesso di una delle più potenti compagnie (quella dei Bardi)—aveva constatato, anzi aveva vissuto il graduale cedere del potere militare e politico a quello economico. Il solenne Re Roberto di Napoli, i pretenziosi Pontefici di Avignone, gli altezzosi imperatori boemi e germanici, gli stessi sovrani al di qua e al di là della Manica, si rivelavano 're da sermone' di fronte ai risoluti e spregiudicati finanzieri italiani. I così detti potenti erano in realtà alla mercé dei 'mercatanti', che imponevano loro non solo titoli e riconoscimenti solenni e taglie pesantissime, ma anche le linee fondamentali della politica, le alleanze e le intese, le decisioni di pace e di guerra. In molte regge d'Europa gli uomini d'affari toscani potevano a buon diritto anticipare l'affermazione baldanzosa di secoli a venire: 'L'Etat c'est nous'. I re di Francia e di Inghilterra avevano dovuto abbassare le armi quando i Peruzzi e i Frescobaldi, loro banchieri, lo avevano imposto perché quella guerra rovinava traffici che molto li interessavano: gli imperatori, da Ludovico il Bavaro a Carlo di Boemia, erano docili strumenti dei mercatanti, che presentavano loro, con risoluti discorsi, eleganti borse rigonfie di migliaia di bei fiorini d'oro; gli Angioini avevano dovuto cessare dalla loro azione contro la Sicilia ribelle (e ormai aragonese) quando i Bardi e i Canigiani, loro tesorieri, avevano smesso di finanziarli, perché il commercio con la Sicilia e la Catalogna era loro vantaggioso; Nicola Acciaiuoli, compagno prediletto del giovane Boccaccio, colla forza della sua banca era divenuto proprio in quegli anni, come scriveva un cronista, 'facitore e disfacitore di re', arbitro dei regni e degli imperi del Mediterraneo. La potenza degli eserciti era soppiantata da quella delle banche e delle compagnie mercantili; la spada e la lancia dal fiorino, il vero dollaro del Medioevo; la strategia militare e politica dalle nuove tecniche economiche, scoperte dalle compagnie toscane con la lettera di cambio, con la partita doppia, con il circolo economico e produttivo. Di fronte alla forza fisica e materiale si ergeva giovanile e baldanzosa la forza dell'intelligenza e dell'avvedutezza umana. Sembrava inverarsi nella storia il mito eterno dell'Orco e di Pollicino, la esemplare vicenda biblica del gigantesco Golia vinto dal piccolo e ingegnoso David.

In questo profondo rinnovamento nella gerarchia dei poteri, in questo rovesciamento del rapporto tra vigore del braccio e vigore dell'ingegno, poteva aprirsi il varco anche una nuova valutazione sociale delle opere dello spirito. Esse potevano essere facilmente sentite quali elementi decisivi e necessari in quel rinnovamento sociale, e non solo quali preziosi ornamenti della vita signorile o quali eleganti esercizi cortigiani o ecclesiastici. Come la nuova *leadership* capitalistica cercava la sua giustificazione teoretica nel pensiero francescano e tomistico, così la nuova classe dirigente si annetteva la letteratura e l'arte più moderne. Non a caso le prime citazioni di Dante appaiono, come ho dimostrato anni or sono, nel diario di Domenico Lenzi, un mercante di grano, e i primi lettori e trascrittori della *Divina Commedia* escono dal cerchio dei notai e dei banchieri. Non a caso i cronisti più impegnati e informati (i Villani e lo Stefani) e i poeti più acclamati in quegli anni (i Frescobaldi, i Rinuccini, i Pucci) appartengono a famiglie mercantili o ai ceti notarili e giuridici legatissimi alla vita commerciale (Lapo Gianni, Cino da Pistoia). Non a caso gli artisti più nuovi e felici, da Giotto ai Gaddi e all'Orcagna, lavorano per le cappelle della nuova borghesia e per le Arti, cioè per le organizzazioni produttive della Firenze, centro finanziario dell'Europa civile.

Proprio in questo quadro sociale e attraverso le esperienze dirette dello scrittore nella vita della nuova classe dirigente si profilano nell'opera del Boccaccio il ritratto e il mito del tutto rinnovati dell'uomo esemplare, dell'eroe. Già nella seconda opera fiorentina, l'*Amorosa Visione* (1342), la gerarchia dei valori e la conseguente proposta di eroi esemplari rivelano un radicale rinnovamento. Il poema introduce, come è noto, nella letteratura il tema anzi il 'genere' dei 'trionfi': uno schema subito dopo ripreso e imposto autorevolmente dal Petrarca e sviluppato poi entusiasticamente, su piano europeo, almeno fino all'autunno del Rinascimento e al Barocco stesso. Presenta i grandi personaggi dell'antichità e dell'evo medio e moderno, fino ai contemporanei, ordinati attorno ai simboli delle forze di cui erano soprattutto rappresentanti esemplari, cioè eroi: la Sapienza, la Potenza, la Ricchezza, l'Amore, la Fortuna che tutti eguaglia e travolge. Non sono semplici enumerazioni, come nella tradizione epica; o cascate di nomi meravigliosi per accrescere autorità, come nel *Carroccio* di Rambaldo o nel *Roman de la Rose* o nel *Tesoretto* di Brunetto (per citare solo tre capofila delle tre letterature romanze). Sono consacrazioni degli eroi delle maggiori forze che agiscono nell'umanità; consacrazioni minutamente calibrate e studiate, proprio—come ho dimostrato in un mio saggio—in senso esemplare ed eroico. Ma accanto alle tradizionali categorie degli eroi della Forza e dell'Amore (in cui ritornano le figure canoniche, da Giove amoroso, da Ercole e Sansone a Orlando e al Saladino, a Paride e Tristano e Lancillotto) è fatto posto, con novità esplicitamente dichiarata, a quelle della Sapienza e della Ricchezza. E in questi due trionfi campeggiano, atteggiate eroicamente, anche figure di contemporanei, o quasi, al Boccaccio: Dante e Giotto, per la prima volta collocati nell'Olimpo dei grandi; e i mercanti del tempo, con a capo proprio un agente dei Bardi, il padre stesso del Boccaccio.

È una novità ardita e sorprendente, in senso letterario e sociale, sul piano della concezione e del costume: sia per i due nuovi valori che risolutamente si impongono fra quelli tradizionali, sia per l'audacia di proporre come eroi personaggi moderni, anzi contemporanei, con una eccezionale apertura alla continuità di certi valori dal mondo biblico a quello classico e a quello moderno. È una novità affermata astrattamente e con gravi rigidezze e incertezze nell'*Amorosa Visione*. Solo vari anni dopo, attraverso le multiformi esperienze di vita e di cultura di un decennio, si invera umanamente e artisticamente nel *Decameron*, il capolavoro e la *summa* della narrativa europea del Medioevo.

Già nella struttura unitaria dell'opera (quale ho potuto identificare e delineare in un volume tradotto ora per la serie della New York University) si riflette quella radicale novità di posizioni. Il *Decameron* infatti si svolge proprio come una calcolatissima rappresentazione di quello che l'uomo può, nel male e nel bene, al confronto delle grandi forze della Fortuna, dell'Amore e dell'Ingegno. Descrive l'itinerario

ascensionale (gotico in certo senso) dello *jedermann* dal vizio rappresentato nella prima giornata alla virtù glorificata nell'ultima,
attraverso le prove fornite al paragone con la Fortuna (nella II e III
giornata), con l'Amore (IV e V giornata), con l'Ingegno (VI, VII
e VIII giornata). Dal campione del vizio, Ciappelletto, protagonista
della prima novella e configurato attraverso un linguaggio caratterizzante in un Giuda moderno, si giunge nell'ultima novella all'eroina
della virtù, Griselda, stilizzata attraverso preziose volute allusive
nella figura della Vergine. Come l'aspra e amara riprensione del
vizio nella prima giornata così l'esaltazione della virtù nell'ultima
coinvolgono i tre ordini della classe dirigente nell'Italia comunale e
dell'autunno del Medioevo: cioè i potenti per forza materiale, per
dominio economico, per preparazione intellettuale. Ma in questa
grandiosa commedia dell'uomo il Boccaccio vuole soprattutto dar
rilievo al nuovo eroe, al mercante: per la sua multiforme intraprendenza si era imposto in quegli anni alla sua attenzione umana,
fino a una figurazione quasi prometeica quando ne aveva descritto—
col suo *De Canaria et insulis noviter repertis*—l'invitta audacia nello
scoprire nuove terre e nuovi mondi.

Per la prima volta nella letteratura europea ricevono così nel
Decameron alta consacrazione il mondo e l'azione delle compagnie
mercantili. È un movimento decisivo, fra Duecento e Trecento, per
la storia dell'Europa e del Mediterraneo: sui relitti dell'ormai
frantumato impero franco-germanico, sulle rovine di quello bizantino
ormai travolto dall'ondata islamica, crea un'unità sociale-economica
da Cadice a Damasco, dalla Tunisia alla Scozia. È un'unità promossa
da veri eroi dell'intraprendenza e della tenacia umana, da un pugno
di uomini eccezionali lanciati alla conquista dell'Europa e dell'Asia,
alla scoperta di nuove terre a Occidente e a Oriente. Isolata ancora
nell'opera di Dante in un cerchio di aristocratico disprezzo per 'la
gente nova e i subiti guadagni' ignorata come inferiore o estranea
dalla raffinata esperienza del Petrarca, questa classe è fatta irrompere
dal Boccaccio nella commedia umana del *Decameron*: e la domina
con la sua esuberante vitalità. Non ci riferiamo solo alla folla di
temi, di ambienti, di personaggi, di usi, di riferimenti vari che
colora con le tinte vivaci e sanguigne, proprie a questo mondo, più
della metà delle novelle (precisamente 60 su 100). È soprattutto la
centralità nello stesso disegno ideale dell'opera, nel suo significato
esemplare e in senso umano e artistico, a configurare la presenza di
questo ceto nella fantasia narrativa del Boccaccio come caratteristica,
anzi insostituibile. Quella leggenda dell'uomo tra Vizio e Virtù non
poteva trovare in quell'età esempi di più potente e prepotente
eloquenza visiva. Dopo le ferree sequenze dei campioni della forza,
dopo le dorate schiere dei cavalieri della spada e dell'amore, è solo

il mondo dei mercanti che fra Duecento e Trecento offre i campioni più vivi ed esemplari nell'agone umano. È in quel mondo che, per ripetere Stendhal, la pianta uomo ormai cresce più vigoreggiante: e offre personaggi capaci di imporsi come eroi da ammirare e da imitare, come incarnazioni e simboli di valori e di forze che ormai danno nuovo senso alla vita. Erano uomini che—come rappresenta il Boccaccio nel *Decameron*—correvano il mondo sempre in lotta con gli agguati della Fortuna, sempre pronti a provare la loro elegante sveltezza umana nelle più diverse avventure d'Amore, sempre protesi a vincere col proprio ingegno le iniziative o le insidie dell'Ingegno altrui. Re e principi, paladini e cavalieri, ecclesiastici e universitari avevano tradizionalmente fornito i personaggi alla letteratura sulle vicende di Fortuna, di Amore, di Ingegno. Sono ora soppiantati risolutamente dalla energia e dalla evidenza di questi nuovi eroi della vita comunale e dell'ultima civiltà medievale: eroi dalla mente aperta, dall'intelligenza pronta, dalla cultura solida, dalle aspirazioni che arrivavano all'ambizione principesca e all'orgoglio regale, tenaci e audaci. Imponevano dappertutto una tale personalità che sollecitava i principi a intimorita blandizia e le popolazioni a ammirato rancore, come per chi aveva fra le mani le loro sorti. E tornavano a casa dalle più lontane contrade onusti di esperienze e di ricchezze, per applicare le une e le altre alla grande politica e alle sublimi creazioni dell'arte, consacrandole negli splendidi palazzi pubblici e privati, nelle chiese e nei conventi, negli spedali e negli Studi, che hanno eternato la civiltà di quel secolo. La stessa evocazione della vita splendida di questi mercanti, come è stato fatta lungo tutta una letteratura—da Gilles li Muisis al Villani—ha i colori di una leggenda dorata ed eroica. Il loro esempio è, per dirla con Renan, 'la plus grande leçon d'énergie et de volonté de l'histoire'.

Per questo il Boccaccio sceglie fra di essi i personaggi per rappresentare esemplarmente la storia dell'uomo: anzi sceglie i campioni-modello per il comportamento di ogni uomo, cioè gli autentici eroi.

La prudenza più sottile e più elegantemente vittoriosa è esemplariamente fermata in Melchisedech (I 3) e la solida fede religiosa, inattaccabile dalle contingenze, in Giannotto e Abramo (I 2). La scrupolosa e invincibile fedeltà agli impegni trova in Alessandro Agolanti il suo campione da apologo, redimito com'è fiabescamente, alla fine della novella, dalla corona del Regno di Scozia (II 3). La castità e la fedeltà coniugale hanno una loro espressione così apodittica in Bernabò e in Ginevra (II 9), che proprio seguendo questa novella saranno poi emblematizzate da Shakespeare nel suo *Cymbeline*. L'amore, l'amore insieme più totale e casto, più abbandonato ed esemplare, è stilizzato in Lorenzo e Lisabetta, in Pasquino e Simona, in Girolamo e Salvestra (IV 5 e 7 e 8). L'avventura più audace e intraprendente fino al rischio della vita, si incarna nei suoi valori umani in modelli insuperabili come Martuccio e Gianni da Procida (V 2 e 6). La gentilezza umana più elevata e più discreta ha i suoi cavalieri esemplari, senza macchia e senza paura, in Federigo e in Torello (V 9 e X 9). La generosità spinta fino alla spontanea offerta della propria vita splende in senso paradigmatico nella favolosa figura di Natan (X 3).

Sono questi (e tanti altri simili) tutti personaggi appartenenti al mondo mercantile: e sono tutti presentati e atteggiati come i veri eroi della nuova umanità. E, col processo consueto nelle epopee e nelle raffigurazioni di società eroiche, agli Achilli e agli Orlandi della mercatura sono opposti i Tersiti e i Gano: ser Ciappelletto abisso di nequizia (I 1), Ambrogiuolo tutto viltà menzognera (II 9), la mercantessa milanese, incarnazione di turpe avidità (VIII 1): quasi a dar maggior risalto, colle tenebre del contrasto, alla luce e alla esemplarità di quei campioni di virtù diverse ma egualmente sublimi.

Si profila così, attraverso di essi, il ritratto nuovo dell'eroe. Anch'egli—come nei miti antichi—bello nella persona e buon parlatore; dominatore non colla forza del braccio ma con quella dell'ingegno e della prudenza; valutatore geniale delle situazioni e delle congiunture mondiali; pronto a cogliere le occasioni, anche le più complesse e remote, come quelle offerte dalle Crociate e dalle trasmigrazioni mongole; aperto e generoso, leale e fedele, sensibile a tutti gli interessi umani.

Sono di questa tempra i campioni di quella invitta intraprendenza, di quella insaziabile curiosità di uomini e di paesi che avevano avuto nella storia il nome di Marco Polo, di Guido e Ugolino Vivaldi, di Niccolò Acciaiuoli e nella leggenda del Boccaccio hanno quelli di Alessandro Agolanti, di Landolfo Rufolo, di Torello di Stra, di Antigono di Famagosta, di Natan e Mitridanes. Emergono, nel *Decameron*, questi nuovi eroi in una luce di crepuscolo come in tutte le epopee gli autentici eroi; come quelli omerici al tramonto della civiltà achea sotto l'uragano dorico. Le crisi e le difficoltà degli anni quaranta—provocate dal nuovo assetto politico europeo nei grandi regni accentrati—erano state fatte precipitare dal terribile flagello della peste del '48, che aveva ridotto a un decimo la popolazione fiorentina. Alla forza espansiva e esplosiva della generazione fra Duecento e Trecento era successo a metà del secolo una più cauta e sistematica organizzazione che mirava esclusivamente al maggior guadagno. Si iniziava il momento riflessivo dell'economia capitalistica toscana: quello dominato dalla legge della 'ragion di mercatura': una ragione ferrea e spietata come due secoli dopo sarà la 'ragion di stato', dura e inumana quale è deprecata nell'introduzione al

Decameron, quale è raffigurata demoniacamente nella prima novella, quale è continuamente bollata dal Boccaccio perché, come egli scrive, 'tutte ha discacciate…le belle e laudevoli usanze' (VI 9,4).

Proprio al tramonto di questa società che nell'autunno del Medioevo aveva creato i presupposti del nuovo vivere civile e sociale, il Boccaccio crea la sua commedia multiforme e umanissima: con una sensibilità ai valori e ai limiti di quel grandioso movimento, desta e risentita, ma che non diminuisce l'ammirazione e il nostalgico vagheggiamento per l'energia vitale di quegli uomini d'eccezione. E di questi veri e nuovi eroi di una umanità fidente soprattutto nella forza dell'ingegno e dell'intraprendenza, sempre tesi verso nuovi orizzonti, tetragoni ai colpi di ventura e giovanilmente fidenti nelle proprie forze e nel proprio destino, egli si fa nel *Decameron* il rapsodo appassionato, l'ispirato *trouvère*.

Al centro dell'epopea dell'autunno del Medioevo in Italia, qual'è il *Decameron*, doveva necessariamente svolgersi la grandiosa *quête* dei più arditi precursori della società moderna; doveva campeggiare in primo piano la *chanson de geste* dei nuovi eroi, dei paladini di mercatura.

La creazione del mito del nuovo eroe è possibile nel *Decameron* perché il Boccaccio aveva acutamente penetrato la eccezionale umanità e la ricca forza spirituale dei grandi mercanti. Al di là di pregiudizi di classe o di apparenze materiali, egli l'aveva identificata come la carica essenziale del loro agire e del grandioso movimento civile che aveva avviato la moderna società capitalistica. Aveva avvertito—come ripete con le sue più luminose raffigurazioni del *Decameron*—che i migliori esemplari di quella nuova borghesia avevano veramente portato la civiltà nell'Europa occidentale e nel Mediterraneo tutto e avevano aperto le vie al progresso, ma senza armi, senza violenze, senza ostentazione di forza brutale. Aveva identificato, il Boccaccio, l'anima di quel loro dinamico impegno e di quel loro grandioso successo nel precetto elevato e umanissimo che stava in fronte a un loro statuto: 'Niuna impresa per minima che sia può avere cominciamento o fine senza queste tre cose: cioè senza potere, senza sapere, senza con amore volere'.

Erano—il potere, il sapere, il volere—tutte doti interiori che lievitate dall'amore configuravano il nuovo eroe al di là degli schemi di forza dei miti antichi e medievali. E questa rottura dei vecchi moduli, questo rinnovamento di valutazioni aveva aperto al Boccaccio, anche al di là dell'ambiente mercantesco, nuove prospettive eroiche. Ne aveva anzitutto ampliato il cerchio tradizionalmente limitato agli uomini. E vi aveva risolutamente immesso le

signore della carne e dello spirito, ardite così nella licenza come nella
virtù, ma sempre palpitanti di umanità, e alle volte veramente
esemplari nelle capacità di male e di bene che caratterizzano l'uomo.
Non erano, come quelle di Ovidio o delle opere giovanili, solo eroine
perché *grandes amoureuses*, secondo la definizione dell'Hauvette; e
non appartenevano solo alle classi elevate, delle principesse e delle
dame della letteratura arturiana o comunque romanzesca. Gilletta,
Ginevra, Andreuola, Simona, Giovanna, Lisa, Griselda, modeste
borghesi o addirittura umili lavoratrici, sono presentate in un'atmosfera di gentilezza e di forza, e con tratti così ammirati e marcati da
non essere in nulla inferiori ai nuovi eroi del *Decameron*. È un
ampliamento, questo, che già raggiunto nel capolavoro troverà
la sua più sistematica affermazione, dieci anni dopo, nel *De mulieribus
claris*. Rovesciando la canonica tradizione classica e medievale dei
trattati sugli eroi e sugli uomini illustri (riconsacrata proprio allora
da un'autorità come il Petrarca col suo *De viris*) il Boccaccio pre-
senterà centosei donne, da Eva alla contemporanea Regina Giovanna, come protagoniste della storia. E accanto a personaggi
illustri egli farà anche posto a donne elevate al rango di eroine
perché artiste squisite (Saffo e Leunzio e Cornificia, XLVII, LX,
LXXXVI); o perché il loro agire esemplare è da citare a modello.
Così proporrà la povera femminetta pugliese che arditamente
soccorse i fuggiaschi Romani di Canne, dichiarandola polemica-
mente superiore allo stesso Alessandro (LXIX); o la barbara Galata
che, novella Giuditta, decapitò il centurione romano che l'aveva
violentata (LXXIII); o le generose e fiere borghesi dei comuni
italiani, Gualdrada e Camiola (CIII, CV); o persino, spregiudi-
catamente, prostitute intrepide e generose, come Leena e Epicare
(I, e XCIII) perché, afferma, 'est [virtus] ubique preciosa, nec
aliter fedatur, scelerum contagione, quam solaris radius ceno
inficiatur immixtus' (la chiara allusione guinizelliana scatta qui
quanto mai significativa per il suo valore esemplario). *Decameron* e
De mulieribus saranno insieme, nel 1370, sullo scrittoio del Boccaccio
per essere riveduti e ricopiati nei due autografi che abbiamo avuto
la ventura di scoprire recentemente, l'amico Ricci ed io, a Firenze e a
Berlino. L'eccezionale ampliamento operato lungo vent'anni di lavoro
letterario nel mito classico e medievale dell'eroe era dunque profonda-
mente presente e operante nel Boccaccio, anche nella sua maturità,
anche nell'entusiastico impegno classicistico degli ultimi vent'anni.

Ma quella visione dell'eroe soprattutto come modello eccezionale
di volontà e di doti naturali, se apre il varco a personaggi sia femminili che socialmente inferiori e fino allora esclusi, amplia risolutamente anche le prospettive in senso spirituale. Il conte d'Anguersa
chiuso nella dignità del suo silenzio di condannato ingiustamente e

di ramingo e mendico come il dantesco Romeo di Villanova (II 8); Girolamo che soffre tacitamente fino alla morte per non compromettere l'amata andata sposa ad un altro (IV 8); messer Ansaldo che supera l'ardore sensuale proprio per cavalleresca pietà verso Dianora (X 5), sono veri eroi che il Boccaccio delinea e presenta con severa commozione e propone a modello. Le vittorie intellettuali e morali non contano meno di quelle materiali o guerresche: anzi caratterizzano meglio l'eroe. Esemplare in questo senso, più altamente di ogni altro, Federigo degli Alberighi (V 9). La sua rinunzia pacata e spoglia di ogni gesto spettacolare, la sua povertà silente e dignitosa, la sua prontezza non ragionata nel sacrificare all'amata (pur sempre ritrosa) l'ultimo ricordo della sua vita gentilesca— l'amato falcone—compongono il suo profilo in una luce eroica ricca di nuovi sensi umani. Per esser candidi e disadorni sono forse più profondi e certo più intimi di quelli raffigurati nei grandi affreschi della generosità di principi e di cavalieri. I gesti umili di Federigo assumono così un'esemplarità solenne non meno del duello eroico d'un paladino per la sua dama: e il cavaliere delle ardue rinunzie interiori, delle lotte silenziose, il cavaliere d'una umanità spiritualmente gentile e generosa, si pone accanto ai cavalieri della spada e della possanza guerresca con una dignità più intima e più persuasiva. Anche in questo senso e anche nel *Decameron* il Boccaccio mostra così una eccezionale apertura alla continuità che, malgrado le apparenze, lega le diverse espressioni umane. Come sentiva l'ininterrotto messaggio della poesia attraverso civiltà e lingue diverse (da Omero a Dante e ai suoi stessi contemporanei, dalle forme più aristocratiche a quelle più popolaresche), così avvertiva e rappresentava l'incontro fra due società che avevano miti e modelli diversi: quella feudale irta di ferro e d'oro, solenne nei suoi atteggiamenti nobilmente statuari, e quella della più splendida età comunale, tutta sapienza e cortesia umana nella misurata eleganza dei gesti e delle parole. Federigo degli Alberighi e Lisabetta da Messina hanno una nobiltà umana non inferiore a Re Carlo d'Angiò o a Ghismonda, la principessa normanna (V 9, IV 5 e X 6, IV 1); Gentile de' Carisendi non è meno cavalleresco di Re Pietro d'Aragona (X 4 e X 7); l'Andreuola ha una fierezza aristocratica non inferiore alla Marchesa del Monferrato (IV 6 e I 5). Non sono, questi personaggi, borghesi o popolari, incoronati o ingemmati come quelli della generazione precedente: ma sono ricchi di un'umanità più profonda e più vicina alla nostra sensibilità, di una capacità di sacrificio più semplice ma più intima, seppure esemplarmente eroica.

Il Boccaccio sembra riprendere più esplicitamente proprio questa contrapposizione di modelli quando, anni dopo, scrivendo a Jacopo di Pizzinga afferma:

in spem venio atque credulitatem, Deum ytalico nomini misertum, dum video eum e gremio sue largitatis in ytalorum pectora effundere animas ab antiquis non differentes, avidas scilicet non rapina vel sanguine, non fraude vel violentia, non ambitione vel decipulis sibi honores exquirere, sed laudabili exercitio, duce poesi, nomen pretendere in evum longinquum, conarique ut possint viventes adhuc volitare per ora virorum.

(Ep. XVIII). Appunto per questi motivi il Boccaccio proclama Jacopo un eroe e un modello.

Nella caratterizzazione attraverso l'ingegno e la virtù interviene ora decisivo il crisma della poesia. Proprio l'essenza e i motivi ideali e sociali della poesia il Boccaccio, negli anni dopo la composizione del *Decameron*, aveva assiduamente meditato. Aveva iniziato nel 1350 la *Genologia deorum gentilium* nel cui finale campeggia la grande sintesi sulle ragioni eterne della poesia; aveva steso nel '51 la prima redazione della *Vita di Dante* in cui quelle ragioni sono riferite a una grande esperienza concreta come quella di Dante; aveva nel '51 discusse quelle sue convinzioni a Padova col Petrarca, leggendo fianco a fianco alcuni testi essenziali (il *Pro Archia*, le pagine petrarchesche nella familiare al fratello Gherardo X 4, e nella metrica a Zoilo II 11).

All'eroe dell'azione, sia essa espressione di potenza materiale o di intraprendenza morale-sociale, si affianca così nella concezione boccacciana degli anni cinquanta-sessanta l'eroe della meditazione e della poesia. È un eroe, che—coerentemente alle convinzioni della nuova società borghese—era già presente nelle stilizzazioni della *Amorosa Visione* (e già prima, in certo senso, nei profili tutti retorici delle più antiche e glossematiche epistole). Le figure di Dante, di Cavalcanti e di Giotto potevano poi a buon diritto prendere il posto nell'Olimpo degli eroi del *Decameron*, tanto erano presentate ed esaltate in senso esemplare, quasi come emblemi della dignità suprema dell'arte.

Ma negli ultimi vent'anni del Boccaccio il mito dell'eroe si sposta risolutamente—in coerenza alle prime aperture e secondo le nuove acquisizioni culturali—sul piano del pensiero e della poesia. Sarebbe naturale la tentazione di vedere in questo spostamento un'evoluzione in senso preumanistico, se l'esempio del Petrarca e della sua scuola non lo smentisse energicamente. Nei continui modelli di eroi, infatti, offertici da lui—dall'*Africa* ai *Rerum memorandarum*, dal *De remediis* al *De viris* (e ancora poi nei suggerimenti per gli affreschi nel salone carrarese con le 36 figure di grandi)—domina assolutamente l'uomo d'azione: e domina ancora negli scritti simili dei più autorevoli discepoli, da Lombardo della Seta a Coluccio Salutati. È del resto questa la serrata e massiccia tradizione classica, da Senofonte e da Plutarco a Svetonio e Cornelio Nepote e Valerio Massimo: una tradizione cui il rinnovato classicismo del Petrarca rimane scrupolosamente fedele. Lo stesso genere biografico, che per sua natura stessa tende a eroicizzare i protagonisti, era rigorosamente limitato ai grandi uomini d'azione guerresca o politica; o se mai, nell'agiografia, a quelli di azione anche più radicale, ai santi. A parte certi filosofi sentiti quali Maestri (come Socrate e Epitteto), di letterati o di artisti si potevano offrire (e si erano offerti da Quintiliano a Svetonio a San Girolamo e Prisciano) notizie biografiche a scopo informativo, utilitaristico, per illustrare l'opera complessiva o singoli testi. Non erano certo biografie di senso esemplare e tanto meno eroico: anzi spesso, dall'età alessandrina e dalla commedia di mezzo in poi, si era affermata nelle biografie degli scrittori una certa tendenza diseroicizzante.

Il Boccaccio interviene energicamente anche in questa tradizione: da una parte rinnova del tutto il genere e dall'altra crea e propone un nuovo mito di eroe. È quello del letterato maestro di coscienze e correttore di costumi personali e sociali. Il mito del poeta-vate si pone così al sommo della scala degli eroi. Infatti, come egli spiega nella *Genologia* (XIV 7), il poeta è caratterizzato e quasi consacrato da un fervore che—come lo Spirito Santo—'ex sinu Dei procedens', è concesso a pochissimi e li rende superiori del tutto agli altri uomini, loro guida e modello. Infatti, continua il Boccaccio, il poeta può e deve

reges armare, in bella deducere, e navalibus classes emittere, celum, terras et equora describere, virgines sertis et floribus insignire, actus hominum pro qualitatibus designare, irritare torpentes, desides animare, temerarios retrahere, sontes vincire, et egregios meritis extollere laudibus, et huiusmodi plura; si quis autem ex his, quibus hic infunditur fervor, hec minus plene fecerit, iudicio meo laudabilis poeta non erit (XIV 7).

Proprio perché investiti di questa alta missione i poeti amano i luoghi solitari e tranquilli, favorevoli alla meditazione. E il Boccaccio, rovesciando la concezione classica della solitudine (sentita dal mito di Bellerofonte in poi come una condanna o un rifiuto antiumano), traccia il ritratto del poeta, solo e meditabondo non per melanconie petrarchesche o romantiche, ma asceticamente per bene dell'umanità:

ob id solitudines incolunt et coluere poetae, quia non in foro cupidinario, non in pretoriis, non in theatris, non in capitoliis aut plateis, publicisve locis versantibus, seu turbelis civicis inmixtis, vel mulierculis circumdatis sublimium rerum meditatio prestatur, absque qua fere assidua nec percipi possunt, nec perfici percepta poemata. Esto non adeo detestabile sit, ut hi arbitrari videntur, habitare silvas, cum in eis nil fictum, nil fucatum, nil menti noxium videatur; simplicia quidem omnia sunt nature opera. Ibi in celum erecte fagi et arbores cetere, opacitate sua recentes porrigentes umbras; ibi solum viridantibus herbis contectum atque mille colorum distinctum floribus, limpidi fontes et argentei rivuli, lepido cum murmure ex ubertate montium declinantes; ibi picte aves cantu frondesque lenis aure motu resonantes bestiole ludentes; ibi greges et armenta, ibi pastoria domus, aut gurgustiolum, nulla domestica re sollicitum, et omnia tranquillitate et silentio plena. . .

Horrent atque recusant turpi atque deformi ypocrisi inertis vulgi mercari gratiam laudesque, et ab ignaris monstrari digito. Horrent fasces nedum exposcere, sed optare, aulas ambire regum, aut procerum quorumcunque assentatores fieri, auro pontificum infulas aucupari, ut ventri et inerti ocio latius indulgere queant, blandiri mulierculis, ut deposita subtrahant, pecunia quesituri, quod meritis quesisse non poterant. Horrent preterea et totis detestantur affectibus caturcenses ob pecuniam in celos evehere, et iuxta muneris quantitatem eis exhibere sedes. Quin imo, quos isti blasfemant, tenui contenti victu brevique somno, speculatione continua et exercitio laudabili componendo scribendoque sibi famosam gloriam et per secula duraturam exquirunt. O species hec hominum conviciis deturpanda, o detestanda solitudo talium!. . .Sed quid verbis insto? Haberem equidem multa, que dicerem, ni spectabilis candor, ni virtus egregia, ni laudabilis vita poetarum illustrium adversus tales se ipsam longe validiori robore tueretur (xiv 11);

mostrano le ragioni delle cose, gli effetti delle virtù e de' vizi e che fuggire dobbiamo e che seguire, acciò che pervenire possiamo, virtuosamente operando, a quel fine che è somma salute (*Trattatello*, xx 11).

L'immagine del poeta acquista così un tono insieme sacerdotale ed eroico. È una voce di maestro e un modello di vita: è poeta vate e poeta eroe.

Quel ritratto ideale non sarebbe stato però nella *Genologia* così preciso e suggestivo se fosse nato soltanto da meditazioni letterarie o filosofiche. È invece chiaramente la proiezione di due incisive esperienze dirette e concrete: quelle che fecero evolvere nel Boccaccio la concezione della poesia da un compito cortigiano ed edonistico a una alta funzione morale e civile. Sono le esperienze discese dallo studio assiduo e dall'ammirazione sempre crescente per Dante, 'prima fax et prima lux' della sua vita, e dai colloqui intimi e ininterrotti col Petrarca 'magister et praeceptor. . .splendidissimum tam morum spectaculum quam commendabilium doctrinarum iubar vividum'. Di fatti nelle pagine che abbiamo citato, Dante e Petrarca sono presenti continuamente come esempi concreti di quel modello ideale, come i nuovi eroi della poesia 'anima mundi'. E come tali sono consacrati nelle due biografie che il Boccaccio dedica loro:

primo esempio, di *vite* non di uomini d'azione, ma di uomini di meditazione e di poesia, proposti a modello, quali capifila di una società, quali espressioni massime di una civiltà: cioè, come eroi. È un dittico significativo in cui—a pochi anni di distanza—appaiono raffrontati e complementari, come sullo scenario di un sublime dialogo tragico, i due massimi poeti moderni (fin dai titoli scanditi sulla stessa sequenza: *De vita et moribus domini Francisci Petrarchi: De origine vita et moribus viri clarissimi Dantis Aligerii*). Le ragioni eterne della poesia sono avvalorate dall'esempio concreto dei due grandi maestri; e i tratti più caratteristici nel profilo ideale del poeta tracciato nella *Genologia* riflettono puntualmente i ritratti concreti dei due poeti (l'amore della solitudine, il disprezzo della popolarità e delle cariche e delle ricchezze, la temperanza nel cibo, la schiettezza, l'impegno nel promuovere una vita virtuosa singolarmente e socialmente). Sarebbe facile indicare tutta una serie di vere trascrizioni fra la vita di Dante e le pagine teoriche della *Genologia*. Anzi sarebbe possibile—come non è stato ancor visto ma come sarà documentato prossimamente—identificare attraverso l'elaborazione della *Vita di Dante* (in tre redazioni diverse, fra il '51 e il '72) un progressivo stilizzarsi del profilo del poeta, come eroe di una nuova civiltà, quella comunale e volgare. Nella prima e più ampia redazione il Boccaccio aveva indulto alla narrazione dell'uomo Dante, anedottica e romanzesca—quasi pettegola. Nella seconda, del '61 (ripresa con piccole varianti nella terza), egli si impegna invece soprattutto nel delineare proprio il poeta vate ed eroe, caratterizzato dall'eterne ragioni della poesia, facendo intervenire anche testi ciceroniani e petrarcheschi. Quel suggestivo dittico Dante-Petrarca si fa così più categorico, più esemplare ed eroico: forse anche perché —come spero che il mio allievo e collega Quaglio potrà dimostrare prossimamente—è stato ridisegnato fra il '51 e il '61 a quattro mani, dal Boccaccio e dal Petrarca con allusiva utilizzazione dei testi di quest'ultimo.

Le figure dei due poeti si fissano attraverso questa impegnata rielaborazione come quelle dei due massimi eroi della storia fra Duecento e Trecento: proprio quella storia in cui il Boccaccio lamentava l'assenza di grandi personalità che non fossero famose solo per iniquità e violenze (ep. XVII; Intr. *De casibus*). Entrano poi a pieno diritto e a piena orchestra, quali uomini di lettere e di pensiero fra i grandi dell'azione, nel *De casibus virorum illustrium* e in una posizione anche superiore—in senso esemplare—alle altre figure (III 14, VIII 1, IX 23 e 27, e anche IV 7, VI 12, VIII 18). E Dante è infine proposto e commentato come vate ed eroe—caso veramente unico—in una chiesa, S. Stefano di Badia, dal Boccaccio stesso nei suoi ultimi anni di vita; proprio con la ripresa martellata e ampliata dei grandi motivi esemplari già sviluppati nel *Trattatello* e nella *Genologia*.

Così si impone il modello del nuovo eroe, ignoto del tutto ancora al Petrarca prima dei suoi incontri col Boccaccio. E questo nuovo mito già signoreggia, sulla fine del Trecento, nelle chiare e dirette riprese di Filippo Villani e di Domenico Bandini, e si sviluppa poi nelle serie biografiche di Leonardo Bruni e di Giannozzo Manetti (che sempre nelle sequenze di uomini illustri affiancano a quelli d'azione quelli di meditazione e di poesia: anzi il Bruni rimprovera il Boccaccio di non aver presentato Dante abbastanza grave. Trionfa poi nei grandi affreschi ormai risolutamente umanistico-rinascimentali del Biondo e del Filelfo.

Ma già quando, il 21 dicembre del 1375, il Boccaccio chiude gli occhi rimane per i contemporanei quasi ieraticamente composto nel modello dell'eroe della poesia 'ex Dei gremio originem ducens...ad omnes virtutes calcar'. Nella lapide che aveva scritto per la sua tomba terragna, nella cara chiesa dei Santi Michele e Jacopo, di cui era stato rettore, il Boccaccio aveva alluso alla sua grandiosa opera solo con una semplicissima frase: 'Studium fuit alma poesis'.

Aveva voluto evidentemente consacrare così soprattutto la fede e la passione che sempre più erano divenute le ragioni stesse della sua vita; aveva voluto insistere con quell'aggettivo *alma* sulla funzione morale e civile del poeta.

Ma quasi rispondendo all'umile nostalgia di fama che aveva sorriso a lui mentre creava il nuovo mito dell'eroe-poeta ('nulla est tam humilis vita que dulcedine glorie non tangatur') Coluccio Salutati sotto quel candido epitaffio scriveva

> Inclyte cur vates, humili sermone locutus,
> de te pertransis?...Etas te nulla silebit.

Lo chiamava esplicitamente *vate* e lo celebrava poi nel carme come *eroe* di sapienza e di poesia. E in quegli stessi giorni il Sacchetti esaltando il nobile ingegno dell'artista tanto 'divulgato e richiesto che infino in Francia e in Inghilterra l'hanno ridotto alla lor lingua', lamentava: 'morte ci ha tolto *ogni valore*'. Riecheggiava così, con naturalezza, il tono dei rimpianti omerici per la morte dell'eroe per eccellenza, Ettore.

Sono, queste, chiare affermazioni del più autorevole classicista e moralista, ma anche *leader* della politica e dell'amministrazione fiorentina, e del più felice scrittore in volgare, ma anche autorevolissimo mercatante. Il Boccaccio viene così non solo posto risolutamente a far trittico accanto a Dante e al Petrarca: ma è egli stesso stilizzato nel nuovo mito dell'eroe che, dal *Decameron* alle *Esposizioni* dantesche, aveva, proprio lui, genialmente e generosamente creato.

University of Padua VITTORE BRANCA

Indico soltanto due distinte serie di opere tenute presenti nella stesura di questa relazione alla V Annual Conference of the Center for Medieval and Early Renaissance Studies della State University of New York at Binghamton, e alle quali mi riferisco alle volte nel testo col solo nome dell'autore.

Opere generali sul concetto dell'eroe e la sua evoluzione

G. BACHELARD, *L'Air et les songes*, Paris, Corti, 1943; *La Terre et les rêveries de la volonté*, Paris, Corti, 1947

CH. BAUDOUIN, *Le Triomphe du héros*, Paris, Plon, 1952

P. BÉNICHOW, *Morales du grand siècle*, Paris, Gallimard, 1957

C. M. BOWRA, *From Virgil to Milton*, London, Faber, 1963

A. BRELICH, *Gli eroi greci; un problema storico-religioso*, Roma, Edizioni dell'Ateneo, 1958

J. CAMPBELL, *The hero with a thousand faces*, New York, Meridian Books, 1956

W. FLITNER, *Europäische Gesittung*, Zurigo, Artemis, 1961

P. GAUTHIER, *La magnanimité*, Paris, Vrin, 1951

R. GRAVES, *The Greek myths*, London-Baltimore, Penguin Books, 1955

M. GREAVES, *The Blazon of honour*. A study in Renaissance magnanimity. London, Methuen, 1964

S. HOOK, *The hero in history; a study in limitation and possibility*, Boston, Beacon Press, 1955

C. G. JUNG, *Métamorphoses de l'âme et ses symboles*, Genève, Georg, 1953

C. KERÉNYI, *Gli Dei e gli Eroi della Grecia*, Milano, Mondadori, 1963

F. MAURER, *Dichtung und Sprache des Mittelalters*, Bern, Franck, 1963

F. R. RAGLAN, *The hero; a study in tradition, myth, and drama*, New York, Vintage Books, 1956

O. RANK, *Der Mythus von der Geburt des Helden*, Leipzig-Wien, Deuticke, 1909

PH. SELLIER, *Le mythe du héros*, Paris, Bordas, 1970

J. M. STEADMAN, *Milton and the Renaissance Hero*, Oxford, Clarendon, 1969

F. TAEGER, *Charisma, Studien zur Geschichte des antiken Herrscherkultes*, Stuttgart, W. Kohlhammer, 1957-1960

E. M. WAITH, *The Herculean Hero*, London, Chatto, 1965

S. WEIL, *L'Iliade ou le poème de la force*, in 'Cahiers du Sud', 1947, n.284 (poi in *La source grecque*, Paris, Gallimard, 1953)

G. WEISE, *L'ideale eroico del Rinascimento*, Napoli, E.S.I., 1961 (vol. I), 1965 (vol. II)

R. and M. WITTKOWER, *Born under Saturn*, London, Weidenfeld and Nicolson, 1963

Opere particolari sul Boccaccio

S. BATTAGLIA, *Mitografia del personaggio*, Milano, Rizzoli, 1968

V. BRANCA, *Giovanni Boccaccio. Profilo biografico*, Milano, Mondadori, 1967 (in *Tutte le opere di G.B.* a cura di V.B., Milano, Mondadori, I)

V. BRANCA, *Boccaccio medievale*, Firenze, Sansoni, 1970³

V. BRANCA, *Boccaccio: the man and his works*, New York, N.Y. Univ. Press, 1974

G. GETTO, *Vita di forme e forme di vita nel Decameron*, Torino, Petrini, 1966²

H. HAUVETTE, *Boccace*, Paris, Colin, 1914

H. J. NEUSCHÄFER, *Boccaccio und der Beginn der Novelle*, München, Fink, 1969

A. D. SCAGLIONE, *Nature and Love in the Late Middle Ages*, Los Angeles, Univ. of California Press, 1963

V. SKLOVSKŸ, *Chudozestvennaja proza*, Moskva, Sevetskij Pisatel, 1961 (trad.it.: *Lettura del Decameron*, Bologna, Mulino, 1969)

On Translating the 'Decameron'

The *Decameron* is untranslatable. Once the truth of this proposition is accepted, the would-be translator is left with a simple alternative: either to leave it severely alone or to embark upon a Herculean labour which he knows from the start to be incapable of fulfilment. In deciding to embrace the second of these alternatives, my own motivations were threefold. In the first place I wished to seize an opportunity that had fortuitously fallen in my path of making some contribution to the notoriously under-nourished Italian section of the Penguin Classics series. One of the editors—now, alas, no longer with us—had written suggesting that I should translate one of Verga's two great novels, and when I pointed out that Verga had been inconsiderate enough to survive until 1922, and that therefore his work was still in copyright, I was sent a list of other possible candidates for inclusion in the series, one of whom happened to be Boccaccio. Knowing that Boccaccio was untranslatable, I hesitated for some little time before being persuaded, against my better judgment, to undertake the task. So it was not a case of marrying in haste and repenting at leisure, but rather, as I had foreseen from the first, of marrying at leisure and repenting in haste. My second reason for deciding to attempt a translation of the *Decameron* was that I was fascinated, and possibly a little hypnotized, by the sheer complexity and magnitude of the various problems that such an assignment entailed, and was sufficiently vain to suppose that I could devise solutions to some of them and that in the fulness of time, the remainder would assume more tractable proportions. But my third and most pertinent motive for choosing to translate the *Decameron* was that the English versions already available seemed, for one reason or another, to fall short not only of perfection but even of an acceptable standard of competence or readability, or both. The truth of the old tag *Traduttore, traditore* seemed to me to be nowhere more persuasively illustrated than in the nine English versions of the *Decameron* we already possessed, and I was convinced that Boccaccio could be better served. Indeed, unless one is fortified by the belief that one can improve upon the efforts of one's predecessors, there can be no possible justification for translating any work that has already been translated, except in those cases where the only earlier versions, whilst possessing considerable stylistic merit, are essentially of their own period. I could not for instance have hoped to match the magnificently florid prose of the anonymous but bowdlerized and inaccurate Jacobean translation of the *Decameron* which was first published in 1620, any more than I could have hoped to emulate the quaintly anachronistic but relatively accurate pre-Raphaelite version of John Payne, published in 1886. It seemed to me that what was needed was a translation that combined the virtues of accuracy and readability, and that attempted to eschew as far as possible the anachronistic vocabulary and linguistic devices to which earlier translators of the *Decameron* had been so incorrigibly attached. It is not for me to judge whether I succeeded in producing such a translation. All I can say is that I tried to do so, and that at the end of my protracted labours my relief was not unmixed with a feeling of dissatisfaction. But since the *Decameron* is untranslatable, my dissatisfaction was not perhaps entirely surprising.

The untranslatability of the *Decameron* arises from its unique combination of various sophisticated stylistic features which are blended into a rich and intricate pattern that is both coherent in all its particulars and wholly inimitable. Boccaccio's prose, in the *Decameron*, resembles a complicated and magnificently-wrought tapestry, consisting of a thousand different threads, of varying colour and texture, which have been interwoven in a uniquely personal fashion to produce an overall effect of breathtaking splendour and harmony. The prose of the *Decameron* is the polished final product of Boccaccio's long apprenticeship in the art of rhetoric, an apprenticeship which had its beginnings in Naples, where he acquired the tools of his craft with the assistance of Paolo da Perugia and Dionigi da Borgo San Sepolcro, and of which his minor works mark the gradual progression towards full artistic maturity.

One has only to read Vittore Branca's masterly analysis of the complexities of Boccaccio's prose structure[1] in order to appreciate the magnitude of the problems confronting the translator. For instance, one of the stylistic devices of the medieval *artes dictandi* to which Boccaccio was particularly attached was the *cursus*, or the configuration of accented and unaccented syllables at the end of a clause or sentence. Each of the different types of *cursus* was associated with a particular mood or sentiment. The commonest were the *cursus planus* and the *cursus velox*, of which the first connoted tranquillity and pensiveness, whilst the second reflected a mood of what one of the medieval rhetoricians, Guadifredus Anglicus, described as *gravitas morosa*, or intense gravity. It is in the minor works, especially the *Filocolo*, that Boccaccio's predilection for the *cursus* is most clearly to be seen. The device is used much more sparingly in the *Decameron*, being confined for the most part to the *Proemio* and the *Conclusione dell'autore* (where, interestingly enough, the pseudo-autobiographical motifs that characterize the minor works are very much in evidence) and to those parts of the work where Boccaccio exercises his rhetorical gifts to the full, such as the Introduction, the amorous entreaty addressed to the Duke of Antwerp by the French King's daughter-in-law (II, 8), Ghismonda's eloquent defence of her love for Guiscardo (IV, 1), the series of homilies directed by the scholar to the hapless widow (VIII, 7), and the deliberately elaborate and long-winded tale of Titus and Gisippus (X, 8), where Boccaccio, by the excessive use of rhetoric, seems to be intent upon parodying the abuses to which a slavish attachment to the norms of the *artes dictandi* could give rise.

In the opening lines of the *Proemio*, Boccaccio makes repeated use of the *cursus planus* (dactyl plus trochee) to heighten the impression of emotion recollected in tranquillity. There are no fewer than seven examples in the opening sentence:

> Umana cosa è l'aver compas*sióne agli afflítti*; e come che a ciascuna persona stea bene, a coloro è massima*ménte richésto* li quali già hanno di conforto *avúto mestiére*, e hannol tro*váto in altrúi* fra' quali, se alcuno mai n'*ébbe bisógno* o gli fu caro o già ne rice*vétte piacére*, io sono *úno di quégli*.

Obviously, Boccaccio's use of the device in these opening line is too deliberate for a translator to be able to ignore, and in my own version of the passage, with the occasional help of another rhetorical device, that of enjambement, the *cursus planus* occurs six times:

> To take pity on *péople in distréss is* a human quality which every man and *wóman should posséss, but* it is especially requisite in those who have *ónce needed cómfort*, and *fóund it in óthers*. I number myself as one of these, because if ever anyone required or ap*préciated cómfort*, or indeed derived pleasure therefrom, *Í was that pérson*.

If Boccaccio's fondness for the *cursus*, in the more formal parts of the *Decameron*, were the only problem with which the translator had to grapple, his task would be comparatively simple. But as Branca has shown, the prose of the *Decameron* is a shining example of a technique described by John Garland in his *Poetria magistri Johannis anglici de arte prosayca metrica et rithmica*, whereby the clauses of a sentence frequently possess characteristics associated with lines of poetry, in other words rhyme or consonance and equality of syllabic length. Boccaccio was not only the greatest Italian prose-writer of the pre-Renaissance period: he had also, in his *Filostrato*, *Teseida*, and *Ninfale fiesolano*, provided Italy with her first substantial body of narrative verse. And the habit of writing in hendecasyllables is carried over into the *Decameron*, to such an extent that there is scarcely a single page where the characteristic structure and rhythms of the hendecasyllabic line—the staple verse-form of Italian poetry— cannot be detected. Two of the scores of examples cited by Branca will perhaps be sufficient to indicate the nature of this fundamental feature of Boccaccio's prose. The story of Calandrino's pig (VIII, 6) begins with a sentence that contains four perfect hendecasyllables:

> Chi Calandrino, Bruno e Buffalmacco
> fossero non bisogna che io vi mostri...;
> per ciò più avanti faccendomi dico
> che Calandrino avea un suo poderetto....

And similarly, the opening sentence of the story of Ludovico and Madonna Beatrice (VII, 7) also contains a string of four hendecasyllables, this time arranged in consecutive order:

> Voi dovete sapere che in Parigi
> fu già un gentile uomo fiorentino
> il qual per povertà divenuto era
> mercatante; ed eragli sì bene....

Walter Savage Landor once wrote that 'prose on certain occasions can bear a great deal of poetry', and the truth of this observation is nowhere more clearly confirmed than in the pages of the *Decameron*. But if Boccaccio was one who, to use Byron's phrase 'both by precept and example, shows / That prose is verse, and verse is merely prose', I think it would be generally conceded that nowadays we are apt to keep the two things separate, and that a translation of the *Decameron* that attempted to reproduce Boccaccio's *prosa ritmata* would sound distinctly odd, to say the least.

But quite apart from the problems posed by the *cursus* and by Boccaccio's *prosa ritmata*, the *Decameron* is studded with examples of almost every rhetorical device to be found in standard manuals on the third and greatest of the liberal arts. This places the translator in an intolerable dilemma. If he expunges the rhetoric, and resorts to a plain and homely style, what will emerge will be, at best, a dull and monochromatic rendering of Boccaccio's lively and multicoloured text, and at worst, a collection of commonplace narratives. Aldington's version, in which an almost total disregard for Boccaccio's rhetoric is combined with an unsure grasp of Boccaccio's meaning, is just such a collection. But in an age, such as our own, that is unreceptive to flights of rhetoric, it would be equally inappropriate for the translator to go to the opposite extreme, and attempt to reproduce all of Boccaccio's linguistic devices with painstaking exactitude. Even if such a thing were possible (and it could only be accomplished, presumably, by one who had served no less gruelling an apprenticeship in medieval rhetoric than Boccaccio himself), the end-product would be highly anachronistic and (to the modern reader) intolerably artificial. The anonymous Jacobean translation comes closest to this particular model, and the quality of the writing is admittedly impressive, even though the text is shot through with inaccuracies.

The systematic use made by the Jacobean translator of the device of alliteration has been carefully analysed by H. G. Wright,[2] who points out that 'it is his delicate ear which is the dominating factor, so that the alliteration is normally based on sound rather than on spelling.' The doctrine enunciated by Lewis Carroll that if you take care of the sense, the sounds will look after themselves, was clearly one to which the Jacobean translator did not subscribe, for he very frequently distorts Boccaccio's meaning in order to preserve an alliterative pattern. A simple phrase like *la chiara acqua*, for instance, with its insistence on the sound represented by the letter *k*, is translated as 'coole current.' But not only does the 1620 translator attempt to preserve Boccaccio's alliterative patterns; he is so strongly committed to this particular device that he often introduces it without any warrant from the original text. A case in point is the alliterative 'Now bestowes he costly bathings on his body', where all that Boccaccio had written was *lavatosi bene*. As Wright has shown, what is most remarkable about the 1620 version is the ingenuity displayed by the translator 'in finding words that usually reproduce the sense of the original and at the same time fit into his alliterative scheme.'[3] The question that arises here, however, is whether any translator is justified in amplifying and embellishing a text which is already well-furnished with decorative elements, simply in order to emphasize a particular stylistic motif. That the 1620 translator was to a large extent gilding the lily is amply confirmed by the examples quoted approvingly by Wright to underline the skill and ingenuity of the translator in this matter of alliteration. To insert, quite arbitrarily, a phrase like 'Fortune is infinite in her fagaries' seems to me not only perverse but also misleading, as it suggests that Boccaccio, too, was given to anachronistic turns of phrase, whereas in fact his vocabulary is for the most part free of such affected and obsolete elements. Nor

does it seem to me that Boccaccio is faithfully served by a translator
who is so self-indulgent as to write 'by soft and stealing steps' for
chetamente, or 'hee both played and sung a whole Bed-role of songs'
for *cantò più canzoni,* or 'the onely iewell of his ioy' for *amata cosa,* or
'stript into his shirt' for *in camicia,* or 'like a vertuous and valiant
Virago' for *virilmente,* or 'venting forth a vehement sighe' for *sospirando.*[4] In all of these cases, the virtue of conciseness is needlessly
sacrificed for the sake of alliterative patterns that are not to be found
in the original text.

Whereas the anonymous Jacobean translator carries his fondness
for alliteration to unwarrantable extremes, so that it becomes the
most obtrusive single feature of his style, Boccaccio himself employs
the device with just the right degree of restraint to prevent it from
assuming a dominant role in the total stylistic pattern. There are
many passages where alliteration is used to heighten a particular
mood created by the narrative, and a good translation will attempt
to reflect this fact. In the tragic tale of Ghismonda, for instance,
Boccaccio describes how the heroine's maidservants gather round
her in a state of bewildered compassion, a mood that is accentuated
by the series of labial consonants that Boccaccio weaves into the
text at this point:

> Le sue damigelle che d'attorno le stavano, che cuore questo si fosse e che
> volessen dire le parole di lei non intendevano; ma da compassion vinte,
> tutte piagnevano, e lei pietosamente della cagion del suo pianto do-
> mandavano invano, e molto più, come meglio sapevano e potevano,
> s'ingegnavano di confortarla.

The sobbing of the maidservants is underlined in my own version by
the use of sibilant alliteration, which is perhaps no less effective than
Boccaccio's labials, albeit I am conscious of having slightly expanded
the original text here and made it more explicit, for the sake of
balance and euphony:

> Her ladies-in-waiting, by whom she was surrounded, were at a loss to
> know what heart this was, nor were they able to make any sense of her
> words, but they too began to cry in unison, being filled with compassion
> for their mistress. They pleaded with her to explain why she was weeping,
> but to no avail; and for all their strenuous efforts, they were unable to
> console her.

Another device which is alliterative in its effect, even though its
main intention is a different one, is that of repetition. This was of
course a favourite ploy of medieval rhetoric, perhaps the most famous
instance of its use being Dante's *cred'io ch'ei credette ch'io credesse,* in

describing his experience in the Wood of the Suicides. A literal translation of that line from *Inferno* XIII ('I believe he believed I believed', or 'I think he thought I thought') serves to indicate that the rhetoric of one age can sometimes be totally inappropriate in another, and whenever I encountered an instance of this particular device in the *Decameron*, I deliberately suppressed it in translation. There are scores of examples, but I shall mention only three, the first two because they are quoted by Branca in the article to which I have already referred, and the third because it is discussed by Guido Almansi in a forthcoming book.[5] In the story of Ferondo and the Abbot (III, 8), Ferondo's wife assures the Abbot that she will keep his secret in terms which, as Branca shrewdly observes, highlight the woman's equivocal moral state. (The phrase used by Branca is in fact *incerta ambiguità morale*, which is tautological). What the lady says is this:

'...io mi lascerei innanzi morire che io cosa dicessi ad altrui che voi mi diceste che non dicessi.'

Obviously, any attempt to employ the same rhetorical device in English would produce a most curious result, and in translating this passage I have concentrated on conveying the exact meaning, using variation rather than repetition:

'...I would sooner die than repeat anything you had asked me to keep to myself.'

The extravagance of the lady's claim ('I would sooner die') is perhaps in itself sufficient to indicate the 'uncertain moral ambiguity' to which Branca draws attention.

The second example is found in the story of Giotto and Forese da Rabatta (VI, 5). As these two illustrious men return astride emaciated hacks from their country villas to Florence, their borrowed and ill-fitting clothes bedraggled and spattered with mud, Forese turns to Giotto and asks him what would happen if they were to meet a stranger:

'...credi tu che egli credesse che tu fossi il miglior dipintor del mondo, come tu se'?'

To which Giotto's reply is:

'Messere, credo che egli il crederebbe allora che, guardando voi, egli crederebbe che voi sapeste l'*a bi ci*!'

As can be seen, in this brief exchange between the two men, the verb *credere* is repeated, in one form or another, no less than five times. In translating into modern English, the repetition must I think be sacrificed. But the loss is amply compensated, or so it seems to me, by the resultant enhanced naturalness of the dialogue. My own translation reads:

> '...do you think he would believe that you were the greatest painter in the world?'
> To which Giotto swiftly replied:
> 'Sir, I think he would believe it if, after taking a look at you, he gave you credit for knowing your A B C.'

The third example is rather different. It occurs in the story of the Genoese merchant, Bernabò, who makes a wager with a fellow-merchant, Ambrogiuolo, that the latter will not succeed in seducing his virtuous wife, Zinevra (II, 9). When Ambrogiuolo presents Bernabò with what appears to be the most convincing proof of Zinevra's infidelity, in other words a description of the mole below her left breast, he drives his point home by repetition of the verb *dire*:

> '...ma poi che tu vuogli che io piú avanti ancora dica, et io il dirò. Dicoti che Madonna Zinevra, tua mogliere,...'

Professor Almansi is almost certainly right when he points out that the repetition, or polyptoton, highlights the streak of viciousness that is present in Ambrogiuolo's personality. But after quoting my translation of the passage, he lets me too lightly off the hook when, in a footnote, he states that 'there is no way of conveying the cumulative effect of the polyptoton in English.' For in this particular instance, the polyptoton could have been preserved, as follows:

> '...but since you want me to tell you more, I will tell you. And I tell you that your wife Zinevra....'

But the question that arises is whether a literal translation of that sort, which retains the undercurrent of vindictiveness, is preferable to a freer but more coherent and less wooden statement, and after weighing up the relative advantages of each, I opted for the second alternative, so that the passage reads:

> 'But since you want me to provide further evidence, I will do so. And I will tell you that...your wife Zinevra....'

This extract from the story of Bernabò offers a clear illustration of a problem with which the translator of the *Decameron* is constantly beset. The texture of Boccaccio's prose is so rich, the implications it carries are so numerous, that unless one attempts a literal, word-for-word translation (which would in any case be quite unreadable), something must inevitably be lost. It is part of the translator's business to see that what is lost is kept within reasonable bounds.

Another of the stumbling-blocks to satisfactory translation is Boccaccio's fondness for paranomasia, the technical term for puns and plays upon words of every description. The *Decameron* is loaded with examples of this device, and some of the stories, such as those of Frate Cipolla (VI, 10), Monna Belcolore (VIII, 2), and Maestro Simone (VIII, 9) depend in large measure on paranomasia for their humorous effect. It was H. W. Fowler, in his *Modern English Usage*, who once wrote that puns 'are good, bad, and indifferent', adding that 'only those who lack the wit to make them are unaware of the fact.'[6] Like Joyce's puns, Boccaccio's puns can be good, bad, and indifferent. It is not always the fault of the translator if one of his puns seems weak or contrived in English, but the translator does have a duty to ensure that whatever force the original pun may have possessed is not too seriously weakened. There are various ways of resolving the problems to which paranomasia gives rise. One can, for example, adopt a literal translation, which was the solution I adopted for the priest of Varlungo's description of the fine cloak that he proposes to hand over to Monna Belcolore in exchange for her favours:

'Io voglio che tu sappi che egli è di duagio infino in treagio, et hacci di quegli nel popolo nostro che il tengon di quattragio;'

The punning here is of limited effectiveness, even in the Italian, and it seemed to me that a fairly low-key, literal rendering was sufficient:

'I'll have you know that it's made of pure Douai, not to say Trouai, and there are those in the parish who would claim that it's Quadrouai.'

It is in the story of Monna Belcolore, in fact, that Boccaccio's delight in wordplay comes triumphantly into its own, and is seen to be a necessary element of the actual narrative, which moves swiftly along by way of a whole series of lively and intricately assembled effusions of verbal humour, from the initial description of Monna Belcolore to the brilliantly equivocal final paragraph, with its account of her eventual conversion to the priest's way of thinking. No translation could ever do proper justice to this high-spirited account of rustic, midsummer passion, with its constant stream of

Florentinisms and double-meanings. The language, round which so much of the humour revolves, is distinctively Florentine in flavour, and to translate it is by definition to remove it from its living context and thereby to lessen its impact. Even the names of the characters play a part in the total comic effect. Apart from Belcolore herself, and her gormless husband, Bentivegna del Mazzo, Boccaccio inserts into the narrative a whole gallery of other characters, whose sole *raison d'être* is to heighten the humour by the very sound of their curious Florentine names: Ser Bonaccorri da Ginestreto, Lapuccio, Naldino, Biliuzza, Lotto *rigattiere*, Buglietto, Binguccio dal Poggio and Nuto Buglietti. None of these has any real function in the narrative: they are simply personalities who flash momentarily into being and then subside, like sparks from a catherine-wheel. And to a certain extent, the same applies to the stream of references to rustic pursuits, such as Belcolore's flair for singing and dancing (*era quella che meglio sapeva sonare il cembalo e cantare 'L'acqua corre alla borrana' e menare la ridda et il ballonchio...con un bel moccichino e gentile in mano*), and the priest's gardening skills that account for the curious presents he despatches to the object of his love (*un mazzuol d'agli freschi,...un canestruccio di baccelli,...un mazzuolo di cipolle malige o di scalogni*). Or again, when the priest hears that Bentivegna is going to Florence, he asks him to remind Lapuccio and Naldino to bring him *quelle còmbine per li correggiati miei* ('those leather thongs for my flails'). There is of course a strong sexual undercurrent in all of these references, and this will emerge in the translation, albeit the uniquely Florentine rustic flavour of the original text is lost. The loss is inevitable, and it seriously weakens the *vis comica* of a story that is one of the most brilliant examples of humorous writing in any literature. How does one convey the rich semantic overtones of so peculiarly Florentine a phrase as *andando il prete di fitto meriggio per la contrada or qua or là zazzeato*, with its economical implication of a feeling of sensual lassitude induced by the heat of the mid-day sun? Or how, similarly, does one preserve the pertness and familiarity of Belcolore's question to her priestly admirer: *'che andate voi zacconato per questo caldo?'*

The wordplay and outlandish Florentinisms of the story of Belcolore are no mere ornaments: they are a function of the narrative itself. But in other stories, such as the one concerning Maestro Simone's initiation into the mysteries of Bruno and Buffalmacco's secret society of hedonists, or the *brigata che va in corso*, the puns and quips and double-meanings are a kind of recurrent leitmotif which highlights and underlines the extreme gullibility of the main character. When Buffalmacco pays Simone the seemingly extravagant compliment, *'voi non apparaste miga l'abbicì in su la mela..., anzi l'apparaste bene in sul mellone*', he is merely laying further emphasis on Simone's stupidity. A literal translation would clearly make no sense here, but by casting round for an alternative play upon words, it is possible to achieve a similar result, and my own version of the passage reads: 'you obviously didn't learn your alphabet from a blackboard..., but from a blackamoor.' In the same story, there is a preposterous conversation between Bruno and Simone, in which Bruno, having on an earlier occasion furnished the gullible physician with a catalogue of the fine ladies who make themselves available to the members of the *brigata* ('*la donna de' barbanicchi, la reina de' baschi, la moglie del soldano, la 'mperadrice d'Osbech, la ciancianfera di Norrueca, la semistante di Berlinzone e la scalpedra di Narsia*', to say nothing of '*la schinchimurra del Presto Giovanni*'), tells Simone that he had grown tired of his regular bedmate, the Queen of England, and sent instead for the '*gumedra del gran can d'Altarisi*'. The problem of anglicizing the titles of those exotic ladies is one that would have taxed the ingenuity of a James Joyce, but the conversation between Bruno and Simone, with its wordplay on names associated with the art of medicine, can be rendered in a way that does not materially lessen the comic force of the original, which reads:

> Diceva il maestro:
> 'Che vuol dire "gumedra"? Io non gl'intendo questi nomi.'
> 'O maestro mio,' diceva Bruno, 'io non me ne maraviglio, ché io ho bene udito dire che Porcograsso e Vannaccena non ne dicon nulla.'
> Disse il maestro:
> 'Tu vuoi dire Ipocrasso et Avicenna.'

In translation, this becomes:

> '"Gumedra?"' said the physician. 'What does that signify? I don't understand these titles.'
> 'I'm not a bit surprised, my dear Master,' said Bruno, 'for I've heard that neither Watercress nor Avadinner say anything on the subject.'
> 'You mean Hippocras and Avicenna,' said the physician.

The stories concerning Calandrino are also richly stocked with instances of verbal humour, and none more so than the account of his search for the heliotrope, whose magical powers are first brought to his attention by that arch-exponent of the practical joke, Maso del Saggio. Maso's mouth-watering description of the land flowing with milk and honey, or to be more precise, with Parmesan cheese and macaroni, prompts Calandrino to inquire how many miles it is from Florence, to which Maso's reply is: '*Piú di millanta, che tutta notte canta*'. The combination, here, of preposterous word-play,

nonsensical meaning, and incongruous rhyme defies translation. The
author of the 1620 version characteristically converted the epigram
into a discourse, and wrote: 'In troth, replyed Maso, the miles are
hardly to be numbered, for the most part of them, we travell when
we are nightly in our beddes, and if a man dreams right; he may be
there upon a sudden.' The 1741 translator ran away from the
problem, and simply had Maso saying 'Many thousands'. This tame
solution is also adopted by W. K. Kelly in the version published in
1855, whilst John Payne, the most scrupulous of Boccaccio's English
translators, has 'A million or mo; you might count them all night
and not know'. J. M. Rigg comes up with a jingle that doesn't quite
scan, at the same time lapsing into his habitual antiquated English:
'more than thou couldst number in a night without slumber'. And
in the version of Richard Aldington, we find the distinctly prosaic
'More than a thousand, going night and day.' Frances Winwar
supplies a neat rhyme, but disregards the wordplay and introduces a
meaning where none was intended: '"Ten score miles and ten, there
and back again," Maso jingled'. My own solution ('More than a
milling, that spends the night trilling') can fairly be claimed to
approach more closely to both the spirit and the letter of the original,
although it fails adequately to reproduce the transparent and un-
compromising lunacy of Maso's deliberately enigmatic reply.

   Wordplay of a slightly different order is to be found in the story
of Frate Alberto (IV, 2), where the vain and foolish Donna Lisetta is
variously referred to, by antonomasia, as *Donna mestola*, *Donna zucca
al vento*, *Madama baderla*, and *Donna pocofila*. The conversion of such
titles into fairly close English equivalents presents no great difficulty:
Lady Numskull, Lady Bighead, Lady Noodle, Lady Birdbrain.

   But the most serious problems of all are encountered in the tale of
Frate Cipolla, whose long and ingenious sermon is shot through from
beginning to end with puns and double meanings. Nor is the translator's job made any easier by the widespread assumption that the
account of his peregrinations, at the beginning of his sermon, contains a series of references to places in Florence. Most of Boccaccio's
Italian editors maintain, in fact, that the catalogue of seemingly far-
flung places which Cipolla claims to have visited—Vinegia, Borgo
de'Greci, Garbo, Baldacca, Parione, Sardigna, and San Giorgio—
is merely a list of localities in and around Florence. The translator
is left with two possibilities: either he can leave the names as they are,
and append a series of footnotes explaining where exactly in
Florence they were to be found, or he can dispense altogether with
the Florentine associations and construct a catalogue of his own
which will enable the English reader to savour both the non-
sensicality of Cipolla's narrative and also the impression he conveys

of having travelled to distant parts of the world. Unlike most of the other English translators of the *Decameron*, I adopted the second solution, and by converting *Truffia* and *Buffia* into Funland and Laughland, and *terra di Menzogna* into Liarland, thus hinting at a possible extension of Cipolla's globetrotting to encompass the Baltic region and the Celtic fringe, the surrealistic fancies of the original text were to a large extent preserved:

> 'So away I went, and after setting out from Venison, I visited the Greek Calends, then rode at a brisk pace through the Kingdom of Algebra and through Bordello, eventually reaching Bedlam, and not long afterwards, almost dying of thirst, I arrived in Sardintinia....After crossing the Straits of Penury, I found myself passing through Funland and Laughland, both of which countries are thickly populated, besides containing a lot of people. Then I went on to Liarland, where I found a large number of friars..., all of whom were forsaking a life of discomfort for the love of God...'

The problems presented, in the second part of Cipolla's sermon, by his irreverent description of the various holy relics which he claims to have been shown by *il venerabile padre messer Nonmiblasmete Sevoipiace, degnissimo patriarca di Jerusalem* are perhaps even more formidable. But I do not have the space to consider them here, or indeed to draw attention to hundreds of other difficulties that Boccaccio posed for his translators. To borrow the words of Friar Cipolla, 'these were so numerous, that if I were to give you a complete list, I would go on for miles without reaching the end of it.'

University of Leicester   G. H. MCWILLIAM

NOTES

1.   V. Branca, *Boccaccio medievale*, 3rd Edn., Florence, Sansoni, 1970. See esp. c.III (*Strutture della prosa, scuola di retorica e ritmi di fantasia*), pp. 45–85.
2.   H. G. Wright, *The First English Translation of the 'Decameron' (1620)*, Upsala, 1953. See esp. pp. 72–115.
3.   H. G. Wright, *op. cit.*, p. 112.
4.   H. G. Wright, *op. cit.*, p. 112.
5.   G. Almansi, *Narrative Technique in the 'Decameron'*, Routledge, 1974 (?). The point in question is discussed in c.V.
6.   H. W. Fowler, *A Dictionary of Modern English Usage*, 2nd Edn. rev. by Sir Ernest Gowers, Oxford, 1965, p. 492.

Alberti as a Writer†

The most striking characteristic of Alberti as a writer,—one which was already evident to his contemporaries—is his versatility. This is apparent immediately in the remarkable variety of subjects treated in his works, and in their disconcerting diversity of language and style. Yet this very multiplicity of activities, backed up by the anecdotes reported in the so-called *vita anonima*, has detracted in many ways from a deeper and more comprehensive understanding of his genius: on the one hand they have promoted the creation around him of the myth of the universal superman, and on the other they have favoured the compartmentalisation of studies on the various aspects of his achievements, as if they were dealing with so many different Albertis and not one alone. The blame rests in good part with Alberti himself, who frequently insisted on 'ingenium...*suum* acre et versatile'[1], and launched his own myth with that auto-biography, based on the *Lives* of Diogenes Laertius, and known as the *vita anonima*[2]. But we should be at fault if we simply took his versatility at face value, as a remarkable miscellany of interests and initiatives to be admired in the protean end-products of his writings. We need to consider it as it really was,—as his quintessential state of mind, his *forma mentis*, the point of departure in many different directions for new and yet-unexplored destinations. Alberti was not only completely aware of this intellectual and spiritual disposition of his: he deliberately made it the basis of a whole programme of life, study and writing, which distinguished him clearly from all his

† This paper was prepared in Italian and read at the conference (in Rome, Mantua and Florence) organised by the Accademia Nazionale dei Lincei in April 1972 to celebrate the 500th anniversary of Alberti's death. With the title: 'Il prosatore latino e volgare' it is published in *Atti del Convegno Internazionale indetto nel V Centenario di L. B. Alberti*, Rome (Acc. dei Lincei), 1974.

In its present English form it was also read to the Alberti symposium organised at the Italian Institute in London in November 1972 by the Society for Renaissance Studies.

contemporaries, and determined the highly varied character of the form and content of his works. This paper aims to clarify this programme in relation to the classical and vernacular traditions he followed or reacted against, and at the same time to throw light on the problems he faced and the results he achieved in his Latin and Italian prose writings.[3]

Cristoforo Landino rather exaggerated when he wrote that Alberti 'in prosa ha avanzato e vinto tutti i superiori'; but he was right when he said 'come nuovo camaleonta sempre quello colore piglia il quale è nella cosa della quale scrive'.[4] Expanding this metaphor one might say that for Alberti precedence and greater importance attached to the 'cosa', and the colours came, if at all, of their own accord: or, abandoning the metaphor, that elegance of expression was never the principal object of his writing. Indeed his prefaces, dedications, and works themselves are strewn with explicit declarations of this kind. I shall look at some of them in detail later on. At this point I wish simply to indicate their general tenor, which is as follows: 'I do not aim or claim to be eloquent; what I have to say is new and important, and it is enough for me if they are intelligible to the reader.' With authors other than Alberti one would be tempted to interpret such statements as protests of false modesty. But in his case they need to be taken more seriously, as they correspond in large measure to the facts and to his linguistic and stylistic attitudes and abilities. One can and should enter some reserves, and I shall do so in a moment; but I believe it is true to say that Alberti had an essentially practical view of languages as means of communication, and that this view was part of his concept of the ideal writer, and consequently of himself, as the perpetual investigator and provider of useful, pleasurable, and preferably unexpected information and ideas. This predominantly didactic attitude towards the functions of the writer, evident in all his works, made him insist continually on their practical and ethical content, and on their intelligibility rather than on their elegance of expression.

Yet Alberti would not have protested so loudly and so often, if he had not also had certain linguistic and stylistic ambitions and pretensions of his own, and if he had not been conscious, not only of the difficulties he had to overcome, but also of other criteria of expression followed or advocated by his contemporaries. This seems to me the only way to explain his continual preoccupation with 'detrattori', with the criticism he foresaw to almost everything he wrote. It is true that we do not possess explicit testimonies of such 'detrattori' and 'invidiosi'; and it is equally true that Alberti was highly, perhaps excessively sensitive to the real or imagined reactions of those around him.[5] But this does not reduce the significance of the fact

that in the literary environment of his time he felt himself to be, and
assumed the attitude of an exceptional, even isolated figure. He
deliberately went against the current. Nor is the fact altered by the
realisation that this spirit of opposition was in part dictated by a
competition within himself as well as with others and with other
traditions.[6] It remains a fact to be reckoned with, because it had
important implications for the form and content of his works in
Latin and Italian.

The position of the two languages in his day was not the same;
and we must make a distinction, not merely between Latin and
Italian, but also between the various uses to which Alberti put them,
in particular between literary works and technical writings. The
Intercenales and *Momus* are his most important literary works in Latin
prose. With them Alberti believed he was filling a gap in Latin
literature, by creating the genre of satire based on the model of
Lucian,—something new, combining usefulness and pleasure,
gravity and humour. Alberti realised or suspected this was not to the
taste of some of his contemporaries.[7] He wrote the *Intercenales* over a
long period of time, collecting them together in 10 books in 1439.
Thanks to Garin's discovery in 1964 of some of the lost books, we
know these compositions better now, and can appreciate Alberti's
intentions from previously unpublished prefaces. For instance, in
the preface to book II he addresses Leonardo Bruni as follows:

> We are not all like you, who combine the best of eloquence with the
> riches of intellect and learning. I am one who regards it as more praise-
> worthy to be able to move plain folk to laughter at street-corners with my
> childish and unpolished sort of eloquence than to grow old collecting
> infinite ornaments of expression and write nothing.[8]

The polemical note hidden here is more apparent in the dedication
of book IV to Poggio:

> There may be some who would prefer me to browse in richer, more
> suitable fields of eloquence. They criticise me for delighting in these very
> difficult compositions and not in those well-known, that are richer in more
> widely accepted eloquence and in the goods of this world. But if they
> consider it a fault that I willingly follow my nature, and spurn all other
> money-making arts, they ought equally to censure all mathematicians, and
> all those who have dedicated themselves to knowledge of the stars and
> investigation of unknown things.[9]

It is clear that, when making this notable and typical comparison
of his own literary inventions with mathematical and astronomical
research, Alberti had a much more serious idea about his own

eloquence than his reference to its being childish and unpolished would imply. But it is an eloquence *sui generis*, certainly different from the Ciceronian eloquence pursued by others. Precisely on such difference he insists in the preface to book VII, again to Bruni. Everyone, he writes, wants to appear eloquent, and thinks to achieve this by studying ancient writers instead of through their own talents; but no one can do this now: rather than try to imitate Cicero, as if his were the only style of expression, it would be better to learn to write well on one's own, and to recognise the rights and merits of a more varied eloquence:

> Nothing that is not buskined and bombastic pleases some; others consider hard and rough anything prepared and published with attention to detail. Some have a taste in reading only for flowery and splendid expressions and well-rounded periods; few recognise in a writer force of intellect and the method and motive of his style. But eloquence is a very varied thing, and even Cicero is not all of one piece. The great thing is to express oneself suitably and well.[10]

One could go on quoting other passages to show that in this genre Alberti on the one hand excuses his style as being 'rudis et inelimatus', while on the other he defends, against contemporary prejudices, its particular elegance and fitness to express serious moral thought 'a bene e beato vivere'.[11] There is no doubt that in the *Intercenales* and similar works (*Momus, Musca,* etc.) he manipulates Latin prose in narrative and dialogue form with extraordinary vivacity and richness of vocabulary. Garin has rightly insisted on 'il gusto che l'Alberti ebbe per le parole e le forme rare e ricercate, al di fuori di ogni concessione agli indirizzi dei contemporanei', and on the need to investigate his sources.[12] Among these would certainly be Latin comedy and his own youthful *Philodoxios*, whose dialogue form closely resembles that of the *Intercenales*. His Latin is natural and fluent, sometimes uneven, but often far more lively not only than the Latin of his contemporaries, but also than his own Italian prose. There is room for a deeper and more detailed study of his writings in this satirical genre. To no other literary genre did he remain so faithful throughout his whole career; and in no other did he seem to succeed so well as a writer in Latin prose.

When he began those *Intercenales* in Bologna, Alberti turned his back on the diffidence and pessimism he had expressed in the *De commodis* in relation to the superior achievements of classical antiquity and the inferior capacities of his own times.[13] From this moment on, in a spirit of rivalry with both past and present, he dedicated his efforts to new ideas and a new prose. Some 20 years later, still in the satirical genre, he prefaced to *Momus* his most explicit statement on the nature and functions of the writer. He recognises that the achievements of the ancients have made it difficult now to be original; nonetheless, he writes: 'I consider it the duty of the writer not to write about anything that is not unknown and unthought of by his readers'. And he goes on to distinguish two kinds of originality:

> In my opinion therefore whoever produces things that are novel, unheard-of and beyond the views and hopes of everyone, is to be considered a truly extraordinary kind of man. Next after him comes the one who deals with known and probably common things in some new and unexpected manner of composition. So, if someone comes along who, while instructing his readers in the improvement of life by the gravity and elegance of what he says, and at the same time provokes laughter and pleasure—a thing which up to now did not exist among Latin writers,— he, I believe, is not to be considered among the common run of men.[14]

We shall see eventually how Alberti fits the first of these categories. Here in *Momus*, he is proud to belong to the second, and to supply a want in Latin literature.

At this point we can say that, as a writer of literary works in Latin prose, at least in the genre he most assiduously cultivated, Alberti has a very precise aim and view of himself. *Mutatis mutandis*, that aim and view are perfectly in accord with his Latin technical writings; and Alberti has already indicated this clearly by making the comparison between his literary research and that of mathematicians and astronomers.[15] But the problems he had to face in scientific Latin prose were different from those of literature, especially in the field of vocabulary. His first important work in this area was *De pictura*, written in 1435, in which he justly claimed he had either dug this art from beneath the ground or brought it down from heaven: it is a prime example of 'res novae et inauditae', which require clear rather than elegant expression. Characteristically he protests at the outset: '...We will express ourselves in cruder terms. And we shall believe we have achieved our purpose if in this difficult subject, which as far as I can see has not before been treated by anyone else, our readers have been able to follow our meaning'.[16] And he adds at the end of the first and most difficult book:

> I have set out the foregoing briefly and, I believe, in a not altogether obscure fashion, but I realise the content is such that, while I can claim no praise for eloquence in exposition, the reader who does not understand at first acquaintance, will probably never grasp it however hard he tries... As they have been explained by me briefly and without eloquence, they will probably not be read without some distaste. Yet I crave indulgence

if, in my desire above all to be understood, I saw to it that my exposition should be clear rather than elegant and ornate.[17]

In view of the difficulties of this technical part of the work, Alberti has succeeded extremely well in expressing himself, taking his language from ancient and medieval writers on mathematics, optics and perspective. Unlike the twin text in Italian, which we will consider later, the problems of interpretation in this Latin text (and they are not many) arise not so much from weaknesses in language as from the author's sometimes eliptical manner of formulating his ideas.[18] In other respects, and especially in some of the descriptions of books II and III, he writes a clear, robust prose, that is certainly not Ciceronian, but neither is it a Latin reduced to vernacular level. One has only to compare the Latin version with the Italian one of 1436 to realise that for Alberti Latin was not only a more precise but also a more flexible instrument of communication.

Similar and even more serious problems faced him when he wrote *De re aedificatoria* some 15 years later. At the beginning of book VI, in a moment of discouragement and perhaps interruption of his work, but conscious as always of beating new paths, he reviews his problems and laments the loss of texts and buildings. His task has proved more arduous than he imagined: 'For there arose frequent difficulties in explaining things, in finding appropriate words, and in dealing with the subject, which deterred me from completing what I had begun'. The only author who survived is Vitruvius, and in a pitiable state, due in the first place to the writer himself: 'for he spoke in such a way that Latins would say he wanted to appear Greek, and Greeks Latin'. However, Alberti was certainly exaggerating, because he had managed to understand quite a lot of Vitruvius and to borrow much from him. But he was not exaggerating the difficulties of understanding and explaining intelligibly to others such a complex subject. He goes on:

To give unified form to such varied material from widely different sources, little known and infrequently dealt with by others; to put it into good order, and treat it in precise terms and with due method; all this required an ability and learning superior to those I possess. Nonetheless I shall not be ashamed if I have achieved my object, so that my readers will see that I preferred to be plain in my expression rather than eloquent. Unless I am mistaken, what I have written is good Latin and sufficiently intelligible.[19]

These are the words of a writer who not only recognised the difficulties he faced, but was aware also of having overcome them; so they are in a sense a protest of modesty. Yet this does not remove the real problem he tackled, nor the importance of the many lexical innovations in *De re aedificatoria*. The glossary of Lucke, when it appears, will make this absolutely clear.[20] At the moment, I wish to stress the typical nature of Alberti's undertaking in the wider context I am trying to illustrate, of his deliberate attempt to create a new prose, new in content and in form.

It is not possible here to review his lesser works in Latin of a technical character; *Elementa picturae, Descriptio Urbis Romae, De statua, De cifris, De equo animante*. I would simply observe that research into the sources, especially of the latter, would show the means whereby Alberti enriched the vocabulary of his prose, not in this case out of taste for the recherché but in order to express his technical information and ideas accurately.[21] Let me conclude this series of observations on Alberti as a writer in Latin with the judgement of Girolamo Massaini, who collected several of Alberti's works for the press in 1500:

> He expresses himself easily even in the most difficult subjects, such is his command in forming his ideas, such his awareness always of the Latin language. One sees some people using excessive licence, and knows they do it out of ignorance, whereas he does it with conscious deliberation; for he was aware what is possible in every kind of writing, and he kept a proper control on himself; mindful of Cicero's dictum, he believed it proper to enlarge the Latin language with the addition of some, but few, new words at his own discretion.[22]

Along the lines of this comment, there is a whole field of enquiry still to be explored.

Critics have observed that Alberti wrote Italian prose as if he had no predecessors and had to make it *ex novo* himself. This is largely true in relation to the varied nature of his production, and it corresponds precisely to that concept of the writer as innovator formulated by Alberti himself. We shall not be surprised therefore to find in his Italian works protests similar to those quoted from his Latin. Yet the position with the vernacular was different, and its traditions more limited and more limiting. Nor was this all. If we believe Alberti, he had to contend with other problems of a personal kind. The *vita anonima* tells how at 29 he wrote in 90 days in Rome the first 3 books of *De familia* 'sed inelimatos et asperos...unpolished and rough, and not Tuscan, for he had been brought up in exile in foreign parts and did not know his mother tongue, and it was difficult for him to write clearly and elegantly in this language, in which before he had not been accustomed to compose'.[23] It is probably true in part at least that his education outside Tuscany made expression in Tuscan somewhat difficult. But it is also true, judging from the chronology of his works in the *Vita*, that he did not begin his vernacular career with those three books but with certain amorous works, which do not show, at least in the known MS tradition, either north Italian characteristics or evidence of difficulty in managing Tuscan. The distinction I made before for the Latin works between literary and technical writings will be valid too for his Italian works. But one has to make a further distinction as well, between prose on amorous themes and prose of moral content. In order to compose during his youth in Bologna, *Deifira* and *Ecatonfilea*, he must have studied the works of the master of the genre, Boccaccio; and it is a noteworthy fact that, though he never mentions Boccaccio, Alberti should have taken up that thread of the vernacular tradition in Bologna, and continued it later, though still in relation with friends of that city like Paolo Codagnello. In this narrower genre Alberti succeeds in writing pleasing and psychologically acute opuscules, which are neither poor imitations of Boccaccio nor over-loaded with Latinate words and constructions. In other words, even where he carries on, without explicit recognition, a particular pre-ceding tradition of the vernacular, he behaves with typical inde-pendence and 'disinvoltura'.[24]

Sending *Ecatonfilea* to Nerozzo Alberti, he wrote: 'Piacerammi Francesco mio...teco la emendi, ché sapete di queste simili cose io sono troppo negligente scrittore, e pure emendata meno dispiacerà a chi la legga'.[25] I will comment shortly on this 'negligenza'. I quote the passage here merely to underline a fact, which may have been in the mind of the author of the *vita anon.* (probably Alberti himself), that a great deal more and a different kind of effort was needed to write vernacular works that were beyond the limits of preceding traditions. In consequence the story of Italian prose in the moral works of Alberti is one of a series of disparate, more or less felicitous, attempts to resolve the problem of adequate and appropriate ex-pression. Apart from the results, one has to ask why on earth he de-cided to take this difficult road, when he had Latin to hand, a language experienced already in all these things. The *vita anon.* tells us he wrote the 3 books *De familia* for the sake of his relatives and to benefit those who knew no Latin.[26] This seems to have been the motive, together with the typical desire to do something new. Those 3 books are not to be seen, at least on the basis of what is known at present, in the context of the discussions about Latin and Italian, which arose shortly afterwards in Florence in 1435. Indeed it may have been in part due to Alberti and this sort of composition that the question arose. But what is certain is that only after such debate, reported in Biondo's *De locutione romana*, do we find Alberti's long defence of the vernacular in the proem to book III added in 1437, and the composition of book IV, which, with its heavily latinised language and style, looks like a deliberate demonstration of the thesis that Italian derived from Latin. I am not concerned to review here the difference in the prose of books I–III, but to advance the hypothesis that these were written with the aim of creating a new genre in Italian, useful to many, and without prejudices concerning the question of linguistic history or 'maiestà letteraria'.

Such problems arise later, from 1435 onwards, and explain the explicit protests in the dedication of *Theogenius* to Lionello d'Este:

> E parsemi da scrivere in modo ch'io fussi inteso da' miei non litteratissimi cittadini. .E fummi caro. .avere te, omo eruditissimo, non inculpatore di quello che molti m'ascrivono a biasimo, e dicono che io offesi la maiestà litteraria non scrivendo materia sì elegante in lingua piutosto latina.[27]

These words take up what he had written some 5 years earlier in the proem to book III of *De familia*:

> A me pare assai di presso dire quel ch'io voglio, e in modo ch'io sono pur inteso, ove questi biasimatori in quella antica sanno se non tacere, e in questa moderna sanno se non biasimare chi non tace.[28]

Inspired by similar sentiments and the same conviction that Italian was as grammatically regular as Latin, Alberti composed in 1443–44 the first grammar of the vernacular. Nor should we omit to mention in this enthusiasm the 'certame coronario' of 1441, and the second one planned for 1442. The pattern would seem to be, therefore, that the original initiative of 1433 with the writing in Rome of the first 3 books of *De familia*, was transformed in the Florentine context amid the linguistic disputes of the middle of the decade, and what had at the outset been an ambitious attempt to create on ancient models a kind of serious literature in Italian prose, developed for Alberti into a positive campaign, for which he strove to forge new weapons with the help of Latin. Between 1436 and 1442 he evolved a much more deliberately Latinate prose, from book IV of *De familia* to *Theogenius* and *Profug. ab aerumna libri*, all written on moral philosophical themes and with the evident intention of demonstrating the virtues and capabilities of the vernacular. This was the most intensive period of his activity as a writer in Italian prose; and everything he wrote at that time seems to me to reflect the linguistic-stylistic programme developed amid the conflicting opinions of his contemporaries; and as usual he is determined to go 'controcorrente' in a spirit of rivalry with both present and past.

It is noteworthy that this period came to an end with his return to Rome in 1443. Outside Florence that stimulus weakened, and he turned to other interests, and again to Latin. His *De iciarchia* (c. 1469) in vernacular is an exception among the major works he wrote in the last 30 years of his life; and in it, if I am not mistaken, his prose lacks the density typical of his Florentine decade: it is far more fluent and easy, and is in my view his best Italian prose. Like the more often praised book III of *De familia*, it too was written outside those preoccupations which dominated the composition of his Florentine works.

Though the major impetus of Alberti as a writer in Italian prose exhausted itself relatively quickly, it was, while it lasted, extremely significant in the variety of its forms, and for succeeding generations a conspicuous example of symbiosis between Italian and Latin.[29] Its many features have yet to be fully explored.[30] I hope we will soon have a complete glossary, and can then see the extent of his lexical innovations, Latinisms, new formations and so on. These were not, of course, confined to his moral works. Indeed, passing to his technical works in Italian, we not only find many new elements of vocabulary, but we seem almost to be confronted by a completely different writer,—a contrast which is all the more remarkable because the works in question were written more or less at the same period as his major moral treatises. The first would be his Italian version of *De pictura*, done in 1435–36 for seemingly practical reasons to reach a wider audience. The result is certainly inferior in clarity and style to the Latin. It is true that much of the material was in itself hostile to elegant expression; but he came off better with Latin than Italian, which here seems to follow its master rather too closely in its syntax. I cannot help feeling he did this in a hurry and with less care than the Latin version. He certainly did not try to raise the level of his Italian prose in this text, as he was to do almost at that same time in his moral writings.[31]

The main explanation for this difference lies in the difference of the subject-matter and the limited experience of the vernacular in this sort of field, making it already difficult to achieve the principal object of 'farsi intendere'. Alberti realised these difficulties in another, related sphere, when he wrote *Ludi matematici* some 10 years later. He commented to Meliaduso d'Este:

Io mi sforzai di scriverle molto aperte; pure mi conviene rimentarvi che queste sono materie molto sottili, e male si possono trattare in modo sì piano che non convenga stare attento a riconoscerle..Molte cose lasciai, e non dissi, benché fussino molto dilettevoli, solo perché i' non vedea modo poterle dire chiaro e aperto come cercavo dirle, e in queste durai fatica non poca ad esprimerle e farmi intendere.[32]

Anyone who reads these *Ludi* will see he was not exaggerating the effort required, and will appreciate how much more difficult it was to bend Italian to such matters than Latin. It is all the more remarkable, therefore, that he never lost courage in such enterprises. The more difficult the task, the more he persisted, with characteristic determination to open the way to new ideas and new expressions. Clearly in these technical works the content came first, and the words, to hand or invented, were merely the means of communicating facts and ideas. So that one can here speak of style as the natural effect, as it were, without pretensions, of that communication:— a kind of Alberti in shirt-sleeves, very different from the Alberti in 'panni reali e curiali' of certain moral writings.[33] His scientific works have a certain air of improvisation; they are of a provisional nature, rather than complete. He recognised the fact himself, preferring to tackle unusual subjects and methods, and put out the results, even in an unpolished and imperfect form, in the hope or expectation that others would eventually add such qualities to what he had begun. At the end of *De pictura* he quotes with satisfaction Cicero's dictum that nothing is born perfect; and at the end of his grammar he claims to have set out at least the first principles, and hopes that others will carry on and reach more complete and elegant formulations.[34] He was satisfied to have shown the way.

This typical Albertian attitude, which is valid also beyond the limits of his scientific works, seems to me essential for a historical understanding of him as a writer. In many things he was, as he himself said, 'negligente scrittore', in the sense that he was a student of contents rather than forms, taking an interest in many subjects and passing rapidly from one to another, and from one language to the other. According to Alberti himself, he was in the habit of dictating his works to friends or scribes. He composed rapidly, citing texts from memory, leaving blank spaces he never returned to fill, correcting his drafts at different times and often on different copies, hardly ever bothering to prepare definitive versions. He knew and used Latin better than Italian; and on the whole he is a better prose-writer in Latin. It is curiously paradoxical, but not inexplicable, that he aimed at greater eloquence in Italian. As we have seen, he opposed certain Ciceronian tendencies of his contemporaries, preferring a medium eloquence of his own more suited to the tone and moral content of satire; nor elsewhere did he pursue in Latin an elevated style. But in Italian, with its more recent and limited traditions, and consequently more open possibilities, he often aimed higher, deploying long, involved periods; and this especially in the works written at the time of the linguistic debate, and probably for the reasons I indicated. It is not difficult to point out the defects and disadvantages of this prose; but it needs to be judged in its historical context and in the intentions of the author. Critics have often rightly admired the balance of style and representation in the first three books of *De familia*, especially on the domestic level of Gianozzo. But it would be unfair to expect that at other, higher levels, and in the climate of the fourth decade of the '400, this same prose could serve Alberti's purposes. For him, as for succeeding generations, this was the nub of the question: how, beyond the confines of the poetic tradition and narrative amorous prose, could one make the vernacular a worthy, noble instrument to express the most varied and the highest human thought. To this question Alberti's prose, with its virtues and defects, offered a new solution, and a first and prophetic example of vernacular humanism.

I would not wish to give the impression in concluding that Alberti's contribution to Italian prose was necessarily more significant than to Latin. It is true that criticism has insisted more on the vernacular; and probably as a consequence, we lack the necessary studies for his and other writers' Latin.[35] As for Alberti, he remained faithful, throughout his long career, to the older language, even in the years of greatest enthusiasm for Italian; but he never treated it as some archival relic set in a particular mode of eloquence. He wanted to make it serve modern needs, and he used it for literary, moral or practical purposes, in his own independent way and even against the prejudices of his own age. Everything he wrote in Latin or in Italian reflects that versatile spirit in continual search of the novel and original, which I have tried to outline in this paper. One must conclude that rhetorical elegance has relatively little part to play in that search; and that if Humanism is Rhetoric, as some would have us believe, Alberti was not a humanist at all. But if we take Humanism to be the cult of human knowledge, formulated in Latin or vernacular and transmitted in a continual discourse between past, present and future, then Alberti must be the humanist *par excellence*.

University of Oxford   CECIL GRAYSON

NOTES

1. The phrase (with *tuum*) is used by the unnamed speaker X in conversation with Philoponius (evidently Alberti) in the *intercenale* entitled *Erumna*, in *Alcune intercenali inedite*, ed. by E. Garin, in *Rinascimento*, vol. IV, 1964, p. 168, line 347. Cf. *ibidem*, p. 169: 'Novi perspicaciam ingenii tui et acre studium, ut cuivis rei intendas, facile assequeris'; and also the conversation with Dati at the beginning of the proem to Alberti's *De cifris* (in *Opera inedita*, ed.

A. Mancini, Florence, 1890, p. 310): 'Tu . . . qui semper istas
recondita artes abditasque natura secutus es'.

2. A note is hardly the place to justify the assertion that this anonymous life (as others, including Bonucci, have thought in the past)
is an autobiography. But, having gone on record to the contrary,
I feel obliged at least to indicate the main reasons why I have
changed my mind. Having read the *vita* many times, and collated
the MS sources with a view to a new edition, I have come to realise
how much it shares that same satirical spirit, between grave and
gay, as informs Alberti's *intercenales*. Furthermore, the *vita*, which
follows the scheme of the *Lives* of Diogenes Laertius (a work much
frequented by Alberti), ends with a characteristic series of *dicta
mirabilia* of Alberti, containing phrases which textually echo some
of the Pythagorean sayings in Alberti's *Convelata* (Garin, ed. cit.
pp. 193–198; cf., for instance, *ibidem*, p. 196, line 98 with the passage
in the *vita*, in *Op. volg. di L. B. Alberti*, ed. A. Bonucci, vol. I, p.CX;
but the whole of this part of the *vita* strongly resembles the sayings
in *Convelata*). See *Rinascimento*, *XII*, 1972, pp. 21–78.

3. A more detailed examination than the present one, though with
different emphases and from other points of view, was published
some years ago by Giovanni Ponte under the title 'L. B. Alberti
umanista e prosatore', in *La Rassegna della Lett. Italiana*, anno 68,
nn. 2/3, 1964, pp. 256–285.

4. Cit. by G. Mancini, *Vita di L. B. Alberti*, 2nd ed., Florence, 1911,
p. 422.

5. For various passages in which Alberti shows concern about detrac-
tors and jealous rivals see *L. B. Alberti: La prima grammatica della
lingua volgare*, ed. C. G., Bologna, 1964, p. xxviii, n. 42.

6. This same spirit informs the portrait of Alberti in the *vita anon.*
(see note 2 above).

7. On the theory and tradition of this literary genre in ancient and
mediaeval writers see E. R. Curtius, 'Jest and Ernest in Medieval
Literature', in ch. IV of his *European Literature and the Latin Middle
Ages*, New York, 1963, pp. 417 ff.

8. *Alcune intercenali inedite*, cit. sup., p. 127.

9. *Ibidem*, p. 140.

10. *Ibidem*, pp. 179–180. The name of the addressee of the proem to bk.
VII is missing, but he can be identified as Bruni, who in the proem
to bk. II is called 'hac etate litterarum princeps'; cf. in proem to
bk. VII: 'ut es fama auctoritateque inter litteratos princeps'.

11. See proem to bk. X (*ibidem*, pp. 207–208), in which, emphasising
the different tastes and talents of men, he exhorts all writers to give
what they can to the common cause: ' . . date, queso, una mecum
operam ut nostra hec tempora, cum iocosis scriptoribus non vacua,
tum eadem posteri non invidie fuisse plena sentiunt'. In similar vein,
and with similar concern for the criticism of others, see the dedication to *Uxoria*, in which he defends his work, 'rudis et inelimata', at
the same time protesting that he strives 'ut scribendo elegantes
simus' (*Op. volg.*, ed. C.G., vol. II, Bari, 1966, pp. 302–304).

12. Ed. cit., p. 126.

13. On this aspect of the *De commodis literarum atque incommodis* see my
art. on the humanism of Alberti in *Italian Studies*, XII, 1957, pp.
40–42. For the text see the recent ed. by Giovanni Farris, Milan,
1971 (with Ital. translation on facing pages).

14. *Momus o del Principe*, ed. by G. Martini, Bologna, 1942, pp. 4–5. On p. 7 see also his typical protest that his is 'nudum proemium' and different from the traditional kind, full of ornamentation and false praise.

15. In the proem to bk. IV of his *Intercenales*, cit. sup., p. 86 (note 9). The comparison is significant in indicating what we might call Alberti's concept of the unity of knowledge without prejudice to any considerations of specialisation,—a concept misunderstood by some critics in the past and equated with dilettantism. It should be added here that my distinction between literary and technical works is not always and completely valid in the sense that some 'technical' works (e.g. *De pictura* and *De re aed.*) are also 'literary' works, and show a remarkable fusion between the humanist and exact sciences.

16. L. B. Alberti, *On painting and on sculpture. The Latin texts of 'De pictura' and 'De statua'*, ed. with translation, introduction and notes by C. Grayson, London, 1972, p. 36.

17. *Ibidem*, p. 58.

18. See, for example, §§ 19–20 of the text in the ed. cit. in n. 16, and the relative note on pp. 113–114. There is a certain ambiguity in the use of the construction 'omnes parallelos habeo descriptos', as it is difficult to see whether he intends a present or past definite tense (under the influence of the vernacular; on this kind of influence cfr. the work of Spongano, cit. infra).

19. The quotations (my English) are from the ed. by G. Orlandi and P. Portoghesi, Milan, 1966, vol. II, pp. 441–445.

20. I would foresee that the glossary of *De re aed.* will show two major categories of lexical novelties: the first of architectural and technical terms, which had fallen into disuse in the medieval period, and are now recovered and restored from a wide knowledge of sources; the second of current terms applied with new significance by Alberti to express technical or aesthetic concepts. I envisage also a third but smaller category of neologisms based on Greek. For an instance of the second category see the fully documented article by L. Vagnetti, '*Concinnitas*; riflessioni sul significato di un termine albertiano', in *Studi e Documenti di Architettura*, n. 2, June 1973, pp. 139–161.

21. Almost every line of the brief *De equo animante* (in *Opere inedite*, ed. G. Mancini, cit., pp. 241–256) contains some rare word found only in specialist treatises on the horse. Alberti gives a list (p. 240) of Greek and Latin authors consulted. The work is an excellent example of his method of research, both for material and related language, in his technical writings.

22. Massaini's ed. is rare (Brit. Mus. IA 27402). I base the above quotation on the preface reprinted by Bonucci in L. B. Alberti, *Opere volgari*, cit., I, pp. CCXXXVIII–CCXXXIX. It is interesting to note that Massaini frames his praise of Alberti in the context of a polemic against some writers of Latin of his own day ('modo affectatiunculis suis .. pueriliter gaudent, modo duri et quantum in se est salebrosi abscondita et exoleta linguae verba perquirentes, vulgo admirationi esse volunt'). For the situation at that time, cf. C. Dionisotti, *Gli umanisti e il volgare fra Quattro e Cinquecento*, Florence, 1968, especially the last chapter, pp. 78 ff.

23. *Op. volg.*, ed. Bonucci, cit., vol. I, pp. XCIV ff.

24. For the texts of *Ecatonfilea*, *Deifira* and *De Amore* (to P. Codagnello) see *Op. volg.*, ed. C. Grayson, vol. III, Bari, 1973; for their MS tradition and chronology, ibidem, pp. 366 ff.

25. *Ibidem*, p. 197.

26. *Op. volg.*, ed. Bonucci, cit., vol. I, p. XCIV.

27. *Op. volg.*, ed. Grayson, cit., vol. II, p. 56.

28. *Ibidem*, vol. I, p. 155.

29. Cf. Landino's comment in his Petrarch 'prolusione', ed. by R. Cardini in appendix to his art. on 'C. Landino e l'umanesimo volgare', in *La Rass. d. lett. ital.*, anno 72, nn. 2-3, 1968, p. 293.

30. Some aspects have been examined in recent years; e.g. by M. Dardano (syntax and style in the *Famiglia*) in *Cultura Neolatina*, XXIII, 1963, 2/3, and in *Annali d. Scuola Norm. Sup. di Pisa*, XXXII, 1963, 1/2 (see also G. Ghinassi, 'L.B.A. fra latinismo e toscanismo', in *Lingua Nostra*, XXII, 1, 1961), and by M. Vena (vocabulary of *De Iciarchia*) in *Lingua Nostra*, XXXI, 2, 1970. See also the art. by G. Ponte cit. sup. in note 3.

31. The relationship between the two versions can be more clearly observed now that the Latin and Italian texts are published on facing pages in *Op. volg.* (Grayson), vol. III, cit., pp. 10–107. The syntactical similarities are fairly evident (for some examples see my art. in *Rinascimento*, IV, 1953, p. 61), whereas in the field of vocabulary Alberti tends not to transfer Latin terms into Italian, preferring to use vernacular words that were possibly then in common use among artists as 'terms of art'. For some lexical innovations in *De pictura* cf. G. Folena's art. in *Lingua Nostra*, XVIII, 1, 1957.

32. *Op. volg.* (Grayson), vol. III, cit., pp. 133 and 173.

33. More like, in fact, the simple style of his letters in Italian (now collected together, *ibidem*, pp. 291 ff.).

34. *De pictura*, ibidem, p. 107; *Grammatica*, ibidem, p. 193.

35. The best study is still R. Spongano's *La prosa letteraria del Quattrocento*, originally published as a preface to his reissue of Pellegrini's ed. of *I primi tre libri della Famiglia*, Florence, 1946, and subsequently republished in his *Due saggi sull'umanesimo*, Florence, 1964.

To fortify or not to fortify?
Machiavelli's contribution to a
Renaissance debate

Machiavelli's straightforwardly technical writings on fortification provided no stimulus to thought or action in later generations. Book seven of the *Arte della Guerra* contained the longest discussion of the subject that had yet appeared in print, but this was based on his knowledge of the sieges of Pisa and Padua,[1] which had ended in 1509, eleven years before he wrote. Both had seemed to show the greater effectiveness of internal defences, while—as was recognized in the much briefer contemporary treatment of the subject by Battista della Valle[2]—future practice was to stress the walls themselves and the building of outworks; and he gave no hint of the importance of geometrically computed proportions which came to play so prominent a role in the literature and practice of fortification. Neither of the two men who later independently claimed to be the pioneer authors dealing with fortifications adjusted to the challenge (fully accepted by Machiavelli) of gunpowder mentioned him, nor did they incorporate any of his suggestions.[3] The terminology and the proposals made in his *Relazione di una visita fatta per fortificare Firenze* of 1526 were more up to date than those of the *Arte della Guerra*, doubtless because he was chiefly recording the comments of the professional soldier and engineer Pietro Navarra. But this was a governmental report and remained unpublished.[4]

In neither work did Machiavelli attempt to put his subject into any sort of political framework, though in the *Arte della Guerra* he made one psychological point: that the existence of successive rallying points within a circuit of walls weakened the resolve of the defenders. It was when he treated fortifications in terms not of ramparts and ditches, but of statecraft and morale, that posterity listened.

In *Il Principe*, before completing his survey of different kinds of principality with the ecclesiastical variety—a topic which, in the circumstances, could hardly be left out but seems to have caused him the same sort of embarrassment that he felt about the most up-to-date section of his Medici-commissioned *Storie Fiorentine*—he pauses to consider in chapter ten 'how the power of every principality should be measured.'[5] He is mostly concerned with princes who do not have armies capable of defending the whole of their territories from invasion, and his advice is that they should 'strengthen and fortify their own towns and not worry about the country around.' Emphasizing the reluctance with which an enemy faces the prospect of besieging a well-defended capital he points to the cities of Germany: they fear neither the emperor nor their neighbours because they have citizen armies, ample stocks for eating and working and 'excellent moats and walls'. This defensive posture has, it is true, its risky side. Ignoring any tactical or technical hazards that can arise from a siege, however, Machiavelli concentrates on the effect on the morale of the defenders of watching their possessions outside the walls being pillaged and burned. Because of the psychological trait that makes men loyal to a leader they have made sacrifices for, and because he is assuming the qualities of bravery and energetic authority in that leader, Machiavelli concludes that 'it should not be difficult for a prudent prince to inspire his subjects with determination during a siege, so long as he has adequate provisions and means of defence'. But this conclusion has been prepared by another assumption, twice repeated: that we are dealing with a prince 'who is not hated by the people', who 'does not make himself hated.'

When Machiavelli returns to the question of fortifications in *Il Principe* it is not in connection with the three chapters he devotes to military affairs, but after five dealing with the qualities and attitudes that are desirable in his ruler. And here, in chapter twenty, after looking back to Rome and across to contemporary cases when walls and citadels have or have not protected princes, he re-formulates that last assumption as a general rule: 'the best fortress that exists is to avoid being hated by the people.' That stone walls have on occasion provided protection, he concedes, nonetheless 'I censure anyone who, putting his trust in fortresses, does not mind if he is hated by the people.'

This treatment of fortification in psychological and political terms, with no hint of the technological interest he was to show in the *Arte della Guerra*, recurs in the extended discussion of the subject in chapter twenty-four of the second book of the *Discorsi*.[6] Fortresses 'cause you to be more violent and audacious towards your subjects', so 'a good and wise prince, desirous of maintaining that character, and to avoid giving the opportunity to his sons to become oppressive, will never build fortresses, so that they may place their reliance upon the good will of their subjects, and not upon the strength of citadels.' Though for the Roman and contemporary instances he cites the chapter is basically an amplification of what he had said in *Il Principe*, the tone has markedly changed. In the earlier work he had not been dogmatic about the disadvantages of fortifications; their usefulness depended on circumstance. His discussion of them in chapter 20 is, indeed, one of the most carefully balanced arguments to be found in the work as a whole. Now there is an unyielding prejudice against fortifications. There is no more mention of the walls and provisions of the German towns; fortifications are lost 'by the violence of the assailants or by famine.' In the *Ritratto di cose di Francia* he had said that France feared no invasion from Italy because of her fortified towns, to pass which, without conquering them, 'would be madness'.[7] In the *Discorsi* border fortresses may serve to gain the invaded ruler a little time, but 'even if they are so strong that the enemy cannot take them, he will march by with his army and leave them in the rear'. Now, as he had not in *Il Principe*, Machiavelli links armies with fortifications. Again, the effectiveness of the latter is disparaged; 'they are not needed by those peoples or kingdoms that have good armies; for good armies suffice for their defence without fortresses, but fortresses without good armies are incompetent for defence...A prince, then, who can raise a good army, need not build any fortresses; and one who cannot should not build any.' Now, once more in contrast with what he had said in *Il Principe*, while it is wise for a prince to fortify his capital, this is only 'so as to be able to resist the first shock of an enemy, and to afford himself the time to negotiate, or to obtain aid from without for his relief.' No: the really wise prince will rely on the love of his people and on his armies in the field. 'Experience proves this to be the case with those who manage their government and other affairs well, as was the case with the Romans and Spartans; for whilst the Romans built no fortresses, the Spartans not only refrained from doing so, but even did not permit their city to be protected by walls, for they wanted to rely solely upon the valour of their men for their defence, and upon no other means.'

There it is. The future chancellor of the *Cinque provveditori delle mura della città di Firenze* decides that fortifications are 'unnecessary' against a foreign enemy and 'injurious' against one's own subjects. The latter point he returned to a few years later somewhat by way of self-quotation. In the *Istorie Fiorentine* he puts a speech into the mouths of a group of citizens who warn the Duke of Athens to moderate his invasions of their traditional liberties; however much he trusts in allies, guards and *cittadelle*, these are no sure defences for a tyrant who has alienated his people.[8] And in a letter to Guicciardini of 1526, referring to plans to strengthen the spur of San Miniato, he warns of the danger to a republic of establishing a potential fortress within its defences; 'if ever in any disorder a powerful man should come to Florence, as did the king of France in 1494, you would become slaves without any way of escape.'⁹ If only Machiavelli had lived to see out the siege of 1529–30, the stoutness of the modified walls, the initial successes of the supporting army, the reactions of the wealthy to the destruction of their property in the *contado*, the effect on morale of famine, plague and fear, the loyalty and treachery that make the story of the Last Republic so suggestive and so haunting a study! We might then have had an account of fortification that balanced the pros and cons of a rapidly changing technology against the aims to be pursued by a ruler and the conditions making for loyalty and self-sacrifice among subjects. Such a work, combining the subject matter of *Il Principe* and the *Discorsi* with that of the *Arte della Guerra* might have added to his repute in our days, but it would have reduced his reputation and influence in the century that followed his death. Balanced views have a tepid *fortuna*, if they have one at all.

Machiavelli's writings prior to 1513 anticipate his later concern with fortifications in a political context hardly at all, though his missions for the Ten took him to many walled towns and citadels. An exception is the reference to Duke Guidobaldo of Urbino in his account of Cesare Borgia's drastic dealings with his untrustworthy captains.¹⁰ When Guidobaldo retreated to Venice, Machiavelli records, he destroyed the fortifications in his duchy which he knew he could not defend, lest the invaders should use them to bridle the loyalty of his subjects. This point, made at some time after 1503, was so pertinent to his views as they developed that variants of it were employed again in *Il Principe* and in the *Discorsi*.

As far as his reading is concerned, influences can, in the main, only be guessed at. But there was, I think, little in the writings of the recent past to act as a growth-point for his observations, especially for the sweep of arguments he mustered in the *Discorsi*. In their treatises on architecture Francesco di Giorgio mentioned the need to protect the seat of government against conspiracy while Filarete's ideal city was unquestioningly surrounded by strong walls; the military writers Valturio and Cornazzano described siegecraft. None, however, can be seen as a precursor of Machiavelli's point of view. Leon Battista Alberti comes nearer. In his *De re aedificatoria* (1449, printed 1485 in Florence) he contrasts the good ruler, who will build a palace in the centre of a city, with the tyrant who, because of the inconstancy of the people, will build a fortress athwart its walls. He also cites the Spartans, who 'gloried in having no walls at all about their city; for confiding in the valour and fortitude of their citizens, they thought there was no occasion for any fortification besides good laws.' Alberti took issue with this openness: 'what is there to be said against adding security to security?'¹¹ Here, at least, were hints which, if known, could have been more suggestive than anything to be found in pre-Machiavellian writers on politics: the occasions and justification of war; the use of armies and the character of the soldier; the need for and the nature of defences, the qualities of the tyrant and discussion as to whether it is better to be loved or feared: these topics, already rather fully dealt with by Egidio Romano in the thirteenth century, were not linked as Machiavelli was to link them. To turn back to the ancients is to come closer to Machiavelli. Aristotle had raised in the *Politics* the doubts expressed (notably by Plato in the *Laws*) as to the military and psychological effectiveness of fortifications, and had disposed of them. 'It is sometimes argued that states which lay claim to military excellence ought to dispense with any such aids. This is a singularly antiquated notion—all the more as it is plain to the eye that states which prided themselves on this point (an allusion to Sparta) are being refuted by the logic of fact.' Again: 'To demand that a city should be left undefended by walls...is like refusing to have walls for the exterior of a private house, for fear they will make its inhabitants cowards.' And these gruff dismissals might have carried even more weight to an early sixteenth century reader because he could see a parallel between the race mentioned in the *Politics* between new siege 'engines' and wall design, and the situation in his own day. 'It is always the concern of the offensive to discover new methods by which it may seize an advantage,' Aristotle wrote 'but it is equally the concern of the defensive, which has already made some inventions, to search and think out others. An assailant will not even attempt to make an attack on men who are well prepared.'[12] This point of view could well have acted as a goad. Machiavelli would also have responded to the passage in the *Laws* where the Athenian stranger praises weapons rather than walls, and lauds the Spartan practice. 'It is a fine saying of the poet, and often repeated, that walls should be made of bronze and iron rather than of earth'; to build a wall 'usually causes a soft habit of soul in the inhabitants, by inviting them to seek refuge within it instead of repelling the enemy.'[13]

In connection with Machiavelli's key phrase 'la miglior fortezza che sia, è non essere odiato dal popolo', the pioneer English editor of *Il Principe*, L. A. Burd, cites three Roman parallels: Seneca's 'unum est inexpugnabile munimentum, amor civium'[14]; Cicero's 'caritate et benevolentia civium saeptum oportet esse, non armis';[15] and Cornelius Nepos' 'nullum est imperium tutum nisi benevolentia munitum.'[16] While the last two occur in a police or military context, only the first is associated with the needlessness, for the merciful king, of fortifications. Professor Gilbert adds a passage from Pliny the younger: 'The unassailable fortress, the impregnable castle is to have no need for protection. In vain he encircles himself with terror who is not surrounded with love, for arms are roused up by arms.'[17] Again, in chapter 24 of the *Discorsi*, Machiavelli writes: 'when a Spartan was asked by an Athenian whether he did not think the walls of Athens admirable, he replied, 'Yes, if the city were inhabited by women.' Father Walker suggests that this could be modified from three similar remarks quoted in Plutarch's *Moralia*.

Even granted the stimulus of Aristotle's summary discussion and a building block or two from elsewhere, Machiavelli's approach to the role of fortifications was so naturally related to the contemporary situations he described, to his enrichment of the theme of effective political and military control and to his constant preoccupation with morale (evinced in his attitude to religion, for instance, or to the use of native troops, or to the de-personalizing influence of fire-arms), that readers of *Il Principe* and the *Discorsi* were faced with opinions apparently new and all the more provocative because closely integrated into an overall vision of the nature of political life. And his approach seemed all the more provocative to succeeding generations because it not only contradicted a re-installed Aristotle but collided with an enthusiasm for the theory of military engineering that was amounting to a cult, and with a wholesale building and re-designing of city walls and citadels. The topic acted, moreover, as a hinge between his fascinatingly frank exposition of princely self-interest and his emphasis on enlisting the willing support of subjects and entrusting them, and not hired mercenaries, with arms. On the one side Machiavelli gave encouragement to the spokesmen for an increasingly 'absolutist' age, on the other he challenged them with his doctrine of the open city.

The new style of bastioned fortification, designed to answer and make use of provenly effective artillery, was largely an Italian development[18] and became an acclaimed orthodoxy in the 1530's. Geometrically based, it depended on the architect-engineer's intelligence because 'forma' was now more important than 'materia'.[19] No longer simply utilitarian, it was looked on as an art in its own right. With printing and overseas exploration it was seen as one of those few areas in which the moderns had outdistanced the ancients,[20] and it made works of the fourteenth and fifteenth centuries seem crassly out of date. And from the mid-sixteenth century interest in refurbishing fortifications or founding them 'alla moderna' was increased by a growing promotional literature. At its end, the debate preceding the construction by Venice of the frontier fortress town of Palma took account of cost, and the usefulness of armies as against fortifications, and the danger of provoking an enemy by a stone show of force, but, on the other side, as well as the favourable strategic argument were others drawing attention to the glory it would bring its sponsors and designers—and to the fact that all princes nowadays protected themselves with fortifications.[21]

For while architects and engineers and *capi di guerra*, supplemented by a growing number of armchair enthusiasts,[22] formed a highly vocal pro-fortification lobby for reasons of up-to-dateness and prestige, governments were in any case building at a hitherto unprecedented rate for severely practical reasons, to stabilize frontiers and to control their populations: the Spaniards in Lombardy, the Venetians in their *terra ferma*, the popes in the Church States—and the Medici in Tuscany. An anecdote told by Bishop Gian Girolamo Rossi points up the contrast between Machiavelli's views and the political inclinations of the time. He describes how he went to see Pope Clement VII (probably towards the end of 1531) and found him reading chapter 24 of *Discorsi*, book two, and, Rossi reports, 'he gave a great laugh, and said "Look at this scoundrel and the fine way in which he would like to dissuade me from building the fortress in Florence. But he will not succeed."'[23] Three years later, after delays caused, in part at least, by the doubts expressed by Machiavelli in his 'fine way', Duke Alessandro's Fortezza da Basso began to be built athwart the city wall. To enemies of the Medici it was 'a thing totally inappropriate to a free city', 'a prison and slaughter-house for the distressed citizens'. To their friends it was a necessary 'yoke for their critics'; the Emperor Charles V made its completion a condition of his continuing support of Alessandro.[24] On the opposite side of Florence, S. Miniato, strengthened as a quasi-independent fortress by Michelangelo and others for the siege of 1529–30, was maintained and garrisoned under Cosimo I, so that in 1576 a Venetian ambassador could report that while both fortresses could be used against an invading army 'they were principally built to keep the people in check' ('per freno dei popoli').[25] In the same year Jean Bodin made the same point; the grand duke needed the fortresses, 'having found out that it was impossible to live securely in the midst of his subjects once he had converted the popular state into a monarchy.'[26] And by the end of the century one arm of the pincers had been reinforced by building the superb Belvedere fortress to strengthen the role hitherto played by S. Miniato. In the *Discorsi* Machiavelli had attacked the view of 'our wiseacres in Florence that Pisa and other similar cities should be held by citadels'. With citadels now gripping Florence itself, and the countryside and frontiers weighted down by the most radical defence programme Tuscany had ever known,[27] Machiavelli's case for the open city and sparsely defended *dominio* might have seemed buried by the evidence.

From a miscellaneous, and by no means systematic, scattering of sources, I shall suggest that it was not. But first the routine cautions of any *fortuna*-hunter must be emphasized. When an author deals with fortifications in what seems to be a Machiavellian way but without mentioning Machiavelli, three points must be borne in mind. Plagiarism was still rife. The citation of classical sources became more usual in the sixteenth century, but contemporaries or near contemporaries were commonly pillaged without acknowledgement, especially if, as was the case with Machiavelli after his works were placed on the index published in 1559, they had provoked scandal or censure. Secondly, the classical sources open to Machiavelli were open to all; others may have arrived independently, with their aid, at Machiavellian conclusions. Borrowing from medieval sources does not, I have suggested, present a similar problem. Thirdly, events, actual situations, produced opinions that could sound like Machiavelli's. Given the financial burden of supporting armies and of building fortifications, there was much debate as to which should be favoured at the expense of the other; it was an argument that delayed the building of Palma for half a century. Or again, if the Fortezza da Basso was seen as a prince's vote of no-confidence in his subjects, the same opposition prevented Venice from proceeding with plans for a citadel in Padua in 1517 and again in the 1540s. The citadel in Antwerp became a notorious symbol of Spanish oppression, as did that of Milan and its guns 'whereof part', Thomas Coryat noted, 'are planted Eastward against the towne, to batter it if it should make an insurrection; and part on the country side Westward against the country if that should rebell.'[28]

It is useful to start by looking at that notorious piece of plagiarism, the *De regnandi peritia* (Naples, 1523) of Agostino Nifo. The clumsy style, the plodding accumulation of gobbets from 'authorities', above all the impertinence of rushing a version of a manuscript of *Il Principe*, all unacknowledged, into print, has secured its author a uniformly bad press. But as an example of how suggestive Machiavelli's treatment of a subject could appear to lesser, if conventionally better-trained minds, Nifo's work is instructive. He sees the importance of the treatment of fortifications in a political context and gathers what Machiavelli had spread between two chapters into one dealing solely with that topic.[29] This was an example Machiavelli himself had by then anticipated in the *Discorsi* and was to be followed, as we shall see, by others. Nifo recognizes the disputative attraction of the subject—'de arcibus semper dubitatum est an construendae ne an destruendae sint a regibus'—and its impetus not only leads him to add to Machiavelli's list of illustrative examples but to filch others from elsewhere in *Il Principe* and adjust them to their new context.[30] He senses the resonance of a central proposition—his version is 'regis enim arx munitissima est ut a suis subditis ametur'; his reading enables him to develop the subsidiary themes hinted at by his author (the relationship between armies and fortifications, the question of martial spirit: 'muri timidos tutantur et arces'); he chops up his chosen text, adds chippings from elsewhere, and there is a *discorso* (indeed, his chapter gives the impression of drawing more on the *Discorsi* than on *Il Principe*) worth offering to a king. To placate his contemnors, it can be pointed out that in spite of his dedicating his book to a monarch, Charles V, Nifo is if anything more outspoken than Machiavelli in connecting fortresses with tyranny. More to the point, however, is Nifo's demonstration of how an old topic, re-handled in a way that made it relevant to contemporary circum-stances, could be absorbed into an argumentative mode which, though its roots lay in the techniques of medieval scholasticism, was to remain characteristic of much sixteenth century scholarly dis-course.

With Guicciardini we move from the atmosphere of the schools to that of the court-house, and to another work. In his *Considerazioni sui discorsi del Machiavelli* (c. 1530) he cites chapter 24 of Book II and one-sidedly rends its arguments. Just because the Romans did not build fortifications in their subject cities, it cannot follow that those who do so now are at fault. However well treated, men are not basically rational, they pine for change; they can yearn after the memory of their last prince, or the sort of liberty they used to enjoy. No ruler, besides, can afford always to adopt measures that are popular. So some element of force is essential. Having hemmed in the open city argument, he turns elsewhere. Fortifications tempt rulers to swagger, to be overbearing? What a frivolous idea! If you follow it, why not insist that they give up guards, weapons, armies as well? Should medicines be jettisoned because their existence can give a sense of false confidence? And after dismissing Machiavelli's contemporary examples for his not taking account of the military and political situation as a whole, he reasserts the usefulness of fortresses to protect against insurrection, to serve as a bridle ('freno') to revolt and to help recover territories that have been lost.[31]

Proceeding chronologically, and taking a group of military writers whose reluctance to name names, other than those of military com-manders, was to remain typical of the *genre*, we find Zanchi in 1554 referring to the argument as to whether it is better to trust walls or hearts ('gli animi de' cittadini') as though it is perfectly familiar. The preference for trusting to hearts he credits to 'many wise men and judicious philosophers' but as he proposes to write for those who need help in putting the opposite contention into effect he brushes their view aside.[32] Writing at about the same date, Francesco de' Marchi gives the opposition more of its due, gives, indeed, the impression of having *Il Principe* beside him as he writes. It is hazardous, he says, to build fortresses in cities or places that have been used to determine their own political fortunes ('città o luoghi che sono usi di vivere liberi') because the resentment they cause can lead to revolt. Moreover, some have suggested that if a prince has a large army he has no need of fortifications. However, an additional form of control is needed where cities have been taken by force or guile or where populations are particularly seditious. In these cases fortresses act as the bit ('freno') in a wild horse's mouth. And as an example he cites the Fortezza da Basso.[33] Both Zanchi and de' Marchi were professional military engineers. Ascanio de Hortensii Centorio was not; perhaps that is why his *Il quinto discorso sopra l'ufficio d'un capitano generale di essercito*, published in Venice in 1562, appears more sympathetically Machiavellian. He cites Lycurgus to the effect that stone walls are useless unless the men within them have adequate martial qualities, but then he points out that the Romans relied mainly on their armies, and that fortifications were chiefly useful in frontier zones or in mountain passes, so that rulers had time to mobilize. Apart from these, given loyalty, men and cash, it would be best not to build them.[34]

After Guicciardini, the first fairly detailed (five pages) treatment of the utility of fortifications known to me occurs in Gianfrancesco Lottini's *Avvedimenti civili* (Venice, 1575). Those who challenge their usefulness, he writes, have to reckon with the authority of Aristotle in the *Politics* as well as 'the universal opinion that security is something you can never have enough of.' However, many join Socrates in praising the Spartan point of view that reliance on walls emasculates the fighting spirit of a people. By referring to the 'ancient verses' about walls of bronze and iron being better than those of earth, he makes it clear that, directly or indirectly, he is citing the *Laws*. And, he goes on, if anyone wishes to save the contradiction by allowing fortifications in frontier regions while forbidding them to capital cities, then his argument is risible ('cosa degna di riso'); in that case, why not give up lances, heavy armour, fortified camps? No, fortifications must be built, though the prince must garrison them wisely to prevent their falling into the wrong hands.[35]

In the next year support for Machiavelli's view in chapter 20 of *Il Principe* that only princes who feared their people should build fortresses came from a curious quarter. It was characteristic of Innocent Gentillet's attack on Machiavelli that when he agreed with any of the opinions expressed in *Il Principe* he misrepresented its intention so sharply that he could, while in fact glossing it, appear to warn his readers against it. Thus he misrepresents Machiavelli as recommending the use of fortresses as the culmination of advice to would-be tyrants. However, as his opinion reflects one view of the experience of his generation, it is worth quoting at some length.

> The invention of citadels (which in our time princes have builded against their subjects) hath bin cause of infinit evils: For all commerce and traffique hath been & is greatly diminished in towns where they have been builded, and there have been and are committed infinit insolences by souldiers against citizens; and there neither hath come nor will come to princes which have builded them other good than great expences and evill will of their subjects. For this construction of citadels is an apparent shew that the prince trusteth not his subject, but especially where they are builded any other where than in the limits and borders of kingdoms and countries against strangers. When the subjects know that their prince distrusteth them they also esteem that he loveth them not. And when the subject is not beloved of his prince, he cannot also love him, and not loving him, he obeys not, but is constrained, and in the end will get his head out of the yoke as soone as there wil fal out a fit occasion. Here is the profit of citadels.[36]

Also in 1576 appeared Bodin's more comprehensive treatment of the subject. In republics only the capital city need be strongly walled, otherwise 'one may be sure that ambition will move someone or other to seize a fortified place and then convert the popular state into a monarchy.' It is at this point that he refers to Duke Cosimo. In a princely state, especially in a large and long-established one, 'it is never expedient for a prince to erect citadels and strongholds except on the frontiers, lest his subjects suspect that he intends to become their tyrant. But if he encircles his kingdom with strong frontier posts, his subjects will believe that they are directed against the enemy, and the prince, at need, can use them either to repel the enemy, or master his subjects should they rebel.'

These crisp, and highly politicised, conclusions are only reached after a general discussion of the pros and cons of building fortifications. Like Machiavelli (whom he nowhere mentions), he sees the subject as one calling for a presentation of alternative views before he gives his own opinions, for 'this is one of the most important problems of policy, and one of the most difficult to solve, because of the disadvantages of either course of action.' Against fortification there is the Machiavellian point that 'citadels and defence works encourage bad rulers to oppress their subjects' and the Machiavellian marginal rubric 'La plus belle forteresse est l'amour des subiects'. Then it is claimed both that 'they turn the inhabitants into cowards' and that they enable subjects to rebel against their rulers; 'for this reason the kings of England do not allow any of their subjects to fortify their houses, even with a moat.' If these arguments are valid, then fortifications 'are harmful and destructive of the common-wealth.' On the other hand, open towns tempt aggression and 'to say that men are the best defence against the enemy is only applicable on the field of battle'; because of age, sex or infirmity, only a quarter of the inhabitants of a city are available to fight, the rest need the protection of the walls. 'It is, moreover, ridiculous to say that men are more valiant if they have no fortifications to rely on...Logically we should then prohibit men from fighting otherwise than quite naked.'[37] So fortifications will have their use, and this will differ according to the nature of a country's political institutions, mon-archical, tyrannical or republican.

In 1577 Raphael Holinshed's *Cronicles* accept that 'it hath beene of long time a question in controversie, and not yet determined, whether holds and castles neere cities or anie where in the hart of common-wealths are more profitable or hurtful for the benefit of the countrie.' But he has no use for balanced arguments. He points to that blatant symbol of oppression, the citadel at Antwerp. He cites Aristotle and 'Timotheus of Corinthum'[38] as being uncompro-misingly opposed to the building of fortresses in a commonwealth. And he clearly would not have agreed with Bodin's interpretation of the comparative paucity of fortifications in England. 'I need not to make anie long discourse of castels, sith it is not the nature of a good Englishman to regard to be caged up as in a coope and hedged in with stone walls, but rather to meet with his enimie in the plaine field at hand strokes.'[39]

Two works of 1589 show, in varying degrees, how the subject of fortification was now taken for granted as a suitable topic within the treatment of political themes. For the authoritarian Brabanter, Justus Lipsius, the question was straightforward. In his *Politicorum Libri sex* he assumes that rulers will need to take precautions against revolt. The wars in France and the Netherlands, however, have shown that siegecraft has overtaken military architecture. While fortresses are useful in frontier zones, within his realm the wise ruler should therefore plant colonies rather than trust to walls.[40] Discussing fortification in *Il Principe* and the *Discorsi*, Machiavelli had not mentioned the rival advantages of establishing colonies in con-quered territories. In both works this topic was dealt with in other chapters, without cross-reference. As the arguments for and against building fortifications developed, however, his readers began to exploit the potential relevance of the two themes and set them together.

Thus, in his *Della ragion di stato libri dieci*, Giovanni Botero, an avowed, if rarely overt, anti-Machiavellian, also expressed a pre-ference for using colonies rather than fortresses to hold down a militant people. He cites the ancient example of the Romans and a modern one: 'Calais, a colony of English men...was the last place which that nation lost there on the continent.' But he adds that it is not just a question of a simple antithesis. Colonies imply fortresses as well. And because colonies plus fortresses take a long time to become established, advice to a present ruler must concentrate on fortresses alone. There is, certainly, the case of Sparta. 'When Agesilaus was asked why the city of Sparta had no walls, he pointed to the armed citizens and said "here they are!", adding that cities should be built, not with wood and stone, but with the strength and valour of their inhabitants.' Yet valour by itself will be worn down in the end, so 'I do not know why anyone should doubt the utility of fortresses to a prince...There is no empire, however great and powerful, which has neither fear nor suspicion of the inclination of its subjects or the intentions of neighbouring powers. In both cases fortresses are a safeguard.'[41]

For Scipione Ammirato, snug in the possession of a grand-ducal pension guaranteed by those bridles against change, the Fortezza da Basso and the Belvedere, Machiavelli's wrong-headedness is an article of faith. He does not name him in the Discorsi...sopra Cornelio Tacito (Florence, 1594), but he quotes from Discorsi, II, 24, and point by point he refutes its author. He begins by accepting the embarrassing discrepancy between Plato's views and those of Artistotle. Aristotle is in the right, but Plato was more in the right than those who distrust fortifications have been willing to concede, for when he commends the Spartans he is talking about the desirability of a valorous civic spirit in a people rather than criticizing walls as such. The following advantages of fortified places he assumes to be unchallengeable: an enemy will hesitate to attack them; they can be defended against many by a few; they are essential places of refuge in adversity; they weary an invader; they serve, in defeat, as a means of extorting better terms; the argument that they can all be eventually taken is less important than the fact that they help you 'to benefit from the advantage of time' and the unguessed-at changes in fortune it can bring.

Now come his direct challenges to Machiavelli. First, the notion that fortresses so encourage rulers to oppress their subjects that they should not be built, lest their sons come to rely upon them rather than on the good-will of their subjects. Not so, counters Ammirato; possession of a standing army is more likely to make a ruler oppressive than are fortresses. Then he [Machiavelli] says that fortresses are useless because they can be betrayed by their castellans. But far more examples can be found of princes who have been betrayed by the commanders of their armies. Next he [still the unnamed Machiavelli] cites examples of famous men whose actions appear to support his distrust of fortifications: Guidobaldo, duke of Urbino, Niccolo da Castello, Ottaviano Fregoso. Again, wrong: what actually happened shows that our author is misinterpreting the events in which they were concerned. And Ammirato brings in Guicciardini as witness for the prosecution, quoting at length from the *Storia d'Italia*. And yet again, 'voglio mi basti l'autorità de' Romani', says our author. But he cannot make the authority of the Romans support him because even if they employed colonies they did not, in fact, distrust fortifications; they employed them, they refined them. Ammirato then concludes by observing that, thanks to all the new fortifications that have been built in Italy, the peninsula has never been so safe from foreign invasion.[42]

Three years later, another commentary on Tacitus was published in Florence. As Filippo Cavriana dedicated his work to Grand Duke Ferdinando, his point of view can be anticipated. A new prince, he writes, cannot expect to be completely safe, because he comes to power either at the expense of an aristocratic or a popular form of government. Even an Augustus (who, thanks to assiduous propaganda had become almost the tutelary deity of the Medici dukes), 'amabilissimo principe' as he was, had to reckon with potential discontent. Certain precautions, then, are necessary, not only the employment of foreign bodyguards, the use of spies, the exiling of seditious persons and the forbidding of subjects to carry arms, but the building of fortresses. And these measures (and he has described those adopted by Ferdinando's predecessors) cannot be dubbed tyrannous, for if well and peacably intended they offend neither the people nor the laws of nature.[43]

With the *Discorsi politici* of Paolo Paruta, published in 1599, shortly after his death, we find the century's most concentrated discussion of the advantages and disadvantages of fortifications. He was at home among the literature of the ancients. He had pondered the *Discorsi*, at least, of Machiavelli, though he affected to ignore rather than to appear to draw back in revulsion from him. He had been an active government servant, had, indeed, been a member of the three-man magistracy that supervised fortifications throughout the Venetian empire. A scholarly man of affairs, he could draw at will on antiquity, Machiavelli and experience.

'Forts and strong holds,' he begins, are of late grown into so great esteem as princes seem now adaies to mind nothing more than these for the security of their states.' But to say whether they are right is a matter of some complexity. He then sets out the arguments against fortifying. Though fortifications are more skilfully designed than they ever have been, the race between attack and defence goes on, and they could, after a crippling expenditure of money, become anachronistic, or, at least, involve continuous extra expense for modifications. By themselves, they are inert and useless, their effectiveness depending on the quality of those defending them, and men of the requisite quality might well be better employed in the field; besides, unsupported by armies to relieve them, the strongest fortress must fall at last. An army is, after all, a sort of fortress itself, but one that can move, can seek out, head off or avoid the enemy as it chooses, rather than waiting to be assaulted or by-passed. Even if, technically, a fortress is invulnerable to attack from without, there is always the possibility of its falling to treachery or heedlessness on the part of those commanding it, or through the insurrection of the inhabitants who may hand it over to a rival prince. 'But if the state be open and not pestered with fortifications, though it may the more easily be lost by sudden assaults, or by ill affected subjects, it will be the more easily regained.' This is why the Duke of Urbino slighted his strong points when he recovered the territories taken from him by Cesare Borgia. It was because Venice had not yet invested heavily in elaborate fortifications for her subject cities that she had been able to recover so quickly the mainland empire she had lost to the allies of Cambrai in 1509. Paruta returns to the question of cost, 'for who can deny but that the excessive charge which princes are at, not onely in building fortresses, but more in muniting and guarding them doth sufficiently exhaust the publick exchequer and necessitate the disbursing of such moneys in times of peace as ought to be kept for the more urgent occasions of war.' And, winding up the case for the prosecution, he says that dependence on walls can lead a ruler to neglect his army and citizens to lose their martial spirit. The walls of iron rather than stone motif is introduced, and Plutarch's anecdote: 'A Spartan being demanded by an Athenian what he thought of the walls of Athens? answered that he thought they were very handsome for a city which was to be inhabited by women.' Finally, a prince 'who thinks he shall be able to curb his subjects, to govern them and rule them as he pleaseth by means of bulwarks and castles, and that therefore he needs not the love of his subjects, is much less mindful of those things which become a good prince, and which purchase affection...And it may be generally observed, that such governments as have lasted longest, have been preserved not by the advantage of strong holds, whereof some have not had any, but by vertue of a good militia, and of the subjects love.'

In favour of fortifications Paruta brings forward five arguments. Both nature and reason prompt us to adopt defences, and men have constructed them from the earliest times. Their design, if not yet perfect, is at least more effective than hitherto. Without them, a country is constantly vulnerable to enemies 'who, whilst they may safely at unawares enter thereinto, not meeting with any obstacle, have it alwaies in their power, if not to prejudice the main affairs of that state, at least to vex the people by fire and rapine, of whose safety and preservation the prince ought alwais to be careful.' Armies cannot be so large as to be in every threatened zone; fortresses act as refuges and rallying points all the more effectively because enemy forces are unwilling to have them in their rear. Lastly, the very existence of fortifications can give a potential enemy pause, for 'in the condition of the present affairs and times, it is seen that as much time is spent in the taking of one onely fort as in former ages... was spent in taking whole provinces.'

'What then is to be resolved upon in this diversitie of allegations?' First, one must distinguish between the policy to be adopted by large states and small ones. The former, especially if they have large armies, should concentrate their fortifications along the frontiers, to give time for mobilization. The latter need fortifications at the centre; their forces will be too small to defeat an enemy in the field, so they must rely on the deterrent effect of well garrisoned defences. All princes must guard against spending so much money on fortifications in peacetime that they cannot find the large sums necessary in an emergency. No prince should trust entirely to armies. Suppose his army should be defeated? He will be utterly lost, 'wheras by the help of fortresses a few are able to resist many and to gain time, the only true remedy of him who is the weaker.' No weight need be attached to the example of the Spartans. Their neighbours were weaker than they, and the whole nation was uniquely dedicated to the art of war. Neither need any heed be paid to the argument that fortifications tempt princes to be harsh to their subjects. Quite the contrary, 'the prince is so much the more bound to preserve the love and loyalty of his subjects in that he stands in the more need of them for the safety of the city thus fortified, for if it should fall into the enemies hands by the peoples rebellion, the loss would be the greater.'[44]

Lest the influence of Machiavelli in shaping discussion of the subject should seem to be either habitual or to be assumed, two more works of 1599 may be mentioned, Cino Spontone's *Dodici libri del governo di stato*, published in Verona, and Girolamo Frachetta's *Il prencipe*...which appeared in Venice. Spontone's book takes issue with Machiavelli, but while he praises the defensive value of fortifications he betrays no response to Machiavelli's having placed their utility in a political context, nor does he compare their value with that of armies. Frachetta lists his sources, including Plato and Aristotle among the ancients, Guicciardini and Bodin among the moderns, without mentioning Machiavelli. He discusses the various zones, one or all of which may be fortified according to the prince's power vis-à-vis his neighbours: cities, *dominio*, frontiers. He compares their value with that of armies—using the image of their likeness to mobile fortresses ('come fortezze vive et mobili'). He points out that while the prince's best protection comes from 'la benevolenza' of his subjects, men are fickle and untrustworthy, so an armed guard is always necessary as a precaution against revolt. But he does not mention walls or citadels in this connection, nor is it easy to see Machiavelli himself as a point of departure for his discussion of the other themes. It is probable that Frachetta omitted Machiavelli from his sources not out of deference to the censorship but because he had not read him.

With the more widely diffused *Tesoro politico*, a collection of tracts and *relazioni* originally compiled by Comin Ventura, we slip back into the mainstream of overtly anti-Machiavellian polemic—at least as far as the anonymous section on fortifications, which first appeared in the edition of 1600–1601, is concerned. Once more, colonies on the Roman model are considered before the author moves to fortresses, those essential 'bridles' for the discontent of both long-established and newly acquired lands. Machiavelli has rejected them as useless, 'but for reasons so feeble and frivolous that one brushes them aside as one would a spider's web.' The lessons of recent history are such, the author goes on, that he merely invites our ridicule. Machiavelli's opinion is as follows: if you have sufficient men under arms you have no need of fortifications; if you do not, they cannot protect you. He posits extremes. Wisdom is to be found in a middle ground. If a prince can raise enough troops to meet a danger at once from his own resources or with the aid of allies, then fortresses are at least no disadvantage to him. If he cannot, then fortresses are essential to delay the enemy: 'as the Venetians say, "who has time, has life."' And if we have to answer the question: which is better for a prince, to build fortifications or maintain a large standing army to control and defend his territories? experience directs us to the former course. Fortifications cost less, and thus the ruler does not have to tax his subjects so heavily. And whereas large numbers of troops quartered around the countryside behave like criminals, rioting and laying waste, as well as forgetting all military discipline, a small force garrisoned in fortified places behaves better and retains its soldier-like qualities.[45]

With a foot over into the next century, let us turn back to review the significance of these references. Of his most famous phrase, 'la miglior fortezza che sia, è non essere odiato dal popolo' we can say little more than that Machiavelli found an already current idea, gave it a little twist (that negative 'not to be hated') and imparted some momentum and accretive power to its passage through other men's thoughts. Burd quotes, without giving the source, a fifteenth century rhyme that had jingled to the effect that princes are busy constructing fortresses and city walls, 'Mais si n'est-il muraille que de gens.' Pre-Machiavellian, again, was Diomede Carafa's advice of c. 1485 to a ruler that 'no castles, no walls will be more nearly impregnable than the defence which consists in having the spirits of your people friendly to you, and to have all your subjects wish you well.'[46] After Machiavelli the instances multiply. In his commentaries on Aristotle, Louis Le Roy mocks the naivety of this Spartan ideal[47], but trust in men rather than walls is expressed again in D'Aubigné's scornful reproach to his mortar-mad fellow countrymen 'Vos ayeux desdaignoyent forts et villes frontieres...Nos cœurs froids ont besoin de se voir emmurez.'[48] On the other side of the channel Thomas Digges stoutly claimed that 'we have no such multitudes of strong townes as other countries: our armes and weapons are our wals and rampires',[49] and it was a fervent royalist, the poet Francis Quarles, who was to declare that 'the surest fort is the hand of thy souldiers, and the safest citadell is the hearts of thy subjects.'[50] Quarles knew both *Il Principe* and the *Discorsi* well,[51] but there are some ideas whose neatness conceals so complex a suggestiveness that the study of their transmission is the province of the folklorist rather than of the historian.

Taking his arguments as a whole, we can say, I think, that Machiavelli moved the issue of the significance of fortifications nearer the centre of current political as well as military debate, and enriched its scope. What he had to say was relevant, in the directest way, to a reawakened interest in the way in which fortifications were constructed, a lavish building programme of citadels, town walls and frontier fortresses, and to a comparatively new feature of contemporary warfare, long sieges which received more publicity than did the pitched battles of the period. He sharply increased the topic's theoretical relevance to those revitalized stand-bys of the medieval schools, whether it is better for a ruler to be loved or feared, and what distinguishes a monarchy from a tyranny. He brought it firmly into connection with another debate, anticipated in the fifteenth but rampant in the sixteenth, about the rival trustworthiness of national as opposed to mercenary armies; and here, as in connection with the reflections we have noted on the rival merits of colonies or fortresses in the retention of new conquests, we must bear in mind the magnetic power of ideas he isolated in separate chapters but which sprang together in the minds of his readers. Finally, the topic was respectable, because it had provoked conflicting views in antiquity, and attractive to those who took it up because it lent itself (if the tone of *Principe* chapter 20 was followed) to judicious parades of pros and cons or (if *Discorsi*, II, 24 were the point of departure) to strenuous concurrence or rebuttal: and in both cases because it enabled scholars to display examples of their knowledge of events both ancient and modern.

'Politike affairs', Montaigne remarked, constitute 'a large field open to all motions and to contestation. . . . As, for example, Machiavel's *Discourses* were very solid for the subject, yet it hath been very easy to impugne them, and those that have done have left no lesse facilitie to impugne theirs.'[52] The *Discorsi* did not stop Clement VII from sponsoring the Fortezza da Basso (nor the French from relying on the Maginot Line) and Machiavelli's views on fortification were impugned by arguments as well as, apparently, by events. But our impression of the past, the issues that concerned it, the modes of thought in which they were expressed, relies in some part on our reading of its contestations. And when they concern fortifications it is legitimate to suspect that they concern Machiavelli, too.

University College London   J. R. HALE

NOTES

1.   Giancarlo Severini, *Architetture militari di Giuliano da Sangallo* (Pisa, 1970) 51–2; V. Bertolini, 'Niccolò Machiavelli a Verona durante la lega di Cambrai', *Atti e Memorie della Accademia di Agricoltura, Scienze e Lettere di Verona* (1959) 273–301.

2.   *Libro continente appertinentie ad capitanii, retenere & fortificare una citta con bastioni . . .* (Naples, 1521).

3.   Giovanni Battista Zanchi, *Del modo di fortificar le citta* (Venice, 1554)4, and Giacomo Lanteri, *Duo libri . . . del modo di fare le fortificationi . . .* (Venice, 1559). In the dedication he is writing about 'la . . . materia delle fortificazioni moderne . . . . per non essersi fino a questo tempo trovato chi ne habbia scritto.' Two years earlier, in his *Due dialoghi . . . del modo di disegnare le piante delle fortezze secondo Euclide . . .* (Venice, 1557) he had been more modest: 'vedendo io quanto pochi siano fin ad hora stati coloro di ciò habbino scritto . . .'.

4.   Now most easily consulted in *Arte della guerra e scritti politici minori*, ed. Sergio Bertelli (Milan, 1961).

5.   Quotations from *The Prince* are from George Bull's translation in the Penguin Classics series.

6.   Quotations from tr. by Christian E. Detmold (New York, Modern Library, 1940).

7.   In Bertelli, ed. cit., 172.

8.   Book 2, section xxxiv.

9. In Allan H. Gilbert, *Machiavelli's* Prince *and its forerunners* (Durham, N. C., 1938) 159.

10. *Descrizione del modo tenuto dal duca Valentino nello ammazzare Vitellozzo Vitelli . . .*, in Bertelli, ed. cit., 44.

11. I quote from the translation by James Leoni, (repr. London, 1955) 82, 86–7.

12. Book 6, ch. xi.

13. Loeb ed. (London, 1967) i, 481. The 'poet' has not been identified. Plato did recommend the ditching and fortifying of frontiers.

14. *De clementia*, i, 19, 6.

15. *Philippics*, ii, 44, 112.

16. *Dion*, 5, 3. He also cites Isocrates, who certainly stresses the need to win the hearts of the masses: 'consider your surest body-guard to be the virtue of your friends, the goodwill of the citizens, and your own wisdom.' 'To Nicocles', *Orations*, tr. J. M. Freese, i. 22–3. But again, there is no connection with fortresses.

17. Op. cit., 160–1; *Panegyricus* (Leipzig, 1933) 49.

18. So, at least, I have argued; 'The development of the bastion, 1440–1534', in *Europe in the late middle ages*, ed. J. R. Hale, Roger Highfield and Beryl Smalley (London, 1965).

19. Niccolo Tartaglia, *Quesiti e inventioni* (Venice, 1546) 69^{r-v}.

20. G. Zanchi, op. cit., 59.

21. Maria Grazia Sandri, 'La progettazione di Palmanova', *Castellum* (1973) ccclxxxix–ccxc.

22. Eg. the complaint from the Venetian *proveditore* in Candia (1591) that his task is complicated by the fact that 'hoggidi pare che ogniuno voglia esser professore della scientia del fortificare'. In Giuseppe Gerola, *Monumenti veneti nell'isola di Creta*, i (Venice, 1905) 352.

23. In Luigi Firpo, 'Le origini dell'Anti-Machiavellismo', *Il Pensiero Politico* (special fascicle, 1969) 37.

24. J. R. Hale. 'The end of Florentine liberty: the Fortezza da Basso', in *Florentine Studies*, ed. Nicolai Rubinstein, (London, 1968) 502–3 and passim.

25. Eugenio Alberi, *Relazioni degli ambasciatori veneti al senato* (Florence, 1839–63) Ser. 11, vol. ii, 363.

26. *Les six livres de la republique* (Paris, 1576). I quote here (p. 170) as later from the translation by J. M. Tooley (Oxford, 1955) and give page references (in this case 764) to the ed. of Paris, 1583.

27. See Raymond de Fourquevaux, *Information au roy . . . touchant les affaires de Florence* [1555], ed. Raoul Brunon (Aix-en-Provence, 1965) esp. 76–7, and G. Spini, 'Architettura e politica nel principato mediceo del cinquecento', *Rivista Storica Italiana* (1971) 797–8 and 827.

28. *Coryat's crudities* [1611], (London, 2v., 1905) i, 249.

29. Lib. II, cap. xvii. No pagination.

30. He names Aristotle, adds Pedianus, Timoleon of Corinth and Pyrrhus, and cites Fabius Maximus in connection with armies versus fortifications, not, as in *Il Principe* chap. 17, with military discipline. He uses Machiavelli's examples of Milan and Forlì, and re-writes the argument of chap. 4, where Machiavelli deals with the conquests of Alexander the Great and the Turkish sultan, in terms of the connection between conquests and fortresses.

31. *Opere inedite*, i (Florence, 1857) 70–74.

32. See note 4. I paraphrase from the Venice, 1560, ed., 3–4.

33. *Della architettura militare* . . . (Brescia, 1599, written 1546–60) book one, ch.s 13 and 18, 3^v and 5$^{r–v}$.

34. 62–69.

35. Ed. B. Widmar in *Scrittori politici del '500 e '600* (Milan, 1964) 593–597.

36. *Discours* . . . *contre Nicolas Machiavel, Florentin* (written 1575, first printed, s.l., 1576). I quote from the translation of Simon Patericke (London, 1602), 348. The translation was made in 1577.

37. Op. cit., French ed., 756, tr. 167–8.

38. Presumably Timoleon, who destroyed the tyrant Dionysius' citadel in Syracuse in 343 B.C.

39. I use the London, 1807–8, ed.; i, 326–7.

40. *Opera omnia* (Wesel, 1675) iv, 73–4.

41. *The reason of state*, tr. P. J. and D. P. Waley (London, 1956) 117–120.

42. Lib. XIX, discorso 4 (Padua, 1642) 393–403. Francesco Patrizi the younger's *Paralleli militari* was published in the same year, in Rome. Patrizi also notes the number of new fortifications: 'Delle fortezze, tante n'hanno fatto a prencipi fabricare, in si picciolo paese quanta è Italia, che il resto del mondo tutto non n'ha altretante.' But he points out that many ('passato il numero di xc') have changed hands. What is the use of them if men ignore the example of the ancients, if good military discipline is lacking?

43. *Discorsi* . . . *sopra i cinque libri di Cornelio Tacito*, 40–41.

44. Venice, 1599, 577–597. Quotations from the tr. by the Earl of Monmouth (London, 1657) 168–178.

45. *Tesoro politico cioè relationi, instruttioni* . . . *discorsi varii*. There is no mention of fortifications in the first (Cologna, 1589) or second edition (Cologna, 1598); the discussion summarized here occurs in the Milan edition in two volumes, 1600–1601, ii, 49–57 and is repeated in subsequent editions and translations, e.g. *Le tresor politique* (Paris, 1611) 410–415.

46. Burd, op. cit.; Carafa quoted from *De principis officiis* (ed. of Florence, 1558) 652 by Allan Gilbert, op. cit.

47. *Les politiques d'Aristote* (Paris, 1568) 890. He dedicated the book to the Duke of Anjou, the King's brother.

48. *Les tragiques* (1st ed., 1616), *Oeuvres*, ed. Henri Weber (Paris, 1869) lines 663–9. The passage continues: 'Et comme les veillards, revestus et fourrez / De rempars, bastions, fossez et contre-mines . . .'

49. *Four paradoxes or politique discourses concerning militarie discipline* (London, 1604, but written before 1595) 69.

50. *Observations concerning princes and states* . . . (London, 1642) no. 66.

51. Felix Raab, *The English face of Machiavelli* (London, 1964) 110.

52. '*Of presumption*', Florio's translation in the Everyman edition (London, 1910)ii, 381–2.

Ginevra and Ariodante

A Deception Motif from Ariosto to Shakespeare

The story of Ginevra and Ariodante is one of the best-known in *Orlando Furioso*, partly perhaps because it appears early in the poem where its impact is the more memorable (Cantos IV–VI), and also because it is largely autonomous and has lent itself readily to translators seeking detachable passages, and to poets and dramatists in search of ready-made plots. Before the end of the 16th century translations and adaptations appeared in France, Spain, England and Germany, and it attracted the attention of Spenser and Shakespeare.[1] Critical commentary has thus understandably been copious, particularly on the connection with *Much Ado about Nothing*, but the understanding of Ariosto's episode itself has been obscured by criticism aimed primarily at its analogues, and also by conceptions of the poem no longer acceptable; and these in turn have affected critical judgements of the episode, and confused the relationship of Ariosto both to Spenser and to Shakespeare.[2] Charles Prouty, for example, in his study of the sources of *Much Ado* states categorically: 'The Ginevra episode is like many another extraneous tale which Ariosto introduced to adorn his romantic epic. It has no hidden meaning, nor any relation to the characters or main events of the *Orlando*: it is a narrative which pleases by its recital of events.'[3] While this is consonant with much 19th and 20th century Italian criticism, recent writers have stressed both the seriousness and the unity of the poem, and the view of the Ginevra episode which I shall present here is one almost diametrically opposed to that taken by Prouty.[4] The purpose of this article is to throw light on Ariosto's episode, in particular by comparing his treatment of its central motif with that of his source (Martorell), one predecessor not a source (Chariton), and three conspicuous analogues (Bandello, Spenser and Shakespeare). I am not concerned here to uncover further sources or to define influences, although clearly the interpretation of Ariosto's story has a bearing on these matters.

Ariosto's immediate source for the major part of the episode was almost certainly the Spanish romance *Tirante el blanco* by Johanot

Martorell, a native of Valencia, where the first edition of his work
was published in 1490.[5] It was soon known in Italy: Niccolò da
Correggio began (but did not complete) a translation in 1501, and
in 1514–19 Lelio Manfredi made a translation of the whole work
published in Venice in 1538. In the third book of this romance
Tirante, an English knight who has rendered great service to the
Emperor of Constantinople against the Turks, falls in love with the
Emperor's daughter Carmesina, and she with him. A maid, Placer-
demivida, acts as go-between. This courtship is disturbed by Repo-
sada, one of the princess's ladies, who has herself fallen in love with
Tirante but is rebuffed by him. She therefore contrives a scheme to
make him think that Carmesina has another lover. She secretes
Tirante in a room overlooking a garden into which he can see
through a high window by means of mirrors, and she then gets
Carmesina to come to the garden and engage with the maid and
herself in some light-hearted masked games associated with the
Corpus Christi celebrations. In these the maid dresses up as the negro
gardener and indulges in some amorous play with Carmesina who is
seen by Tirante laughing at the 'negro's' caresses and then dis-
appearing into his room with him. Tirante weeps, but still rebuffs
Reposada, and soon after goes and kills the unsuspecting gardener.
He says nothing to Carmesina, preferring to ignore her, and is about
to sail away when the anxious Carmesina sends her maid to find out
what has gone wrong. The mistake is thus cleared up and the lovers
effectively reconciled, but Tirante's boat then breaks away in a
storm and a further series of adventures separates the two from each
other.

Such *peripezie* derive ultimately from the Greek *novelle*, a common
one being that of the faithful wife accused of adultery but cleared and
restored to her husband's favour.[6] There is a similar episode in
Chariton's romance where Chaereas is deceived into thinking his
wife Callirhoe unfaithful, a former suitor having wooed the maid
and got her to let him into the house in full view of the concealed
husband. In the Greek version the angry Chaereas assaults his wife,
who seems to be dead, is buried, and then discovered by a pirate
who breaks open the tomb; and a long series of adventures follows
before husband and wife are eventually re-united.

The kernel of this episode, the attempt to frustrate the course of
true love by a jealous rival who deceives the lover into thinking his
lady unfaithful, becomes the central motif of Ariosto's story of
Ginevra. Here Ginevra's serving maid, Dalinda, is rescued by
Rinaldo from some assassins who have been set on to her by her
lover Polinesso. Dalinda tells Rinaldo how, through her love of
Polinesso, she agreed to help him win the King of Scotland's

daughter, Ginevra, by dressing up as her mistress and accepting Polinesso on Ginevra's balcony one night—not knowing that Polinesso had hidden his rival Ariodante where he could witness the scene and be deceived into thinking that Ginevra, who truly loved him, was unfaithful. Ariodante, says Dalinda, went off in despair and flung himself from a cliff into the sea, whereupon Ariodante's brother, Lurcanio, denounced Ginevra's unchastity and invoked the 'aspra legge di Scozia' which required a woman guilty of fornication to be burned, unless a champion appeared to defend her reputation in armed encounter against her accuser. Rinaldo denounces the injustice of this law as penalising women for offences that men boast of. He then rides with Dalinda to the Scottish court, where an unknown champion has appeared to challenge the accuser, Lurcanio. Rinaldo denounces Polinesso, challenges and defeats him and forces a confession from his dying lips. The unknown champion is now revealed as Ariodante, who had jumped into the sea with the intention of committing suicide, but changed his mind, swam out and came back to save his lady. Thus Ginevra and Ariodante are happily re-united, and Dalinda retires to a convent.

At the centre of both Martorell's and Ariosto's story is the dramatic reversal of fortune of the lover who is plunged from the joy of passionate reciprocated love to the despair of apparent rejection and betrayal. Both Tirante and Ariodante have overwhelming evidence of their ladies' devotion to them, yet their happiness is suddenly shattered by the visual proof of the ladies' infidelity. The shock of this sudden reversal of fortune, highlighted by three lines of verse in the Greek prose story, is similarly emphasised by Martorell:

> podéis pensar lo que su ánima podía sentir, que el día antes estaba tan pomposo y contento por haber alcanzado esposa de tan alta dignidad y señoria que era la cosa que él en este mundo más deseaba ¡y después ver de sus ojos tan gran dolor, cuita y miseria! (III, cl)

It is this scene which provides the central inspiration for Ariosto's episode. It is prepared and presented, like the Spanish source, with considerable care and precision, the emphasis being thrown on the successive moments of Ariodante's confusion and despair—from the first false claims by Polinesso of his success with Ginevra (V, 27–8), and Ariodante's confident rejection of them, followed by Polinesso's offer of visual proof (V, 40) and Ariodante's first fears:

> Resta smarrito Ariodante a questo,
> e per l'ossa un tremor freddo gli scorre.

Then comes the balcony scene itself which is vividly and dramatically

presented with each of the participants set tensely in place, one after
the other: Lurcanio watching his brother, Ariodante concealed in
the shadows, Polinesso signalling to Dalinda, and the latter, all
unawares, decked out in her mistress's finery in the moonlight:

> Le veste si vedean chiare alla luna; . . .
> Vien Polinesso, e alla scala s'appoggia
> che giù manda' gli e monta in su la loggia.
>
> A prima giunta io gli getto le braccia
> al collo, ch'io non penso esser veduta. . .
> Egli più de l'usato si procaccia
> d'accarezzarmi, e la sua fraude aiuta.
> Quell'altro al rio spettacolo condutto,
> misero sta lontano, e vede il tutto. (V, 49–51)

It is a vivid and highly poetical scene, a dramatic recreation of the
perils to which love exposes its victims and the fears which lie half-
suppressed in their minds: it impresses us, as it was surely meant to
do, as the most moving and memorable moment in the story (—all
the more remarkable perhaps in that it is all given in the words of
Dalinda who is thus forced to report to Rinaldo the dialogue of the
rival lovers, and of the brothers, neither of which she has witnessed).
And we are reminded of other scenes in the *Furioso* where lovers are
suddenly brought face to face with their partners' infidelity: Olimpia
deserted by Bireno (X, 20), Rodomonte jilted by Doralice (XXVII,
107), Astolfo and Iocondo cuckolded by their wives (XXVIII,
21, 44), the husband in the story of Melissa (XLIII, 38), and, most
prominent of all, Orlando confronted with the evidence of Angelica's
love for Medoro (XXIII, 103). The deception of Ariodante is therefore the first in a gallery of portraits of lovers whose world has suddenly collapsed about them. It is clearly a topic of deep interest to
Ariosto and one on which he plays a wide range of variations, exposing the fragility of man's emotional and moral life beneath the
capricious hand of Fortune.

This is of course a leit-motif of the *Furioso*, and the Ginevra episode
presents us with an early variation on it. In the Spanish source
Tirante's reason was inhibited by the disordered state of his emotions, which confuses his senses, notably his eyes. He thinks he sees
something which is really something else:

> 'por mis ojos he visto poseer quietamente a un moro negro lo que yo no
> he podido alcanzar ni con ruegos, trabajos, ni peligros. . .' (III, cli).

But for his emotional involvement he would have questioned the
extraordinary evidence with which he is confronted; but he never

does so, and it is left to Carmesina to uncover the mystery. In Ariosto's story the same visual proof of the lady's infidelity is promised to Ariodante:

> Suggiunse il duca; 'Non sarebbe onesto
> che noi volessen la battaglia tòrre
> di quel che t'offerisco manifesto,
> quando ti piaccia, inanzi agli occhi porre.' (V, 40)

And Ariodante's last words before his suicidal leap underline this:

> '...dille poi, che la cagion del resto
> che tu vedrai di me, ch'or ora fia,
> è stato sol perc'ho troppo veduto:
> felice, se senza occhi io fossi suto.' (V, 58)

This motif, simply but explicitly presented by Martorell, is developed by Ariosto with considerable skill. Another deception is practised on the serving-maid who is deceived by Polinesso into thinking that he loves her: but this too was a 'show', a false appearance which the infatuated girl could not see through:

> Perché egli mostrò amarmi più che molto,
> io ad amar lui con tutto il cor mi mossi.
> Ben s'ode il ragionar, si vede il volto,
> ma dentro il petto mal giudicar possi. (V, 8)

So a double deception is enacted: Ariodante is deceived into thinking that his lady is false to him when she is really devoted; and Dalinda is deceived into thinking that her lover is devoted to her when he is really false.[7] We have already seen in Canto I Ariosto's comment on Angelica's much-vaunted virginity, which the infatuated Sacripante takes on trust:

> Forse era ver, ma non però credibile
> a chi del senso suo fosse signore;
> ma parve facilmente a lui possibile
> ch'era perduto in via più grave errore.
> Quel che l'uom vede, Amor gli fa invisibile,
> e l'invisibil fa vedere Amore. (I, 56)

After Ginevra we find the story of Alcina, who deceives her lovers with cosmetics and magic arts so that she seems beautiful when she is really an ugly old hag; then comes Olimpia, deceived by Bireno, who is no villain but simply an inexperienced youth who deludes himself as to the true nature of his feelings for Olimpia. And in due course the havoc that love wreaks on the senses will reach its climax in Orlando who loses his reason completely when his belief that Angelica returns his affection is shown up as a delusion. Angelica's deceitfulness and Orlando's self-deception combine to form a grand illusion the shattering of which provokes the crisis on which the whole poem is built.

Simulation between the sexes however is only part of a wider problem of deceit in social and political life, an issue prominent in Machiavelli's political thought and certainly considered by Ariosto in this wider context, as the proemio to Canto IV shows:

Quantunque il simular sia le più volte
ripreso, e dia di mala mente indici,
si truova pur in molte cose e molte
aver fatti evidenti benefici...

And in the Ginevra episode deception brings a solution: the traveller is deceived into thinking he saw Ariodante commit suicide and his false report prepares the way for the disguised lover to come to his lady's rescue.[8] But the warning is against credulity at any level, and the moral is brought right home to the Estense court, when Ippolito is praised for (or urged towards?) shrewdness in passing judgement:

...che s'ognun truova in voi ben grata udienza,
non vi truova però facil credenza. (XVIII, 1)

The *peripezia* of the lover plunged from bliss to despair is then the structural centre of Ariosto's episode, and the deception motif is treated as part of a wide-ranging enquiry into the effects of love upon the senses, and of passion upon the reason. In this respect Ariosto takes up and elaborates the moral already drawn by Martorell, whose Carmesina rebukes Tirante for his tirade against Fortune: 'Queréis saber qué os ha forzado? vuestro poco saber que dejó la razón por seguir la voluntad desordenada' (III, clxi). But to Martorell's episode, the basis of the Ginevra story, Ariosto adds two further elements; the long initial incident where Rinaldo hears of the 'aspra legge di Scozia' which requires women accused of fornication to be burned unless proved innocent by a defender; and also the dénouement in which the lover, Ariodante, returns incognito to fight for the lady he still believes guilty. Both these passages have various literary precedents which were known to Ariosto and which it is unnecessary to examine here.[9] The dénouement is necessitated of course by the sentence of death on Ginevra which has either to be carried out (with a tragic conclusion similar to that in Juan de Flores) or to be over-ridden by a defending champion—which allows for the dramatic re-appearance of Ariodante incognito, for which there are a number of precedents in Arthurian romance well-known to Ariosto.[10]

However if the dénouement is determined by the presence of the 'aspra legge di Scozia', what led Ariosto to couple the latter motif to the deception scene he took from Martorell's romance? This link does not occur in some of the most successful analogues—in Bandello for example, or in the *Faerie Queene* or in *Much Ado*. The reason I think is implicit in the deception motif itself: a false charge can be exposed and makes little impact if a simple enquiry by the accused brings the truth to light, as it does so flatly in *Tirante*; when the maid hears the reason for Tirante's despair she produces the mask and shows him it was all a game. For the story to have any effect the consequences of the deception must be serious, fatal or nearly so— and in its development in Renaissance times, the classical and medieval motif is led in two different directions—the accused lady is sentenced to death according to a pre-ordained law, or she is so shocked by the charges made against her that she swoons and seems to be dead. Bandello and Shakespeare took up the second of these alternatives, Ariosto the first, which offered him scope to pursue a favourite topic of his, the male–female controversy.

In the Ginevra episode therefore Ariosto pieces together from a complex variety of sources a story that fits precisely into the structure of his poem as a whole and serves the moral purpose underlying it. So too he is distinguished from his sources in the method of presentation of this material in several ways which have a significant bearing on the subsequent literary tradition. The confrontation of an unsuspecting lover with the evidence of his lady's infidelity can lend itself to farcical comedy at one extreme, and to tragedy at the other: the lover may become the cuckolded fool of the comic stage, or the suicidal hero of the tragic. The comic cuckolds of the Boccaccesque tradition are not to be found in Ariosto's poem: indeed it is significant that whereas Boccaccio regularly presents this situation from the viewpoint of the intruding adulterer, Ariosto is almost always concerned with the reaction of the unhappy spouse or fiancé, for whom however the results are rarely tragic. What is characteristic of Ariosto's treatment is that he underlines the suffering of the betrayed lovers but also shows us their capacity for recovery—the potentially tragic ends in the comic, which is the formula of tragicomedy.[11] In the Ginevra episode the stage is to be set for a sequence of such stories, and for this curtain-opener a tragic note would be particularly inappropriate—and Ariosto takes pains to avoid it. Firstly, there is no infidelity: it was all a mistake, the only one of its kind in the poem. After this we have the real infidelities of Bireno, Angelica etc. Secondly, the tragic hero is cut down to size in typically

Ariostesque fashion: Ariodante takes a suicide plunge into the sea, changes his mind and swims out. Thirdly the pathos of Ginevra's misfortune and Ariodante's despair is toned down by the adoption of a remote setting which takes it out of real life and sets it firmly in the world of romance[12]—we are in Arthurian Britain ('la selva Calidonia') among 'i cavallieri erranti/incliti in arme, di tutta Bretagna': Rinaldo sets off to save 'il fior di quante belle donne/ da l'Indo sono all'Atlantee colonne,' (IV, 61) and hears from Dalinda a tale of romance:

> ...Tu intenderai
> la maggor crudeltade e la più espressa
> ch'in Tebe o in Argo o ch'in Micene mai
> o in loco più crudel fosse commessa. (V, 5)

—ending with an unknown knight, all in black, appearing from nowhere to save the princess from the stake, a striking contrast with the source where Carmesina's maid in a down-to-earth interview with Tirante wants to know why he is sulking in his ship; and equally distinctive from Bandello's version which constantly impresses the veracity of the story on us with historical comments and everyday detail. Thus while the Ginevra story is serious in tone (Ariodante's failed suicide providing the only comic touch) it is far removed from the pathetic and near-tragic notes sounded later in the poem.

The second significant feature in Ariosto's treatment of his theme is his extension of the deception motif to a second group of characters, (that is to Polinesso and Dalinda). There is no equivalent situation in Martorell—or in Chariton. In each of these precedents a serving maid is the unwitting instrument of a jealous rival out to undermine a devoted relationship; in Chariton the maid is seduced by Chaereas's rival whom she lets into the house, giving a signal at the door which the concealed Callirrhoe witnesses. But this is the maid's only part in the episode, and we know nothing of her feelings or subsequent actions. In Martorell the maid, Placerdemivida, has a prominent rôle but the trickery is devised by a jealous *woman* who is pursuing Tirante, and Placerdemivida is not emotionally involved in any way.

Ariosto substitutes a scheming *male* rival in place of Martorell's female: having decided to couple the death-penalty with the deception motif and to use this as an exemplum of unjust male sexual attitudes, it was natural that he should make the villain of the piece a man. What is more significant is his expansion of the serving-maid's role and her relationship with the rival into a secondary plot quite as interesting as the main one. So we have two parallel relationships, one between Dalinda and Polinesso, the other between Ginevra and Ariodante, linked of course by Polinesso's transference of his attentions from Dalinda to Ginevra. The effect is morally more convincing and artistically richer, with a pattern not only of anti-thetical deception situations as we pointed out earlier, but also of types of amorous passions: Ariodante's chaste and self-sacrificing love contrasts with Polinesso's lustful and selfish one; Ginevra's chaste and correct devotion is set against Dalinda's sensual and illicit passion. The ultimate triumph of chaste and unselfish love in this first episode in the poem (where Ariodante fights his own brother to save the lady he no longer claims) prefigures effectively a similar situation in the very last canto where Ruggiero returns incognito to fight Bradamante so that his rival, Leone, may have her.

The most significant contribution, however, made by Ariosto to the literary tradition is in the field of narrative technique. The bulk of the story, as we have seen, is given us in Dalinda's words spoken to Rinaldo when he rescues her from her would-be murderers: a large part of the action is therefore complete when Rinaldo, (and with him the reader) enters the action—the wooing of Dalinda, and of Ginevra, the balcony scene, the flight of Ariodante, and Lurcanio's denunciation of Ginevra are all set in the past and are given us as a flash-back—after which the action continues in chronological sequence with the return of Dalinda and Rinaldo to the court, the exposure of Polinesso and the revelation of Ariodante's return. This disturbance of the chronological order of events is peculiar to Ariosto's version of the story and is characteristic of his technique in the *Furioso*.[13] Martorell preserves the chronological order with a story told in the author's words, the narrative following in turn the activities of Tirante, his lady Carmesina, and the scheming Placer-demivida; it is the same technique as that employed by Chariton who tells the story from his own point of view, causing us to follow one at a time Chaereas, the seducer, the maid, Chaereas again and so on, giving us the actions and the mental processes of each in turn.[14] Bandello preserves a meticulous chronological sequence, and so, effectively, does Spenser, his flash-back taking in the whole story. Ariosto's method has various advantages, among them being the link of the episode to the main action by the intervention of a main character at a critical moment—here heightening the suspense but also fostering an illusion of the continuum of life into which our individual activities are slotted.[15]

It also has the advantage of re-creating some of the ambiguity of human experience: instead of an account by the all-seeing author exposing magically the minds of his characters we have the story as it might indeed have appeared to one of the participants. We only know as much of Ginevra's, Ariodante's and Polinesso's motives as

Dalinda, with her limited contact with them and her disturbed state of mind, can surmise. The remarkable volte-face of Ariodante in swimming to safety is not explained: neither he nor Ginevra are defined in any detail: and Polinesso's villainy is particularly obscure: did he really love Dalinda at one stage and only later aspire to the princess (as Dalinda suggests); or was Dalinda only his tool from the beginning? And what of Dalinda herself: was she really so gullible as to accept Polinesso's plan without sensing the risk to her mistress? Polinesso, it will be remembered, gives two successive unlikely explanations for his courting Ginevra (first, that if Dalinda helps him to marry the princess he will keep Dalinda as his mistress; and later that if Dalinda lets him make love to her in the princess's clothes he will be able to rid himself of his obsession for Ginevra). Dalinda, in retrospect, seems to accept the first of these but to question the second. Spenser and Shakespeare apparently found the motivation for the maid dressing as her mistress unsatisfactory and substituted different explanations, but Ariosto's treatment is quite consistent with the moral of the episode as a whole even if taken at its face value: Dalinda's judgement is so confused by her infatuation with Polinesso that she cannot see through his deceit.

Another interesting consequence of making Dalinda the narrator is to bring the four main characters effectively into balance. Whose story is it? Peter Beverley in his 16th century version entitled it 'The Historie of Ariodante and Genevra'—and the most recent English version calls it 'The Misfortunes of Dalinda'[16]—we might add 'The Treachery of Polinesso'. It is reported initially to Rinaldo as the story of Ginevra, the Scottish princess, and it is her misfortune that he sets out to rectify: then he meets Dalinda who claims most of the episode as *her* story: yet the arch-schemer who binds together the two sub-plots and holds the stage throughout is Polinesso; and the obvious hero who suffers the harshest blow and triumphs over it in a dramatic final appearance is Ariodante. The action therefore is a subtle blend of interacting personalities and motives, in which (in Pirandellian fashion) no-one is content to be a 'minor character'.

There is not the space here to consider Ariosto's analogues in any detail, but I should like to draw attention to certain features of the versions of the story by Bandello, Spenser and Shakespeare which bear on the points I have made in relation to Ariosto. Bandello, for example, in his story of Timbreo and Fenicia stresses Timbreo's credulity ('fui troppo credulo') in accepting the evidence of his eyes ('dal velo di gelosia accecato'), evidence which had been treacherously falsified by his jealous friend, Girondo.[17] The basic deception motif is repeated, though it is treated very differently: it is the lover here, not his brother, who denounces the lady, an extension of Ariosto's moral on hasty judgements (leading even further in Spenser and Shakespeare to the themes of intemperance and discourtesy), and this denunciation causes the apparent death of Fenicia with the consequent repentance of Timbreo, who is lured into marrying a substitute, his revived lady in disguise.[18] The return of the apparently dead Fenicia parallels that of Ariosto's would-be suicide, Ariodante, so that deception brings a cure in the end to the ills it had caused earlier. Noteworthy is the absence of the serving-maid, so prominent in other versions of the story, and hence of the double-plot used by Ariosto—there is no distraction here from the story of Fenicia. Significant also are the changes in presentation: Bandello follows closely the chronological sequence of the action moving to and fro between the actors and pacing his narrative with great skill; he persuades us to accept the extraordinary deception and final marriage scene by his patient uncovering of his characters' motives and a good deal of historical and realistic corroborative detail which contrasts markedly, as we have seen, with Ariosto's conscious adoption of romance modes and diction.

Spenser's material for his story of Phedon and Philemon (*FQ.* II(iv)) clearly derives from Ariosto:[19] Philemon thwarts his friend Phedon's courtship of Claribell by showing him a lover being admitted to the 'inner bowre' of what seems to be his lady, really the serving-maid decked out in her mistress's clothes by the scheming Philemon. But the alleged lover is 'a groome of base degree', the motive for Philemon's treachery is obscure, and a more plausible reason is given for the handmaid's compliance (Philemon persuades her that she would be as beautiful as her mistress if she wears her clothes).[20] The main difference however is in the reaction of the lover who gives way to rage and desire for revenge, (as in Chariton and Martorell), kills Claribell and Philemon, and pursues the maid with the intention of killing her too. Spenser gives us explicitly an example of intemperance, thus turning Ariosto's story to a quite different purpose. Ariosto's hand-maid, or his villain, Polinesso, could have ensampled Intemperance, not the lover Ariodante whose response to his 'betrayal' is a dignified silence and withdrawal. The main function of the Ariosto story here is to explain how a lover could mistakenly believe his lady guilty of infidelity (hence revenge is wrong, as it is conceived in anger and may be misplaced). In general terms however Spenser follows Ariosto in using the deception motif to exemplify a type of love, and also in the structure of his tale: it is after all Guyon who releases Phedon (just as Rinaldo released Dalinda), and the episode is thus drawn into the main plot by the involvement of a main character. The tale is then told by the rescued person (Phedon/Dalinda)—although Spenser largely ignores the dramatic character of his source: the dull monochrome of Phedon's brief report contrasts notably with the tension and excitement of Dalinda's account.

When he wrote *Much Ado about Nothing* Shakespeare was clearly familiar with these three versions of the deception motif; Ariosto's, Bandello's and Spenser's, and he exploited all three as well as other sources of a somewhat different nature.[21] Much has been written on the sources of *Much Ado* and I only propose here to add a footnote on the relationship of Shakespeare's comedy to the *Furioso* in the light of the interpretation of the Ginevra story offered above. First I would stress the continuity of the deception motif from Martorell and Ariosto to Shakespeare: in *Much Ado* it is clearly of prime importance. A central theme of the play, as F. P. Rossiter has suggested, is the functioning of illusion, shown in a series of 'misapprehensions, mis-prisions, misunderstandings, misinterpretations and misapplications' —leading, it has been suggested, to 'self-recognition', 'the journey from confusion to clarity, knowledge of one's own truth'.[22] We have shown the germ of this in Martorell, and its growth in the Ginevra episode to a double and antithetical deception situation based on the confusion of the senses operated by passion, this episode itself forming part of an extensive and complex pattern of illusions at the peak of which is Orlando's madness.

Second in importance perhaps we should note the significance of the double-plot. Most striking in *Much Ado* is the way in which what seemed the sub-plot (Beatrice/Benedick) overshadows the main plot (Hero-Claudio): the running of the two plots alongside each other makes for a rich and witty counterpoint of character and action, foreshadowed in Ariosto's two pairs of lovers. Indeed Ariosto alone of the most likely sources of *Much Ado* uses a double-plot: elsewhere we find only a triangular relationship between the main characters.

On the genesis of Shakespeare's play there has been much conjecture: particularly concerning his creation of Beatrice and Bene-dick as a sort of compensation for the dull Claudio and Hero. Certainly Ariosto's Ariodante and Ginevra are sketchy, pallid characters compared with the forthcoming maid and her scheming seducer; and if Shakespeare was led to create Beatrice and Benedick as a foil to the two 'main' characters, one could point to the prominent allusions at the beginning of Ariosto's story to the male/female controversy as perhaps leading him in the direction of the lively exchanges between Beatrice and Benedick in *Much Ado*. If Claudio is the epitome of the unromantic lover he still is not so far removed from Ariodante who seems not only a suspicious, but also a cautious,

lover (beside Polinesso) even before he makes his unromantic escape
from the sea—indeed Claudio's repentance and readiness to marry
Hero's 'sister' is the result of a change of heart foreshadowed by
Ariodante's return to fight his own brother in order to save Ginevra.[23]

Ariodante's challenge to Lurcanio is in many respects the closest
parallel in any of the sources to the challenges issued by Benedick
(and Antonio) to Claudio, and it serves essentially the same function.
None of these challenges in fact needs to be put into action—they
signify however the 'gut reaction' of the lover in accepting the
promptings of his heart and his imagination rather than those of his
head and his eyes.[24] In spite of everything, Ariodante returns to
champion Ginevra; and in response to Beatrice's startling demand
'kill Claudio', Benedick poses what for him is a new question 'Think
you *in your soul* the Count Claudio hath wronged Hero?' and he
accepts the promptings of his soul in making his challenge to Claudio.

There remains the thorny problem of the maid Margaret's part in
the deception scene. Borachio says that the watchers shall 'see me at
her chamber window, hear me call Margaret Hero, hear Margaret
term me Claudio'—for which the *Furioso* seems the only likely
source. Dalinda is persuaded really to act the part of her mistress,
whereas Spenser's Pryene merely takes her clothes in order to look
more beautiful. But how can one reconcile Borachio's words with
Shakespeare's insistence on Margaret's innocence? One assumes,
with Miss Trenery,[25] that *Borachio's* intention is to make Claudio
think that Hero and Borachio are 'making mock of his honourable
suit'; and one accepts A. P. Rossiter's view that this is a sufficient
explanation for Borachio's words. Nevertheless this still leaves us to
make surmises about the story he spun to Margaret to persuade her
to participate, and about *her* motivation. Clearly we cannot expect
explanations for everything that occurs in a romantic tale and Dover
Wilson's hypothesis of an earlier version superseded by the present
text is not necessary on this account. If there is some confusion about
Margaret's part in the plot it is surely enough to look for it in
Shakespeare's sources which left him, as we pointed out above, with
two different explanations of the maid's motives, neither of which was
particularly relevant to the story as he had envisaged it. It seems at
first sight strange that Ariosto, in his narrative poem, should put the
balcony scene so vividly before us (even though in Dalinda's con-
jectural account), and that Shakespeare with the resources of the
theatre declines to do so—but times had changed and the balcony
scene might well have seemed stale by the time of *Much Ado*—and
then we should remember, in comparing these different versions of
the same motif, not only the differing cultures and intentions of the
authors and the different genres which they adopt, but also the

promptings of independence which urge them to strike out into the areas of their topic not previously explored by their predecessors.

We should not therefore look on the Ginevra story as a mere romantic tale only fully exploited by Ariosto's successors. It is in fact a rounded, subtle and poetic portrayal of the working of love and it is typical in conception and presentation of many of the poet's later episodes. The point of departure is a dramatic scene, a critical moment in a relationship between two people, most often a moment of truth when an ideal is tested or an illusion broken; such a scene is then related to the wider philosophical or moral thesis of the poem, of which it exemplifies a particular facet; or it is connected to a particular contemporary issue—the 'querelle des femmes', misogyny, chivalry. Characteristic also is the setting of the tale in the words of a participant, the skilful disturbance of the chronological sequence, and the intrusion into the episode of a main character essential for its resolution and also for the reader's enlightenment. These it seems to me are significant and distinctive features of Ariosto's narrative method, in which the episode contains its own truth and its own poetry as essential components of the total art of the poem.

University of Edinburgh   C. P. BRAND

NOTES

1. See G. J. Ferrazzi, *Bibliografia Ariostesca* (Bassano, 1881); G. Fuma-galli, *La fortuna dell'*'O.F.' *in Italia nel secolo XVI* (Ferrara, 1912); A. Benedetti, *L'*'O.F.' *nella vita intellettuale del popolo inglese* (Firenze, 1914) p. 22. A. Cioranescu, *L'Arioste en France* (Paris, 1939), p. 309; G. Chevallier, *L'Arioste en Espagne* (Bordeaux, 1966), pp. 183, 269, etc.

2. See e.g. A. Momigliano, *Saggio su l'*'O.F.' (Bari, 1928): 'L'episodio non è rimasto fra quelli indimenticabili del poema . . .' (p. 210). W. B. C. Watkins writes of the 'cynical Ariosto' with his 'tongue-in-cheek morality' (*Shakespeare and Spenser* (Princeton, 1950) p. 112); and V. Kostic: 'The story of Ginevra, like most tales from Ariosto, allows a multiplicity of morals to be drawn from it, but warrants none . . . Ariosto is not concerned with morality' ('Ariosto and Spenser', *English Miscellany* 17 (1966) pp. 157, 169).

3. Charles T. Prouty, *The Sources of 'Much Ado about Nothing'* (New Haven, 1950) p. 20. In respect of moral seriousness 19th and early 20th century criticism is a reaction against 16th century allegorisa-tion (Fornari, Valvassori etc.). In respect of lack of unity the charge dates from 16th century neo-Aristotelian criticism: cf. Paolo Beni's objection that Rinaldo goes off in search of adventures when he should be recruiting in Scotland: he should have come upon Dalinda by accident! (*Comparatione di Homero, Virgilio, e Torquato* (Padova, 1607) p. 249).

4. Note particularly the critical essays of R. Spongano, R. Battaglia, G. De Blasi, N. Cappellani, C. Segre.

5. Quotations are from the edition by Felicidad Buendia (*Libros de Caballerias Españoles*, Madrid 1960). See Book III, Chapters cxlix–cl.

6. See S. Trenkner, *The Greek Novella in the Classical Period* (Cambridge, 1958) pp. 60–1. For deception motifs see Stith Thompson, *Motif-index of Folk Literature* (Bloomington, 1932–6); D. P. Rotunda, *Motif-index of the Italian Novella in Prose* (Bloomington, 1942); Lefebure, *Romans et contes egyptiens de l'époque pharaonique* (Paris, 1949), pp. 137 ff.

    For Chariton I have used the Latin translation by J. J. Rieskius *Chairea et Callirrhoe*, ed. J. P. D'Orville (Amsterdam, 1750), Book I. There is no evidence that Ariosto knew Chariton whose romance was not published until 1750 (first Italian translation 1752). There are also points of similarity with Heliodorus's story of Knemon and Demainete (*Ethiopica*, I). I have not been able to see G. Kentenich, *Die Genovefa legende* (Trier, 1927).

7. See Valvassori's allegory in his edition of the *Furioso* (Venice, 1554, 1566): 'Lurcanio si crede d'haver veduta Ginevra trarsi in casa un suo amante, quantunque nel vero non lei, ma Dalinda veduta havesse: s'esprime la potenza d'una fallace credenza, e mala informazione' (Allegory to Canto V).

8. The imminent duel between Lurcanio and Ariodante is neatly analysed in a 16th century commentary: 'L'abbattimento di Lurcanio con Ariodante è di due nature: che Lurcanio combatte il torto, credendo aver ragione: ed Ariodante, credendo d'avere il torto, combatte per la ragione: in modo che più giustamente combatte colui il quale secondo l'intenzion sua muove l'armi contro la giustizia; che l'altro il quale intenda di difenderla' (see the *Parere in Duello d'incerto autore sopra l'Orlando Furioso* in the Valvassori edition of the *Furioso* (Venice, 1567)).

9. See P. Rajna, *Le fonti dell'O.F.*, Florence, 1900, pp. 149–63. For Rinaldo's complaint against the injustice of the law, cf. Madonna Filippa in the *Decameron*: 'le leggi deono essere comuni e fatte con consentimento di coloro a cui toccano' (VI, 7). A similar law, in a Scottish setting, is described in *Amadis de Gaula* and in Juan de Flores' *Grisel y Mirabella*, where the law requires the death of the one of the two lovers responsible for the offence ('el que mas causa fuesse al otro de haber amado . . .'), which leads to a lengthy debate on the general question of whether men or women are responsible for sexual offences, very much in tune with Rinaldo's speech.

10. See particularly versions of Lancelot returning incognito to Guinevere (e.g. in *Li Chantari di Lancellotto* (London 1874), C. II); and for Polinesso's murder attempt on Dalinda see the *Tristano Riccardiano* (Bologna, 1896), I, 61).

11. E.g. Olimpia, abandoned by Bireno, accepts another husband (XI, 80); Rodomonte, rejected by Doralice, seeks compensation with Isabella (XXVIII, 98); Iocondo and Astolfo end up reconciled to their wives (XXVIII, 74), as does Anselmo (XLIII, 143); Orlando's loss of his senses is of course tragi-comic. The only really tragic lover is the husband in the Melissa story (XLIII).

12. 'Un colorito apertamente romanzesco . . .', according to M. Turchi, (*Ariosto o della liberazione fantastica* (Ravenna, 1969), p. 206).

13. Cf. for example the stories of Olimpia (IX) and Isabella (XIII) into which we break, in mid-course, with the ladies' own accounts of their adventures.

14. See Tomas Hägg, *Narrative Technique in the Ancient Greek Romances* (Stockholm, 1971), pp. 115 ff.; Remy Petri, *Über den Roman des Chariton* (Meisenheim am Glan, 1963).

15. Cf. Orlando's intervention in the Olimpia story (IX, 21); Ruggiero in the Ricciardetto episode (XXV, 8); Bradamante in the Rocca di Tristano (XXXII, 69) etc.

16. *Orlando Furioso*, translated by Richard Hodgens, Vol. I (London, 1973: Pan/Ballantine).

17. Cf. another of Bandello's stories (I, 24) where a would-be lover gets a servant to hide under the innocent lady's bed and thus persuades the husband she is guilty—but not the lions to which she is exposed and which do not harm her. Again the target is excessive credulity: 'Deverebbe nel vero ciascuno non essere molto facile a credere ciò che se gli dice, e massimamente quando gli è rapportato male d'alcuno...' (*Tutte le Opere*, ed. F. Flora (Milan, 1934) Part I, Novella 22, p. 308). A similar moral is drawn by Giraldi in *Gli Ecatommiti* (Introduzione, Novelle 9 and 10) where a husband is falsely persuaded that his wife is unfaithful: 'in cosa di tanta importanza, di quanto è mettere l'onore della sua donna a rischio non si dee luomo lasciare vincere, né all'ira, né all'altrui falsità'. (Florence, 1834, p. 1807) See also *Gli Ecatommiti*, Day V, Novella (i).

18. Note also the change in the relative social status of the lovers—whereas Ginevra is a princess to whom the visiting knight aspires, Fenicia is poor and Timbreo thinks he is demeaning himself by marrying her—which helps to explain his open denunciation of her later. Bandello seems here to be contrasting poor virtue with rich arrogance, and to show the triumph of the former: the friendship of the rival lovers is not stressed.

19. See S. J. McMurphy, *Spenser's Use of Ariosto for Allegory* in the University of Washington's *Publications on Language and Literature*, 21 (1924). The extensive literature on Ariosto and Spenser (Neil Dodge, E. Koeppel, H. H. Blanchard, A. H. Gilbert etc.) has little to say on this episode. Some of the points made here are elaborated in my article 'Tasso, Spenser and the *Orlando Furioso*' in *From Petrarch to Pirandello*, ed. J. A. Molinaro (Toronto, 1973) pp. 95–110. See also A. Thaler, 'Spenser and *Much Ado About Nothing*', *Studies in Philology*, 37 (1940) 225–35.

20. A. Thaler misunderstands Ariosto's purpose when he suggests that 'the maid's part in all this is progressively strengthened as it develops through Spenser to Shakespeare' (article cited, p. 233).

21. Among the vast bibliography note especially C. T. Prouty, *The Sources of 'Much Ado About Nothing'* (New Haven, 1950); G. Bullough, *The Narrative and Dramatic Sources of Shakespeare* (1958), Vol. II; Mariella Cavalchini, 'A Re-evaluation of the Italian Sources of *Much Ado About Nothing*', *English Miscellany*, 14(1963), 45–56.

22. See A. P. Rossiter, *Angel with Horns* (1966), p. 77; J. Wain, 'The Shakespeare Lie-detector: Thoughts on *Much Ado About Nothing*', (*Critical Quarterly* (1967), 29). See also Graham Storey's comment: 'The play's true centre is in fact ... a theme', man's 'irresistible propensity to be taken in by appearances' (*More Talking of Shakespeare*, ed. J. Garrett (1959), p. 135).

23. J. R. Mulryne's comment that Shakespeare's mature comedies 'all submit various briefly-created types of personality to the disciplinary experiences of love' is almost transferrable to the *Furioso* although not many of Ariosto's lovers are truly 'disciplined' by their experiences! (see J. R. Mulryne *Much Ado About Nothing* (1965) pp. 38 ff.)

24. See John Russell Brown, *Shakespeare and his Comedies* (1957), pp. 109 ff.

25. See the Introduction to her edition of *Much Ado* (1924) pp. xvii–xix; Rossiter, pp. 67 ff.

A new autograph of Sperone Speroni's *Canace* and its relationship to the textual tradition of the play*

The task of preparing for publication the most important documents in the debate on tragic principles which stemmed from Sperone Speroni's horror play, *Canace e Macareo* (1542), has raised many problems, some of attribution which have been dealt with elsewhere, others chronological and textual.[1] One of the most difficult of those in the last category, the absence of any definitive text of the tragedy itself, has been partially solved by the fortunate discovery of an unknown autograph copy in the Vatican Library. This has not only thrown valuable light on the text of the play but has also made it possible to fill in some of the gaps in the rather curious story of its composition and publication. It is with this manuscript, *Vat. Lat. 4820*, and its relation to the textual tradition of the *Canace* that this essay is mainly concerned.

In preparing my text I have taken into account all the versions of the *Canace* that I have been able to identify up to and including those published by Forcellini (Speroni, *Opere*, 1740), that is four manuscripts and seven printed editions. I append a summary list of them with the initials to be used in my edition.

Manuscripts

P Padova, Biblioteca Capitolare, *Carte Speroniane*[2], vol. VIII, cc. 43r–77v. Autograph draft of the play.
VAT Biblioteca Vaticana, *Vat. Lat, 4820*, cc. 1r–39v. Autograph.
M Milan, Biblioteca Ambrosiana, *N. 250. Sup.* cc. 92r–129v.
VEN Venice, Biblioteca Marciana, *Mss. Ital. Cl. 9. n.309 (6079)*, cc. 10r–34r. Incomplete.

* I am indebted to many people for help and advice during the writing of this article but am most particularly grateful to Professor Cecil Grayson for his comments on the first draft, to Professor Vittorio Fanelli for information about Angelo Colocci and his library and to Madame J. Bignami Odier for giving so generously of her time and guiding me so surely through the labyrinths of the early catalogues of the Vatican Library.

Editions

D   *Canace tragedia di messer Sperone Speroni nobile padovano*...In
     Fiorenza per Francesco Doni, 1546.

V   *Tragedia di M. Sperone Speroni*...In Vinegia appresso Vincenzo
     Valgrisi, 1546. With a dedication by 'Il Clario'.

B   *Giuditio sopra la Tragedia di Canace e Macareo*...*con la Tragedia
     appresso*...In Lucca per Vincenzo Busdrago, 1550.

G   *Tragedia di M. Sperone Speroni*...In Vinegia appresso Gabriel
     Giolito de Ferrari, 1562.

F   *Giudicio sopra la tragedia di Canace et Macareo*...*con la Tragedia
     appresso.* In Venetia, 1566. No printer's name but the device is
     that of Domenico Farri.

A   *Canace tragedia del Sig. Sperone Speroni. Alla quale sono aggiunte
     alcune altre sue compositioni*...In Venetia, 1597. Presso Giovanni
     Alberti. Edited by Speroni's grandson Ingolfo de' Conti.

FOR *Opere di M. Sperone Speroni degli Alvarotti tratte da' mss. originali,*
     vol. IV. In Venezia, 1740. Appresso Domenico Occhi. Edited
     by M. Forcellini.
         pp. 5–70, *Tragedia.* (Reprint of V).
         pp. 283–340, *Tragedia riformata.* (Edition of P).

The most striking fact about the text of the *Canace* which a collation
of these manuscripts and editions has confirmed, is that the autograph
P stands by itself, being substantially different both in contents and
arrangement from all the other versions. Our first task, therefore,
must be to consider its characteristics and try to determine its relationship to the other texts. It is obviously important because it is
the only text of the play among Speroni's papers in Padua and is
dated by Speroni himself, 9th January–9th March, 1542.[3] These
dates for the composition of the play are confirmed by other evidence.
A page of autograph notes about a production of the tragedy which
the *Accademia degli Infiammati* hoped to stage under the presidency of
Luigi Cornaro with Ruzzante as producer, shows that it must have
been far advanced by the 17th March 1542 when the project had to
be abandoned owing to the death of Ruzzante.[4] By the summer it
was in circulation since it is mentioned by Pietro Aretino in a letter
dated 25th July[5] and Claudio Tolomei states that he was present at
a reading of it in the house of Monsignor di Brescia in Rome in
1543.[6]

Marco Forcellini, the conscientious eighteenth century editor of
Speroni's works, was well aware that P is different from the printed
texts (he did not know about the other manuscripts) but he maintained, and his view has been generally accepted, that it is not the
first draft of the tragedy as these dates would seem to show, but a later
revised version produced by Speroni in reply to criticisms contained

in the anonymous *Giudizio*, dated 1543 though not published till
1550. He therefore published two versions of the *Canace*, a reprint of
V, followed by the autograph P which he entitled *Tragedia riformata*.[7]
There is little doubt that he was mistaken. His rather cavalier dismissal of Speroni's dating, implying as it does an intention to deceive
on the part of the author, is not convincing and furthermore the
differences between P and the other texts have no connection with
points raised in the *Giudizio*.[8] More important, the manuscript has
all the characteristics of a first and very tentative draft, being full of
cancellations and alternative readings, with sometimes as many as
two or three different versions of a single speech.[9] This impression is
confirmed by comparing these cancellations and variants with the
relevant passages in the other texts of the play. 105 examples of
sentences or words which had been crossed out and replaced by an
alternative rendering were examined. In 96 cases it was found that
all the other texts gave the uncancelled second version. In five of
the nine remaining passages the cancelled reading was reproduced,
in three the cancelled version was found in all the texts except M,
and in one case only there was a different reading, not found in P at
all. A further study of 79 examples of passages which give alternative
versions, neither of which is cancelled, revealed that all the other
texts reproduce the same variant except once when M has a different
reading. These statistics seem fairly conclusive. It is difficult to conceive that Speroni could have revised his tragedy after its publication
by providing alternative suggestions only to cross them out and
return to the published text. Furthermore the fact that in the texts
other than P the same choice between alternatives was always made
seems to suggest the existence of another version in which the author
had already resolved his uncertainties.

    A further and no less cogent reason for believing that P is an early
draft lies in those very differences in order and subject matter between P and the other versions which Forcellini had interpreted as
proofs of its later revision. These differences, though substantial, are
not quite so radical as Forcellini makes out when he says, 'prende
quasi quella tragedia nuova forma e figura.'[10] P is considerably
shorter, 1844 lines instead of 2069 as in V, and the order of Acts and
Scenes is different making the play less logical and coherent, but
these omissions and changes occur only in Acts II and III, the contents of Acts I, IV and V are the same in all versions.[11] A brief
synopsis of the *Canace* is here necessary to make these differences
comprehensible. The tragedy, one of the first in Italy to take its
subject matter from classical mythology, is based largely on Ovid,
Heroides XI, and tells of the incest between Canace and Macareo,
twin brother and sister, children of Aeolus, King of the Winds, and

his wife Deiopea. In all the texts except P the main plot develops as follows: *Act I*. In a kind of prologue the ghost of the unfortunate child to be born from the incestuous twins prophesies his own death. The play then opens to show a joyous Aeolus giving orders to his Councillor for the fitting celebration of his children's eighteenth birthday: later the Councillor, left alone, predicts, in a lugubrious monologue, that Aeolus' present joy will soon be changed to sorrow. *Act II*. Deiopea describes to her *cameriera* a worrying dream that she regards as prophetic of misfortunes to come. The *cameriera* recounts his mother's dream to Macareo and his *famiglio* whereupon Macareo confesses both his love for Canace and their sin. There follows an important scene between Macareo and Canace's *nutrice* in which he is dissuaded by her from committing suicide and exhorted to live in order to save Canace and his child. This scene is incomplete. The Act ends with a monologue by the *nutrice*, 'Sciocchi a mio danno...' in which she laments the difficult situation in which she finds herself, torn between her conflicting loyalties, to Canace, her charge, or to Aeolus, her employer.[12] *Act III* opens with Canace, near to her time, invoking the help of the goddess Lucina. She is comforted by the *nutrice* and persuaded to retire to her room. The rest of the Act deals with the *nutrice*'s arrangement for putting into practice her dangerous plan of smuggling the baby out of the palace in a basket of flowers. *Act IV*. The *famiglio* gives a dramatic account to the Chorus, here appearing for the first time, of the disastrous failure of this scheme, the discovery of the child and the fury of the King. Aeolus orders his Councillor to offer Canace a choice between a sword and poison: the *nutrice* must use the method which Canace rejects. Deiopea pleads in vain with Aeolus to save her children. *Act V*. Macareo learns of the deaths of Canace, the *nutrice* and his child and resolves to die too. Aeolus is now overcome by remorse but too late to prevent the suicide of Macareo which is described to him by the *famiglio*. The play ends, rather irrelevantly, with a prophecy of the destruction of Charles V's fleet off Algiers (October 1541).

Acts II and III, as they appear in P, differ in two main respects from the version summarized above. All the scenes with Macareo in Act II are missing, Canace's first appearance and her scene with the *nutrice* come at the beginning of Act II (instead of Act III), while Deiopea's dream is placed at the beginning of Act III. The defects of such an arrangement are obvious. The hero does not appear at all until Act V: Deiopea's dream in Act III cannot be called prophetic since we are already aware of Canace's plight and the role of the *nutrice* is diminished and the action of the play confused by the omission of her negotiations with Macareo in Act II. It would seem difficult to maintain that these differences are improvements on the published text, while the reverse could certainly be argued.

Having shown, therefore, that P is shorter, differently arranged, and earlier than the other texts, we must now consider more closely this second version of the play which they represent. Leaving aside for the moment the manuscripts M, VEN and VAT, our collation of the printed texts showed that they follow two traditions, one being substantially more correct than the other. The first, in which the play is called *Canace*, derives from D, the *editio princeps* (1546) and is found again in B(1550) and A(1597). The second, with the title *Tragedia*, stems from V(1546). It corrects many of the errors of D and these corrections are reflected in G(1562) and sometimes, but not always, in F(1566).[13]

Both D and V are of some typographical interest. D, riddled with mistakes, appeared under the imprint *In Fiorenza per francesco donì*. Doni wrote immediately to Speroni denying all responsibility and accusing Curtio Trajano Navò, a minor Venetian printer, possibly of French origin, of having perpetrated this horror.[14] A comparison of the type used in D with that in other books printed by Doni and Navò, although not conclusive, has shown that he was probably speaking the truth. It closely resembles type used by Navò but has little in common with Doni's printing.[15] It is also significant, perhaps, that some copies of this edition do not have the imprint of Florence nor the name Doni.[16]

The second edition of 1546 (V) was published by Vincenzo Valgrisi, another Venetian printer of French origin.[17] It is clearly stated on the title page that it purports to correct the errors of D,

> se nel fine di questa sana, intiera e corretta si guarderà, si troverà annotato quanto lacera, tronca, e corrotta sia quella, che da altri, che da noi, e contra il voler dell'Auttore, e senza licenza veruna occultamente è stata stampata e intitolata *Canace*.

In a foreword signed 'Il Clario' the editor, whose identity will be discussed later, states that the publication of the *Canace*, with so many errors, against the wishes and without the knowledge of Speroni, has emboldened him to publish the version of it which he had kept locked away for two years and more. At the end of the volume are two pages listing the *errata* of D.

There is no doubt that this text is far superior, not only to D, but also, as has been shown, to the autograph P. When I first started work, however, there was a serious objection to using it as the basis for a critical edition, namely the lack of any documentary evidence to show that Speroni himself had ever approved the alterations that had taken place between the writing of P and the printing of D and

V. Indeed Speroni's own views seem to indicate that he hadn't, since he disclaimed all responsibility for the printed text. In the unfinished *Apologia*, a defence of his play against the criticisms of the *Giudizio*, on which, to judge from notes scribbled on the backs of dated letters, he appears to have been working around 1552/3, he describes how he composed the *Canace*, handing it as he wrote it to the *Approvatori* of the *Accademia degli Infiammati*, how it circulated throughout Italy and was published two or three times, 'non solamente senza i suoi cori, ma senza il capo e senza il nome che poi le posero gli stampatori'.[18] In the lectures by which, in December 1558, he publicly defended his tragedy before the *Accademia degli Elevati*,[19] he declared even more explicitly, 'che ella poi non fu mai né veduta, né da me, né da altri, che se io avessi voluto farla pubblicamente vedere, l'averei data fuori intera se non perfetta'.[20] These protestations are largely true. The *Canace* as we have it, even in the Valgrisi edition, is unfinished, without choruses, without prologue, just as Speroni says, nevertheless there is now evidence that he himself had done a great deal of work on it since he first drafted P and was indeed responsible for 'Il Clario's' text.

   This brings us at last to the Vatican manuscript (VAT). It is to be found in the miscellaneous Codex *Vat. Lat 4820*, and consists of an autograph of the *Canace*. That it has remained undiscovered for so long is due to the fact that it is listed in Alessandro Ranaldi's seventeenth century inventory[21] as *Euripidis Ecuba Sperono Speroni interprete ipsius manu scripta*, a mistaken identification easily explained by the resemblance of the opening scene of the *Canace* to that of Euripides' *Hecuba*.[22] It is written out clearly on sheets (294 × 216mm) which are numbered 1–39 in a different hand. At the end (c.39v), again in a different hand, is written, 'Tragedia di M. Sperone Speroni scritta di sua propria mano.' Unlike P with its cancellations and alterations this is obviously Speroni's fair copy and it has many interesting features. Firstly, it provides the authority that was lacking for the new arrangement of the play since it follows the order of D and V. Secondly, although it is unfinished, no title, no list of *dramatis personae*, no prologue, no choruses except for the last, the scene in Act II between Macareo and the Nurse incomplete, it shows quite clearly that Speroni intended to finish that particular copy for he has left blank pages for the Choruses and also at the end of the unfinished scene between Macareo and the *nutrice*.[23] Lastly, there is little doubt that it is the actual manuscript mentioned by 'Il Clario' in his preface and used by Valgrisi for the printing of his edition.

   I am led to this conclusion in the first place by the fact that the text of V is an almost exact reproduction of VAT. There are about twenty-four variant readings of which only three make any dif-

2

i ----
ii ----   10 A   A. ----V
iv ----
iii ----   8

38

Vat. Lat 4820, c.2r showing the five series of printer's marks

ference to the sense and these can be accounted for by misreadings
of Speroni's handwriting.[24] A further twelve are definite mistakes or
misprints or the result of different spelling habits,[25] while the remainder could be interpreted as attempts to correct the autograph,[26]
or even to improve the scansion.[27]

It is not only the text of VAT that is reproduced in V but also the
punctuation and even the layout of the pages. Speroni's punctuation
is idiosyncratic in that he never uses the apostrophe and writes as one
word articles and nouns which to-day would be separated, *delloffese*,
dellalma, *dellonferno*, *lira* (for *l'ira*) and so on. All these forms appear in
V and the placing of commas (before *et* and relatives), full stops and
question marks, is also followed exactly: there are no accents in
either text. The only significant difference is in the use of capital
letters. V begins each line with a capital and uses them for the names
of characters, whereas Speroni only does so after a full stop. The
pages do not correspond exactly as to contents, those in the manuscript having 33 to 34 lines[28] compared to 28 or 29 in the book, but
their arrangement is very similar. The names of characters on stage
are written in full across the centre of the page while those speaking
are identified by abbreviated names in the left hand margin. These
abbreviations are not always the same in both versions and as a rule
Speroni's abbreviations within the text such as *'m*, *'n*, for *mm*, *nn*,
fia'ma, *do'na*; *ꝑ* for *pre*; *ꝓ* for *pro*; *v.* for *vostro*; *dolciss:*, *breviss:*, for
dolcissimo, *brevissimo*, have been written out in full by the printer.

Finally, the most conclusive evidence that VAT is the actual manuscript that Valgrisi used lies in the printer's marks on the autograph.
The signatures on the printed book (Coll: 8 A–E.[8] 38 cc. n. [1]2–39
[40]) start from the title page, though this is unsigned.[29] Apart from
this the first four sheets of every gathering are signed: thus p. 2r with
'Il Clario's' foreword is signed Aii and the text of the play (p. 3r)
starts at Aiii. The last three pages (Evii[v], Eviii[r], Eviii[v], all unsigned)
have the list of *errata* from Doni's edition and the printer's device and
date. The A signatures on the manuscript, which do not tally
exactly with those on the book, show that the compositor had some
uncertainties before finally adopting this system. On cc. 1r–6r of the
manuscript which correspond to the A gatherings, five separate series
of signatures, each fairly consistent within itself, can be identified. I
number them (i) to (v) for ease of reference (see illustration on facing
page). (i)–(iv) are in the left hand margin, (v) on the right, (i) and
(v) in one hand, (ii), (iii) and (iv) in one or possibly two others. After
the A signatures, that is from c. 6r onwards, (ii) and (iv) are dis-
continued, (i) and (v) combine while (iii) continues consistently
throughout the manuscript.[30] (ii) and (iv) need not detain us long.
(ii) [Arabic numerals and large capital letters, ends of pages indicated

by a line] starts at 7A at the beginning of the play and ends at p^a B
on c. 5r (l. 275). It is thus two pages ahead of the book in which the
text of the play starts at A5 (p. 3r, signed Aiii). It does not correspond
exactly to Valgrisi's pagination. (iv) [Arabic numerals and no
letters] starts at 6 and ends at 16 on c. 5v (l. 317) which coincides
with the top of p. 8v in V but it has many uncertainties *en route*,
numbers 12–15 are missing and there are two 7s, the first being cancelled. (i) [Arabic numerals and lower case letters] starts at 5a in
agreement with V's gatherings, though not with its pagination. It
allows 26–28 lines to a page instead of 29 and has many cancellations.
After the A signatures the order of the letters and numbers is reversed and it continues from b. p^a to b5 (c. 9v, l. 467). The signatures
then cease but the series continues with a sign ◆— or a line across the
manuscript corresponding to the signatures of (v). This series [small
capitals and small roman numerals in the A gatherings, then small
capitals and arabic numerals] goes right through the manuscript. It
starts at Ai (l. 27, bottom of p. 3r in V) and continues to F2 (c. 39v,
l. 2069) which corresponds to Evii^r in the book. It does not coincide
with the printed pagination. The series which agrees most consistently
with V is (iii) [Arabic numerals and capital letters except for 5 and 6
of the A signatures which have no letters: ends of pages indicated
by a short upward slanting line]. It starts at 5 like the V gatherings.
After 8A it remains two lines behind V's pagination. Most of its A
signatures are cancelled but from B onwards it coincides with V's
gatherings and pagination and continues to do so throughout the
manuscript, although in the E signatures this agreement is achieved
by a correction which moves the signature two lines back.

Two further instructions to the compositor concern spaces to be left
at the end of scenes. 'Tre righe di spacio' is recommended on c. 13r, l.
708 which corresponds to a wider space than usual in V, p. 15r. A
similar instruction on c. 30r, 'cinque righe di spatio', has not been
followed by Valgrisi since the gap occurs at the end of a page (V. p. 31r).

However, the most significant measure of agreement remains that
between Valgrisi's text and the signatures of series (iii). It leaves
little room for doubt that this was the printer's manuscript. The false
starts in the A gatherings can be explained by his uncertainty about
the length of the foreword and the nature of the title pages. They are
of some interest as showing how a book was made up.

We may, conclude, therefore, that VAT represents the best available text of the *Canace*, but questions remain to be answered both
about the manuscript and the text. How and when did it come to the
Vatican? Who was 'Il Clario'? What is its relationship to the other
two manuscripts M and VEN in the chronology of the play's
composition?

The codex *Vat. Lat. 4820* is a folio volume (347×247mm), bound in vellum and containing a miscellany of works of which the *Canace* is the first. It consists of 117 sheets numbered through the codex as follows: 115 cc.n. [1] 1–39, 41–116[117] and includes six different works or groups of works, written on six different sizes of paper.[31] Part of the volume, at least, belonged to the humanist Angelo Colocci (1474–1549). The second item, a speech against the Turks, is in his hand, while the last, an index of first lines of Provençal poems, has his notes on the title page. On a piece of paper, stuck in the inside cover, is written in a seventeenth century hand, V. 4820 *Colotii fragmenta/Drammatica italice* and the number 4820 is repeated on the first page of the *Canace*. A list of the contents in French, also stuck in the cover, indicates that it was among the codices sent to France by Napoleon in 1797[32] and this is confirmed by the stamp of the *Bibliothèque Nationale* on cc. 1r, 80v and 116v, and also by a note in the margin of Ranaldi's inventory, 'Dato ai francesi'. The present binding dates from around the same time since it bears the arms of Pius VI and Cardinal Zelada.[33] There is no doubt, therefore, that by 1797 the Codex was bound as it is now. Indeed, the classification slip inside the volume and the detailed entry in Ranaldi's catalogue which corresponds to the present contents and numbering, allow us to go further and say that the works in it must have been together before 1623.[34] What they do not tell us is whether they all belonged originally to Colocci.

The story of his famous library has been told and the contents identified by G. Mercati, S. Lattes, V. Fanelli and most recently by Madame Bignami Odier.[35] It came into the Vatican in three stages: a case of books selected by Sirleto which Mercati has identified as the list for 22nd June 1549 in Cervini's accessions register;[36] the bulk of his library deposited by his heirs in the *guardaroba* and listed in 1558;[37] a final batch included in Fulvio Orsini's library and received in 1602.[38] There is also an earlier catalogue compiled possibly by Colocci himself.[39]

Speroni's tragedy does not figure in any of these inventories, but it is included in one of twelve surviving lists of additional accessions to the library made by the *custodes* Federico and Marino Ranaldi, sometime between 1565 and 1590.[40] These lists have been studied by P. Petitmengin who has shown how books received after the completion of the catalogue compiled by Ruano between 1548 and 1555, were classified later and added to shelves and cases that were not yet full.[41] The *Canace* is no. 58 of the additional inventory for case 6 of the section known as the *Magna Secreta*,[42] one of five cases to which books from the Colocci inventory of 1558 were added.[43] But although it is catalogued among his books it is doubtful that it ever actually belonged to Colocci since it appears also in a list of books for which the library paid twenty *scudi* to a certain Francesco Amadei on 17th February 1565.[44] The most likely sequence of events would seem to be that when the Colocci books in the *guardaroba* were divided according to subject matter and absorbed into the main library some time after 1565, more recent accessions, of which the Canace was one, were catalogued with them.

Are there any clues to its whereabouts before 1565? We know that for two years or more before its publication in 1546 it had been in the possession of 'Il Clario', the editor of V.[45] He can be identified as a certain Giovanni Antonio Clarus, a native of Eboli, who came to Venice and made a small reputation for himself as an editor of learned works.[46] This identification is confirmed by his dedication of the *Canace* to a Neapolitan, Bernardo Martirano, and by his reference in the foreword to his patrons the Giuliani brothers of Eboli.[47] Very little is known about him and the only other edition that I have found attributed to him is a rare anthology of orations, *Orazioni di diversi rari ingegni*, Venice, 1546.[48] He was in Venice by early 1544 and apparently moving in circles where he could easily have met Speroni, for he was in touch with printers such as Manuzio and Giolito de' Ferrari and in correspondence with Lodovico Dolce and Bernardo Tasso.[49] By 1553 he was no longer in Venice[50] and in 1560, according to Annibal Caro, writing from Rome, he was acting as a kind of postman between Caro and the Neapolitan poet Bernardino Rota.[51] So he might well have brought the manuscript to Rome and sold it to Francesco Amadei, whoever he was, or he could have returned it to Speroni who was himself living in Rome from 1560–64. Or perhaps Valgrisi kept it? In the absence of further evidence we can only speculate.

It remains to try and establish the development of the text between the autographs P and VAT and to do this we must consider briefly the other manuscripts, M and VEN. What is their relationship to each other, to P and VAT and to the *editio princeps* D?

They have certain characteristics in common: they are not autograph, nor are they divided into Acts, the choruses are missing and they follow the arrangement of VAT and the printed texts, not that of P. But here the resemblances end. VEN is incomplete, ending at l. 1118 (V p. 22v just after the beginning of Act IV), has the title *Tragedia* and a list of *dramatis personae*; M is complete but has no title and no list of characters.

Changes in the position of the *nutrice*'s monologue, 'Sciocchi a mio danno' enable us to show that in order of time M is an earlier draft than VEN and VAT and all the printed editions. In all the texts, except M and P, this monologue occurs in Act II directly after the unfinished scene between the *nutrice* and Macareo.[52] In P, however, this scene does not exist and the monologue is placed after the conversation between the *nutrice* and Canace, which in P, as we have already seen, is at the beginning of Act II.[53] Now M has the scene between the *nutrice* and Macareo which is missing in P but it is followed immediately, not by 'Sciocchi a mio danno,' but by the opening scene of Act III in which Canace invokes the help of the goddess Lucina. The monologue is then placed, as in P, after the scene between Canace and her nurse (Act III, sc, 2 in M). That Speroni changed this position deliberately in the later versions is shown by a series of alterations to the text which are found in VEN and VAT and the printed editions and which are necessary if the speech is to make sense in its new place. In P and M the *nutrice* is speaking about Canace only and refers to her in the feminine singular, in the other texts where the speech follows the scene in which the *nutrice* had exhorted Macareo to save his sister, she discusses both the lovers and her remarks have been changed into the masculine plural throughout. Thus *questa infelice* > *questi infelici, suo figlio* > *suoi figli, ne' suoi* > *ne'lor, la mia donna* > *il mio signore e la mia donna, la sua vita e il suo honore* > *lor vita e lor honore*. Furthermore two verses in P and M which refer to Canace's future child, *mentre io li tengo ascoso | quel che scoprir non deggio*, are omitted in all the other texts since Canace has not yet appeared. In VAT this monologue is written on a separate sheet of paper which shows that Speroni considered it something that could be moved.

A further proof that P and M are earlier than VEN and VAT is furnished by a series of variants in which VAT reproduces and then crosses out the reading of P and M and two from the scene in Act II, missing in P, where VAT crosses out the reading of M.[54]

The chronology of VEN is more uncertain. It is found in a codex of the *Marciana* containing works by Ruzzante which Lovarini thinks were probably transcribed shortly before his death (17th March, 1542).[55] It is certainly later than M since 'Sciocchi a mio danno' is in its final position but its relationship to VAT is more difficult to determine. It must be independent of it since it has readings which reappear in D and are not found in VAT or V and is possibly earlier because of the verse, *Consumi sospirando te medesmo* of M and VEN which is found in D but in VAT has been cancelled and then changed to *Te medesmo consumi sospirando*.[56]

What can we learn from the *editio princeps* D? Many of the errors in this edition are simple misprints due to the carelessness of the printer, but there are thirty or so which appear in M or VEN but not in VAT. It is obvious that D does not depend directly either from M (Sciocchi a mio danno) nor from VEN (incomplete) and it is also certain that Navò did not know of the existence of VAT. We can only surmise that it is based on a manuscript similar to M and VEN which has not survived.

The remaining printed editions show no signs of later alterations by the author. B is an incorrect copy of D, G a reprint of V, F has characteristics of both B and V while A, edited by Ingolfo de' Conti, Speroni's grandson and supposedly based on the *Carte Speroniane*, is nothing more than a careless copy of B, arbitrarily divided into Acts and Scenes with the addition of a prologue by Venus.[57]

In conclusion, therefore, it is possible to suggest the following partial reconstruction of the story of the writing of the *Canace*. P, the first draft, written by Speroni during the spring of 1542 never left the author's possession and was not made public until it was published by Forcellini in 1740. Speroni immediately set about revising and rearranging the tragedy before showing it to his colleagues in the *Accademia degli Infiammati*. He presented it to them piece by piece and it seems likely that manuscripts like M and VEN, which represent an early stage of this revision, were soon in circulation and that Navò used one of them for his pirated edition. Meanwhile, possibly somewhat later, but almost certainly by late 1543, Speroni made a fair copy of the still unfinished tragedy which came into the possession of Giovan Antonio Clario and was published by Valgrisi. And this brings us back full circle to *Vat. Lat. 4820*, whose importance, both as the most authoritative text of the *Canace* and as a manuscript of some considerable bibliographical interest, I hope to have demonstrated.

University of Oxford   CHRISTINA ROAF

NOTES

1. The following documents will be published by the *Commissione per i testi di lingua* of Bologna. 1. *Canace* by Sperone Speroni. 2. *Giudizio d'una tragedia di Canace e Macareo con molte utili considerazioni circa l'arte della tragedia e d'altri poemi*. This interesting criticism of the *Canace* has for long been attributed to the Florentine scholar diplomat, Bartolomeo Cavalcanti, but I believe that it was written by G. B. Giraldi Cinzio. I am led to this conclusion by the close resemblances, both in contents and style, between the *Giudizio* and the critical works of Giraldi, especially the *Discorsi intorno al comporre de i romanzi, delle comedie e delle tragedie*. See C. Roaf, 'A sixteenth century *anonimo*: the author of the Giuditio sopra la tragedia di Canace e Macareo,' *Italian Studies*, XIV, (1959), pp. 49–74. 3 and 4. Speroni's replies to the *Giudizio*, part of the defence which he started to formulate after the publication of the latter in

1550. They consist of an unfinished *Apologia* (1552/3) and a course of *Lettioni* delivered to the *Accademia degli Elevati* in Padua (December 1558). 5. A Latin letter from G. B. Giraldi in reply to the *Lettioni* (27th December, 1558).

Although all these works were collected together by Forcellini in Vol. IV of his edition of Speroni's *Opere*, Venice, 1740, they are not easily obtainable and no satisfactory text of any one of them exists.

2. Speroni's papers are preserved in the Biblioteca Capitolare in seventeen folio volumes. Most of those connected with the *Canace* are in Vols. VIII and XIII. I would like to record here my gratitude to the librarian Don Bellinati for his advice and assistance and also for allowing me to number the pages of the above two volumes.

3. *Carte Speroniane*, VIII, c. 43r, 'Cominciata dì viiii di gennaio 1542.' c. 77v (i.e. at the end of the tragedy), 'finita dì viiii di marzo del medesimo anno.'

4. *Ibid*, c. 78v. Speroni stipulates a very realistic setting and also gives instructions for a dinner party to follow the performance.

5. P. Aretino, *Lettere*, Paris, 1609, vol. II, p. 300, Aretino to Speroni, 25.vii.1542.

6. C. Tolomei, *Lettere*, Venice, 1747, p. 46, Tolomei to Giovanfrancesco Bini, 26.v.1543.

7. See *supra*, p. 138 and Speroni, *Opere*, vol. I, p. xix, '. . . che sia cosa posteriore alla stampa, cui l'autore dopo la critica del Cavalcanti, senza farne motto però od uso alcuno, preso abbia a riformare . . .' Forcellini accepts the date of 1st July 1543 for the *Giudizio*. It is found on one of the manuscripts and also on the 1550 edition of the text but there are indications, such as the very precise quotations from B. Tomitano's *Ragionamenti della lingua toscana*, Venice, 1545, that it was actually written later.

8. Speroni, *Opere*, vol. V, pp. xxix–xxx. Forcellini notes that Ingolfo de' Conti, in his edition of 1597, had not realized that the autograph P was a later revision since he was misled by the dates on the manuscript. He comments, '. . . né'l carattere mostra per verità che stesse gran fatto altrimenti; ma tutto il resto scopre poscia l'arcano.'

9. For example the *famiglio*'s speech, 'O femminil natura' (V p. 21v, P c. 57r) and Deiopea's 'In vano t'affatichi' (V p. 27v, P c. 62v–63r). In the description of Canace's death, 'al fin conversa al letto in che giacea' (V p. 34r. P cc. 69v–70r) fifty lines have been crossed out and the pages later stuck together, perhaps by Forcellini who omits these cancelled versions.

10. Speroni, *Opere*, vol. I, p. xix.

11. Only P, followed by Ingolfo de' Conti (1597), is divided into Acts, but the divisions are made clear in the other texts by the word *Coro* at the end of each Act. I have divided my edition into Acts and Scenes for easier reference.

12. See *infra*, p. 146 for the position of this monologue in M.

13. F includes the *Giudizio* as well as the *Canace* and is probably following B in maintaining the title *Canace* while correcting some of the errors in accordance with V.

14. A. F. Doni, *Lettere*, Firenze, 1547, p. 48, letter 23, dated 23.ix.1546.

15. The texts compared were; P. F. Giambullari, *Il Gello*, Fiorenza, 1546; G. B. Gelli, *I capricci*, in Fiorenza presso il Doni, 1546, both published by Doni, and *Dialogo di M. Tullio Cicerone dintorno alle*

partitioni oratorie . . . . In Vinegia, per Curtio Traiano di Navò, 1545.
For an account of Doni's short-lived printing press see C. Ricottini Marsili-Libelli, *Anton Francesco Doni, scrittore e stampatore*, Firenze, 1960; S. Bongi, *Vita di A.F. Dino* . . . in A.F. Doni, *I Marmi*, ed. Fanfani, Firenze, 1863 and *Annali di Gabriel Giolito de' Ferrari*, Rome, 1890, vol. I, p. 260 *et seq*. Not much is known about Navò but see *ibid*, vol. I, p. 262.

16. I have seen such copies in the Vatican Library, (*Dramm. Allacciana* 78) and the British Museum (11715. a. 68).

17. See M. Maittaire, *Annales Typographici*, Hague, 1725, vol. III, pt. 1, p. 249; G. Fumagalli, *Lexicon typographicum Italiae*, Florence, 1905, p. 492; E. Pastorello, *Tipografi, editori. librai a Venezia nel secolo XVI*, Bibl. di Bibliografia italiana, vol. V, Florence, 1924, p. 92.

18. Speroni, *Opere*, vol. IV, p. 94.

19. For this Academy, whose existence is denied by Forcellini (Speroni, *Opere*, vol. V, p. xxix), see G. Gennari, 'Saggio storico sopra le Accademie di Padova' in *Saggi scientifici e letterari dell'Accademia di Padova*, Padova, 1786, ch. iii, p. xxiv and B. Brunelli, *I teatri di Padova*, Padova, 1921, p. 39.

20. Speroni, *Opere*, vol. IV, p. 175.

21. *Inventarium librorum latinorum Mss. Bibl. Vat.*, Vol. V. For more information about this catalogue see *infra*, n. 34.

22. Speroni's play, it has no title, opens with the appearance of the shade of Canace's unborn child, 'Uscito dello'nferno/vegno al vostro cospetto, ombra infelice . . . .' Euripides' *Hecuba* starts with the ghost of Polydorus, 'I come from vaults of death, from gates of darkness,/Where from the Gods aloof doth Hades dwell,/Polydorus . . .' (Euripides, trans. A. S. Way, Vol. I, Loeb Classics, 1912, p. 249. See also *infra* n. 44.

23. The following pages of the manuscript are blank: bottom of 6r, 6v, 7r, 7v, for the Chorus at the end of Act I; half of 13r, 13v for the end of the scene between the *nutrice* and Macareo in Act II (which Speroni himself had said was unfinished, *Carte Speroniane*, vol. VIII, c. 238v, unpublished notes for the *Apologia*, 'lasciò imperfetto il ragionamento della nutrice con Macareo'); half of 14v, 15r–v, 16r for the Chorus at end of Act II; half of 21v, 22r–v, 23r for Chorus at end of Act III; half of 30v, 31r–v, 32r for Chorus at end of Act IV.

24. They are: *del* instead of *e il* (V p. 6r, l. 177), *quante* instead of *quanto* (V. p. 25v, l. 1308), *cesta* instead of *vesta* (V p. 27v, l. 1401). V readings are given first. References are to the page number of V and to the number of the line which in my edition will be numbered straight through the play.

25. *che* for *chi* (V p. 13v, l. 625), *saperei* for *saprei* (V p. 14v, l. 677), *lo offesa* for *l'offesa* (V p. 16r, l. 749), *puo* for *po* (V p. 19r, l. 921), *figliuola* for *figliola* (V p. 20r, l. 987), *giovinil* for *giovenil* (V p. 21v, l. 1068), *vorebbe* for *vorrebbe* (V p. 28r, l. 1444), *delalma* for *dellalma* (V p. 28r, l. 1450), *sua* for *tua* (V p. 30v, l. 1572), *luo* for *tuo* (V p. 30v, l. 1577), *tosto* for *tosta* (V p. 30v, l. 1592), *dentro, di fore* for *dentro e di fore* (V p. 32r, l. 1662).

26. *palazzo* for *palazo* (V p. 4r, l. 74), *dilaceraro* for *dilaciraro* (V p. 4r, l. 81), *de suoi figli* for *di suoi figli* (V p. 16r, l. 754), *facci* for *faci* (V p. 23r, l. 1138), *ho pur* for *hor pur* (V p. 33v, l. 1734), *a i piedi* for *a piedi* (V p. 33v, l. 1750).

27. *Signor* instead of *Signore* in the line *d'Eolo nostro signor, mi fa temere* (V p. 8r, l. 308), *dolor* instead of the second *dolore* in the line *di dolore in dolor, fin che'l nipote* (V p. 10r, l. 421) and possibly in the example *esser* for *essere* in the line *mi fa esser in dubbio della vita* (V p. 36v, l. 1909).

28. The lines on each page of the manuscript have been counted and the total written at the bottom, but not by Speroni.

29. This seems to have been a fairly frequent practice of Valgrisi's. I examined a random sample of 40 books published by him between 1541 and 1549. In 28 the gatherings were numbered, as in the *Canace*, straight through from the title page.

30. The signatures in the manuscript are numbered 1–16, that is one for each page of the gathering, not 1–8, one for each sheet, as in the book.

31. The six sections can be distinguished as follows: I, ir–39v (294 x 216mm), the *Canace*. II, 41r–48v (folio size): 42r–47v a summary in Colocci's hand of a speech against the Turks by Giovanni Lascaris. V. Fanelli dates this about 1526 (see F. Ubaldini, *Vita di Mons. Angelo Colocci*, ed. V. Fanelli in 'Studi e Testi' 256, Città del Vaticano, 1969, p. 79, n. 145), S. Lattes identifies it with an entry in a 1558 inventory of Colocci's books, *Vat. Lat, 3958*, c. 196r, no. 29, (see S. Lattes, 'Recherches sur la bibliothèque d'Angelo Colocci' in *Mélanges d'archéologie et d'histoire*, vol. XLVIII (1931), p. 329). III, 49r–58v (313 x 220mm), a notebook with a collection of items in a secretary's hand; 50r–53r, *Novella di ms Leonardo d'Arezzo*. 'Non sono molti anni . . .' This is Leonardo Bruni's story of Seleuco of Antioch and Stratonica. 55r–55v a fragment of a Latin letter, the beginning is missing. 55v–56v, letter from Cecina to Cicero, 'Quod tibi non tam . . .' (*Familiares*, VI, 7). 56v–57v, C. Matius to Cicero, 'Magnam voluptatem . . .' (*Familiares*, XI, 28). IV, 59r–66v (217 x 142mm): 60r–64r *Epistola di M. Francesco Petrarca mandata al famosissimo huomo M. Nicola Aciaroli gran senescalco nel reame di Napoli sopra la incoronatione del Re Aluvise*. An Italian translation of Petrarca, *Familiares*, XII, 2. 64v, a sonnet, 'Specchio sereno e chiaro e non di vettro', in the same hand as Petrarch's letter. V, 67r–80v (236 x 165mm), a *centona* of religious poems in a secretary's hand. I have not identified them but they do not seem to be by Colocci. VI, 81r–116v (145 x 100mm): 81r–104r, *Lemosini per alphabetum*, the title in Colocci's hand. An index of first lines of Provençal poems arranged in alphabetical order. (See Ubaldini, op. cit, p. 97, n. 172). 104v–116v are blank.

32. See E. Müntz, 'La bibliothèque du Vatican pendant la révolution française' in *Mélanges Julien Havet*, Paris, 1895, pp. 579–591 and J. Bignami Odier, *La bibliothèque vaticane de Sixte IV à Pie XI*, Studi e Testi, 272, Città del Vaticano, 1973, p. 189. The manuscripts were handed over in fulfilment of one of the clauses of the Treaty of Tolentino. Most of them were returned in 1816.

33. Francesco Saverio Zelada was Cardinal librarian from 1777–1801. See J. Bignami Odier, op. cit, p. 184.

34. Vol. V of Alessandro Ranaldi's Inventory reflects, on the whole, acquisitions made under Paul V and Gregory XV, that is between 1605 and 1623, though many of the codices were acquired earlier. See J. Bignami Odier, op. cit. pp. 77, 101, 106, 112. For a detailed account of the making of this inventory and of the work of members of the Ranaldi family in the Vatican Library see P. Petitmengin,

'Recherches sur l'organisation de la Bibliothèque Vaticane à l'époque
des Ranaldi (1547–1645)' in *Mélanges d'archéologie et d'histoire de
l'école française de Rome*, vol. 75 (1963), pp. 561–628.

35. G. Mercati, *Opere minori*, vol. IV, Studi e Testi, 79 (1937–41),
pp. 539–545; S. Lattes, op. cit. pp. 308–44; V. Fanelli, 'Le lettere
di Mons Angelo Colocci nel Museo Britannico di Londra,' in
Rinascimento, vol. X (1959), pp. 107–35; F. Ubaldini, op. cit;
J. Bignami Odier, op cit, p. 58, n. 30. See also P. de Nolhac, *La
bibliothèque de Fulvio Orsini*, Bibl. de l'école des hautes études, 74,
(1887) and various articles in *Atti del Convegno di Studi su Angelo Colocci,
Iesi, 13–14 settembre 1969, Iesi, 1972*.

36. G. Mercati, op. cit, pp. 542–44. He published the list which is in
Vat. Lat. 3963.

37. *Vat. Lat. 3958*, cc. 184r–196r, 'Inventario delli libri del Colotio di
sacra scriptura fatto alli 27 d'ottobre MDLVIII' It is studied by
Lattes, op. cit.

38. See P. de Nolhac, op. cit, pp. 334–396.

39. *Arch. Bibl.* 15, cc. 41r–60v. The subject headings are in Colocci's
hand. Further fragmentary lists of Colocci's books are found in
Barb. Lat. 4871, cc. 171r–172r, *Vat. Lat. 3903*, cc. 222r–227r,
Vat. Lat. 4817, cc. 210–211.

40. *Vat. Lat. 8185*, II, cc. 336–366r. Federico and Marino were the
first representatives of the Ranaldi dynasty to work in the Vatican,
and are not to be confused with Domenico and Alessandro who
compiled the *Inventarium*.

41. See. P. Petitmengin, op. cit, pp. 571–575.

42. *Vat. Lat. 8185*, II, c. 364v. 58. 'L'hecuba di Euripide tradotta da
Speron Speroni et scritta di sua mano in cartoncino.' I am indebted
to Madame Bignami Odier for the information that this particular
list of additional books (cc. 358r–364v), headed 'in 6 capsa 2 Plutei
ad dextram ingressi bibliothecae magnae secretae', is in the hand
of Federico Ranaldi. It contains 61 items among which it is possible
to identify most of the present contents of *Vat. Lat. 4820*. Nos 59,
'Novella di Antioco et di Stratonica' (4820, 50r–53r), and 60,
'Discorso sopra le cose de' Turchi' (4820, 42r–47v) are easily
recognizable and it is probable that no. 61 'Versi, tavole et notationi
diverse in un libro lunghetto in cartoncino' is in fact the notebook
containing an index of first lines of Provençal poems (4820, 81r–
104r). A copy of Petrarch's letter to Acciauoli (4820, 60r–64r) is
listed at no. 46. This leaves the fragments of Latin letters (4820,
55r–57v) but since they are in the same hand as Bruni's story they
can probably be included under 59, and lastly, the *centona* of *rime
spirituali*. This is more difficult to identify but perhaps corresponds
to the *rime spirituali* found at no. 47. It should also be noted that
Nos 54, 55, 56 are listed as in Colocci's hand. It seems possible to
conclude, therefore, that *Vat. Lat. 4820* was made up of a rather
haphazard collection of unbound items (they are all listed by
Ranaldi as *in cartoncino* or *in carta*) taken from Case 6, some but not
all of which had originally belonged to Colocci.

43. The cases are listed by Petitmengin, op. cit, p. 574. See also his
plan of the library as it was reorganised after 1592, fig. 3, p. 610.
Case 6 contains *Vat. Lat. 4616–4845*.

44. *Arch. Bibl.* 15, f. 12r. 'Tragedia del Sperone scritta di sua mano in
f°.' At the top of the page is written 'Per la presente confesso io

Franc⁰ Amadei haver ricevuto dal Mag°⁰ ms Federico Ranalli custode di libraria di N. Sʳᵉ scudi vinti di moneta in tanti pauli, quali sono per più libri scritti in penna et stampati, quali dice haver compri (sic) da me per la libraria apᶜᵃ et in fede del vero ho fatto la presente di mia mano q⁰ dì 17 di Febr⁰ 1565. In Roma. Idem Francˢ Amadeus.'

The list contains 29 items, 2 printed books and 27 manuscripts, of which at least three in addition to the *Canace* can be identified with manuscripts in Ranaldi's additional list for Case 6. They are: 'Trattato di conscientia in spagnolo' (Vat. Lat. 8185, II, 361v, n. 42), 'Lancilotti Pasii carmina in 4⁰' (*ibid*, c. 351v, n. 22) and 'Dominici Basili carmen in laude barth⁰ Coglioni ex. perg⁰ in rubro' (*ibid*, c. 351v, n. 25). The fact that the *Canace* is here listed simply as *Tragedia* shows that it was Federico Ranaldi, who first identified it with Euripides *Hecuba*. I have been unable to discover anything about Francesco Amadei.

45. See his foreword to the Valgrisi edition.

46. Conrad Gesner, *Bibliotheca* . . . Tiguri, 1574, 337, 'Joannes Antonius Clarus, Ebolitanus, Venetiis libros quosdam a doctis aliquot viris nostri temporis compositos, in publicum edidit, et in tragoediam nobilis et eruditi viri Speronis Speroni praefatus est'. This entry does not appear in the 1545 edition of the *Bibliotheca* but it is found in the later ones. See also N. Toppi, *Biblioteca napoletana*, Naples, 1678, p. 124, who is following Gesner and C. M. Riccio, *Memorie storiche* . . . . Naples, 1844, p. 102.

47. For Bernardo Martirano, 1490?–1548?, author of a mythological poem entitled *L'Aretusa*, see F. Pometti, 'I Martirano' in *Atti R. Accademia dei Lincei*, s. 5, vol. IV (1896), pp. 58–186. 'Il Clario' mentions four Giuliani brothers, Thomaso, Jacopo, Girolamo and Cristoforo. Toppi, op. cit, p. 297 lists a 'Tomaso Giuliani, d'Evoli, eletto Avvocato Fiscale nelle Provincie di Principato Citra e Basilicata' and on p. 64, 'Christophero de Iulanis della terra d'Evoli, Secretario delle Provincie Principato citra et ultra, e in Basilicata'.

48. E. A. Cigogna, *Iscrizioni veneziane* . . ., Venice, 1834, vol. IV, p. 59, mentions a copy of this work edited by 'Il Florido' but says that he knows of other copies signed 'Il Clario' whom he identifies with the editor of the *Canace*. The only copy I have been able to see, which is in the Marciana, is edited by 'Il Clario'.

49. P. Gerardo, *Novo libro de lettere*, Venice, 1544, p. 89, L. Dolce to G. A. Clario, 26.i.1544 in which he asks to be remembered 'al Signor Iolito et al Magnifico M. Paolo Manutio'. B. Tasso, *Primo libro delle lettere*, Venice, 1549, p. 303, undated letter, but probably written early in 1545 after Tasso's return from the Piedmontese wars (cfr. E. Williamson, *Bernardo Tasso*, Rome, 1951, p. 14, n. 59). Tasso speaks of Clario's departure from Naples to seek his fortune and invites him to return to the south.

50. P. Lauro (*Lettere*, Venice, 1553, p. 141), in an undated letter to G. A. Clario speaks of him as no longer there. Many of P. Lauro's translations of the classics were published by Valgrisi during the 1540's.

51. A. Caro, *Lettere familiari*, ed. Aulo Greco, Florence, 1957, vol. III, letters 588, 593, 595.

52. V pp. 15r–16r, ll. 709–60

53. See supra p. 140.

54. P *quanto e*, M *quanto ei*, VAT *quanto* crossed out and replaced by *quel che ei* (V p. 9r, l. 350); P *potremmo*, M *potremo*, VAT *potremmo* crossed out and substituted by *possiamo* (V p. 11r, l. 459); M *frale*, VAT *frale* crossed out and substituted by *brieve* (V p. 11v, l. 515); M *vol*, VAT *vuole* crossed out and substituted by *sà* (V 12r, l. 532).

55. E. Lovarini, *Studi sul Ruzzante e la letteratura padovana*, ed. G. Folena, Padua, 1965, p. 147. Perhaps it was Ruzzante's own copy to be used for his production of the play. It would then mark the stage which Speroni had reached in his revision by 17th March 1542, when Ruzzante died.

56. V p. 14v, l. 671.

57. See Speroni, *Opere*, vol. IV, p. 201. Speroni summarizes this prologue in the third of his 1558 lectures. An autograph draft of it is in the *Carte Speroniane*, Vol. VIII, c. 42r–v.

Pier Vettori and Lionardo Salviati

It was as a composer of fashionable orations that Lionardo Salviati scored his first literary and social success. His orations in praise of Cosimo de' Medici's son Garzia in 1563, and the ensuing quarrel with Corbinelli, brought him to the attention of Florentine literary society. Between 1563 and 1575 he wrote fifteen orations of various kinds.[1]

By 1585 he had been unproductive in this genre for ten years, devoting himself to the activities of the courtier, the grammarian, and the reviser of Boccaccio. On 19th December 1585 he took up his pen once more, at the request of the Florentine Academy, and wrote an oration which was subsequently delivered in the Church of Santo Spirito on 27th January, 1586. The oration was Salviati's funeral oration for the great Florentine humanist and teacher, Pier Vettori.[2]

The occasion to reappear as a public orator was appropriate, for the significance of Vettori in Lionardo Salviati's life is profound and decisive. Yet the contacts between the two men, though undoubtedly close and constant over many years, have so far been documented extremely thinly. So before proceeding to an attempt to interpret their friendship it will be useful to examine coherently for the first time such published and unpublished documents as bear witness to their relationship.

For an initial link between Pier Vettori and Lionardo Salviati's early life it suffices to look at Salviati's own circle of friends—Francesco Buonamici, Lorenzo Giacomini, Giovanni Rondinelli, Vincenzo Borghini, Baccio Valori the younger, Lorenzo Lenzi, Ascanio da Ripa, Alberto Bolognetti (not to mention his arch-enemy Jacopo Corbinelli)—all of them pupils of Vettori, educator of a whole generation of Florentines.[3] The orientation of Lionardo himself in his earliest years—his sound Greek scholarship, his early interest in the interpretation and study of the *Poetics*, the part played by Demetrius (a text to which Vettori had dedicated much time and attention, and on which he had lectured before producing his edition in 1562) in his quarrel with Corbinelli, and above all the method and discipline which characterised his philological activities, vernacular as well as classical, bore the stamp of the school of Vettori. And if this were not enough, he declares himself, in the *Orazione*, apostrophising Vettori, to be a 'persona da te medesimo ammaestrata'.

Vettori had, by his own admission, no family links with Lionardo, though he was quoted in 1569 as saying that he 'ha conosciuto et conosce m. Lionardo inducente, quale cominciò a conoscere da pueritia di esso m. Lionardo.'⁴ But he does not, as far as is known, ever expressly state that Lionardo was his pupil. Salviati, on the other hand, openly recognises him as his master, in his funeral oration and elsewhere.

Praise and recognition of the stature of Vettori as a teacher is contained in one of his earliest orations, the funeral oration written for Benedetto Varchi and delivered in February 1566, when he writes of Varchi: 'E chi dirà che egli della Greca piena ed esquisita cognizione non avesse? Poscia ch'egli ebbe nell'apprenderla per precettore il *Vettorio*, uomo (dirollo con le stesse parole, con le quali io l'ho detto pubblicamente ragionando altra volta) uomo dico, del quale oltre l'universal notizia di tutte le scienze, nella cognizione delle lingue non fu mai il maggiore', and goes on to praise his extreme kindness and generosity to his pupil.

Throughout his whole life Salviati was to exalt Vettori as a teacher. And he is no doubt absolutely right to do so because, as we shall see, Lionardo's vision of Vettori as a teacher provides the key to the whole character of Salviati's conception, adoration and appreciation of him.

But it is not until 1566 that we have concrete evidence of direct contact between the two men. This is in the form of a hitherto unpublished letter (one of the very few letters of Lionardo which are autograph throughout) dated 8th March, 1565 (i.e. 1566) from the young Salviati (he was then twenty-six), of which the following is the text:

Molto Mag. co S.r mio
Egli m'è stato da piú persone domandato dell'opera di V.ra Sig.ria. A tutto ho risposto, che non so niente; hanno mostro di non lo credere, tanto che m'hanno fatto scandalizzare, peroche sapendo io di non n'havere parlato a persona, mi sono maravigliato, e non vorrei, che V.S. pensasse, che ella uscisse da me. Pure hiersera me ne parlò un frate, e mostrandomene io nuovo, mi disse; come—non n'ho io parlato poco fa con ms. Piero stesso e mi parve, che mi dicesse che glien'haveva parlato il Rondinello in bottega d'un libraio franzese. Ma per quello, che io nel ritraggo, in bottega de' Giunti se n'è parlato. In somma io n'ho dispiacere, e non vorrei haver biasimo, ò cadere in sospizione dove io non ho colpa. Perciò che dove io mi reputo il favore fattomi da V.S. per uno de' mag-

giori, che mi potesse esser fatto, se ella facesse del fatto mio qualche
sinistro concetto, mi parrebbe che la mia fosse stata sventura.

Quanto all'opera, io cammino, ma adagio, si per queste mie diavolerie,
si per che io ci pongo tutta la mia diligenza. Io haveva cominciato a
toccar qualche cosa per conto del numero, ma ho pensato poi, che i
numeri sono come i colori neri, che mai non s'affanno, anzi ha sempre
tanta diversità tra loro, che non si possono accozzare insieme senza troppo
apparente discordante (sic). Però il mio studio sarà tutto su l'osservare
della lingua, su le parole, e su le locuzioni. Io non credo mancare di
renderla al tempo promesso. Et a V.S. mi racc.do. Che Dio la feliciti.

Di Casa agli 8 di Marzo 1565

Di V.S. Ill.a

Osser. mo Ser.re Lionardo Salviati.[5]

For both men this letter has substantial biographical interest.
Vettori has entrusted to Salviati some text of his, and although
Salviati's references to the work in progress are rather vague and
ambiguous, the gist of the letter seems to suggest that he is revising it
linguistically. There is the possibility that the subject of the letter is
not a revision but Salviati's translation into Tuscan of Vettori's
Liber de laudibus Joannae Austriacae, of which the original was published in Florence in 1566 on the occasion of the marriage of
Francesco de' Medici, Cosimo's son and Prince of Florence and
Siena, to Joan of Austria.[6] (On the same occasion Salviati himself
wrote a madrigal to celebrate the ill-fated marriage, beginning 'O
di terrestri dii / o di celesti eroi / nodo felice'. On the whole, however,
Salviati's phraseology—'cominciato a toccar qualche cosa per conto
del numero'. . . 'il mio studio sarà tutto su l'osservare della lingua, su
le parole, e su le locuzioni' makes it far more likely that it is a question here of a linguistic *revision*. Likewise, his use of the expression
'renderla' suggests that he will be 'handing back' to Vettori his own
work and would not seem to be quite appropriate to the circumstances of a translation. The question arises of which language.
Despite Salviati's stress on the honour entailed in the task, it seems
most unlikely that Vettori would have done him the honour of entrusting him with the linguistic revision of a *Latin* text. The terms
which Salviati uses would seem, in view of Vettori's competence and
reputation as a Latinist, to exclude the possibility. Then it must be a
text in Tuscan. It seems much more likely that some known published
text of Vettori is involved here (and clearly both Salviati's consciousness of the responsibility which has devolved upon him, and
Vettori's concern for the language must indicate an intention to publish), in which case the work concerned must be Vettori's only
'volgare' work printed in his lifetime, namely the treatise on the
cultivation of the olive, eventually published in 1569.[7]

This possibility—and it must be stressed that it is only a possibility —has interesting reverberations. For long after Vettori's classical philological prowess and work as a humanist educator was forgotten by all but the specialist his reputation as a writer rested virtually entirely on this little booklet on the cultivation of the olive, written of course, like Alamanni's work on the bee, under the influence of his Latin models. And of the merits of the work the chief one was its 'pure Tuscan' language. The Accademia Fiorentina accepted it as a 'testo di lingua'. Of its language Niccolai writes: 'Alla leggiadra compostezza dello stile si aggiungono a render caro questo libretto i pregi della lingua, la quale risente nell'uso di quella castigatezza, proprietà e fecondità di frasi per cui piacciono tanto a noi le opere rustiche di Varrone, pur dal Vettori lette e studiate'.[8] Indeed, the language has a polished Tuscan character which recalls more the refinement of the late Cinquecento 'volgare' specialist than the professional classicist-cum-amateur 'volgarista'. Niccolai, once again referring to 'questo libretto, che è l'unica scrittura volgare che egli abbia accuratamente limata', continues: 'Piace moltissimo anche a noi vedere unita a tanta purezza e toscanità di lingua una grazia non comune di lingua'.[9] The quality of the language of this treatise has for centuries been considered one of the keys to Vettori's position vis-à-vis the 'volgare', the practical illustration not only of his competence but of his 'volgare' linguistic orientation generally. The 'pure Tuscan' of the work, its extraordinary confidence, have been considered to reveal the direction of his thought as far as the use of Tuscan was concerned and consequently to be a pointer to his attitude to the culture of his times. There now appears to be a distinct possibility that this prose is to be attributed not to Pier Vettori but to Lionardo Salviati.

At all events the work on which Lionardo is at this point engaged is of sufficient importance (again perhaps a pointer to the *Delle lodi et coltivatione*) for all literary Florence to be involved in it and to be avid for news of it, if the 'letterati' of Florence are discussing it amongst themselves and are so constantly importuning Lionardo for news of it that he has become seriously worried in case Vettori should think he is responsible for the leak of what was meant to be a secret between the two of them. The picture of the curious Florentines, meeting in bookshops and printers' offices is an amusing and precious one.

But even more interesting is what the letter reveals of the relationship between Vettori and Salviati. The outwardly formal terms of address do not conceal the easy familiarity characterising that relationship. Lionardo's attitude is that of the reverent and respectful pupil. He is nevertheless at ease with his master, able to express himself in simple, unaffected terms without artificiality of style. Particularly interesting, and illustrating the dominant pupil–master relationship, is his concern for Vettori's opinion of him. This is all the more striking when we compare the tenor of the letter with that of others belonging to these years, where Lionardo reveals an opinion of himself amounting to gross conceit. To Varchi, Corbinelli, even to Cosimo de' Medici he vaunted his equality, in literary and linguistic matters, with any man in Florence.[10] In this context the admiration, respect, gratitude and overwhelming desire to please expressed in this letter are even more striking and revealing. It also tells us much about the prestige of Pier Vettori in Florence that Lionardo Salviati is conscious only of the honour implied in being chosen by the master.

At the same time it adds to our understanding of Lionardo's own position in Florence to find that Pier Vettori has singled him out. Plenty of Vettori's other ex-pupils considered themselves experts in the *volgare*, including that very Giovanni Rondinelli who had spoken about the work in progress to the 'frate'.[11] And it was not Salviati who had translated one of Vettori's earlier works, published in 1563.[12] Since then, however, Lionardo's career had advanced significantly. The epoch-making *Orazione in lode della fiorentina favella* had come in 1564, then the funeral orations for Michelangelo and Varchi and election to the Accademia Fiorentina.[13] His comedy *Il Granchio* was ready for performance and in just a fortnight he was to become Consul of the Academy with all its attendant prestige and honours.[14] Nevertheless, the letter adds significantly to our picture of a Salviati rapidly becoming, in the eyes of his authoritative fellow-citizens, a foremost authority on the vernacular. Who was in fact responsible for the leak is of minimal importance to us. Salviati's reaction, on the other hand, when he fears suspicion might fall on him is most significant.

No less interesting is the second documented contact between the two men, again in the form of an unpublished letter from Lionardo to Vettori, written approximately three years later on 23rd March, 1569. Salviati is in bed with a fever. The illness (though he was never strong) may well have had an emotional as well as a physiological origin, since this extraordinary letter reveals Salviati to be in a state of extreme agitation. Too ill to rise from his bed, or to write more than a few lines in postscript, Salviati dictates a letter to Vettori:

Molto Mag.co Sig.r Mio hon.mo
V.S. per la lr̃a che io scrissi al E.I. vede la miseria nella quale io son caduto. Io gliele mando aperta, affin che ella mi faccia grazia di leggerla, et habbia per fermo che io non habbia potuto scrivere a gran pezza la

cosa tanto quanto ell'è. Cio che v'è scritto è verissimo, così del passato, come di quello che avverrà, se io non ho la grazia. E dico piú oltre a V.S. quello che non direi a S.E., che se io non ottengo questa grazia, io voglio andar disperso per il mondo, e non mi lasciar mai più vedere in questi paesi. Il che se ben parea, che m'avvenga giustamente, havendo io fatto quello che io non doveva, con tutto cio ho 'pensato di poter trovare misericordia nel pietoso animo di V.S. più che in nessuno di coloro, che in questa miseria mi possono aiutare: tanto l'ho conosciuta sempre benigna e misericordiosa verso ognuno generalmente, et in particolare verso di me, non per alcuno mio merito, ma per non so quale mia buona fortuna. A lei adunque e nelle sue benigne braccia humilmente mi raccomando, e la prego per l'amore di Cristo, e per la carità a noi debita, che V.S. habbia pietà di me, e mi campi la vita: che come servatrice della mia vita riconoscerò sempre V.S. se ella m'impetra dal Sig.r Duca questa grazia, la quale a detto d'ognuno con due sole delle sue righe scritte in raccomandatione del fatto mio, ella mi puo agevolmente impetrare. Percioche ognun sa, quanto il Sr. Duca le creda, e quanto le conceda e se a V.S. s'apparecchiò mai occasione di fare un'opera pia e da doverne acquistar merito da Dio e grazia, e lode dagli huomini, questa è dessa. Dove ella ripara che un povero anzi miserissimo giovane (il quale se ben non val niente, ha però desiderato, e desidera di valere) non perda la roba, e l'honore, e non rovini, e se ne vada in precipizio, et in esterminio. il quale riconoscerà sempre la vita da lei e sempre andrà predicando questo benefizio, se bene io so che ella non pensa a questo. Io la supplico addunque, per quell'amore, che morendo per noi Iddio benedetto ci ha mostro, e per quelle cose, che piú la possono muovere, che ella scriva per me, et in raccomandatione di me, e di questa grazia, che io chieggo: che ella scriva, dico, quattro righe all'Ecc.za dell'Ill.mo Sig.r Duca mio Sig.re e me la mandi per l'apportatore insieme con l'inclusa mia a S. E. I. le quali io manderò subito alla corte per una staffetta a posta, accio che in questo mentre quei meschinacci non andasser via. Se io potessi esprimere in parole l'affetto del mio cuore, io crederrei impetrare da qualsivoglia, non che da V.S. che è pietosissima con ognuno, cio che io chiedessi sopra questo. Sig.r mio, io ho fallito, io ho fatto quel ch'io non debbo, e merito gastigo. ma io sono huomo e son giovane e non ho ancora imparato a dominare i primi moti: come spero in Dio, ch'io faro per l'avvenire. Io aspetto con ugual desiderio da V.S. questo favore, che da S. E. I. la grazia, e subito che io l'ho da lei mi quieterò, e saro sicuro d'havere la grazia. Io mi raccomando humilmente a V.S. e pregole ogni felicità. Di Firenze. A 23 di Marzo 1568.
Di V.S.
    Obligatiss.o S.re
    Lionardo Salviati
Desidero che l'apportatore non sappia nulla di questi intrinsechi.

Then, in the hand of Salviati:

Io ho havuta tutta notte la febbre dimaniera che io non ho potuto scriverle di mia mano, non che venire presenzialmente a supplicarla di questo favore. Piacendo a V.S. l'apportatore, ò per dir meglio l'apportatrice, ò altri, tornerà da V.S. quando ella le commetterà.[15]

Salviati is in disgrace. By his own admission he has merited this.
What his misdeed consists in we do not know. What he does reveal—
and it is certainly in keeping with his somewhat choleric temperament as manifested elsewhere—is that he has lost control of himself
and offended in high places. From his sick-bed he now encloses with
his letter to Vettori another letter which he has written to court, in
the hope that Vettori, having read it, will add a note to the Duke
requesting a pardon for the offender. On the details of his misdemeanours, however, Salviati is tantalisingly silent. Whatever he
has done—and the effects certainly dogged him for some time—
he is moving with speed and efficiency, despite his fever, to repair the
damage as quickly as possible. Salviati's extant correspondence contains nothing comparable to the anguished despair of this letter. As
already mentioned, he was quick to anger, especially for a slight, real
or imaginary.[16] But otherwise he was normally coldly reserved. It is
therefore all the more surprising to find such a wild and unrestrainedly emotional outburst, suggesting that his normal control has completely broken down. The rambling nature of the letter, the manner
in which he repeats the same ideas over and over again, even suggest
a mild mental derangement compatible with his fever.

But again the letter illuminates for us the relationship between the
two men. It is to Vettori that Salviati turns in his despair, confident
of sympathy and help. He reveals that in the past Vettori has always
shown him great kindness and special favour, and now the way in
which Lionardo is prepared to open his heart to him shows a genuine
bond of friendship on which he feels he can rely. Interesting is the
light the letter throws not only on the personality of Vettori as
Lionardo sees it, but also on his general prestige and reputation, his
standing with Cosimo, if Lionardo can say to him: 'ognun sa, quanto
il Sig. Duca le creda, e quanto le conceda', and refer to 'questa
grazia, la quale a detto d'ognuno con due sole righe scritte in
raccomandatione del fatto mio, ella mi può agevolmente impetrare.'
Vettori was of course a senator. But again, despite the wildly emotional character of the letter, the pupil–master relationship is again
discernible, when Salviati describes himself as a 'giovane, (il quale
se ben non val niente, ha perú desiderato, e desidera di valere) . . .'
and excuses himself as an immature youth.

The paucity of factual detail is unfortunate, since it might have
illuminated Salviati's subsequent relations with the Medici court, not
only with Cosimo, who seems to have given him (or at least promised
him) his patronage as early as 1563, and from whom in October 1564

Lionardo had requested (though it appears without success) a
Canonicate in the Propositura di Prato,[17] but especially with
Francesco, to whom he had dedicated, in 1564, both his *Orazione in
lode della fiorentina favella* and his *Della poetica lezzion prima* and to
whom Tommaso del Nero had presented the printed edition of
Salviati's comedy *Il Granchio*.

It is important in this respect to note that Salviati does not in fact
say that his own letter is to the Duke himself. When he refers to
Vettori's contribution he uses terms—'Sig.r Duca, Ecc.za dell' Ill.mo
Sig.r Duca mio Sig.re'—which make it quite certain that it is to the
Duke that he wants Vettori to write. Furthermore, he makes it clear
throughout that it is from the Duke that he hopes for the pardon, and
thus when he uses the initials S.E.I. (Sua Eccellenza Illustrissima)
in the sentence 'Io aspetto con ugual desiderio da V.S. questo favore,
che da S.E.I. la grazia', it is to the Duke that he is referring. It must
be taken into account, however, that as used elsewhere the initials
S.E.I., E.I. (Eccellenza Illustrissima), and S.E. (Sua Eccellenza)
could conceivably, in themselves, refer to Francesco de' Medici,
Cosimo's son, for whom the same term as 'Principe di Siena' was in
normal use. Referring to his own letter Salviati does not at any point
use the word 'duca' which would have cleared away all doubt, but
only 'la lettera che scrissi al E.I.', 'quello che non direi a S.E.' (i.e.
a reference to the content of his letter), 'l'inclusa mia a S.E.I.' Even
the fact that the two letters are to be sent to the court by the same
messenger is by no means decisive, and is all the more intriguing
because Salviati elsewhere, and not too long afterwards, shows himself to be very conscious of the fact that he has at some point in the
not too distant past fallen foul of Francesco. In a letter of 24th April,
1571, published by Contin, he admits his past errors, again asks for
pardon, and promises exemplary behaviour in the future.[18]

The tone and content of this letter of 1571 reveal to us quite beyond
doubt that the events of 1569 remain very much alive in Salviati's
mind, and whether or not the letter to Vettori refers directly to
Francesco there is the moral certainty that the 1571 letter relates to
the same events and that Francesco was somehow involved. There is
always a cloud over Salviati's relationship with the morose Francesco
(noted for the grudges he held over long periods), something unde-
finably unsatisfactory in his dealings with him, for the rest of his life.
Occasionally Salviati's resentment against him bursts through his
screen of self-control.[19] It is just conceivable that Francesco's continual coldness in the future towards Salviati, (except for brief
periods when Salviati could be particularly useful to him personally,
as when he was at the Court of Rome), his callous and ungrateful
treatment of him, may have derived not only from Francesco's own

unpleasant character, which led him naturally to despise intellectuals, academics, and other men of the stamp of Lionardo, but also from this incident, whatever it was, which Lionardo, even two years later, was well aware would still be in the forefront of Francesco's mind.

It is also possible that a curious, and obviously allegorical *sestina*, 'D'Arno gentil su la fiorita sponda', has some connection with this event. In it Lionardo tells how he grew 'di vecchio tronco giovinetta pianta' on the banks of the Arno, untroubled by excessive heat or by tempest. Suddenly a violent storm uprooted the 'pianta' and the swollen river carried it away from the bank. The poem continues:

> Vaga m'apparve al fin lucente fiamma
> Ch'allumò intorno, e l'una e l'altra riva,
> E vicina mostrò più d'una pianta,
> Ond'io versando lagrimosa pioggia
> Tutto rivolto alla felice sponda,
> Feci di prego humil risonar l'onde.

> Tutte in un tempo s'aquetaron l'onde
> Al lampeggiar, che la divina fiamma
> Fece al mio prego, ond'io venni alla sponda
> Tosto, e toccai la fortunata riva,
> Ov'io non ho mai poi sentito pioggia,
> E al bel lume mi sto sagrata pianta.

Clearly, the composition has a biographical basis, and it is fairly certain, given the context of Lionardo's poetic activity, that it dates to an early period in his life.[20]

Interpretation of the references in this poem must remain conjecture. What we do know for certain, however, is that Salviati did express, poetically, his esteem for Vettori in a sonnet beginning: 'Se di senno, e virtù, VETTORIO, quanta', in which he praises him for the part he played in the education of the young Duke in whom 'Il tosco gregge mio si gloria, e vanta.' Unfortunately, there is some likelihood that this poem was originally written for another person and subsequently modified to become a sonnet in praise of Vettori.[21] A greater tribute, perhaps, was that about this time, or the previous year, Salviati began work on his commentary on Aristotle's *Poetics*, a text on which his master Vettori spent much time, and over which there was no doubt much collaboration between the two, in view of Salviati's almost complete approval of Vettori's translation and commentary. In the final text of his own paraphrase and commentary Salviati frequently refers to the Latin translation by Vettori and states categorically that it is the best available.[22]

Whether or not Vettori did come to Lionardo's assistance in his distress, Salviati seems to have been swiftly rehabilitated in ducal favour, since one of the next things we hear of him is that in June 1569 he is a candidate for a knighthood in the Order of St. Stephen, the military order created by Cosimo in 1562. As an aspirant to the grade of 'cavalier sacerdotale' he presented his family arms to the Balì Raffaello de' Medici, and a 'consulta' was appointed to examine his claim to nobility. This was eventually confirmed (though not without delay whilst some check was made on his ancestors from Iesi). To check the authenticity of the seventeen traditional 'claims' put forward by Salviati, largely concerning 'la vita et costumi sua et de sua antenati' as the records put it, several witnesses were called. Amongst these was 'Piero di Jacopo Vettori'.[23]

To a certain extent Vettori's testimony was a formality. He merely had to confirm the 'claim', his confirmation being recorded in bureaucratic jargon. He had not personally known Lionardo's paternal grandfather and great-grandfather, he said, though he knew them by reputation. He had, however, known Lionardo's father Giovambattista, and his maternal great-grandfather Piero Ambrogini da Iesi. He even confirmed Lionardo's claim that Piero Ambrogini came to Florence as 'podestà' and that he 'fu et era huomo famoso di lettere'. But it is what he says about Lionardo himself which interests us most. We have already seen that on this occasion he says he has known Lionardo from his boyhood. On the subject of Lionardo's 'claim' in the 'sestodecimo capitolo' that he was a 'giovane di buona vita, costumi et qualità et ha atteso alle lettere et in bonissima aspettatione vissuto sempre honoratamente, ecc.', the documents record Vettori as having said 'che ha conosciuto il detto m. Lionardo da pueritia di esso m. Lionardo et ha visto che è vissuto sempre honoratamente et da gentilhuomo et ha implicato tutto il tempo alle buone lettere et è stato et è di gran dottrina et elegantia et ingegni sublimi sì nelli studii come nella poesia et è in grande aspettatione di tutti i litterati et è sempre moderno (sic 'modesto'?) et di buona vita et costumi et comunemente per tale è tenuto et reputato.'

It is not without significance that on this 'capitolo' Pier Vettori takes the opportunity to expatiate on Lionardo's talents as a man of letters. Admittedly he was very likely the only one of the witnesses to be able to give an authoritative opinion, but he could presumably perfectly well have done what the others did, namely repeat more or less word for word the claim and leave it at that. That he did not, in fact, stop there, but took the opportunity of praising in this way Lionardo and his works, both scholarly and poetic, is a small but valid confirmation of what Lionardo had said of him four months earlier, namely that he showed a particular affection and regard for

Lionardo. Clearly, by 1569 there is a close bond of mutual friendship uniting the two.[24]

And so with Vettori's assistance Lionardo Salviati became on 12th August, 1569 Il cavalier Lionardo Salviati. Whilst the title was much to his liking, his association with the Order was not an unmixed blessing.[25]

It is not until he was acting as 'Ricevitore' (virtually debt-collector) for the Order in Rome that we have further documentation of his connections with Vettori, in December 1578—nine years after the *Provanza*, though it is worth noting that Alberto Bolognetti, to whom Salviati wrote his sonnet 'Da questo al surger mio terreno avverso' was a friend of Vettori and highly regarded by him. The tone of this poem, expressing frustration over conditions in Florence and the desire to get away is characteristic of a period which is also one of close friendship between Vettori and Bolognetti, that is to say the years 1576–78 when Bolognetti was Apostolic Protonotary in Florence. In 1578 it was Vettori who wrote seeking the help of his disciple in furthering at the Papal Court a request for the dissolution of his grand-daughter's marriage. To plead the cause he has sent his grandson Francesco, a trained lawyer, to Rome. We do not have Vettori's letter, but we do have Salviati's reply. Obviously he is delighted to receive the request, and extremely keen to show his worth in giving practical assistance to Vettori. Knowing Francesco was in Rome he had already made a point of seeking him out and putting himself at his disposal. At this point in his life Salviati was particularly well placed to be of effective assistance, being employed in some personal secretarial capacity by Giacomo Buoncompagni, son of the then Pope, Gregory XIII, and Castellano di Sant'Angelo, and coming into intimate daily contact with some of the most important and influential ecclesiastics of the time. Just what part Francesco de' Medici had had in placing him in this post is uncertain, but what is quite certain is that Salviati, aspiring at this time to be a Medicean court favourite, was playing a double game, using his position in Rome (with the information on affairs in the Court of Rome to which it gave him access) in the service of the Grand Duke of Tuscany, for whom he acted as a spy.[26] Being so close to Buoncompagni (who in his turn was extremely close to his father the Pope) he was excellently placed to acquire inside information on the progress of the case and to put in a word on behalf of Vettori with influential ecclesiastics. Thus even before Vettori had written to him personally he had got wind of the affair, and had begun both to exercise his good offices with Buoncompagni and others on his old master's behalf. So the third of Salviati's unpublished letters to Vettori is the one in which on 6th December, 1578 he reports to him on the current situation.

Molto Mag.co et Ecc.mo Sr. mio

Molto prima che V.S. mi scrivessi mi era offerto a M. Francesco suo nipote, et in quel poco, ch'io haveva potuto haveva cercato di servirlo, introducendolo, raccomandandolo al sig.r mio, come da esso m. Francesco le sarà stato scritto. Hora S. Ecc.za per amor di V.S. la quale stima quanto dee, e per qualità della causa, che le par degna d'aiuto, et anche, ardirò di dirlo, in qual che parte per favorir me suo non discaro serv.re farà quanto m. Francesco conoscerà per gli effetti, che sarà, spero, molto piú che i ss.ri non sogliono comunemente; che le giuro che l'ho veduto far dimostrazione di molta compassione, e spero in Dio, che quel conforto, che si potra dare a V.S. per alleggerimento de' suoi travagli sarà porto prontamente. Non ha havuto bisogno il S.re che io lo 'nformi della pistola scritta da V.S. a N.S. ne della grata dimostrazione riportatane da S. S.ta perche molti giorni innanzi n'havevamo ragionato, e l'assicuro che 'l Papa stesso, quanto comporta la persona di Giudice supremo ha speziale affetto nella causa di V.S. si che, se harà ragione come io tengo per fermo non ha da temere, ne d'allungamenti ne d'altro. A questi giorni il Cardinal Farnese me ne parlò mostrando, che gl'increscesse di non potere in questa causa favorire V.S. per l'antica servitù, che havevano gli avversarii con casa sua, onde gli conveniva starsene di mezzo, e fu egli che spontaneamente mosse il ragionam.to e tutto feci subito intendere a m. Francesco, accioche non fondasse le sue speranze nel patrocinio di quel Sig.re. Il qual m. Francesco suo mi pare, che si porti in questa cosa quanto si possa disiderare il migliore, e così sento dire da ognuno. Meco non occorre che V.S. faccia mai cirimonie, che sono obbligato a servirla amandola, come Padre, osservandola come maggiore, et havendola in reverenza, come maestro: si che avvertiscami pure m. Francesco giornalmente di tutto quel ch'io posso fare, che quanto piú harò occasione d'affaticarmici, tanto ne sentirò più piacere. Degnisi raccomandarmi et offerirmi a m. Jacopo suo figliuolo, e qui fo fine baciandole le mani et pregandole felicità. Di Roma alli vi di dicembre, 1578. Di V.S. molto mag.ca et Ecc.ma.

    S.re Aff.mo,
       Lionardo Salviati[27]

The letter marks a striking contrast with his previous one of 1569. Now it is Salviati who is putting himself about to do all he can for Vettori, and at the same time revelling, true to character, in his important contacts and his own position of influence. There is certainly the desire to show his old master that he has made good, and probably some exaggeration, in the process, of the importance of his own role.[28] But the main feature of the letter is the enthusiasm to please Vettori, and his respect and esteem for him are as strongly present as ever. There is great warmth and genuine affection in his insistence that 'Meco non occorre che V.S. faccia mai cirimonie, che sono obbligato a servirla amandola, come Padre, osservandola come maggiore, et havendola in reverenza, come maestro.' He asks only to be told what to do, and 'quanto più harò occasione d'affati-carmici, tanto ne sentirò più piacere.'

The loyalty to Vettori demonstrated here is all the more remark-able in that loyalty was frankly not one of Lionardo's outstanding features. One by one he betrayed his most intimate and trusting friends—Borghini, Guarini, Panicarola. The most one can say in his favour was that it was occasionally a question of conflicting loyalties, and we might give him the benefit of the doubt with regard to the next recorded contact between the two men, a further unpublished letter from Salviati to Vettori dated 17th December, 1580, when Salviati was still with Buoncompagni in Rome. Again it begs a favour, but this time it is one of minor consequence:[29]

Molto mag.co et Ecc.mo Sig.r mio oss.mo
L'Ecc.mo sigr. Jacopo mio padrone non confidando, che altra persona di costà lo sia per compiacere piu amorevolmente, ne con piu prontezza di V.S. disidera per mezzo suo d'havere una nota di tutti i libri ebraci (sic) della libreria di San Lorenzo per chiarirsi se egli, che fa professione d'averne assai, e molto rari, ha ancora a far gran cammino per venire a quel segno della detta libreria: e quali gli restano a procacciare. Ma perche malvolentieri entra in concetto di curioso di queste cose, la prega a cercare questa cosa, come da se, et à mandarmela quanto prima le sarà comodo: che son certo, che le verrà fatto agevolmente per la sua autorità, e per l'amicizia, che ha con maestro Baccio, col quale, ne con altri, S.Ecc.a non vuol esser nominato: la quale all'incontro sarà sempre pronta a far piacere a V.S. come merita la virtù, e bontà sua singolare, et io di cuore me le offero, e raccomando e pregole lunga e felice vita. Di Roma alli 17 di dicembre 1580.
   Di V.S. m.to mag.ca et Ecc.ma
      Aff.mo S.re e figliuolo
         Lionardo Salviati.

In this case the encouragement to Vettori to use his friendship with Baccio Valori for the purpose of deceiving him is perhaps not very representative, since it is done only to save Giacomo Buon-compagni's face and avoid public knowledge of what might seem to be vulgar curiosity. Yet one might have thought that Salviati would hesitate to deceive Valori even to this extent, given his own great debt to him. Valori was the first to recognise Salviati's latent talents and give him, during his (Valori's) consulship, the opportunity to make his maiden appearance before the Accademia Fiorentina. The result was the *Orazione in lode della fiorentina favella* which really made Salviati's name at a time when, as Salviati tells us, the requests to give lectures far exceeded the possibilities of satisfying them.[30] But the issue is comparatively trivial and the letter is brief, businesslike and to the point, lacking the intimacy which was such an interesting feature of the others.

Perhaps it was the influence of his post, for Salviati had by this time been in Buoncompagni's service for three years. Unlike the period immediately before (the years 1564–1577 had produced, in addition to *Il Granchio* and the poems, a stream of orations) his years in Rome had yielded little.[31] Nevertheless they were not lost to his studies, for they were used to deepen Salviati's already unrivalled knowledge of the language of the Florentine trecento, the indispensable prerequisite for his edition of the *Decameron* which came out in 1582. Here too he remembers Pier Vettori—in a manner which recalls Bembo's treatment of Ercole Strozzi in the *Prose della volgar lingua*.[32] Works *in* the *volgare*, not about it, and translation into it, best serve its cause, was what he repeated constantly, and when faced with the accusation that the Florentines do not devote themselves as wholeheartedly as they might to this task he points out that like any other people at any time Florence has her share of men of four categories: those who can write well in the *volgare* and do, those who cannot and don't, those who can't but still do, and those who could but don't. It is on this last category that he could pin his hopes. They are many: 'chi impedito da altri affari, che a lui più rilievano, chi da studj più gravi, chi ritenuto da qualche altro riguardo.' And he gives a long list of them and their qualities, predicting a glorious future for both them and for Tuscan if the latter could have all their concentrated attention.

But this category possesses one man who towers above all. Lionardo, beginning his list, writes: 'a cui potrebbe mai esser dubbio, che Pier Vettori, accioch'io tolga il principio dal più nobile, e più sovrano, e da colui in brieve, cui per maestro hanno tutti, che Pier Vettori, dico, il quale scrive in guisa nella latina lingua, che tra 'l suo stile, ed il migliore del miglior secolo, i più intendenti huomini, e più pratichi di quello studio, non sanno scernere alcun vantaggio; qualora egli a dettar chechè sia nel suo natìo idioma l'animo disponesse, altrettale, ò maggiore non fosse per apparire.'[33]

For him Pier Vettori is a giant who would add lustre to whatever medium he chose to employ. But why, one wonders, is there no reference to *Delle lodi e della coltivazione degli ulivi* which was published in 1569 and was already well known? The phrase 'qualora egli a dettar chechè sia nel suo natìo idioma l'animo disponesse' is positively weird, since it virtually says that hitherto he has in fact written *nothing*—at least for publication—in *volgare*: which is tantamount to saying that his *Coltivazione degli ulivi* is not his work, or at least that the language of it is not his work. One might go further and even say that if much of Florence knew in 1566 that he was in some way revising a work of Vettori, and that that work was *Delle lodi e della coltivazione*, then he had no choice but to ignore it now in his remarks on Vettori's potential in the *volgare*. Whatever one's conclusions, the statement is most odd, since by far the more natural thing to do would have been to refer to the one existing example of Vettori's prowess in the *volgare*.

This is the last tribute during his lifetime to the person whom Salviati considers Florence's greatest man of letters. In December of the following year Vettori died, and on 27th January, 1586 Salviati delivered the master's funeral oration in Santo Spirito on behalf of the Accademia.

The unique character of this work in the context of Salviati's oratorical production can only be appreciated through a comparison with his other orations, largely shallow rhetorical exercises in which content (though Salviati often insinuates into them polemical statements of his own convictions) is entirely subordinated to form. As a term of comparison we might take the funeral oration on Varchi, a tissue of self-conscious and embarrassing rhetorical excesses which emphasise, rather than hide, the insincerity of the orator, who is clearly without any bond of sympathy with his subject. As always in such cases Salviati allows himself to be carried away by the attraction of his rhetorical figures into the most blatant absurdities.[34]

With this latter work the oration in praise of Vettori forms the greatest contrast. There is of course conscious and very obvious artifice, but for once the real subject of the oration is the ostensible one, with the orator aiming at communicating to his hearers his own conception of, and admiration for, this great man, his own old teacher. Some of the material for the anecdotes scattered through the oration is derived from a document on Pier Vettori prepared for him for the purposes of his oration by Francesco Vettori.[35] But much is obviously based on personal reminiscence and longstanding close acquaintance. This personal character is stressed by his remarks on Vettori's philological method, which tie up so closely with what he said about his own in the first book of the second volume of the *Avvertimenti*. At one point, and with a plea to his hearers to forgive him for doing so, he introduces an anecdote concerning himself, and tells how Vettori reproved him for including words of praise for him, Vettori, in his oration on Varchi.[36]

We can be sure that in the case of the *Orazione delle lodi di Pier Vettori* what Lionardo said came from the heart. Yet respect and gratitude do not in themselves fully explain the intimate relationship between the two. It is clear that Salviati felt that he had something absolutely fundamental in common with Pier Vettori, and that a deep identity of view bound them together. At first sight this seems impossible. Salviati was the pugnacious supporter of the *volgare*, asserting at all moments in his life its independence, its supreme contemporary relevance, and its superiority. Vettori we think of as the culmination of two centuries of humanistic classical philology, indefatigably emending and restoring corrupt texts of the classics, expounding them to generation after generation of eager Florentines.

Yet one does not really need to look far to see just why Pier Vettori was Salviati's idol. The key lies in the nature of his humanism and his position in the development of Florentine humanism as it led from Salutati to Salviati himself. For Salviati he was obviously—and on close inspection it could not be otherwise—a living confirmation of, and vindication of, Salviati's own ideas in respect of contemporary culture and a unique link between two vital moments, with Salviati the representative of the later of those moments.

For Vettori saw himself, first and foremost, as an *educator*, in the tradition of all the great humanist educators. It was as an educational medium in the fullest humanist sense that he saw his own classical philological studies, for what he in practice represented was the highest point of the humanist educational programme, which conceived the study of the classics as the means to perfect the man of the present. From his first appointment he saw his instruction as having three aims—firstly a literary one, to make his pupils more sensitive and receptive to literature, and to make them more at home in it: his second aim, following directly from that, was a moral one: and his third aim might be described as a general educational one, for like all good humanists he saw literature as that 'elementary philosophy' which trained and developed man. From the process of the education and refinement of taste and the development of linguistic ability generally it was a natural corollary that the *volgare* would benefit no less than Latin and Greek, for the qualities which it produced and trained were to be seen as quite separate from the medium used—in his case the classical languages. Indeed, it would be the *volgare* which would benefit principally, as Vettori never tired of stressing, as it took over functions hitherto fulfilled by Latin and Greek. His aim in teaching, as he repeated constantly, was not to make his pupils into classical philologists but to *educate* them in such a way that they could then proceed to fulfil their own potential, in their own way, in whatever medium they chose.

Seen from this point of view Vettori pointed straight towards Salviati, who from the time of the *Orazione in lode della fiorentina favella* of 1564 or even the quarrel with Corbinelli of 1563 had been dedicated to the promotion of the *volgare* conceived as the contemporary means of expression. Just as Vettori saw the classics, both language and literature, as developing the Man, who could then employ the education acquired in the best and most appropriate way, so Salviati declared that despite his passionate campaign for the *volgare* he himself was not against classical studies as such. Speaking in the *Avvertimenti* of 1584 of the baneful influence of the influx into Italian of lexical latinisms, the main cause as he saw it of the 'peggioramento della favella', and warning his contemporaries to keep away from them when writing Italian he adds:

> Potrà parere ad alcuno, che noi per le cose dette infin quì, gli scrittori del volgar nostro dallo studio, ò dall'uso della latina lingua, cerchiamo di spaventare, quasi eglino, impacciandosi con esso lei, debol progresso sien per fare in quest'altra. Il che è senza dubbio lungi dal parer nostro. Perciocchè noi stimiamo allo 'ncontro, che chi non ha buon gusto nel latino idioma, e non ha per le mani gli scrittori suoi più solenni, in questo nostro piccolo spazio avanti proceder possa, ò nella prosa, ò nel verso. E perchè 'l gusto in quella guisa si fa migliore, e più fine; utilissima cosa, al dettar bene in toscano, reputiam senza fallo l'esercitarsi nello scriver latinamente: poichè dal pregiudicio, che ciò potesse arrecargli, quanto alla purità, Dante nel suo Poema, il Petrarca nel Canzoniere, il Boccaccio nelle Novelle, e ne' moderni tempi Messer Giovanni della Casa nel suo purissimo Galateo, ciascun de' quali fu sempre involto nella latina lingua, ci abbiano insegnato a guardarcene.[37]

This is entirely in line with the thinking and the practice of Vettori as far as the educational function of the classics in refining taste and increasing awareness is concerned. There is here the separation of this educational function of the classics from the choice of language in which to exercise the taste and discernment acquired through them. Vettori, above all people, was a man 'involto' in classical studies, yet able to put them in this sense at the service of the *volgare*. Vettori was convinced, for example, of the utility, indeed necessity, of the study of Horace for anyone who wished to write lyric poetry in Italian. On this score he cited Luigi Alamanni and the benefit he believed Alamanni had acquired from the study of Greek poets.[38] Vettori and Salviati represented two complementary faces of the final stages of that Florentine humanism which whilst concentrating on the general, irreplaceable educational function of that supreme body of works which constituted the classics, nevertheless recognised the inevitable move towards the rehabilitation of the *volgare* and with it its greatest representatives. Vettori concentrated on the process of education in itself and Salviati concentrated on the development of the *volgare* as an independent entity on which the influence of the classics was to be limited to such benefits of taste and discernment as its users could derive from being educated through the medium of those classics. In this way they understood each other perfectly and saw their tasks as complementary.

Whatever text Vettori was commenting on he constantly stressed its use for Italian, and in particular quite naturally he saw this as applying to the classical rhetoricians, with their general (as he saw it) ability to heighten linguistic awareness and ability. He considered their precepts to be universally valid on a plane of eloquence, and thus no less important for, and applicable to, Italian.[39] For Vettori, too, saw the *volgare* as the natural means of expression of his age, and as we have seen be conceived his own instruction to be in final analysis directed to the most useful cultivation of it. But his own *volgare* production was not large. Indeed, Salviati virtually suggested in 1584 that it did not exist at all. Nevertheless evidence of a great deal of activity by him in Italian abounds. He had read and studied Dante and Petrarch and utilised their works in the education of his grand-children. He did not scorn to use Dante in the illustration and interpretation of classical authors. He himself annotated and glossed the text of the Comedy, wrote a work in *volgare* comparing Dante with Euripides, Virgil and other classical authors, and produced several collections of Tuscan works with comment.[40] It is quite clear therefore that not only was his attitude to the *volgare*, and its relationship to the classical languages, one which fully vindicated its contemporary use on the soundest possible humanistic grounds, bringing him into line with Lionardo Salviati, but also that he took an extremely active interest in it. He even went so far at one point as to make a clear-cut statement on the superior qualities of Tuscan.[41]

Dante, Petrarch, Machiavelli, and Guicciardini were amongst the authors in Italian whom Vettori admired. But his was a much more active involvement in the *volgare*. His love for, and interest in it was indicated by the all-important fact that he was one editor of the 1527 *Decameron*, to which his philological training made him an important contributor. It is further indicated by his action after the 1573 expurgation of that work, when he pleaded eloquently to his friend Cardinal Sirleto against further interference with the text, saying amongst other things 'non voglio entrare in celebrare il frutto, che se ne cava, pel grande ornamento di parole, e per la copia di belli concetti, che sono in questo libro, che senza esso resterebbe monca, e storpiata la nostra lingua, la quale oggi è in gran pregio.' Shortly afterwards he wrote to this same correspondent requesting him, as having a certain influence in such matters, to assist him to gain permission for the printing of the works of Machiavelli (now firmly on the Index), expurgated and rendered harmless, in religious terms, by two (unnamed) grandchildren of the author. 'Io già non le ho viste' he writes of the new version of the works 'nè posso far fede, che la cosa stia così (i.e. that the editors had 'levatone tutto quello, che potesse dispiacere alla Santa Romana Chiesa'); ma stimo bene, che trattone tutto quello, che potesse nuocere alla vita Cristiana, il darle di nuovo fuora emendate, e viste prima, e approvate da V.S. Reverendiss. non potesse essere, se non di giovamento a chi si diletta delle memorie antiche, perchè egli fu uomo di grande ingegno, e molto pratico delle cose del Mondo, e io sentiva dire in quei tempi, che elle uscirono fuora, che egli aveva insegnato cavar vero frutto delle Storie.'[42]

What emerges from all this—from Vettori's own activity, from his letters, from his own work on *volgare* authors is a strong sense not only of the *volgare* itself but also of its literary tradition. The more one examines Vettori's career and literary activity, the more one is impressed by the extent to which it is inspired by a tender love for Italian, and the easier it is to see just how Vettori, with his universal fame as a classical philologist, yet at the same time a man who was one of the most insistent supporters of the *volgare*, could come to occupy a special, a unique place in the pattern of Salviati's vision. Hence comes the literary friendship, hence the ring of sincerity in the funeral oration.

The story of the relationship between Vettori and Salviati is a valuable addition to our picture of Pier Vettori's status in his native Florence, where for several decades he occupied a unique position as an 'educator': unique for the sound scholarly influence which he exercised, unique for the spirit of unity which he brought to the world of Florentine letters.

Though he advanced along personal paths which could not have been Vettori's, stressing the independence of the *volgare* tradition, its ability both to set its own standards and to some extent to take over the educational function for which Vettori's own specialism and training led him to use the classics, Lionardo seems to have understood that continuity which bound his own work to that of the great classicist, and to have appreciated the extent to which his own further progress was made possible by the achievements of Vettori. And so when Giovanni Battista Attendolo, writing to Salviati in March 1586 speaks of the 'tributo di rispetto, e di maggioranza, che debbono al gran Salviati non solo i letterati della Italia, o altra, ma coloro etiandio che sono amatori delle lettere. Chiamerollo maestro commune, e sign. mio particolare, nel valor di cui, non meno che nella oration funerale, può consolarsi la patria, e il Mondo, dopo la perdita di Pier Vettori', Salviati cannot but have concurred that comparison with Pier Vettori was the highest tribute one could offer, and he cannot but have been flattered that he, Lionardo Salviati, should be looked upon as the successor of the man for whom he, for the best of reasons, cherished supreme respect, admiration and affection.[43]

University of Hull   PETER M. BROWN

NOTES

1. Fourteen of these (the exception is the real *Orazione seconda in lode di don Garzia* which was printed only once, separately from the other *Garzia* orations, in Florence by the Giunti, in 1563) were printed in the volume *Il primo libro delle orazioni del cav. Lionardo Salviati*, Florence, Giunti, 1575.

2. *Orazione funerale del cav. Lionardo Salviati delle lodi di Pier Vettori, senatore e Accademico Fiorentino. Recitata pubblicamente in Firenze, per ordine della Fiorentina Accademia, nella Chiesa di Santo Spirito, il dì 27 di Gennaio, 1585, nel consolato di Giovambattista di Giovanmaria Deti*, Firenze, per Filippo e Jacopo Giunti, 1585 (i.e. 1586). But n.b. that whilst the title page of the 1586 edition, and the dedicatory letter to Francesco Panicarola (who was to present the oration to Sixtus V) states the date as 27 January, the title as repeated on the first page of the text runs 'il dì *25* di gennaio 1585'.

3. F. Niccolai, *Pier Vettori*, Florence, Seeber, 1912, pp. 96–130 lists those known to have been his pupils, citing the source of information. Salviati's known relationship with Ascanio da Ripa and Alberto Bolognetti, both of them devotees of Vettori, is limited to poetic exchanges.

4. Pisa, Archivio dello Stato, Archivio di Santo Stefano, 'Provanze di nobiltà', Filza 7, Parte prima, No. 3. See also my 'Lionardo Salviati and the Ordine di Santo Stefano', *Italica*, XXXIV, 2, (June 1957), pp. 69–74.

5. Unpubl. letter Salviati to Pier Vettori, London, British Museum, Add. MS. 10278, f. 48r, dated 8.3.1565 (i.e. 1566). All autograph. The MS. in which this letter is found forms a collection of letters to Vettori, in both Italian and Latin, from friends and acquaintances, ranging from Bartolommeo Cavalcanti to Ascanio da Ripa. The contents of these MSS., from which were taken the other letters to be included in this article, were listed by Cecil Roth, 'Un carteggio inedito di Pier Vettori', in *Rivista storica degli archivi toscani*, Vol. I (1929), pp. 154–185. See also C. E. Pollak, 'Carteggio di Pier Vettori nel Museo Britannico', Estratto dalla *Rassegna bibliografica della letteratura italiana*, I, 3 and III, 5, 6, Pisa, 1895.

6. *P. Victorii liber de laudibus Joannae Austriacae, natae Reginae Ungarie et Boemiae*, Florentiae, 1566, 4to. Salviati's translation was published in the *Primo libro delle orazioni del cav. Lionardo Salviati*, cit., with the title *Orazione delle lodi della Regina Giovanna d'Austria*. Introducing this translation in this volume the editor, Don Silvano Razzi, writes: 'Quantunque questa traduzione fosse pubblicata senza il nome dell'autore, e così fino a ora si sia stata . . . I have not been successful in tracing this publication—if indeed the statement does refer to a printed edition.

7. *Trattato di Pier Vettori delle lodi et della coltivatione de gl'ulivi*, Florence,

1569. Salviati says in March 1566, as we have seen, that he is proceeding 'slowly' with this work, which could account for some of the time which passed between then and the actual publication of the treatise. The fact that this was the only work of Vettori (apart from letters) which was published, does not of course mean that it was the only one ever *intended* for publication. There is the essay *Viaggio di Annibale per la Toscana descritta da Pier Vettori*, edited eventually by Francesco Saverio Gualtieri (Naples 1780, presso Giuseppe Campo). The dedicatory letter to Cosimo de' Medici of this work, however, bears the date 15 July 1559. This makes the likelihood that the letter refers to this particular work rather less likely, as does the fact that it was not published in Vettori's lifetime, but not of course impossible. The language of the work seems to have nothing which would contradict Salviati's linguistic principles.

8. Niccolai, *Pier Vettori*, cit., p. 51.

9. *Ibid.* He also states: 'il pregio maggiore di questo libretto è quello della lingua e dello stile.'

10. See in particular the letter Salviati to Duke Cosimo, dated 12.10.64, published by G. Contin, *Lettere edite e inedite di Lionardo Salviati*, Padua, 1875, in which he asks Cosimo to employ him on the translation of the classics of antiquity into Tuscan: 'Al che fare io mi crederei essere alto quanto alcuno altro sì per molte altre ragioni, di che io V.E.I. farei capace, sì spezialmente per questo che io sono in età che potrei sperare di fornirle, oltre la grande agevolezza che io ho nello scrivere . . .' This is only one of the numerous passages in the letter in which he sings his own praises.

11. Indeed, Lionardo himself was to bestow lavish praise on Giovanni Rondinelli in the *Avvertimenti* where amongst many others he lists, as some of those individuals who have brought lustre to the *volgare*, Bastiano Antinori and 'Giovanni d'Alessandro Rondinelli suo, e mio virtuosissimo amico, nelle lingue, che più non vivono nella voce del popolo, ha gusto sì esquisito, e nel volgar materno è così raro nell'altezza del verso, chente lo mostrano le sue tragedie, magnifiche oltr'a misura.' (*Avvertimenti della lingua sopra 'l Decameron*, Vol. I, Bk. II, 'Proemio', Naples, Raillard, 1712, p. 137). His continued association with him in the intervening years is illustrated by a letter from Ercole Cortile, the Ferrarese ambassador in Florence to Alfonso II, in which he writes: 'Il cav.re Salviati procurerà d'haver in mano molti fogli della Historia di quel frataccio che scrive contro quella del Pigna, essendo ch'egli l'ha di nuovo fatto pregare per il Sig. Giovanni Rondinelli, che la voglia correggere, et subito che li haverà mi ha promesso che me ne darà la copia.' (Letter Cortile to Alfonso II, Modena, Archivio dello Stato, 'Ambasciatori Firenze', 1576, quoted in G. Campori, 'Il cav. Lionardo Salviati e Alfonso II duca di Ferrara', in *Atti e memorie dei R. R. Deputati di Storia Patria per le prov. mod. e parm.*, Vol. VII, Modena, 1874, pp. 143ff). The 'frataccio' in this case is Borghini.

12. *Orazione . . . nella morte dell'Illus. Donna Leonora di Toledo, Duchessa di Firenze . . . Tradotta in Lingua Fiorentina, da N. Mini*, I Figliuoli di L. Torrentino, Fiorenza, 1563, 4.

13. On the quarrel with Corbinelli see P. Soldati, 'Jacopo Corbinelli e Lionardo Salviati' in *Archivum Romanicum*, XIX (July–Dec. 1935), pp. 415–423, and for details of its significance in the context of Lionardo's career see my own article: 'Jacopo Corbinelli and the

Florentine 'Crows' ', in *Italian Studies*, XXIII (1971), pp. 68–89.

14. For publication-details of these and any other works of Salviati
    mentioned (apart from poems) see S. Parodi, 'Una lettera inedita
    del Salviati', *Studi di filologia italiana*, XXVII, pp. 146–174, of which
    pp. 162–173 are devoted to a bibliography of the works of Salviati.
    For MS. and details of printed editions of the poems, see my
    'Manoscritti e stampe delle poesie edite e inedite del cav. Lionardo
    Salviati', *Giornale Storico della letteratura italiana*, CXLVI (1969),
    pp. 530–552.

15. Unpublished letter Salviati to Vettori, 23.3.68 (i.e. '69), London
    Brit. Mus., Add. MSS. 10281, ff. 86r–87r. In an unknown hand
    (including the signature) except for the latter part of the post-
    script, which is autograph.

16. See especially (a) Salviati's angry letter to Varchi, dated 24.3.62
    (i.e. '63); (b) his letter to Lodovico Martelli, dated 24.2.64 (i.e. '65)
    on the occasion of the Mascherata degli Ermafroditi, both pub-
    lished by Manzoni, *Prose edite e inedite del cav. Leonardo Salviati*,
    Bologna, Romagnoli, 1873, and Contin, op. cit.; (c) his furious
    letter to Jacopo Corbinelli (no date, but early 1563), published by
    Manzoni and Contin but mistakenly considered by both of them
    to be addressed to Alessandro Canigiani.

17. See the letters Salviati to Cosimo of 12.10.1564 and 24.10.64,
    published by Contin, op. cit.

18. For the use of the title 'Sua Eccellenza Illustrissima', see Salviati's
    letter to Francesco of 12 December 1564, published in my 'L'edi-
    zione del 1873 delle prose edite e inedite del cav. Lionardo Salviati'
    in *Rinascimento*, VIII, 1 (June 1957), pp. 111–129. The letter is on
    p. 117. In the letter to Francesco, Salviati writes: 'Io so ch'io col
    non m'essere così bene governato come io harei dovuto, ho qualche
    volta per l'addietro dato di me qualche non così buona soddisfazione.'

19. For one example among many, see Salviati's indiscretion to the
    Ferrarese ambassador, Ercole Cortile, who on 4 February 1576
    wrote of Salviati in a despatch to his master Alfonso: '. . . lui si è
    risoluto di non andare mai nelle camere del Sig.r Duca (Cortile
    does not call Francesco 'Granduca' since the Este did not recognise
    the title) et che sia il vero, mi ha accompagnato due o tre volte
    sino al Palazzo, et poi se n'è subito tornato addietro, facendo scusa
    con me che mi terrà compagnia in tutti i luoghi eccetto che in
    palazzo . . .' (pub.d Campori op. cit.).

20. L. Manzoni, *Rime del cavalier Leonardo Salviati*, Bologna, Romagnoli,
    1871 (series: Scelta di curiosità letterarie inedite o rare', no. 117).
    The *sestina* is on p. 10ff.

21. There are two extant versions of this sonnet. One is to be found in
    the Cod. XIII, D 52 of the Bib. Naz. Cent. Vittorio Emanuele,
    Naples, the other in the MS. collection of Salviati's poems in the
    Cod. Magl. VII, 306 of the Bib. Naz. Cent., Florence, and in Cod.
    2849 of the Bib. Riccardiana, Florence. In the case of the first
    version the poem has no dedication, and the first line reads: 'Se di
    senno, e virtù, al mondo quanta', and lines 5–8 run: 'A voi, che dee,
    che fida opra e tanta / Le fuste, ancor per men sicure strade /
    Appoggio fermo, onde non torce e cade / Ma s'erge al Ciel la sua
    più cara pianta.' In the second instance the poem is dedicated to
    Pier Vettori, the first line is: 'Se di senno, e virtù, VETTORIO,
    quanta', and lines 5–8 fittingly read: 'A voi che dee, che sì fid'opra

e tanta / Scrivendo, date alla futura etade / Onde dalla paterna alta pietade / Non pieghi mai la sua progenie santa.' There is reason to believe that the first version (that of the Naples MS). represents the original, but this is by no means certain. For details see my article, 'Manoscritti e stampe delle poesie inedite del cav. Lionardo Salviati', *Giornale storico della letteratura italiana*, CXLVI (1969), Fasc. 456, pp. 530–552.

22. Cf. f.372 of Salviati's *Commentary*, of which the surviving section is in the MS. in the Bib. Naz. Cent., Florence, Cod. Magl. VII, 87. Vettori's commentary came out in 1560 (*Petri Victorii Commentarii, In primum librum Aristotelis de Arte Poetarum*, in officina Iuntarum, Florentiae 1560) and his version of the Greek text in 1564. Salviati must have begun his own work about 1566–67 if in the dedicatory letter of the corrected *Decameron*, written in its original form in May 1582, Salviati could speak of 'le mie fatiche della Poetica, le quali già sedici anni hanno occupato della mia vita.'

23. For details of the 'Provanza di nobiltà', as it was called, see the MSS. quoted in note 4, and for an account of the 'Provanza' and transcriptions of some of the main documents, see my article 'Lionardo Salviati and the Ordine di Santo Stefano', quoted n. 4.

24. There is of course just the possibility that he was there precisely because he was capable of pronouncing a judgement on Lionardo's literary talents, since these would be called into play in the execution of his duties as a 'cavalier sacerdotale o cappellano'. In practice, however, this is unlikely, and it is infinitely more probable that he was there simply as a Senator. The other witnesses were (1) Il Mag. co m. Agnolo di Girolamo Guicciardini, who said he knew that Lionardo 'ha atteso alle lettere et di presente vi attende et non è scandaloso ma persona costumata et sana.' (2) Il Mag.co Carlo di Ruberto Acciaiuoli, who said he 'ha atteso alle lettere et è stato di buona vita, qualità et costumi', (3) Alamanno di Antonio di (illegible) who declared he 'ha visto che ha atteso alle lettere et vi ha fatto buon profitto et è di buona aspettatione et di suavità et costumi esemplari.' (MS. cit. of the 'Provanza', Pisa, Archivio di Stato).

25. There is a copious correspondence between Salviati and the Consiglio dell'Ordine di Santo Stefano in the Archives of the Order in the Archivio dello Stato in Pisa, in the *Registri di lettere missive* and the *Filze di Lettere Originali al Consiglio* for the relevant years.

26. Salviati entered the service of Giacomo Buoncompagni in the second half of 1577, and not in 1578 as is frequently stated (see my article 'L'edizione del 1573', cit., p. 125) and there are several indications in his correspondence that he was virtually placed there by Francesco de' Medici, to whom he pleaded his loyalty even if it conflicted with his duties towards Buoncompagni: 'Basta,' he says, 'che io so qual è l'ufizio di buon suddito e qual è quello di buon servidore e per quanto io saprò e potrò farò sempre l'uno e l'altro ingenuamente. E dove nascesse l'incompatibile conosco quel che mi s'appartiene. (Letter Salviati to Grand Duke Francesco, 16 October 1580, published Contin, op. cit., No. 21). The voluminous correspondence between him and Francesco during these years, especially the minutes of the Grand Duke's letters, reveal how he used his position to acquire information which he then passed on to the Grand Duke.

27. Unpub. letter Salviati to Vettori, from Rome, dated 12 December 1578, (London, Brit. Mus. Add. MS. 10272, p. 130r and v). Only the signature is Salviati's. The rest is in the hand of his amanuensis.
28. The journey of Francesco to Rome in connection with the legal battle is documented also in another letter of 12 October 1578 to Guglielmo Sirleto, in the *Prose Fiorentine*, ed. Carlo Dati, Florence 1661–1723, Part IV, Vol. 4, pp. 34–35, beginning: 'Francesco mio nipote porgerà questa alla Signoria Vostra Reverendiss. che viene costì per conto d'una nostra lite per aiutarla, come Giurisconsulto, che egli è.' He also indicates the nature of the case, continuing: 'Iacopo mio un anno fa, maritando una sua figliuola, fu ingannato e tradito da un suo amico fedelissimo, e la dette con grossa dote, e tutte le buone parti dell'animo, e del corpo a uno stupido, e furioso prima, e poi, come è noto a tutta la Città. E questo è ora quel, che noi siamo dietro di dissolvere questo matrimonio pieno di miserie per noi, e di vergogna, e la causa si agita costì, come intenderà, o forse ha già inteso V.S. Reverendiss. A questo io non mi posso accordare, perchè è ingiuria troppo atroce, e che si tira dietro tutti i pericoli e danni. La mia nipote è con esso noi in casa, e stette pochi giorni col falso marito, *rediitque integra*: e si gitterebbe prima *in mediam flammam*, che tornare a vivere con un pazzo pubblico.' He then asks Sirleto to give him what help he can. All this confirms that Francesco, as Salviati's letter suggested, had already been in Rome for some time when Lionardo wrote to Vettori. (N.B. that it was to this same Sirleto that Vettori had written on 16 December 1569 asking him to plead with the Pope for an allowance which would enable him to send this same Francesco, then 18, to Pisa to study law, which he did. *Prose fior.*, cit. Parte IV, Vol. 4, pp. 19–21.)
29. Unpub. letter Salviati to Vettori, London, Brit. Mus., Add. MS. 10278 f. 46r. Only the signature is in the hand of Salviati. The rest is written by his usual amanuensis.
30. Salviati gives us much information on his relationship with Valori, and particularly on the circumstances of this first lecture, in the dedicatory letter to Valori of his edition of Passavanti's *Specchio di vera penitenza*, Florence, 1585.
31. The *Discorso intorno alla ribellione di Fiandra* and the *Discorso sopra le prime parole di Cornelio Tacito* both seem to date from this Roman period. The former was published by Manzoni, *Prose inedite*, cit. The second appeared in appendix to Giorgio Dati's Tuscan translation of Tacitus' *Annales*, Venice, Bernardo Giunti e Fratelli, 1582, and was almost certainly influenced by Scipione di Castro, who was with Salviati in Buoncompagni's service in Rome.
32. *Prose*, Book II. The story will be found on pp. 40–41 of the U.T.E.T. edition, ed. Dionisotti, Turin, 1931.
33. *Degli Avvertimenti della lingua sopra 'l Decamerone*, Naples, Raillard, 1712, Vol. I, 'Proemio' to Book III, p. 137.
34. L. Salviati, *Nell'esequie di M. Benedetto Varchi*, Firenze, Giunti, 1566. The dedicatory letter, dated 8.2.1565 (i.e. '66) is to Mons. Lorenzo Lenzi.
35. The memorandum, from which Salviati took a lot of information on Vettori's public life, and some of his more dramatic actions, is still extant and unpublished in the Biblioteca Nazionale Centrale in Florence, Cod. Magl. IX, 64, headed 'Instruttione al Sr. Cav.r Salviati'. Internal evidence makes it quite clear that the

author is Francesco Vettori, though the words 'ANON. Vita di
Pier Vettori' have been inserted in a modern hand on the unnumbered fol. 1 of the Codex. The extent and nature of Salviati's
use of this life of his grandfather by Francesco Vettori is an interesting study on which the present writer is now engaged. Niccolai also
made liberal use of it in his quoted book on Pier Vettori.

36. *Orazione delle lodi di P. Vettori*, ed. cit., p. 6 (in fact unnumbered) of
the oration '. . . sentendomi egli pubblicamente in uficio simile a
questo, anche allora d'ordine vostro, celebrar le lodi d'un mio
onorando, e suo caro amico, dove quelle d'esso Vettorio in alcun
luogo fui costretto di mescolare; per quelle, ch'io diedi al comune
amico, con parole molto notabili alla mia allora giovane età volle
dare animo, com'alcun di voi si rammenta, e ciò, che maggior fu
assai, nelle nobilissime sue scritture viva lasciarne la ricordanza:
ma delle lodi rendute a lui, quasi io avessi, in facendolo, travalicata
la verità (che a tutti parve il contrario) fieramente restò crucciato.'
I do not know in which of his works Vettori makes favourable
mention of Salviati's oration on Varchi, as is implied here. See p. 2
for the extract from Salviati's oration on Varchi to which this
episode refers.

37. *Avvertimenti*, ed. cit., Vol. I, Bk. II, Particella VIII, pp. 80–81.

38. On this detail, whilst agreeing with the theory, Salviati would have
had particular reasons for disagreeing with Vettori over Alamanni,
of whose attempt to reproduce Greek metres in Italian he could
not approve, since he interpreted it, not as applying to the use of
another language qualities of taste and discernment learnt through
the medium of the classics, but as applying to the *volgare* certain
standards—in this case of metre—which were natural to Greek but
unnatural to Italian. The process thus exceeds the bounds of
Vettori's otherwise valid educational theory. Salviati says this in
so many words in his unpublished Commentary on Aristotle,
Florence, Biblioteca Nazionale Centrale, Cod. Magl. VII, 87,
fols. 187v and 188r.

39. Niccolai, op. cit., p. 60. To have a full picture of the relationship as
Vettori saw it between the study of the literary art and rhetoric of
classical antiquity on the one hand, and composition in the *volgare*
on the other, it suffices to read the references (a) in the posthumous
publication *Petr. Vict. Epistolae et orationes XIII et liber de laudibus
Johannae Austriacae*, Florence, Giunti 1586, particularly the *Orationes*
IV and VIII; (b) the so-called 'varie lezioni', of which several
editions, e.g. *P. Victorii variarum lectionum libri xxxviii . . . quorum
librorum veteribus editionis addite sunt quaedam*, Florentiae, 1582.

40. See Niccolai, op. cit., pp. 45–50, who gives detailed information on
the *volgare* production of Vettori which includes: (a)(Published)
*Viaggio di Annibale per la Toscana descritto da Pier Vettori con due lettere
del medesimo a Corrado de' Ricci su l'istesso argomento*, Napoli, 1780,
presso Giuseppe Campo (edit. by Francesco Saverio Gualtieri):
Trattato di Pier Vettori delle lodi e della coltivazione degli ulivi, Florence,
Giunti, 1569. (b) (In MS.) *Spiegazione d'alcune parole della lingua
italiana: Canti di Dante confrontati con Euripide, Virgilio, ecc*: Raccolta
di termini toscani adoperati dall'Aldobrando: *Ristretto della potenza
de' Principi, all'Illustrissimo ed Eccellentissimo Sig. Cosimo de' Medici,
Principe di Siena, mio Signore*. These unpublished works are all in
Munich, (see Halm & Laubmann, *Catalogus Codicum Latinorum*

Bibliothecae Regiae Monacensis, Monachii, a. 1868). Many *volgare* letters of his are published in the *Prose fiorentine,* cit.

41. In the context of a discussion over the origins and development of the *volgare* he writes, on the subject of Tuscan: 'Noster tamen sermo suavior politiorque servatus est, quod aut caeli benignitate aut regionis situ asperitate factum est, quamvis non parva laus etiam tribui debeat maioribus illis nostris florentinis poetis qui labore et industria sua eum expoliverunt et ex magno acervo inconditoque vocabulorum elegantiora splendioraque studiose collegerunt.' (*Epistolae et Orationes,* cit., Oratio VIII.)

42. *Prose fiorentine,* cit., Parte IV, Vol. IV, p. 25, letter 6.2.1573 (i.e. 1574) to Guglielmo Sirleto.

43. Letter Attendolo to Salviati, printed with *Lo 'Nfarinato Secondo, ovvero dello 'Nfarinato Accademico della Crusca, risposta al libro intitolato Republica di Camillo Pellegrino, ecc.,* In Firenze, per Anton Padovani, 1588.

Marino and Donne†

I should perhaps begin by indicating the context in which I think
that a comparison can properly and profitably be made between
these two poets, each of whom is associated in his own country with a
characteristic manner of poetry, and each of whom has enjoyed
great acclaim and endured great disapproval as the pendulum of
critical taste has swung. They were, of course, almost exact contemporaries. Marino was fifty-five years old when he died in 1625,
and Donne may have just reached sixty when he died six years later.
But this fact alone provides scant justification for linking the two,
especially since there is, as far as I am aware, no substantial evidence
for thinking that Marino exercised any direct influence on Donne,
and indeed the majority of the *Elegies* and the *Songs and Sonnets* were
already probably composed when the first edition of Marino's *Rime*
appeared in 1602, For Marino's influence on a number of English
poets a little later in the century, of whom the most celebrated is
probably Crashaw, there is clear documentation in the form of
translations and close adaptations, but for any direct influence on
Donne there is no such evidence.

Nor do the personalities and careers of the two men appear to have
much in common. The story of the Cavalier Marino is that of a
flamboyant extrovert creating his own legend in his own lifetime, a
public man of letters achieving position and wealth through the
power of his pen, a self-proclaiming, self-advertising V.I.P. who,
despite three spells of imprisonment for moral and/or political
offences, won favour in three capitals, first Rome, then Turin, and
finally Paris, before returning to his native Naples a year before his
death. Donne on the other hand, whose verse was published post-
humously, achieved no such public honours and wealth. A secret
marriage to his patron's niece early put paid to any hopes of a

† This paper is a revised version of a lecture delivered on 7th January
1967 to the Annual General Meeting of the Society for Italian Studies
chaired by Professor Whitfield.

brilliant career which the worldly young Jack Donne might have had, a growing family brought domestic and economic cares, hopes of advancement were disappointed, there came illness and the death of his wife, and it is the passionate, sombre voice of Dr. John Donne, Dean of St. Paul's, which speaks in the *Holy Sonnets* and the *Hymns*. Careers as dissimilar as these seem unlikely to offer many points of contact, and indeed it may well be that when we read Marino and Donne, it is the differences between them which will eventually strike us most.

In the meantime, however, is there some common basis on which we can begin to construct a comparison between the two? I think that there is, and that it is to be found in the fact that they are both poets in revolt. Each of them is attempting novelty, each consciously, even ostentatiously, refusing to conform. If one comes to Marino and the Marinisti straight from a representative selection of Cinquecento lyrics, or to Donne's *Elegies* and *Songs and Sonnets* straight from the Elizabethan sonnet sequences of the 1590s, one cannot but feel that in both the gesture of dissent looms large. And if it can be agreed that in both cases it is the fading idiom of sixteenth century Petrarchism which is being rejected, then we have at least an approximate starting-point from which to begin to consider the two poets together. This, at all events, is the way in which I wish to look at them in turn—as major representatives in their respective countries of a move away from the broad Petrarchan tradition which had dominated the lyric of the sixteenth century.

In its stylistic extravagance Marino's verse has all the appearance of literary revolt. Marino is well aware that he is breaking with literary tradition and glories in his originality. His letters, for example, while not containing any explicit statement of a consistent aesthetic theory, show clearly enough that he is aiming at novelty. Writing to Tassoni from Ravenna in 1610, he decries excessive reliance on tradition and pours scorn on those 'poeti tisicuzzi, i quali non sanno fabricare se non sopra il vecchio, né scrivere senza la falsa riga'.[1] And some of his comments on his own works show clearly the direction in which he aims to travel. His *Galeria* is a 'libro curioso per la sua varietà' (*Lettere* p. 143), while his *Dicerie Sacre* he describes as 'cosa stravagante ed inaspettata', and claims that 'faranno stupire il mondo' (*Lettere* p. 167). Poets who cannot achieve brilliance and animation are failures—'I poeti che dettano rime senza vivezze, fabricano cadaveri, non poesie' (*Lettere* p. 420). Literary tradition and authority must thus give way to the needs of the present, and in the interests of this brave new modernism Marino lays valiantly about him. In a letter to Girolamo Preti, for instance, written a year before his death, he claims as a particular virtue his refusal to conform to traditional precepts—'Io pretendo di saper le regole più che non sanno tutti i pedanti insieme, ma la vera regola (cor mio bello) è saper rompere le regole a tempo e luogo, accomodandosi al costume corrente ed al gusto del secolo' (*Lettere* p. 396). Gone are Bembo's decorum and reverence for tradition. Contemporary taste, Marino perceives, makes other demands, and he feels well qualified to meet them and is delighted to do so, for he is a worldly poet openly in search of wealth and position. His craving for recognition and reward is insatiable, and his arrogance will often leave readers of a less uninhibited epoch speechless with incredulous rage. Courtier, literary lion and wit, his capacity for self-display is equalled only by his capacity for self-righteousness, so that when, at Turin, he narrowly escapes assassination at the hands of his exasperated rival Murtola, he does not fail to see in his deliverance the hand of God, and immediately writes to invite his friends to rejoice at this sign of divine favour and protection for himself.

The same impregnable self-esteem supports him in his literary ambitions. He suggests that he is the equal of Tasso—'Iddio mi dotò (la sua mercé) d'intelletto tale, che si sente abile a comporre un poema non meno eccellente di quel che si abbia fatto il Tasso' (*Lettere* p. 141). Unorthodoxy and novelty are the hallmarks of genius, and it is only the elect spirit who ventures to leave the beaten track and strike out on his own:

> Conviensi a non vulgare
> spirito peregrino
> dal segnato sentier sviarsi alquanto,
> e per novo camino
> dietro a novi pensier movere il corso.
>   (*La ninfa avara*[2])

Novelty is the watchword, and Marino is anxious to provide it, but this does not mean that he has no literary roots. On the contrary, his verse is steeped in the Classics, his debt to his beloved Ovid being only one of many, and in a letter to Achillini on the delicate question of imitation and plagiarism, he gives an illuminating account of his own procedure:

> Dal primo dí ch'io incominciai a studiar lettere, imparai sempre a leggere col rampino, tirando al mio proposito ciò ch'io ritrovava di buono, notandolo nel mio zibaldone e servendomene a suo tempo: ché insomma questo è il frutto che si cava dalla lezione de' libri. Cosí fanno tutti i valenti uomini che scrivono. (*Lettere* p. 249)

Thus Marino's verse, whose qualities are aptly described in a favourite phrase of his own as 'sapere e sapore', presents a curious mingling of imitation and novelty, tradition and rebellion, in which material derived from wide reading and study is fashioned to serve an aggressive, new aesthetic. For whereas Petrarch's artistry had been directed towards an ideal of harmony and repose, and the doctrines bequeathed to the Cinquecento by Bembo aimed at a noble, balanced, decorous eloquence, Marino deliberately seeks the audacious and spectacular. The obvious determination to be 'different' from the Petrarchists of the Cinquecento manifests itself in a variety of ways, some of them trivial. For instance, in addition to the golden tresses and alabaster brow of Petrarchan tradition Marino sings also of the dusky charms of his *Bruna Pastorella* (Ferrero p. 509), and in *La Lira* has a sonnet beginning 'Nera sì, ma se' bella', whose pattern was exploited by several of his followers. 'Serva sei ma sei vaga' says Sempronio (Ferrero p. 761), and 'Vecchia sei ma leggiadra' echoes Salomoni who employs the formula with sardonic playfulness (Ferrero p. 908).

It is by combining originality of invention with spectacular stylistic virtuosity that Marino hopes to excel, for these are the qualities he draws particular attention to in his works. Of the *Dicerie Sacre*, for example, he says 'Spero che piaceranno, sí per la novità e bizzaria della invenzione, poiché ciascun discorso contiene una metafora sola, sí per la vivezza dello stile e per la maniera del concettare spiritoso' (*Lettere* p. 167), and in the *Murtoleide*, the satirical series of sonnets ridiculing the unfortunate Murtola, he includes a tercet which is often quoted as a statement of his poetic.

È del poeta il fin la meraviglia
(parlo de l'eccellente, non del goffo):
chi non sa far stupir, vada a la striglia. (Ferrero p. 627)

Hence his constant search for striking stylistic effects and for striking subjects, particularly in the realm of descriptive poetry, for he delights in all opportunities for descriptive bravura. A great lover of the figurative arts, and, as his letters show, himself an avid collector, he composed in the *Galleria* a heterogeneous series of short poems specifically on pictures and sculptures, but his acute pictorial sense is apparent throughout all his writings. He welcomes the challenge of unconventional subjects which he examines with indefatigable interest and curiosity. The stanzas in Canto 5 of the *Adone*, for instance, in which he describes the revolving stage with its variety of scenery and its intricate mechanism, are typical of this descriptive zest. And the cantos dealing with the Garden of Pleasure, with the delights of each of the five senses anatomised in turn, provides further outstanding examples. The lines describing the appearance and function of the nose in Canto 6 and the mouth in Canto 7 are impressive achievements of sheer verbal ingenuity. Singularity of subject is matched by virtuosity of style as he extravagantly exploits rhetorical figures and demonstrates his mastery of rhyme and rhythm in ostentatious tours de force. There is, for example, in Canto 7 a sequence of five stanzas, recalling but exaggerating a shorter passage in Poliziano's *Stanze*,[3] in which he creates a surging Bacchic rhythm by putting three proparoxytones into each line:

Or d'ellera s'adornino e di pampino
i giovani e le vergini più tenere,
e gemina ne l'anima si stampino
l'imagine di Libero e di Venere. (*Adone* VII. 118–122)

As an exuberant technical demonstration the passage is a triumph. Apart from this mastery of rhyme and rhythm, Marino has also at his command all the resources of a rich and wide-ranging vocabulary, and his ear is ever alert to the sensuous, onomatopoeic potential of words. From all his descriptive verse one example must suffice—the splashing fountain in *Adone* 9. It is a fitting choice, for in this century of Baroque fountains, water scenes figure prominently among his impressive descriptions:

Trasformasi l'umor liquido e molle:
volto in raggi, in comete, in stelle il miri.
Miri qui sgorgar globi, eruttar bolle,
là girelle rotar con cento giri,
spuntar rampolli e pullular zampilli,
e guizzi e spruzzi e pispinelli e spilli. (*Adone* IX. 108)

Akin to this zest for onomatopoeia is a liking for assonance and alliteration which can be illustrated by any random page. The swarms of Cupids lamenting the death of Adonis, for instance:

e sfaretrati e con spuntate frecce,
rotte le reti d'or, sciolti i legami,
gittate a terra fiaccole e focili,
fanno a le triste essequie ossequi umili. (*Adone* XVIII. 189)

I have not space to attempt any exposition of the whole range of Marino's rhetorical repertoire—audacious metaphors, plays on words, various repetitive figures, antithesis, oxymoron. It is a formidable armoury, constantly drawn on, often with little regard for psychological verisimilitude. Venus weeps for Adonis, and as she

watches her human lover die, she laments that she, as an immortal,
cannot join him. This is the climax of her grief, but she retains
sufficient presence of mind to play elaborately on words in expressing
it:

Perché per dura ed immutabil sorte
mortalar l'immortal non può la Morte? (*Adone* XVIII. 183)

The demand for verbal ingenuity in final couplets overrides all other
considerations. This verbal sophistication is a constant in Marino's
verse. Even in poems describing events about which he presumably
feels deeply, this is the elaborate form which his expression normally
takes. The canzone on the death of his mother, for instance, opens
with a verbal subtlety:

Torno piangendo a riverir quel sasso,
ove, chi nove lune in sen mi chiuse,
chiuse lasciò le 'ncenerite spoglie. (Ferrero p.409)

This flamboyance is more successful when, as often happens, the
subject matter is itself exotic and colourful. Marino delights in the
stranger manifestations of Nature in all her variety. Beasts and birds,
plants and trees are described exuberantly and profusely in terms
highly charged with pictorial or dramatic potential. Passages like the
last part of the *Orfeo*, where the verse becomes a riot of colour as he
portrays the effect on trees and animals of Orpheus' playing, illustrates this descriptive audacity at its most brilliant:

Il purpureo granato
si ruppe il fianco d'oro, e le nascoste
viscere di rubin tutte gli aperse. (Ferrero p.442)

It is a vision of Nature audacious both in its dwelling on realistic
detail and in the way in which it dramatically animates the world
surrounding mankind. The whole universe lives, breathes, moves
and glitters, and fruitful and bejewelled, it impinges excitingly on all
man's senses. All Nature is sentient and vital, and the poet portrays
it in bold strokes and strident colours. It is an audacious vision
expressed through a hazardous technique. Often the result is taste-
lessly extravagant, and rarely are the good moments sustained. But
amidst much wildness and aesthetic incoherence are to be found
occasional scenes startlingly impressive in their imaginative power,
not only in Marino himself, but in his followers too. Here is a
quatrain of Anton Sale describing springtime succumbing to the
killing heat of summer's dog-days:

De l'arrabbiato Can sotto i latrati,
sotto il ruggir de l'anelante fiera,
io t'ho visto esalare, o primavera,
di moribondo odor gli ultimi fiati. (Ferrero p. 968)

It is a killing savagery and a fleshly dying. And the same intensity
is found in Fontanella's description of a drought, where once more
the metaphors succeed:

Son de la terra i fior bocche funeste,
e sospiri gli odor, lingue le frondi. (Ferrero p. 846)

It is in the vibrant excitement of such descriptive poetry as this that
the greatest positive achievement of the Marinisti is to be sought.
Marino and those who follow him display a close interest in the world
which surrounds them, if only for the fact that it presents a challenge
to their powers and techniques. Their lyrics are filled with little
descriptive vignettes, often extravagantly wrought, often moralistic-
ally commented on. A woman drying her hair, a girl binding books,
a Roman fountain, the hospital of the incurables at Naples—these
are some of the sketches which enliven the pages of the typically
erratic Gianfrancesco Materdona. This is the water falling into his
fountain:

Liquida è l'onda e pur gelata appare,
né di lassù trabocca altro che gelo;
poi se ne forma un curvo e crespo velo,
che si frange in sui marmi e cangia in mare. (Ferrero p. 776)

But this close awareness of the physical world can become a trivial,
quizzical contemplation of the abnormal or the deformed. In avoiding the golden tresses of Laura's descendants the Marinisti sing the
praises not only of dark ladies, but of more grotesque ladies too. In
the wake of the *bella bruna*, there appear *la bella nana, la bella zoppa,
la bella balbuziente* and *la bella tartagliante, la bella losca,* and even *la
bella pidocchiosa.* This last example, from a sonnet of Narducci
(Ferrero p. 820) in which the fauna are described as 'fere d'avorio
in bosco d'oro' was lampooned by Salvator Rosa in his satire *La
Poesia* and thus acquired notoriety as an example of Seicento taste-
lessness. One wonders though how seriously such poems as these
were ever intended, for in a literary atmosphere as sophisticated as
this irony is always a possibility. Marino himself is quite capable of
poking fun at the high-flown style and bejewelled metaphors of
contemporary love-poetry. Eyes of sapphire and mouths of ruby and

pearl, says his aptly-named nymph Filaura in the *Ninfa Avara* are not to be bought with sighs and protestations, but with gold.

More significant evidence of a concentration on repulsive aspects of reality can be found outside the love-poetry, in for example Marino's *Strage degli Innocenti*. This work he himself rated very highly, but to us the narration of the horrors of the massacre with a wealth of realistic physical detail and a complete lack of psychological or emotional participation in the tragedy depicted, will probably seem a repellent piece of writing, which exposes starkly the author's limitations. As one atrocity follows another, and the babes are butchered in a minutely described variety of ways, no pity is generated and the scene remains emotionally inanimate. Marino's effective appeal as a poet is to the senses, not to the emotions or the mind. He can paint a scene so that colours, shapes, movements make an exciting impact, but he cannot fill his scene with people or tell of human predicaments. He is no narrative or dramatic poet and hence the failure, as a whole, of the *Adone*. True, in the Ovidian atmosphere of the *Adone* there is much which his particular gifts can exploit, for the world of classical mythology, with its opportunities for descriptive embellishment and hence stylistic display, is his most congenial habitat. But a tragic theme like the slaughter of the innocents finds him virtually destitute. The absence of the human element from his scenes, much more than any stylistic extravagance, is the great weakness of Marino. There is a fundamental failure, despite, or perhaps indeed because of, his technical brilliance, to create a coherent idiom for dealing with the emotional and psychological lives of human beings, and this ultimately invalidates his poetic world. The deeper emotional and spiritual aspects of experience elude him. The physical he portrays excitingly.

The best known passages of the *Adone* illustrate how the sensuous and the physical predominate in his verse—the stanzas in the third canto, for example, where Venus sings the praises of the rose which brought about her meeting with Adonis, or the voluptuous eighth canto describing the consummation of their love. Beauty is physical, woman a creature to be caressed and enjoyed. The kiss, which for the Neo-Platonists symbolised the mingling of souls, and in the *Aminta* belonged to an innocent world of the senses, becomes in Marino's verse a frequently treated subject for sophisticated sensualism. Some of his writing is frankly lascivious, and indeed one of his reasons for publishing the *Adone* in Paris was the tactical one that he feared its 'lascivette amorose' might incur criticism in Counter-Reformation Italy. He had no moral scruples on the subject, and swept the whole matter aside with the cynic's traditional disclaimer that 's'oscena è la penna, è casto il core' (*Adone* VIII. 6). And he claims the *Adone*

to be a moral poem because it shows, ultimately, how sensual pleasure
ends in sorrow!

Però dal vel, che tesse or la mia tela
in molli versi e favolosi e vani,
questo senso verace altri raccoglia:
smoderato piacer termina in doglia. (*Adone* l. 10)

Marino marks the end of an epoch. He is the last of a line of Italian
poets, beginning with Petrarch, who were regarded throughout
Europe as authoritative writers. Between the first and last of the line
there is a vast difference, both in temperament and in aesthetic aim.
Petrarch is painfully introspective, Marino exuberantly extrovert.
Petrarch's aesthetic aims at harmony and repose, Marino's at excitement and wonder.

And yet, despite the cult of *novità*, Marino in one fundamental way
maintains and strengthens the established tradition of Italian verse—
by accepting the craft-concept of poetry and maintaining, even indeed accentuating, the life-literature dichotomy dominant in Italian
verse from the Sicilians onwards. By making the craft element in
poetry more spectacularly conspicuous, he reinforces even further the
already solid rhetorical tradition of Italian verse.

Let us now turn to Donne and the English poetic scene in the
years just before and after 1600. In Donne, as in Marino, there is
evident a desire to speak in an idiom different from that of others.
Indeed Donne may well appear the more radical of the two, for
whereas it could be argued that Marino aims at individuality by
concentrating on and exacerbating rhetorical tendencies already
present in the tradition before him, Donne seems to be at pains to
reject tradition ostentatiously, lock, stock and barrel. Petrarchan con-
ventionalism, first introduced by Wyatt and Surrey, and later
definitively established by Sidney's *Astrophil and Stella*, had taught
English poets many valuable lessons and culminated in the sonnet-
vogue of the 1590s when the sonnet sequences poured from the
presses. If one comes to Donne directly from these sequences, one
cannot but be struck immediately, on reading the Ovidian elegies or
the more 'scandalous' of the *Songs and Sonnets*, by the element of protest in them and their utter rejection of the Petrarchan tradition. It
is a rejection so complete as to appear like a deliberate polemical
gesture, and if we accept Professor Helen Gardner's persuasive
dating of many of these aggressive lyrics in years before 1600, that is
in the decade of the sonnet sequences, we will find little difficulty in
agreeing with Mario Praz that 'Donne must have actually felt in
opposition to the poetry of his day'.[4] This spirit of opposition, whilst

it does not, of course, comprehensively define Donne's whole literary position, does make itself strongly felt. He must indeed have felt a rebel against the prevailing poetic fashion, and as is the wont of angry young men, he sardonically expressed his refusal to conform in as extreme a manner as possible, rejecting completely, point by point, the conventionalisation of love which he found in the Petrarchan lyric, turning away from the sonnet form, and cultivating an intensely personal, dramatic tone. His abhorrence of the derivative is stated with characteristic virulence in *Satire 2*:

> But hee is worst, who (beggarly) doth chaw
> Others wits fruits, and in his ravenous maw
> Rankly digested, doth those things out-spue,
> As his owne things. (ll. 25–28)

Certainly Donne himself, as far as the Petrarchan tradition is concerned, cannot be accused of being derivative, for his attitudes are, as often as not, diametrically opposed to those of the Petrarchists. The convention takes the lover's constancy as a matter of course, so Donne, at times, ostentatiously champions promiscuity:

> I can love her, and her, and you and you,
> I can love any, so she be not true. (*The Indifferent*[5])

Marino too writes of his *Amore Incostante*:

> Non ha sol un oggetto
> il mio bramoso affetto:
> cento princìpi e cento
> trov'io del mio tormento;
> sempre che vada o miri,
> sempre ho nove cagioni ond'io sospiri. (Ferrero p.399)

Thematically this is similar to Donne's *The Indifferent*, but stylistically and in artistic intention it has nothing in common with the monosyllabic directness of Donne. 'Sempre ho nove cagioni ond'io sospiri' creates a very different effect from 'I can love her, and her, and you and you'. Women, says Donne in this mood, exist for men's pleasure, to be taken, rejected, or just ignored, at will:

> But they are ours as fruits are ours,
> He that but tasts, he that devours,
>   And he which leaves all, doth as well:
> Chang'd loves are but chang'd sorts of meat,
> And when hee hath the kernell eate,
>   Who doth not fling away the shell? (*Communitie*)

Instead of Petrarchan submissiveness, outrageous masculine sexual arrogance sweeps poem after poem along. But at least there is equality of the sexes, for women have the same freedom:

> Foxes and goats; all beasts change when they please,
> Shall women, more hot, wily, wild then these,
> Be bound to one man, and did Nature then
> Idly make them apter to'endure then men?
> They'are our clogges, and their owne; if a man bee
> Chain'd to a galley, yet the galley'is free. (*Change*)

Professor Gardner mentions Tasso's 'O bell'età de l'oro' as one of two main literary sources for Donne's advocacy of sexual freedom as a reflection of Nature's laws (the other being Ovid). In a very general sense this may be so, but Donne's earthy argumentativeness and his urgent, colloquial, first-person, here and now tone are far removed from the evocative lyricism of Tasso's musical chorus celebrating a remote world of myth and innocence.

Just as he replaces traditional constancy with a cynically witty championing of promiscuity, so Donne replaces spiritual adoration with a physical passion which is frank and intense, and often proclaimed with polemical aggressiveness:

> Who ever loves, if hee doe not propose
> The right true end of love, hee's one which goes
> To sea for nothing but to make him sicke. (*Loves Progress*)

Intense moments of physical lovemaking are freely depicted, and at times the tone becomes openly licentious. But the erotic excitement which animates his poems does not derive from physical description. The visual element in his verse is relatively slight, and this constitutes another important difference between Donne and Marino. The world of Marino is brilliantly sensuous, outward, visual, audible, tactile; that of Donne is dramatic, personal, inward. The women Donne cajoles, caresses, bullies or reviles, are dynamically present in the effect they have upon him and as receivers of his reactions, but they are not themselves much described. Description as such is too static an element to have much place in the essentially dramatic, argumentative texture of his verse.

Throughout the Elegies and in certain of the Songs and Sonnets, such as those I have quoted, the aggressively 'scandalous' element is strong. Tradition is being defiantly flouted and the outrageous openly proclaimed. Much of the vitality of such poems consists in the flourish of wit with which a startling attitude is imposed, startling both in relation to the conventions of love-poetry and current social morality. The piquancy and ingenuity of these anti-demonstrations are the poems' main concern, and their spirit is akin to that of the wilfully disputatious prose of the *Paradoxes and Problems*. Indeed the very violence of the tone of dissent and protest contained in poems of this sort comes to constitute paradoxically a bond between them and the convention they are rejecting, and in a sense Donne thus remains within the orbit of European Petrarchism. We feel him to be utterly impatient at the selective and formalised myth which the relationship between man and woman has become in the sonnet sequences, and determined to shatter the myth and talk more realistically about what goes on between the sexes.

More important than the rebellious substitution of an image of ardent sexuality for the conventional image of decorous idealisation, and of cynicism and its attendant realistic details for traditional adoration, is the stylistic revolution which accompanies this process. For Donne aims to create an impression of actuality by establishing a colloquial conversational level of discourse, more akin to the briskness of the stage than to traditional concepts of lyrical eloquence. The vigorous forward movement of argument or illustration leaves no room for surface ornament, and thus mythological embellishments, indeed the whole world of classical mythology so dear to Marino, have no place in his verse. The lyric verse-form of the 1590s, the sonnet, which by its very architectonics imposes a formal pattern on material, he discards. Instead he uses in the *Songs and Sonnets* a variety of stanza forms, whose very diversity, when one reads through the whole collection, helps to create and maintain an impression of the directness and restlessness of untrammelled speech. The mingling of long and short lines to produce varying rhythms, copious use of elision and synaloepha, the sharpness of direct questions and monosyllabic imperatives, the frequency of personal pronouns and demonstratives, the use of irregular speech pattern to render metrical pattern less obtrusive, the employment of unemphatic rhymes—all these features aim at urgency and are designed to set up the poem from the outset as a dramatic actuality. They are quite different stylistic features from the expansive rhetorical figures of Marino. Marino attempts to revivify the poetic idiom via a brave new inflation, Donne cuts it down to sinew and bone. The *Songs and Sonnets*, and the religious poems too for that matter, abound in vivid openings which impose a situation with striking power, and this trenchant dramatic attack, utterly different in its objectives both from the harmony of Petrarch and the *maraviglia* of Marino, remains characteristic of Donne throughout the whole range of his verse, even after he abandons the programmatic, anti-Petrarchan role of cynical amorist and enriches his love-poetry by introducing moods and attitudes encompassing the most disparate experiences of love. There is the impatience of youth at the sedate advice of mature wisdom in the young lover's cry of 'For Godsake hold your tongue and let me love'. There is a contentment and confidence in love so secure that it can relax and indulge in the playfulness of

> Busie old foole, unruly Sunne,
>   Why dost thou thus,
> Through windowes, and through curtaines call on us?
> (*The Sunne Rising*)

The sad sweetness of a tender parting inspires poems like

> Sweetest love, I do not goe,
>   For wearinesse of thee. (*Song*)

And the same tender sense of complete involvement in and identification with his beloved produces

> If yet I have not all thy love,
>   Deare, I shall never have it all. (*Loves Infiniteness*)

These poems vary in mood, but the initial dramatic attack is the same in all of them. They are not musing soliloquies, but are presented as direct address, demanding a hearer. From first and second person openings such as these the poems spiral away into debate or illustration or dialectical discourse which may be seriously intensifying or wittily detached. The attitude may be tender or critical, serious or mocking, or, as often as not, ambiguous in its mingling of diverse intonations, but at all times the poem aims at creating an impression of a movement forward, a theme which is growing even as the words are being uttered. Here are no past tenses. Instead we hear the language of an evolving, contemporaneous actuality. Sometimes it is an actuality of authentic-sounding sentiment we are offered, sometimes a half-acknowledged pseudo-actuality of dialectical cleverness. In either case the initial imaginative assault is strong, the aesthetic objective original, and the conceits employed are not decorative, as in Marino, but structural, bearing the argument of the poem along.

Inevitably Donne at times employs traditional Petrarchan themes, but what probably strikes the reader who recognises the Petrarchan situation is the way in which Donne's individual tone utterly transforms it. The monosyllabic dramaticity of the openings, the sinewy intellectual tone of the developing argument, the original twists of sentiment, all give quite new character to traditional themes. The transplanting of the heart from mistress to lover or vice-versa, often a topic treated in terms of subjection and constancy, becomes in *The Legacie* a subject of almost clinical scrutiny as the poet opens up his breast and finds, not his own heart, but hers. The comment is factual and wryly disconsolate:

> Yet I found something like a heart,
>   But colours it, and corners had,
>   It was not good, it was not bad,
> It was intire to none, and few had part.

In the same way the dream or vision of the beloved receives a highly original treatment from Donne. As he sleeps, his mistress enters the room where he is dreaming of her, and wakes him as his dream reaches a climax:

> Therefore thou wakd'st me wisely; yet
> My Dreame thou brok'st not, but continued'st it,
> Thou art so true, that thoughts of thee suffice,
> To make dreames truth; and fables histories;
> Enter these armes, for since thou thoughtst it best,
> Not to dreame all my dreame, let's do the rest. (*The Dreame*)

The theme of lovers parting he also handles in a highly distinctive manner in the four *Valediction* poems, exploring a whole range of emotions, far from consistent or homogeneous in character, but each conveying a convincing version of the same human situation. *A Valediction: of Weeping* depicts a self-abandonment to the sheer grief of separation which, though honest in itself, serves also to block disquieting glimpses into future danger or anxieties, the foreboding that something vital is dying, the fear that a sterile oneness lies ahead. In *A Valediction: of my Name in the Window* one at least of these anxieties comes to the fore, for here he clearly doubts her fidelity, and his chief concern in engraving his name in glass is to keep his memory before her when he is gone. *A Valediction: forbidding Mourning* has no room for fear or suspicion, for here the love celebrated is one which rises above the senses and can triumph over physical separation:

> Our two soules therefore, which are one,
>   Though I must goe, endure not yet
> A breach, but an expansion,
>   Like gold to ayery thinnesse beate.

And the famous compass image illustrates how indivisibly linked they are. The fourth treatment of the theme, *A Valediction: of the Booke*, generates less emotional tension than the other three. It wittily enthrones love as the supreme experience from which men of all types can learn wisdom, but the nature of the bond which links the lovers is nevertheless quite seriously defined. It is complete, secure and satisfying, encompassing as it does both 'abstract spirituall love' and 'Something which they may see and use', and his confidence in its stability is such that he can afford to be philosophical about the prospect of separation:

> How great love is, presence best tryall makes,
> But absence tryes how long this love will bee.

The moods of the four *Valedictions* are thus quite different, but together they offer a varied treatment of a single situation and illuminate it richly by the multiplicity and power of their differing dramatisations of it. Perhaps un-Petrarchan, rather than anti-Petrarchan, is how we should describe the range of Donne's love-poetry outside the ostentatiously scandalous moments. What impresses most is the powerful tone of conviction he can give to a diversity of attitudes extending from tenderness to recrimination, from platonic idealism to a confident sharing of physical pleasure with his partner, from joy and wonder to satiety and disillusionment. In these poems the traditional Petrarchan reference points are gone, and instead Donne is free to examine uninhibitedly all the potential aspects of the emotional and physical experience of being in love. Sometimes one aspect is thrown into relief, sometimes another as the mood varies between a resentful, jagged individualism to a feeling of peace in the bliss of physical and spiritual union. In the course of his self-explorations and self-dramatisations he discharges many roles and shows himself, with varying degrees of seriousness, in a variety of attitudes and voicing the most diverse sentiments. The unrequited lover of the *Broken Heart* can be the supremely contented lover of the *Anniversarie*. The joyous, passionate rapture of *The Sunne Rising* and the intimate affection of *Loves Infiniteness* can be replaced by the wounded bitterness of *Twicknam Garden*. The impatient desire of 'For Godsake hold your tongue, and let me love' in *The Canonization* can, in disappointment, become 'imposture all' and 'the short scorne of a Bridegroomes play' in *Loves Alchymie*, and the consummation of love can leave 'A kinde of sorrowing dulnesse to the minde' in *Farewell to Love*. This portrayal of the love relationship as a complex phenomenon involving the whole of the human personality and not as a literary myth organised along conventional, literary lines, combined with his stylistic originality and his intensely dramatic conception of the dynamics of a poem, makes Donne's an utterly distinctive voice.

And yet, if we look back over the last decades of the sixteenth century in England, when Italian influence was at its peak, Donne's reaction can be recognised as the radical expression of a tendency latent all along in the English literary consciousness. And it was a tendency which in the ultimate analysis ran counter to one fundamental feature of the Italian legacy. By and large, Italian poetry tended to look to literary tradition as an authoritative controlling factor, and accepted an autonomous formalism as a motive force in writing. Among the Elizabethans, even while still learning from the Italians, there became apparent a desire to accord more importance to the urgency and drama of real experience and to make writing more relevant to and expressive of living. Thus Sidney himself, in his *Apology for Poetry* stresses 'forcibleness' as an essential ingredient of poetry, and attacks contemporary love poetry for its lack of conviction:

> But truly many of such writings as come under the banner of unresistible love, if I were a mistress, would never persuade me they were in love; so coldly they apply fiery speeches, as men that had rather read lovers' writings...than that in truth they feel those passions.[6]

And Samuel Daniel too, who in his sonnet sequence *Delia* appears as the most Italian in spirit among the Elizabethan sonneteers, later speaks in a different tone in his *Defence of Ryme*:

> Eloquence and gay wordes are not of the Substance of wit, it is but the garnish of a nice time,...Hunger is as well satisfied with meat served in pewter as silver.[7]

And at another point he declares:

> The most iudiciall and worthy spirites of this Land are not so delicate, or will owe so much to their eare, as to rest uppon the out-side of wordes, and be intertained with sound.[8]

This difference in spirit is, it seems to me, confirmed and well illustrated by the comparison between Marino and Donne which I have attempted to make. Marino, confronted with a declining poetic idiom, aims to revive it by a potent injection of rhetorical violence. Donne's reaction is to reject it and to substitute for it a style which is sinewy, colloquial, and in any traditional sense 'unpoetic'. Marino's verse invites the reader to wonder at the musical and decorative quality of language and the virtuosity of the craftsman-poet. Donne's introduces him with monosyllabic urgency to drama, to argument, and to human predicament.

University of Birmingham DAVID REES

NOTES

1. Giambattista Marino, *Lettere*, ed. M. Guglielminetti, Turin, 1966. p. 110. All references to Marino's letters in the body of the article are to this edition.
2. *Marino e i Marinisti*, ed. G. G. Ferrero, Milan, 1954, p. 534. All verse quotations from Marino and his followers in the body of the article are from this anthology.
3. *Stanze*, Book 1, 111–112. The passage, which also describes a Bacchic scene begins
    Vien sopra un carro d'ellera e di pampino
    Coverto Bacco, il qual due tigri guidono.
4. Mario Praz, 'Donne's relation to the poetry of his time', p. 71, in *John Donne, a collection of critical essays*, ed. Helen Gardner, Englewood Cliffs N.J., 1962.
5. All quotations from the *Elegies and the Songs and Sonnets* are from the edition by Helen Gardner, Oxford, 1965. The titles given at the end of each quotation provide sufficient identification.
6. Sir Philip Sidney, *An Apology for Poetry*, ed. G. Shepherd, London, 1965. p. 137.
7. Samuel Daniel, *Poems and a Defence of Ryme*, ed. A. C. Sprague, Phoenix Edition, 1965. p. 145.
8. ibid. p. 154.

Quattro Capitoli inediti di Michelangelo
Buonarroti il Giovane

I quattro Capitoli, o epistole, in terzine sono indirizzati a Niccolò Arrighetti, e figurano nel codice marucelliano A37, fra molti altri componimenti dello stesso autore, ivi comprese le nove satire che sono a stampa; il codice è autografo, e fu riconosciuto come opera del Buonarroti un secolo e mezzo fa da F. Del Furia.[1] Le cc. 83–94 recano la prima stesura, o minuta, con molti pentimenti; nelle cc. 67–79 si legge la 'bella copia', o seconda stesura. La dedica porta la data del 2 luglio 1637.

Il Buonarroti doveva avere da tempo legami d'amicizia coll'Arrighetti,[2] che era più giovane di lui di diciott'anni: come il Buonarroti, anch'egli apparteneva almeno dal 1612 all'Accademia Fiorentina, di cui anzi era stato console, e dal 1603 all'Accademia della Crusca, davanti alla quale aveva recitato orazioni; era discepolo di Galileo, poeta lirico e scrittore di drammi e commedie (il Buonarroti aveva dettato gli Intermedi per la sua commedia *La Gratitudine*, rappresentata nel carnevale del 1628[3]), grecista, filosofo e studioso di Platone e dei classici italiani: insomma, un congeniale compagno di studi, oltre che di passatempi.

I quattro capitoli evocano e commemorano un soggiorno del Buonarroti nella Villa Montedomini, situata a una quindicina di chilometri da Firenze, a nord della strada che conduce a Prato, villa che l'Arrighetti si era sforzato di ingrandire e di abbellire, edificandovi un 'bello oratorio',[4] ed iniziando proprio allora i lavori per costruirvi 'Un gran salone, e più innanzi una loggia/Da farvi a qualche tempo un bel convito'.[5] Il Buonarroti, che vi si trattenne otto giorni,[6] afferma che era questa la sua prima visita;[7] ma la Satira prima, dedicata appunto all'Arrighetti, e scritta certamente nel 1632,[8] dimostra che doveva già conoscere bene non solo la sua ubicazione ('fra Monte Morello e Cantagrilli', v. 11; tra i 'valdimarini poggi', v. 28–9) ma anche le occupazioni a cui l'amico attendeva in villa: o che avesse risieduto nelle vicinanze, o che vi fosse fuggevolmente passato; certo è che ancora nel 1633 l'Arrighetti, scrivendogli da Montedomini, deplorava che egli non vi avesse mai soggiornato: 'S'io credessi ch'ella venissi la 'nviterei a venir a star otto giorni da me, che forse non le dispiacerebbe la stanza'.[9]

I quattro componimenti presentano le medesime caratteristiche di gran parte dei lavori poetici del Buonarroti, e in particolare delle satire: hanno lo stesso tono bonario e discorsivo, lo stesso andamento un po' prosaico, come, del resto, si conveniva al tema, che è la descrizione e celebrazione della Villa Montedomini, e dei piaceri della vita che vi si conduceva; argomento quanto mai adatto alla musa di un poeta che era sensibile agli stimoli della vita rustica, amava la campagna e godeva di osservare i contadini nel loro ambiente. I versi, le terzine fluivano facili dalla sua penna; troppo facili, forse; sì che anche questi capitoli soffrono del difetto di quasi tutti i suoi lavori poetici: la prolissità, il moltiplicarsi delle digressioni, al punto che occorrono non meno di 799 versi a concludere l'argomento. È ben vero che solo nei primi due capitoli, pur perdendo spesso il filo del discorso, e lasciandosi distrarre ad ogni istante, e verso tutte le direzioni, l'autore si attiene all'assunto, e cioè descrive la villa dell'amico ed il sito che essa occupa, nonché l'accoglienza che vi aveva ricevuto. Negli ultimi due non sembra che tenti nemmeno di attenersi ad uno svolgimento ordinato e, saltando di palo in frasca, si dà a narrare una serie di episodi, quali più e quali meno divertenti, allo scopo di illustrare la serenità dell'ambiente e l'ameno succedersi delle giornate in quei luoghi giocondi e spensierati. Egli stesso è consapevole di dilungarsi più del dovuto, e non manca di deplorare a più riprese il suo vizio: 'Mutar non so l'intrapreso costume, / Mi fermo a ogn'osteria, m'arresto a i ponti, / Si spegne ognor di mia lanterna il lume';[10] ma poi gli bastano appena nove versi di considerazioni simili a questa per rimettersi in carreggiata! Il fatto è che egli non poneva troppo impegno nella composizione delle sue epistole, e magari non le teneva in gran conto; altrove egli afferma: 'Il mio comporre è opra di granata / Che, trascurato e lasciato alla polvere, / Ne fa di quando in quando ragunata'.[11]

Eppure, errerebbe chi credesse che queste benevole chiacchierate, piene di garbo, non ripaghino la fatica di spolverarle e farle conoscere dopo tre secoli e mezzo di oblio. Certo il loro pregio precipuo sta nello strumento di cui disponeva il Buonarroti: il puro, ricco, fluido idioma fiorentino.[11a] Se spesso il diluito dettato fa languire l'attenzione del lettore, l'interesse linguistico non viene mai meno; da quel consumato cruscante e lessicografo che era, egli aveva sulla punta delle dita un imponente corredo di vocaboli tolti dalla parlata toscana, di fiorite locuzioni, di eleganti proverbi e modi proverbiali: non per niente era stato 'pars magna' di ben tre edizioni del dizionario della Crusca. Ma aveva altresì nutrito la mente di letture degli autori del 'buon secolo', e il suo discorso è adorno qua e là di vere e proprie citazioni, soprattutto del prediletto Dante (per es., Cap. I, v. 175; Cap. II, v. 93), ma anche del Petrarca (Cap. II, v. 70); né mancano quelli che dovevano essere già allora veri e propri arcaismi ('sozzopra', nella prima stesura del v. 183, Cap. II; 'sucitar', v. 197, ibid.; 'guarnello', v. 175, Cap. III). Quanto allo stile, esso si rifà, se mai, agli scrittori del Cinquecento, o magari a quelli dei secoli precedenti, più che ai contemporanei; Firenze si mantenne quasi del tutto estranea alla moda del marinismo, e in questi componimenti non si rinvengono che rari esempi di bisticci, come 'orti senz'ortica' (Cap. II, v. 22), 'voglia svogliata' (ibid., v. 30), 'se da inalzar lor versi io versi avessi' (Cap. IV, v. 45).

I motivi d'interesse non si esauriscono, peraltro, nell'aspetto linguistico o stilistico. Non meno delle satire, i quattro Capitoli ci tramandano un ritratto fedele della simpatica figura dell'autore, attristato di tanto in tanto, 'com'uso è de' vecchi' (Satira V, v. 45), da preoccupazioni e accessi di malinconia in questi anni di età oramai avanzata ('I pensier dico che torbidi, e neri / Vengonti intorno ognor mosche culaie,[12] / Né si lascian quetar pungenti, e fieri', Cap. I, vv. 13-15), ma fondamentalmente ottimista e pronto al sorriso, e amante delle liete brigate, come quella che gli aveva dato il benvenuto a Montedomini: 'Ma giunti a casa di quivi a un po' / Se vi si fe' di risa un carnovale / Ditel voi, gli altri il dicano, io 'l dirò' (Cap. IV, vv. 94-6); insomma, qui, 'Dov'appesi i pensier tutti ad un chiodo / O nelle tazze di rubin sommersi' (Cap. IV, vv. 175-6) egli si sentiva veramente libero da ogni cura e felice, qui poteva dimenticare il peso del vecchio dilemma 'città-campagna', così vivo in questo cortigiano e frequentatore di accademie che pure era un innamorato della vita rustica, abbandonarsi allo spensierato godimento di ciò che massimamente gli era gradito, e sgombrare per qualche giorno la mente dall'irresistibile attrattiva che, suo malgrado, la città esercitava su di lui:

> Quest'è 'l vero goder; quest'è lo spasso;
>   Perché non son io nato un contadino,
>   Ma un contadin de' contadin papasso,
> Ch'abbia sempre il suo spillo al botticino,[13]
>   Dietro all'uscio di camera il prosciutto,
>   E buon pollaio con qualche latticino?
> Tutto 'l resto del mondo mi par brutto
>   Fuor che dove si gode quel che piace.[14]

Così questo assiduo cultore della poesia rusticale vagheggiava l'ideale di un'esistenza in campagna, irrealizzabile per lui, ma sinceramente sentito ed espresso; e si deve a questo punto sottolineare come il sentimento della natura parlasse al Buonarroti assai più che alla maggior parte dei suoi contemporanei o perfino degli uomini delle due o tre generazioni seguenti; nei quattro Capitoli, poi, esso è vivo e spesso viene in primo piano; non si vuol già dire che egli fosse un romantico avanti lettera, ed avvertisse il fascino della natura incolta e selvaggia: era ancora troppo presto; ma apprezzava la campagna curata dalla mano dell'uomo, adorna e amena, o utile per le sue messi e i suoi prodotti; e fin qui niente di notevole o di diverso dai modelli tradizionali dei secoli precedenti e dell'antichità. Quello che si rinviene, di veramente nuovo e fresco, è che, a guardar bene, egli non si rifà a questi modelli, non ripete meccanicamente formule annose, ma, si direbbe, descrive dal vero, ed esprime con spontaneità i moti del suo animo, e il piacere delle sane gite pei colli; sono questi i momenti più felici dei quattro Capitoli, perché il realismo della narrazione tempera un poco il dimesso tono della musa del Buonarroti e, se non accende la fiamma della poesia, pure porta una nota di vivacità:

O che piacere, o che spasso, o che gioco
   Di selva in selva far soavi gite,
   Sudati, e stanchi riposarsi un poco;
Agevolar le ripide salite
   Col dar lo sguardo alla campagna amena,
   Onde riconfortarvi il cuor sentite;
E quando quella valle è più serena
   Sedersi spensierati in sur un sasso,
   Su le frasche, su l'erbe, su la rena
(Sare' poltroneria un materasso)
   Tenendo gli occhi rivolti allo 'n giù,
   Star a veder su la riviera il passo,
Lettighe, e some andar di giù, e di su,
   Star a udir (che vi rimbomba l'ecco)
   Venire i vetturali a tu per tu.
. . . .
Che gusto andar di lieta compagnia,
   Quest'a pie', quel su l'asin, quello in sella,
   E pe' boschi talor smarrir la via;
Posarsi a un fonte e più di una novella
   Contare or vera, e ora imaginata.[15]

E soprattutto c'è il sapore concreto, ricco di particolari colti dal vero, di una vita di campagna ormai scomparsa e irricuperabile, che esala da questi versi, proprio come accade talvolta quando, aprendo un vecchio armadio, se ne sprigiona un odore d'altri tempi. Né vi sono soltanto i dettagli del costume secentesco, dei giochi che allora si facevano, dei cibi che si cucinavano:

Dar mano agli stidion[15a] puliti e netti,
  E gran tegami apparecchiar lardati;
Cuocerne arrosto, e lessi, e far guazzetti,
  Stufati, marinati, e fricassee,
  E refriggeri,[16] e pasticci, e tocchetti,[17]
Caricarne le barche, e le galee,
  E le some, mandarne a' monasteri
  Per rinvertirli in torte, e in treggee,[18]
E in quei calicion[19] morbidi e leggieri,
  In cotognati, e in quei marron franciosi,
  Che sarebbe me' dir datteri veri;
O più tosto in quei fior miracolosi,
  Fior d'arancio in conserva, e confettati
  Che Sant'Agata[20] fa sì saporosi.[21]

Ci balzano anche agli occhi continuamente i bozzetti di tipici abitanti della campagna, per lo più senza gusto di parodia, amorosamente osservati e ritratti in pochi tocchi, parlanti, da un poeta rusticale che univa al godimento della vita agreste il piacere di studiare il carattere dei villani, la loro rozza parlata, la loro salubre esistenza. Il primo che incontriamo è il prete di Travalle, martire della gotta:

Ci venne incontro, e sopra le mutande
  Il copria la camicia, e sopra quella
  Un zimarron che 'n sino a' pie' si spande.
Altra non gli vid'io giubba, o gonnella,
  Ch'avea cenato, e volev' ire a nanna
  Dalla gotta inchiodato che 'l martella,
E sta sempre fra 'l letto e la ciscranna[22]
  E si dispera, e la sacra, e la taglia
  (Un ch'ha la gotta va tu e lo scanna).[23]

Assai più singolare è Tabosso, lo sfaccendato del villaggio, che per campare si esibisce ai villici in qualità di mangiatore di ranocchi e di uccelli vivi, a pagamento, come è naturale, e con una tariffa che varia a seconda dell'animale da inghiottire:

Che dirò del magnanimo Tabosso
  Che si mangia i ranocchi belli e vivi,
  Né gli fan mal, né 'l corpo gli fan grosso!
E gli augelletti garruli, e lascivi,
  Becco, pie', penne ingoia per quattro soldi;
  Vuol pe' ranocchi sei giuli effettivi.[24]

Leggermente più caricaturale è il bozzetto dedicato ai due bellimbusti che ronzano attorno alle figlie della cerusichessa; ma uno di loro esce scornato dall'innocente avventura, e si trova un bel giorno ridotto dall'indisposizione della sua amata ad accontentarsi di far la corte... alla madre di lei; i termini arcaici con cui sono ritratti i due 'leggiadri amanti' danno risalto alla caricatura:

Difficil, dura e perigliosa impresa
  Della cerusichessa le figliuole
  Alzare al cielo, e soma è che mi pesa.
. . . .
Folle la madre di bellezze tali,
  Che vagheggiate, o 'n chiesa o su pe' canti,
  Paion far convertir gli huomini in pali:
Sempre hanno dietro due leggiadri amanti
  Che le servon di coppa e di coltello,
  E vengon via su duo destrier volanti.
Ciascun di lor vestito di guarnello,[25]
  In calzette scarnate,[26] adorno il crine
  Di viole, e di brucioli[27] il cappello.
In appressarsi a quelle alme, divine
  Bellezze (ch'han così di dirle usanza
  Quei che nel cor sentono d'amor le spine)
Saltan di sella e ciascun la sua amanza[27a]
  Mette a cavallo, e fa da servitore,
  E parli il sol toccar per la baldanza.
Ma ingrato, crudo, e dispietato amore,
  Fato nemico, e stelle empie, e funeste,
  Ch'una inchiodata in letto il suo amatore
Fa stare in doglia: e voi meco il vedeste
  Svogliato parer mordersi le mane
  Quando, salendo per l'alte foreste,
Sudando, ansando, trottando l'alfane,[28]
  Con la sorella non la vide in coppia,
  Arrabbiando d'invidia com'un cane.
Rigna,[29] si strugge, e ponza, e sbuffa, e scoppia
  Per ché la dama sua non può servire,
  Massime che 'l dolor gli si raddoppia,
Che vede l'altro innanzi al suo desire,
  Innanzi all'alma propria, al proprio core,
  Che per dolcezza sta per isvenire.
Per lui non v'ebbe partito migliore
  Che por la madre ove dovea star lei
  E lei far cavalcare, e farle onore.[30]

Poco o nulla ci rivelano i quattro capitoli intorno all'Arrighetti e alla sua famiglia, all'infuori dell'ospitale accoglienza che avevano fatta al poeta; non apprendiamo che i nomi, o poco più, della sua consorte Gostanza, dedita a raccontar pettegolezzi, come aveva fatto un giorno 'tornando dalla chiesa, / Dove n'è sempre una grande abbondanza'[31] e di due figli, 'Noferi vostro e Gian Luigi', i quali con la feroce lor sirocchia / Giucando venir sogliono a' litigi';[32] ma forse era figlio di Niccolò Arrighetti anche quell'adorabile Cosimino, suonatore di zufolo,

> Che mentre il suona, e torce quel bocchino,
>   E con le dita d'ebano il percuote,
>   Vi volta a sghembo un cotal occhiolino[33]

(notazione colta dal vero, questa, e di notevole modernità).

La lettura di questa pacata cronaca di giornate serene lascia, insomma, nell'animo l'immagine di un momento felice nell'esistenza del Buonarroti; un breve momento, ché ben presto il destino non gli avrebbe più consentito di trovar rifugio dai pensieri a Montedomini; due anni dopo, infatti, l'Arrighetti moriva in età ancor vegeta;[34] ma è bello apprendere come il più che settantenne poeta, ad onta delle difficoltà economiche che lo assillavano in quegli anni, si sia allora preso cura di uno dei figli dell'amico scomparso, e lo abbia avviato agli studi.[35]

*University of Cambridge*UBERTO LIMENTANI

Ragioni di spazio impediscono di pubblicare in questa sede l'intero testo dei quattro Capitoli; se ne dà un saggio, trascrivendo la parte centrale del Capitolo I.

> O mesi dell'autunno almi, e beati,
>   Fra tutti gli altri voi sete i più industri;
> 45 Vo' chiamar gli altri mesi scioperati.[35a]
> Altro ci vuol che rose, e che ligustri;
>   Abbiasele per sé l'aprile, e 'l maggio;
>   Voi sete i mesi più chiari, e più illustri.
> L'agosto, è ver, che vien col carriaggio,
> 50 E col trionfo di Cerere bionda,
>   E 'l giugno, e 'l luglio mena assai formaggio.
> Palla col frutto dell'amata fronda[36]
>   Ci fa (ma troppo rado) ugner le macini[37]
>   Nella stagion che più di neve abbonda.
> 55 Ma contro a lor settembre vien co' gli acini,
>   Pesta, e gli ammostatoi mette in lavoro,
>   E par che qua, e là penzoli[38] stracini.
> Ma ritornando com' i frati in coro
>   Che fur chiamati da un campanello
> 60 Ch'ebbe tirato qualch'amico loro,

Vengo a contar di paese sì bello
    La posta[39], il sito, i commodi, e i piaceri
    E fommi a dir di lui da Settimello,[40]
Dove la via si parte in due sentieri,
65   Un che va a Prato, e l'altro va a Bologna,
    Come v'è scritto a caratteri neri.
A chi capita quivi gli bisogna
    Legger la storia a non smarrir la strada
    Come fa chi è ebbro, o fa chi sogna,
70 Che vede o riva, o prato che gli aggrada,
    Colà si getta, e coglier fior desia
    Ond'avvien che 'l meschin dal letto cada.
Di San Donato a destra è la Badia,[41]
    Anzi la Pieve volta a mezzodì,
75   Ch'ire in Val di Marina ne fa spia.[42]
Torcendo adunque il viator di lì,
    E lasciando a sinistra Calenzano,
    In zucca ha poco sal s'ei si smarrì.
S'insacca, volto il guardo a tramontano,
80   In una valle, ma non dico amena,
    Passasi un fiume assai diverso, e strano,
Ch'assetato talor secca ha la vena,
    Talor briaco gonfia e fa pazzie,
    E vaneggia, e si scaglia per la pena.
85 Di là su la man manca fra le vie
    Che si posson lodare una n'è tale
    Che non ha gambe chi non la salie.
Industria, senno, architettura vale
    A far che l'huom ghiribizzando impari
90   I nugoli scalar senza aver l'ale.
Forza d'ingegno, e virtù di danari,
    Costante, e ferma voglia, sal mi sia,[43]
    Sa far volare a Empoli i somari.
Ora straccisi[43a] qui la Musa mia,
95   E mi venga a servir Febo in farsetto,
    Minerva abbia, e Mercurio in compagnia,
Perch'io lodi il valor dell'Arrighetto,
    Che sa far delle selve gallerie,
    E per gli scogli ritrovar tragetto;
100 E da queste, e da quelle alte macie,[44]
    Come suol farsi per la bassa rena,
    Spianarsi agevolissime le vie.
E s'assorte[45] del monte in su la stiena
    Piantate, com'io credo, un gran colosso,
105   Un gigante, un dragone, una balena,
Un Ercole ch'a Caco infranga il dosso,
    Sì che si vegga dal vostro palazzo,
    Più quel di Rodi celebrar non posso.

Un ampio e grande stradone, uno spazzo[46]
110   A quel ti mena senza alcuno sbaglio,
E parte serve per starvi a sollazzo.
Ivi per la pillotta, ivi pel maglio,
Pel pallon, per la lotta, e per la rulla,[47]
E per ogn'altro giuoco avvi buon taglio.
115   Tu ti conduci quasi come 'n culla
All'alto albergo non ancor finito,
Ben ch'a me paia non vi mancar nulla,
Dove far vo' avete stabilito
Un gran salone, e più innanzi una loggia
120   Da farvi a qualche tempo un bel convito,
Da starvi al sole, da fuggir la pioggia,
Da tenervi a giucar conversazione,
Massime allor che forestier s'alloggia.
Il che fate con somma discrezione,
125   E con tal arti, che palesi, e certe,
Non però il forestier tengon prigione.
Però che s'ei le vede pur scoperte,
Può finger non conoscerne gran parte,
E fuggir del complir le vie tropp'erte.
130   Vo' avete d'onorar perfetta l'arte,
Halla la vostra gentil compagnia,
Della famiglia ognun fa la sua parte.
Pur dura condizione era la mia,
Ch'ospite vostro mi pareva strano
135   Dissimular cotanta cortesia.
Io mi vedea venir di sottomano
Vari vantaggi, e non parea lor fatto;
E io me gli godea pian pian pian piano.
Spesso mi vedea far scacco[48] d'un piatto,
140   Come s'io fossi il prior del convento,
E io non stava in sul fare a ricatto.[49]
In favor mio tirava ogni vento,
Ogni trionfo in mano a me venia,
Io era della scena l'argomento.
145   Questo sia detto in andando per via;
E torno a dir che 'n luogo io mi trovai
Ch'io dissi: quest'è arte di magia.
Perché, venuto per più gineprai,
E per un fiume ch'ha per rive i monti,
150   Vidi poi campi dilettosi e gai,
Vidi, per quanto a gli occhi vaghi, e pronti
Concedea, spento il sol, l'ombrosa sera,
E bramai che novello il sol su monti.
La cortesia, l'accoglienza, la cera
155   Che ne fu fatta dalle mura stesse
Richiede a dirne una giornata intera.

Per quanto l'ora, e 'l tempo ne concesse,
Così in compendio quel luogo squadrai,
E pregai 'l ciel che lo benedicesse.

160   Condotto in parte ov'io mi riposai,
Da poi ch'io ebbi un po' ripreso lena,
Che prima io non vi fui me condennai.

NOTE

1. F. Del Furia, *Di alcuni scritti di Michelangelo Buonarroti il Giovane esistenti in un cod. ms. originale della Pubblica Libreria Marucelliana*, Firenze, Tipografia all'Insegna di Dante, 1828; il lavoro del Del Furia è anche negli *Atti dell'Imperiale e Reale Accademia della Crusca* (*ibidem*, vol. II, 1829, pp. 67–72).

2. Sull'Arrighetti (1586–1639), v. la voce relativa nel *Dizionario Biografico degli Italiani*, e opp. ivi cit.

3. M. Buonarroti il Giovane, *Opere varie in versi ed in prosa*, a cura di P. Fanfani, Firenze, F. Le Monnier, 1863, pp. 293–310.

4. Cap. II, vv. 34–51.

5. Cap. I, vv. 119–20.

6. Cap. III, v. 55: 'Tu m'hai interi otto dì date le spese'.

7. Cap. I, v. 162: 'Che prima io non vi fui me condennai'.

8. U. Limentani, *La satira nel Seicento*, Milano-Napoli, R. Ricciardi, 1961, pp. 76–8.

9. M. G. Masera, *Michelangelo Buonarroti il Giovane*, Università di Torino, Fondo di studi Parini-Chirio, 1941, p. 83.

10. Cap. II, vv. 121–3.

11. Satira VIII, vv. 175–7.

11a. V., a questo proposito: T. Poggi Salani, *Il lessico della 'Tancia' di M.B. il G.*, Firenze, La Nuova Italia, 1969; v. pure: G. Petrocchi, 'Società contadina e società borghese nel teatro di M. B. il G.', in *Atti del Convegno sul tema: La poesia rusticana nel Rinascimento*, Roma, Accademia Nazionale dei Lincei, 1969, pp. 223–32.

12. Mosche cavalline.

13. Cioè, che abbia sempre modo di spillare vino dalla botte.

14. Cap. II, vv. 229–36.

15. Cap. II, vv. 199–213; 217–221.

15a. La voce 'stidionata' figura nella *Tancia* (I, Interm, V.14); cfr. T. Poggi Salani, *op. cit.*, p. 179.

16. Cibi cotti, conservati per essere mangiati freddi.

17. Intingoli, manicaretti.

18. Confetti di dimensioni minute.

19. Sorta di dolce.

20. Il convento di S. Agata, che era situato in Via S. Gallo, a Firenze.

21. Cap. I, vv. 29–42.

22. Seggiola di legno a braccioli.

23. Cap. II, vv. 157–65.

24. Cap. IV, vv. 28–33.

25. Antico panno tessuto d'accia e bambagia; il termine doveva essere già un arcaismo ai tempi del Buonarroti.

26. Incarnatine, rosee.
27. I cappelli di brúciolo erano fatti di un'erba simile alla paglia; se, peraltro, il B. intese dire 'adorno il cappello di brucioli,' il significato sarebbe: che avevano adornato il cappello di fronde di una specie di olivo.
27a. Cfr. T. Poggi Salani, *op. cit.*, p. 25.
28. Cavalcature.
29. Ringhia.
30. Cap. III, vv. 160–2; 169–201.
31. Cap. III, vv. 157–9. Gostanza di Noferi Bracci aveva sposato l'Arrighetti nel 1617.
32. Cap. IV, vv. 4–6. Noferi Arrighetti visse dal 1620 al 1715.
33. Cap. III, vv. 61–3.
34. Il 29 maggio 1639.
35. M. G. Masera, *op. cit.*, p. 25.
35a. Per le accezioni di questo termine nel B., cfr. T. Poggi Salani, *op. cit.*, pp. 128–9.
36. L'oliva.
37. S'intende, le macine dei frantoi.
38. Due o più grappoli pendenti da uno stesso tralcio.
39. La posizione.
40. Paese situato a circa 12 km. a nord-est di Firenze, fra Sesto Fiorentino e Calenzano.
41. Il villaggio di San Donato sorge su un colle a nord-est di Calenzano, a poca distanza da questa località.
42. Indica la strada di Val di Marina. La valle del torrente Marina scende dalle colline situate a nord-est di Calenzano.
43. Salvo mi sia; Dio mi scampi. La locuzione figura anche nella *Tancia* (cfr.: T. Poggi Salani, *op. cit.*, p. 156).
43a. V. T. Poggi Salani, *op. cit.*, pp. 336–7.
44. Ammassi di pietre. Il termine 'Macia' si rinviene anche come toponimo nella zona (Macia di sotto); una villa situata a breve distanza dalla Villa Montedomini, ed appartenente ad Andrea Arrighetti (1592–1672, figlio di Giulio ed allievo di Galileo; primo cugino ed intimo di Niccolò Arrighetti), si chiamava appunto, e si chiama tuttora, Villa di Macia. Per un'accezione metaforica del termine, cfr. *Tancia*, V, VII, v. 949.
45. Per sorte; se accade che.
46. Uno spazio di terreno.
47. Pillotta: una specie di palla da gioco; maglio: martelletto di legno usato nel gioco della pallamaglio; rulla: disco di legno usato come gioco.
48. Rara accezione di questa frase, già usata dal Buonarroti (Satira II, a Jacopo Soldani, v. 181: 'Ma per non far di rima in rima scacco / Di concetti, e pensier troppo discosto, / E che paiano aver duro l'attacco, / Ripiglio e dico . . .'); vorrà significare: mettere accanto; V. anche Cap. IV, v. 81.
49. Non cercavo di rifarmi, di prendere la rivincita (conformemente alla locuzione: riscattarsi, o ricattarsi, nel gioco). La voce 'ricattarsi' in questo senso di 'rifarsi', nella *Tancia*, V, V, v. 396; cfr. T. Poggi Salani, *op. cit.*, p. 155.

Wordsworth, Isola, Lamb

The influence of Italy on England has been deep and significant. In the field of literature alone the names of scores of English poets and men of letters immediately come to mind. How much Chaucer owed to Boccaccio! What inspiration Shakespeare drew indirectly from Italian renaissance sources! Wyatt, Surrey, Spenser, Milton, and in more modern times, Shelley, Byron, Swinburne, Meredith, Browning, Landor, these names are obvious. On reflection the list can be doubled, but it is safe to say that the name that does *not* occur to one naturally is that of William Wordsworth. What had that highly individual and very English Englishman to do with Italy?

The young Wordsworth went as a student to St John's College, Cambridge, in October 1787, where he remained until he took his Bachelor of Arts Degree in January 1791. He has given us a poetical commentary on his life and feelings at that period in his remarkable autobiographical poem *The Prelude or Growth of a Poets Mind*. From that, and other sources, we learn that he did not take very kindly to the regular studies of Mathematics and Classics, but that he loved to range beyond them in his reading and meditations:

> I did not love
> (As hath been noticed heretofore), the guise
> Of our scholastic studies; could have wished
> The river to have had an ampler range,
> And freer pace;[1]

Instead of diligently following the normal course, he went in search of hidden intellectual sweets, what he called 'wild wood honey'. There is no doubt that one of the most important objects of pursuit in his scholastic truancy was the Italian language and literature. Years later, at the age of 77, the poet dictated some autobiographical memoranda in which, referring to his first year at Cambridge, he wrote that he got into rather an idle way; reading nothing but Classic authors according to my fancy, and Italian poetry. My Italian master was named Isola, and had been well acquainted with Gray the poet. As I took to these studies with much interest, he was proud of the progress I made. Under his correction I translated the *Vision of Mirza* and two or three other papers of the Spectator into Italian.[2]

During the long vacation of 1790 Wordsworth had his first sight of Italy. Accompanied by a friend, with a bundle on his back, he went on foot through France to Switzerland and then for the inside of a week, over the Alps into Italy. He saw little of the country on that occasion, only the lakes Maggiore and Como, but it was enough to leave a lasting impression of natural beauty and humanity. Beautiful as those places still are, they were far more beautiful then, before the days of motor-roads and crowded villas. I quote from a letter of Wordsworth to his sister:

The shores of the lake consist of steeps covered with large sweeping woods of chestnut, spotted with villages...nor was the surface of the lake less interesting than its shores; half of it glowing with the richest green and gold, the reflection of the illuminated wood and path, shaded with a soft blue tint. . . . At the lake of Como my mind ran through a thousand dreams of happiness, which might be enjoyed upon its banks, if heightened by conversation and the exercise of the social affections.[3]

The inhabitants of this natural Paradise impressed him no less than the scenes they inhabited:

I was also much pleased with what I saw of the Italians during the short time we were among them. We had several times occasion to observe a softness and elegance which contrasted strongly with the severe austereness of their neighbours on the other side of the Alps. It was with pleasure I observed, at a small inn on the lake of Como, the master of it playing upon his harpsichord, with a large collection of Italian music about him.[4]

In the *Prelude* he returned to this Italian experience in memory:

>   I spake
> Of thee, thy chestnut woods, and garden plots
> Of Indian corn tended by dark-eyed maids,
> Thy lofty steeps, and pathways roofed with vines
> Winding from house to house, from town to town,
> Sole link that binds them to each other, walks
> League after league, and cloistral avenues
> Where silence is, if music be not there.[5]

With his enthusiasm for Italy increased by this first visit beyond the Alps, the student returned to Cambridge and to his studies with the old Italian-master who was so proud of the progress of his student.

Agostino Isola (b. 1713) is said to have left Milan and come to England for political reasons in the middle of the eighteenth century. It has been stated[6] that the possession of a forbidden English book was the cause of his exile, but the tale seems to me rather unlikely. In 1764 he was appointed assistant at Cambridge by the Rev. Mr Brockett, Professor of Modern History. On Brockett's death (after a fall from his horse) he was succeeded in the Chair of Modern History by no less a person than Thomas Gray the poet. Isola remained as Gray's assistant and continued to be the chief teacher of Italian at Cambridge until his death at the ripe age of 84 in 1797.

The study of modern languages had not then attained the respectable stature at Cambridge and Oxford it has today. But in regard to Italian it went far beyond instruction in the language itself, as a consideration of Isola's activities proves. The practical knowledge of foreign tongues was, however, the chief aim of the reform set in motion early in the eighteenth century with the support, and in the name, of the Hanoverian George I, who incidentally could not even talk English himself. The draft scheme contained these words:

> The two Universities being intended for a nursery of learned and able men, not only for the service of the Church, but also of the State; and the service of the State by reason of continual correspondence with foreign courts and agencies therein, requiring in a peculiar manner the knowledge of the modern or living languages, both in speaking and writing, for which no provision hath yet been made in either of the Universities. By reason of which not only the Secretaries of State and others who are employed by his Majesty in the public administration at home, but also those who are sent abroad upon embassies and other affairs, are sometimes obliged to employ under them persons of foreign nations; and from the same defect, the nobility and gentry of these Kingdoms are frequently under the necessity of employing persons of foreign extraction to accompany their sons in their travels.

At each University a Professor of Modern History was appointed with the requirement that he should provide and pay out of his own salary two teachers of modern languages. It will be seen that teachers of modern languages were in a very inferior situation as compared to properly established Professors and lecturers in other subjects. They were the humble assistants of the Professor of Modern History. Isola only drew £25 per annum from his official master and therefore had to maintain himself by giving private tuition and writing books. We are not therefore very surprised to read the following advertisement in the local paper, *The Cambridge Chronicle*, of 17th November, 1764.

> *To the Gentlemen of the University.* Signor Agostino Isola who was some months ago appointed by the Rev. Mr Brockett, Professor of Modern History and Languages, to teach Italian in this University, begs leave to inform such gentlemen who are desirous of being acquainted with that language that he will wait on them, by giving him notice at his lodgings, Mr Munns, Tinplate-worker in the Market-Hill Cambridge.

Some months previously (3rd March, 1764) a paragraph in the same newspaper had reported Isola's appointment, and described him as 'a modest and moderate man of unexceptional morals, and equally well qualified for the employment which he has undertaken.'

It is from his published works that we can learn what, and how, Isola taught. They are as follows:

> 1. *Italian Dialogues* consisting of familiar expressions upon various subjects. Dedicated to the Lovers of the Italian Language in the University of Cambridge by A.I. Cambridge 1774. Price 1/6.
> 2. *Pieces Selected from the Italian Poets* by Agostino Isola (Teacher of the Italian Language) and translated into English verse by some gentlemen of the University. Cambridge 1778. (2nd Edition 1784).
> 3. *Elegia* [*Translation of Gray's Elegy*] 1782. [A new edition of the version made by Giuseppe Torelli.]
> 4. *The Gerusalemme Liberata of Tasso* with explanatory notes on the syntax in obscure passages, and references to the author's imitations of the ancient classics. To which is prefixed a compendious analysis of Italian metre by Agostino Isola Teacher of the Italian Language in the University of Cambridge (2 vols.). Cambridge 1786.
> 5. *Orlando Furioso of Ludovico Ariosto* with an explanation of equivocal words and poetical figures and an elucidation of all the passages concerning history or fable by Agostino Isola Teacher of the Italian Language in the University of Cambridge. 1789. (4 vols.).

The Dialogues show that he favoured the conversational method. Here are twenty-six pages of selected everyday subjects: *Per cavalcare, Per pregare Dio, Per giocare (alle carte), Per cantare, Per andar alla caccia.*

We get a glimpse of the ruddy-faced young students of the time who spent as much, if not more, time in the fields as in the libraries, and who probably learnt Italian as a preliminary to the Grand Tour of Europe.

> Dov'è stato Signore che pare così affaticato?
> In questo momento vengo dalla caccia con altri miei amici.

In the pieces selected for translation by his pupils there is evidence of a typical 'Arcadian' taste. There is one example each from Guarino and Marino, two from Tasso and Tassoni, three from Petrarch, five from Ariosto and twenty-six from Metastasio. This is one of the books used by Wordsworth as we shall presently consider.

Isola had considerable influence in directing the taste of many generations of young Englishmen towards Italian literature. Amongst his pupils was the younger Pitt, William Hayley (the prolific poet of whom Southey wrote 'everything about that man is good except his poetry'), Lort Mansel, later Master of Trinity College, Jacob Mountain who became first Anglican Bishop of Quebec, T. J. Mathias who lived so long at Naples, translated much from Italian authors and wrote numerous original poems in Italian. Amongst his private pupils Isola taught several young ladies, one of them Matilda Betham, to whom we are obliged for an interesting piece of information, namely that the old master in his enthusiasm for Ariosto, Tasso and Metastasio did not neglect Dante. Matilda had come to Cambridge in 1796 especially to take lessons from Isola, her interest having been kindled by reading Hoole's translation of Metastasio. A year later this devoted pupil penned an elegy to her master who died on 5th June, 1797.

O Isola! When that glad season comes,
Which brought redemption to a ruined world,
And, like thee, hides beneath the snow of age
A gay, benevolent, and feeling heart,
I hop'd again to hear thy tongue repeat,
With youthful warmth and zealous energy,
Those passages, where Poetry assumes
An air divine and wakes th' attentive soul
To holy rapture! There you promised me
The luxury to weep o'er Dante's muse
And fair Italia's loftier poets hail.
. . . .
        Dear, guileless friend!
Thou read'st mankind, but saw not, or forgot
Their faults and vices; for thy breast was still
The residence of sweet Simplicity.
Daughter of lettered Wisdom, and the friend
Of Love and Pity. Happy soul, farewell!
Long shall we mourn thee! longer will it be,
'Ere we shall look upon thy like again!'

The most distinguished pupil of this well-beloved old teacher was, of course, William Wordsworth. There is in the Fitzwilliam Museum at Cambridge, a most interesting relic of their association, Wordsworth's own copy of Isola's *Pieces selected from the Italian Poets*, in which the poet has written alternative versions in his own hand.[7] For many years these had remained unpublished, but in 1947 they appeared in an Appendix to Vol. IV of the Selincourt-Darbishire edition of the Poetical Works.[8] It may be of interest if I quote a few lines of Wordsworth's translation from Metastasio:

Placido zeffiretto
  Se trovi il caro oggetto
  Digli che sei sospiro
  Ma non gli dir di chi.
Limpido ruscelletto
  Se mai t'incontri in lei
  Dille che pianto sei
  Ma non le dir qual ciglio
  Crescer ti fè così.

Gentle zephyr
  If you pass her by
  Tell her you're a sigh
  But tell her not from whom.
Limpid streamlet
  If you meet her ever
  Say with your best endeavour
  That swoln with tears you come
  But tell her not of whom.

At various epochs of his life Wordsworth translated from very many Italian authors, octaves from Orlando Furioso,[9] poems of Michelangelo, including the reply to Giovanni Strozzi's epigram on the statue of Night in the Medici Chapel in Florence, a sonnet of Tasso and numerous epitaphs and elegies of Chiabrera. It is not my purpose to indicate the extent or the limitations of the influence of such Italian authors as these on Wordsworth's own poetry. I will however mention that Wordsworth wrote three articles in 1810 on the subject of Epitaphs, a consideration directly arising from his interest in Chiabrera.[10] Three years before, Foscolo had published his *Sepolcri* in Italy. I have no evidence that Wordsworth had read this great poem though he had met the poet, but I am sure that no Italian can read such passages as the following without thinking of that *Corrispondenza d'amorosi sensi* that is the root idea in the *Sepolcri*, or of Foscolo's insistence on commemoration in garden surroundings.

Almost all nations have wished that certain external signs should point out the places where their dead are interred. Among savage tribes unacquainted with letters this has mostly been done either by rude stones placed near the graves, or by mounds of earth raised over them. This custom proceeded obviously from a two-fold desire; first to guard the remains of the deceased from irreverent approach or from savage violation: and secondly, to preserve their memory. ...As soon as nations had learned the use of letters, epitaphs were inscribed upon these monuments ...

Compare:

Dal dì che nozze e tribunali ed are
dier alle umane belve esser pietose
di sè stesse e d'altrui, toglieano i vivi
i miserandi avanzi che Natura
con veci eterne a sensi altri destina.

Let a man only compare in imagination the unsightly manner in which our monuments are crowded together in the busy, noisy, unclean and almost grassless churchyard of a large town with the still seclusion of a Turkish cemetery, in some remote place; and yet further sanctified by the grove of cypress in which it is embosomed. ...

A village churchyard lying as it does in the lap of Nature, may indeed be most favourably contrasted with that of a town of crowded population; and sepulture therein combines many of the best tendencies which belong to the mode practised by the Ancients. ...

Compare:

Non sempre i sassi sepolcrali a' templi
fean pavimento; nè agl'incensi avvolto
de' cadaveri il lezzo i supplicanti
contaminò...

            Ma cipressi e cedri
di puri effluvî i zefiri impregnando
perenne verde protendean su l'urne
per memoria perenne...

Pietosa insania che fa cari gli orti
de' suburbani avelli alle britanne
vergini...

Wordworth continues to praise precisely the sort of burial Foscolo advocates as it is most favourable to

that communion between living and dead which the conjunction in rural districts of the place of burial and place of worship tends so effectually to promote.

Compare:

> Celeste è questa
> corrispondenza d'amorosi sensi,
> celeste dote è negli umani.

I do not propose to make a close analysis or comparison between these two works but, making full allowance for the fact that authors writing on a similar theme will say similar things, the extent and nature of the similarities here incline me to the belief that Wordsworth had read the *Sepolcri* and, if so, we must think of Foscolo as well as Chiabrera in this connexion.

It is quite reasonable to suppose that old Isola spoke to his pupils of other things than *canzonette* of Metastasio. He must have shared the common feeling of regret for the political degradation of his country. If so, it would have helped to inspire liberal sentiments such as these expressed in a letter of Wordsworth of 1811[11]

> Now I think there is nothing more unfortunate for Europe than the condition of Germany and Italy...could the barriers be dissolved which have divided the one nation into Neapolitans, Tuscans, Venetians etc. and the other into Prussians, Hanoverians etc, and could they be once taught to feel their strength, the French would be driven back into their own land immediately. I wish to see Spain, Italy, France, Germany formed into independent nations.

His sonnet *On the Extinction of the Venetian Republic* (written 1802) was founded on a real sentiment of admiration and regret:

> Once did she hold the gorgeous east in fee;
> And was the safeguard of the west: the worth
> Of Venice did not fall below her birth,
> Venice, the eldest Child of Liberty

Nor were the words he wrote in 1837, on leaving Italy, empty rhetoric:

> What thou dost inherit
> Of the world's hopes, dare to fulfil; awake
> Mother of Heroes, from thy death-like sleep!

It is a tragedy that Wordsworth postponed his first real visit to Italy until he was 67 years old and feeling his age. 'It is too late', he said to Crabb Robinson, and in regard to creative poetry he was right. The poems collected under the title *Memorials of a Tour in Italy* are not amongst his best. There are poems on Rome, Florence, Naples,

La Verna, Vallombrosa and (in memory of Chiabrera) Savona. As
an old man he often pondered on these Italian scenes as he sat
musing at Rydal Mount. An Italian pavement, with the word *salve*
on it, was at the threshold, and on the staircase hung a picture by
Luca Giordano for which he wrote a sonnet at the age of 80 a few
years before his death.

> Giordano, verily thy Pencil's skill
> Hath here portrayed with Nature's happiest grace
> The fair Endymion couched on Latmos-hill;
> And Dian gazing on the Shepherd's face
> In rapture, ...

To the last, classical and Italian influences surrounded him. Old
Isola's Italianate classicism still influenced one of the most romantic
of English poets.

The association of the family of Isola with English men of letters
did not cease at the death of Agostino. He left a son, Charles, who for
seventeen years (1797–1814) held the honourable ceremonial post of
Esquire Bedell of the University of Cambridge. Charles married a
Cambridgeshire girl and had a number of children of whom Emma,
the third child, is of special interest. On the death of her father in
1814, and her mother in 1815, the little girl of seven years old was
left an orphan. She first went to live with an aunt, Miss Humphreys,
but soon after she became known to Charles Lamb and his sister
Mary. There was something in the little girl (and probably that
something was Italian), that instantly appealed to Lamb's sensitive
nature. Until his death in 1834 Lamb cherished the child with a deep
paternal love. Descriptive phrases in Lamb's letters give us some idea
of Emma's dark, thoughtful charm—'a girl of gold', 'our nut-brown
maid', 'something of a pensive cast', 'the silent brown girl'. After
some visits to the home of her new friends Emma was adopted as a
daughter into the Lamb household at Enfield. The essayist and his
sister took their duties very seriously and started to teach the little
Italian girl Latin, ''tis like feeding a child with chopped hay from a
spoon'. She made them laugh by translating *Blast you* by *Deus afflet
tibi*. Mary Lamb wrote a poem on the subject of Emma's Latin
studies:

> Droop not, dear Emma, dry those falling tears
> And call up smiles into thy pallid face,
> Pallid and care-worn with thy arduous race;
> In few brief months thou hast done the work of years,
> To young beginnings natural art these fears. Etc.

Whatever her shortcomings in Latin, Emma read aloud so well in English that Coleridge admitted she read Milton better than he. The instruction was not all one way, for when the Lambs began to read Dante, Emma was able to help them with the Italian. A remarkable scene! The brilliant, whimsical essayist, the elderly woman with face marked by the strange quality of her aberrant mind, the solemn Italian child, all three poring over the pages of the *Divina Commedia*. But there was plenty of laughter too—Lamb delighted in the odd side of life. Witness a letter written to a doctor in Enfield:

Dear Sir,

Some draughts and boluses have been brought here which we conjecture were meant for the young lady whom you saw this morning, though they are labelled for Miss Isola Lamb. No such person is known in the Chase Side, and she is fearful of taking medicines which may have been made up for another patient. She begs me to say that she was born an *Isola* and christened *Emma*. Moreover that she is Italian by birth and that her ancestors were from Isola Bella (Fair Island) in the kingdom of Naples [*sic*]. She has never changed her name and rather mournfully adds she has no prospect at present of doing so. She is literally I sola, or single, at present. Therefore she begs that the obnoxious monosyllable may be omitted on future phials,—an innocent syllable enough, you'll say, but she has no claim to it. It is the bitterest pill of the score you have sent her. When a lady loses her good *name*, what is to become of her? Well she must swallow it as well as she can, but begs the dose may not be repeated.

Yours faithfully,

Charles Lamb (not Isola).

Emma did not remain single long, for on 30th July, 1833, she was married to Edward Moxon the publisher.

Before her marriage Emma had been bitten by the fashionable craze for keeping an Album and Lamb solicited many of his friends on her behalf. It was a remarkable collection containing autograph contributions by nearly all the leading men of letters of the earlier nineteenth century. Amongst them: Lamb, Keats, Wordsworth, Moore, Tennyson, Leigh Hunt, Thomas Hood, James Hogg, Southey, Campbell, Dibdin, Landor, Rogers, etc., etc. The Album was later cut up for the value of its MSS.

Lamb wrote various poems to or about Emma. On her twenty-first birthday he wrote as follows:

Crown me a cheerful goblet, while I pray
A blessing on thy years, young Isola;
Young but no more a child. How swift have flown
To me thy girlish times, a woman grown
Beneath my heedless eyes!

. . . .
. . . .
Grandchild of that respected Isola,
Thou should'st have had about thee on this day
Kind looks of parents, to congratulate
Their pride grown up to woman's grave estate.
But they have died, and left thee, to advance
Thy fortunes how thou may'st, and owe to chance
The friends which Nature grudg'd.

Lamb has given an endearing portrait of Emma in his poem *To a
Friend on his Marriage, 1833* [Moxon]:

. . . . .A mind exempt
From every low-bred passion, where contempt
Nor envy, nor detraction, ever found
A harbour yet, an understanding sound;
Just views of right and wrong; perception full
Of the deformed, and of the beautiful,
In life and manners; wit above her sex,
Which as a gem, her sprightly converse decks;
Exuberant fancies, prodigal of mirth
To gladden woodland walk, or winter hearth;
. . . .
And beauty, which some hold the chiefest boon,
Is in thy bargain for a make-weight thrown.

It is sad to recall that after Moxon's death (in 1858) Emma fell on
evil days. A subscription was organised for the benefit of the now
almost destitute widow. The Editor of *Notes and Queries* made a
moving appeal for her in that periodical (28th February, 1874):

To the last, Lamb loved the child of his heart with an unselfish love, and
a part of the little he had to leave fell, after his sister's death to Mrs
Moxon. The 'dark days' however to which Lamb alluded, came still
darker than he had contemplated them. . .the Emma Isola who was the
youth of Lamb's house stands before the world, blameless but in an almost
destitute position. . . .The spirit of Charles Lamb, if it can be moved by
any earthly action, will assuredly smile on all who show active beneficial
sympathy with Emma Isola.

Other descendants of Agostino Isola multiplied and led obscurer
lives on lower rungs of the social scale. Emma's brother Frederick was
a baker of the Cambridge suburb of Chesterton. His daughter was
the washerwoman described by a visitor in 1915 as

a good old soul, blessed with an unusual vocabulary with a decided liking
for words that resounded...It was little of a definite nature that she could
tell me. She possessed nothing relating to the Isolas, no book, picture or
scrap of paper. She understood that her father, Frederick Isola, was a
Bluecoat boy, and his father too. She had heard as a child that her
grandfather, Charles Isola, wore a long silk gown with gold 'epeletts', that
he could talk Greek, and looked a gentleman...

Other descendants of Agostino survived till quite recently and
there is still a generation of them though now of course far more
Cambridgeshire than Milanese. One was a cook to a Cambridge
Professor, another was a taxi-driver. The name has varied and
become corrupted—Isolo—Isoli—Isloa—and more commonly Issler.

In the early years of this century there was a character about the
town of Cambridge, known as 'Doggy Issler', so-called from the remarkable ability he showed in pulling live rats out of a sack with his
teeth. Italian genius is many-sided! It is sad that the English branch
of the Isola family has come down in the world. They did not boast
a Panizzi or a d'Israeli, but nevertheless they have their niche in
English literary history and provide yet another example of the
fruitful result of Italian–English collaboration.

Kingston St Mary, Taunton   E. R. VINCENT

NOTES

1. Prelude, III, vv. 507–510.
2. *Memoirs of W.W.*, Christopher Wordsworth, 1851, I. p. 14.
3. Ibid. pp. 59–60.
4. Memoirs of W.W., Christopher Wordsworth, 1851, I, pp. 63–4.
5. *Prelude*, VI, vv. 594–599.
6. T. N. Talfourd, *Letters of Charles Lamb*, 1837, II. Ch. XIV, p. 141.
7. Three in his own hand, two in that of his sister.
8. Pp. 369–370.
9. *Poetical Works*, 1947, IV, pp. 367–8.
10. But I suggest that Arcadia (unlikely as it may seem!) played some
    little part in the formation of Wordsworth as a nature poet. One
    only has to read Professor Mario Praz's able translation of the
    Verses written near Tintern Abbey and notice phrases such as the follow-
    ing to realise how well they fit in to an 'Arcadian' context.

    > Quest'erte eccelse rupi
    > Quand'io salivo come un capriolo
    > Su pei monti, lunghesso i fondi fumi
    > (It then seems to require:
    >   Io adoravo Filli!)

Ed anelli di fumo salir vedo
E di tra mezzo gli alberi, un silenzio
Quali indizi d'erranti abitatori
Delle inospiti selve, e della grotta
D'un eremita, dove l'eremita
Presso al suo fuoco solitario sta.

11. See *Memoirs of W.W.*, Christopher Wordsworth, 1851, I, p. 416.

Fortuna del Leopardi

Non è strano che in Inghilterra il Gladstone, bene informato, se altri mai, di cose italiane, solo nel 1849 si rendesse conto dell'importanza e singolarità del Leopardi. E non è strano che a rendersene conto egli giungesse per la via lunga e ingrata, che oggi nessuno più si attenta a battere, del *Gesuita moderno* di Vincenzo Gioberti. A distanza di cento anni e più, le cose che finiscono col non essere strane, richiedono però, a chi voglia intenderle, una qualche ricerca e un poco di riflessione. Per il Gladstone, la documentazione edita e a tutti accessibile è più abbondante e precisa che per alcun altro suo contemporaneo inglese: è insomma, indipendentemente dall'importanza storica dell'uomo, un passaggio obbligato della ricerca sui rapporti fra Inghilterra e Italia nell'Ottocento. Come da questa documentazione risulta, il Gladstone non cessò mai, dal 1832 innanzi, di ampliare e perfezionare la sua conoscenza della lingua e letteratura italiana. Benché subito, nel 1833, al ritorno dal suo primo viaggio in Italia, egli avesse intrapreso una carriera politica, i suoi interessi allora e per un buon tratto ancora, fino alla sua piena maturità, furono letterari e religiosi piuttosto che politici. Il nesso che per lui, come per tanti altri suoi contemporanei in Inghilterra, era fondamentale, fra letteratura e religione, fondamentale anche era e appariscente, *mutatis mutandis*, nell'opera del Manzoni. Si spiega che l'attenzione del Gladstone si appuntasse sul Manzoni, la fortuna del quale del resto fu in Inghilterra maggiore che non quella di altro moderno scrittore italiano. Ma fondamentale in Italia non era allora il nesso fra letteratura e religione: era fra letteratura e politica. Pertanto la posizione antagonistica assunta dal Leopardi nei confronti del Manzoni appariva in Italia ristretta e irrigidita nei termini linguistici e letterari della polemica fra classicisti e romantici, e d'altra parte irrilevante o comunque insufficiente e inaccettabile in termini politici. Il potenziale antagonismo fra i due, Manzoni e Leopardi, si era manifestato nel 1827, quando entrambi, non a caso, avevano dimesso l'abito, tradizionale in Italia e che prima era stato anche loro, della poesia, e si erano presentati al tempo stesso sulla scena in veste di prosatori. In quell'anno la polemica fra classicisti e romantici, intempestivamente riattizzata nel 1825 dal *Sermone sulla mitologia* del Monti e poi subito discesa al livello e ristrettasi nell'ambito dei *Lombardi* di Tommaso Grossi, dava chiari segni di aver esaurito la pazienza, nonché l'interesse del pubblico. Per contro in quello stesso anno la scomparsa del Foscolo e la previsione della ormai imminente scomparsa del Monti aprivano nella repubblica delle lettere italiane una crisi di successione. Il candidato più forte, di gran lunga, era il Manzoni, e tanto più forte era, anche e in ispecie a paragone dei predecessori, Monti e Foscolo, per il suo disinteresse e riserbo, pari alla sua indipendenza e dirittura. Ma era il rappresentante della nuova scuola romantica: non era tale in Italia da poter ottenere l'assoluta maggioranza, nonché l'unanimità. Poteva ottenere e di fatto ottenne una maggioranza relativa, senza che per ciò l'opposizione desistesse, come del resto era suo diritto, dalla ricerca di un valido antagonista. Il Giordani ad esempio, che non poteva aspirare alla successione, ma che certo aveva, già allora, l'autorità e l'ambizione del *kingmaker*, non era né sarebbe mai stato disposto ad accettare la presidenza del Manzoni sulla letteratura italiana, se non come una fatale, inevitabile degradazione. Ma nel 1827, e subito dopo, per quante riserve suscitassero in Italia i *Promessi sposi*, tante più e maggiori in Italia che non fuori, a nessuno poteva passare per il capo che le *Operette morali* reggessero al paragone. Già qui saltava agli occhi che, movendo in una direzione diametralmente opposta a quella del Manzoni, il Leopardi giungeva a risultati analoghi, altrettanto e più sconcertanti: più netta era la rescissione del nesso fra letteratura e politica, e per compenso alla letteratura era imposto il compito, tanto più rischioso e ingrato alla maggioranza, che non fosse quello impostole dal Manzoni, di combattere contro la religione. La cultura italiana non era in quel momento disposta a prendere sul serio la religione, come il Manzoni avrebbe voluto, ma ancor meno era disposta a prendere sul serio una filosofia eversiva della religione. Prima e più che la religione, era in causa la filosofia, qualunque essa fosse: il fatto che, restando ignoto e isolato il Galluppi e ancora non essendo comparsi sulla scena il Rosmini, il Mamiani e il Gioberti, figurasse in Italia come gran maestro della filosofia a paragone dell'Europa un Romagnosi, basta a dimostrare quale fosse l'atteggiamento allora della cultura italiana nei confronti della filosofia in genere, e in ispecie di una filosofia che non fosse al servizio della politica. Si tornava così alla rescissione, inaccettabile in Italia, del nesso fra letteratura e politica: onde la preferenza, storicamente ineccepibile, accordata dall'Accademia della Crusca nel concorso del 1829–30 al Botta, piuttosto che al Leopardi. Il vecchio Botta, antiromantico sfegatato e antimanzoniano a segno che per suo decoro non avrebbe concorso al premio se suo competitore fosse stato il romanziere Manzoni, aveva le carte in regola: era impegnato fino al collo nella politica dell'età sua, era nazionalista fino all'osso, benché cittadino francese, e come storico era ostentatamente immune dal contagio della moderna filosofia.

Dopo il 1830 la situazione politico-letteraria dell'Italia appare diversa, e conseguentemente anche diverso il rapporto a distanza fra il Manzoni e il Leopardi. Il primo si apparta e non dà piu segni di vita, se non la promessa o minaccia di un'opera sulla lingua. Sarebbe stata a quei chiari di luna una minaccia incredibile e comunque ridicola in ogni altro paese: non in Italia, come noi stessi sappiamo per la nostra esperienza, posteriore d'un secolo e più. Ma anche in Italia, in quella che pur era la giovane Italia degli anni trenta dello scorso secolo, qualcosa più ci si attendeva dal successore di Vincenzo Monti che non fosse una nuova *Proposta*. Il Manzoni restava inattaccabile per quel che aveva fatto nel decennio precedente e perché impensabile era che avesse rinunciato a fare, ma inevitabilmente, col passar del tempo, sempre più si mescolava al rispetto e all'aspettazione il disagio per quella sua pacifica assenza da una scena, che in Italia e nella vicina Francia proponeva esperimenti nuovi e rischiosi. Per parte sua il Leopardi riapparve in quel giro d'anni nella figura sua propria di poeta. Qualunque fosse, la figura del poeta sempre aveva esercitato un irresistibile fascino sulla cultura italiana. Né il fascino venne mai meno per tutto l'Ottocento e oltre, fin quasi all'età nostra. Ma accadde che per l'appunto in quel giro d'anni, subito dopo il 1830, la cultura italiana a un tratto si capacitasse di quella conversione del Manzoni alla prosa, che dapprincipio aveva deplorato. Al riconoscimento e alla fortuna della prosa contribuiva anche, nel campo avverso al Manzoni, la crescente autorità del Giordani. E finalmente contribuì, al di sopra delle parti e però su di una linea esemplarmente diritta, il successo dell'*Antologia* di Firenze, primo periodico che in Italia assumesse una importanza nazionale. Accadde insomma che dal 1831 innanzi, per quanto ancora avanzava di vita al Leopardi, la stagione dei *Canti* coincidesse con una alluvione prosastica, quale non si era mai verificata prima nella letteratura italiana. Basti ricordare la pubblicazione nel 1832 delle *Mie prigioni*, cioè del solo libro italiano in tutto il secolo, paragonabile per il successo editoriale ai *Promessi sposi*. Poi subito la scena si affollò dei seguaci e oppositori del Manzoni nella nuova moda del romanzo storico: nel 1833 l'*Ettore Fieramosca*, nel 1834 il *Marco Visconti*, nel 1836 l'*Assedio di Firenze*. Quanto questa disparata alluvione prosastica fosse tutt'insieme estranea al Leopardi, non occorre dire, ma è chiaro che l'estraneità stessa finì coll'avere un peso decisivo sulla vita di lui e sulla fortuna dell'opera sua fra i contemporanei. Sarà stato un caso, ma un di quei casi che mirabilmente corrispondono all'imposizione degli eventi, che l'originario isolamento di lui, finalmente rotto fra il 1825 e il '33, fra Bologna e la Toscana, nel bel mezzo della scena letteraria italiana, si risaldasse definitivamente, dal 1833 innanzi, a Napoli. Da Firenze riparando a Napoli, egli si sottraeva all'alluvione, che fin là non era giunta né poteva giungere, ma anche rinunciava a far sentire la sua voce di poeta vivo al resto d'Italia. Non che andando a Napoli sapesse di dover rinunciare: non poteva sapere e s'illudeva, ma nel 1835, dopo l'edizione Starita e dopo aver conosciuto l'ambiente arcaico e ai suoi occhi ridicolo, seppe. Non gli restava più che l'illusione di Parigi; di fatto l'appello ai posteri. È impensabile che l'autore dei *Paralipomeni* s'illudesse di poter stampare l'opera sua in Italia. Nel suo supremo isolamento, aveva riconosciuto a Napoli la comicità meschina dell'intiera scena italiana. Si spiega che in Italia l'isolamento finale del Leopardi perdurasse al di là della morte di lui, e a maggior ragione valesse per gli stranieri, all'infuori dei pochi che lo avevano conosciuto di persona. Fra questi pochi non risulta che alcun Inglese si rendesse conto d'aver conosciuto un uomo eccezionale. Non risulta finora, ma la documentazione inglese sull'Italia per quegli anni è tanta che nessuno, credo, può illudersi di averla scorsa tutta. Resta che in quegli anni, dopo il 1830, nella cultura inglese cominciava a manifestarsi una ben giustificata sazietà della moda italiana divampata quindici anni prima. E resta che, seguendo la moda, gl'innumerevoli Inglesi ospiti dell'Italia finivano col trovarsi ivi, a Firenze e Napoli in ispecie, come a casa loro, disposti sì a guardarsi attorno, ma piuttosto per verificare e apprezzare il già noto, che non per far paragone di sé coll'ignoto. Affatto diverso, per ovvi motivi, l'atteggiamento degli Americani: onde, nella documentazione in lingua inglese, generalmente avara di riferimenti precisi alla letteratura italiana contemporanea, fanno spicco le *Letters from abroad to kindred at home* dell'americana Catharine Maria Sedgwick, apparse a Londra in due volumi nel 1841. Poiché di una donna si tratta, vien subito fatto di pensare a Mrs Trollope, che a spese dell'America aveva iniziato dieci anni prima la sua tarda e fortunata carriera di scrittrice, e il cui libro sull'Italia, *A Visit to Italy*, anche in forma di lettere, anche in due volumi, apparve a Londra nel 1842. Ed è un libro interessante, dove qualcosa traspare della società e cultura toscana, dove a un tratto persino appare, incredibile e vera, la Giovane Italia. Ma sono figurine introdotte qua e là con mano scaltra e leggera per aggiungere un pizzico di novità al quadro tradizionale: per Mrs Trollope, che del resto aveva sessant'anni suonati e che già deplorava il declino dell'interesse inglese per l'Italia, a paragone di quel che era stato trent'anni prima, la letteratura italiana restava, qual'era per l'appunto trent'anni prima, compresa fra Dante e l'Alfieri. L'americana Miss Sedgwick, fiera della sua origine e smaniosa di non essere scambiata per inglese, dovunque andasse in Italia, da Torino a

Napoli, mirava diritto alla realtà presente e viva, a ogni segno che le
apparisse di una nazione che cercava se stessa nel futuro, al di là del
mostruoso assetto che il passato e la prepotenza della vecchia Europa
le avevano imposto. Che i segni le apparissero chiari a Torino e a
Milano, a colloquio col Pellico e col Manzoni, ai quali l'aveva
indirizzata il Confalonieri, già esule in America, non stupisce. Più
notevole è che, giunta a Napoli nel febbraio del 1840, subito s'imbat-
tesse in uno, prudentemente designato colla sola iniziale L., il quale
considerava 'Count Leopardi the finest poet since Alfieri', e si offriva
di guidarla nella lettura. E certo 'the bitter invectives and keen sar-
casms of the poet' non sarebbero stati facilmente comprensibili da uno
straniero senza una guida esperta. Ma il seguente commento mostra
che la lettura non si fermò alla protesta e al sarcasmo: 'certainly there is
great power in some of the things we read, and oh it gives us such a
feeling, such a realising sense of the mental suffering endured here by
men who have one spark left of that love of freedom which seems to be
God's universal gift, who have their eyes open to what is passing round
them and aspirations after better things'. Nel 1840 pochissimi erano
quelli che nel Leopardi riconoscevano il maggior poeta italiano
dell'età nuova, maggiore del celeberrimo Manzoni, e che si pro-
ponevano di rompere l'isolamento in cui egli era da ultimo vissuto e
che durava oltre la morte. L'isolamento non poteva più, a quella data,
essere rotto in Italia, dove la scomparsa dell'*Antologia* di Firenze aveva
tolto di mezzo il solo punto di riferimento e centro di raccolta di una
letteratura nazionale, e abbandonando al loro destino le singole
regioni aveva reso incolmabile il distacco della zona centro-meridio-
nale. Neppure poteva però essere rotto senza il contributo italiano:
al riconoscimento del Leopardi filologo erano bastati, lui vivo, e a
maggior ragione ora, nel precipitoso declino e naufragio della filologia
italiana, bastavano e avanzavano gli stranieri; al riconoscimento del
poeta no. La Germania in ispecie non era più quella del Goethe, che
vent'anni prima aveva deciso il successo europeo del Manzoni.
L'Inghilterra sempre era stata ed era fuori questione: attenta e
ospitale ma estranea, sufficiente a se stessa e al mondo, prima che
all'Europa. La Francia, per contro, dal 1830 innanzi aveva ritrovato
intero il suo slancio, la fiducia e la forza del suo primato intellettuale.
Ma ancora non bastava a se stessa: a differenza di quel che era stata
nell'età rivoluzionaria e imperiale, e di quel che sarebbe tornata ad
essere col secondo Impero, ancora si preoccupava di accogliere e
intendere, piuttosto che di sottomettere, quel che di estraneo e nuovo
le si parava innanzi. Conseguentemente sulla Francia si affisava
sempre più la cultura italiana, che vent'anni prima si era provata a
guardare, bene o male, in direzione della Germania e dell'Inghilterra.
E in ispecie alla Francia faceva capo, dovunque si trovasse, quella

parte ormai importante della cultura italiana che aveva dovuto prendere la via dell'esilio. Si spiega insomma che una svolta decisiva nella fortuna del Leopardi si verificasse in Francia prima che in Italia, sotto l'egida della superiore cultura francese, rappresentata dal Sainte-Beuve e dalla *Revue des deux mondes*, ma non senza il concorso di iniziative italiane, così dei pochi amici del Leopardi rimasti in Italia come degli esuli. La svolta può essere disegnata in modo semplice e chiaro, elencando, collegando fra loro e riconsiderando un per uno i seguenti dati bibliografici:

(1) Ristampa a Parigi nel 1841 dell'edizione napoletana dei *Canti*, che in Italia era stata ristampata una volta sola, a Firenze nel 1836. La ristampa parigina è notevole perché nello stesso volume aggiunge e implicitamente sottopone ai *Canti* una scelta di poesie d'altri autori moderni, cioè Foscolo, Pindemonte, Arici e Mamiani, l'ultimo dei quali, notoriamente congiunto e avverso al Leopardi, era in quel momento esule a Parigi e in amichevoli rapporti coll'editore. Questi, A. Ronna, non era un esule; era un modesto e benemerito insegnante di lingua italiana a Parigi, E certo non aveva bisogno dell'imbeccata altrui, né del Mamiani né del Tommaseo, per citarne due soli, certo manifestava il suo proprio convincimento, quando metteva in guardia i lettori: 'Noi non parteggiamo per le dottrine filosofiche del Leopardi . . .noi crediamo non poter l'uomo inclinato allo scetticismo, come fu il Leopardi, conseguire quella dose di felicità cui è dato aspirare, né muoversi a giovare agli altri con efficacia'. Ma così scrivendo, e concludendo a suo discarico e a conforto dei lettori che 'le pratiche del Leopardi furono sempre in contraddizione colle sue dottrine', il Ronna sapeva bene che la sua iniziativa editoriale, accompagnata da quelle riserve, intendeva soddisfare 'in parte al desiderio vivissimo di vedere riprodotte tutte le opere di lui [Leopardi], che vanno da lunga pezza manifestando i colti Italiani residenti in Parigi, i quali sperano in esse nuovo lustro alla patria'. E a tal punto il Ronna era consapevole di poter contare sull'appoggio altrui, che nella stessa avvertenza ai lettori ardiva rimbeccare, abilmente ma senza mezzi termini, l'autorevole e temibile Giordani: 'e rispondiamo anche in sì fatta guisa alle accuse che il Giordani, indotto certo in errore, scagliò colla magia delle sue prose contro agli Itali-Parigini per avere, a creder suo, dissuasa la riproduzione dei libri del Leopardi, cui egli dà seggio fra migliori vati d'Italia'. Il Ronna alludeva alla lettera che il Giordani aveva indirizzato il 15 settembre 1839 al marchese di S. Tommaso, implicitamente denunciando l'atteggiamento ostile al Leopardi del Tommaseo. A questo tentativo di far leva sulla notoria malignità e sulla dubbia italianità del Tommaseo per risolvere la controversia leopardiana in termini nazionalistici, nel tradizionale contrasto fra Italia e Francia, l'iniziativa editoriale parigina rispondeva dimostrando

col fatto che il contrasto non si applicava al Leopardi e che anzi in Francia si era disposti a fare per lui quel che la vecchia guardia, rappresentata dal Giordani, avrebbe dovuto e magari voluto, ma non sapeva fare in Italia.

(2) Pubblicazione a Parigi nel 1842 degli inediti *Paralipomeni*. Questo 'libro terribile', come ebbe poi a definirlo il Gioberti, che primo e solo, fino all'età nostra, bene o male riuscì a far profitto di quella ambigua e sottile terribilità, non poteva certo essere pubblicato in Italia. Ma neppure poteva essere appetito e digesto dalla assoluta maggioranza degli Italiani esuli. Non stupisce che anche in Francia apparisse quasi clandestinamente, senza che il Ronna o altri si azzardasse a presentarlo. Ma apparve, e trattandosi di un inedito non giovanile, dell'estremo periodo napoletano della vita del Leopardi, direttamente trasmesso da Napoli a Parigi, servì a dimostrare che in Italia la giovane guardia, rappresentata dal Ranieri, non era più disposta a far causa comune con la vecchia guardia rappresentata dal Giordani. Per la sostanza del libro e per il modo della pubblicazione, era ormai chiaro che l'eredità del Leopardi si era disincagliata dalle secche della polemica fra classicisti e romantici e fra Italia e Francia.

(3) Seconda ristampa a Parigi nel 1843 dei *Canti*. Era la stessa raccolta apparsa due anni prima, in cui al Leopardi si accompagnavano Foscolo, Pindemonte, Arici e Mamiani, con la sola giunta di un sonetto del Mamiani 'Sulla Tomba di N. Machiavelli'. Ma anziché in un volumetto a sé stante, la raccolta riappariva compresa in un massiccio volume di *Poeti italiani contemporanei maggiori e minori*, dove era preceduta da opere poetiche scelte del Parini, del Casti, del Monti, del Manzoni, del Grossi e del Pellico, che lo stesso editore aveva già pubblicato in singoli volumetti, ed era seguita da una sezione dedicata al Niccolini e da tre altre dedicate a più di cinquanta poeti minori o comunque ancora *in minoribus*, fra i quali parecchi esuli, come il Berchet e il Tommaseo. A schermo di quel che in un volume cosiffatto poteva esserci di politicamente troppo scottante, seguiva in fine, a cura del Ronna, 'un saggio di rime di Poetesse Italiane antiche e moderne'. È probabile che allo stesso scopo dovesse servire il 'Discorso preliminare intorno a G. Parini e il suo secolo' del Cantù, messo in fronte al volume. E finalmente serviva insieme a salvaguardare e riaffermare l'intenzione di fornire un quadro della poesia italiana contemporanea il frontispizio, dove i sei medaglioni realistici del Casti, del Parini, del Monti, del Niccolini, del Carrer e del Pellico facevano corona a un medaglione più grande e idealizzato del Manzoni. Fuori questione dunque era il principato, ma anche era chiaro che l'autorità del principe lasciava largo spazio alla dissidenza.

(4) Pubblicazione nel settembre del 1844, nella maggior rivista letteraria della Francia e, a quella data, dell'Europa, di un ampio

saggio sul Leopardi del maggior critico francese, Sainte-Beuve. Superfluo dire che era di gran lunga il più importante saggio mai apparso sull'argomento. Ma poiché bravo è chi si raccapezza nella *Bibliografia leopardiana* del Mazzatinti e del Menghini, compilata alla meglio e in fretta per il centenario del 1898 e malamente messa a stampa da altri più di trent'anni dopo, converrà precisare che in Italia, prima del 1844, chi non avesse sotto mano i pochi necrologi apparsi qua e là nel 1837 o poco dopo, fra i quali indubbiamente notevole per la sede e per il contesto quello di Fruttuoso Becchi negli Atti dell'Accademia della Crusca, altra informazione sul Leopardi non poteva reperire che quella fornita dall'articolo di Giuseppe Ignazio Montanari nella raccolta biografica del De Tipaldo. Vedo che nella citata *Bibliografia leopardiana* è anche compreso il *Saggio sulla storia della letteratura italiana nei primi venticinque anni del secolo XIX* di Ambrogio Levati, apparso a Milano per i tipi del leopardiano editore Stella nel 1831, e che l'inclusione è giustificata dalla seguente nota: 'Naturalmente vi si tratta del Leopardi'. Naturalmente il Leopardi è ricordato in questo saggio a pp. 33 n.,124, 125–6, ma solo come traduttore di poeti greci, *unus multorum*. A rigore, nei limiti cronologici prestabiliti dal Levati, solo le *Canzoni* rientravano, ma quei limiti non vietavano certo al Levati di intrattenersi sul clamoroso successo dei *Promessi sposi*. Resta che l'autore di un libro apparso a Milano nel 1831, qualunque fosse l'editore, 'naturalmente' ancora poteva ignorare l'importanza del Leopardi. E resta che, se nel 1844 affatto diversa ormai era la situazione anche in Italia, il saggio del Sainte-Beuve segnò una svolta decisiva nella fortuna del Leopardi, d'un colpo sottraendolo alla meschinità del culto municipale e partigiano, che gli era toccato in sorte in Italia, e isolandolo, secondo la verità storica, come autore vissuto e vivente nell'Europa. A tanto la cultura dell'Italia risorgimentale non poteva né voleva giungere: era però ormai pronta a fare del suo meglio perché anche in Italia l'importanza nazionale del Leopardi fosse generalmente riconosciuta.

(5) Pubblicazione a Firenze nel 1845, a cura del Ranieri, delle *Opere* in due volumi, subito seguiti dal terzo volume degli *Studi filologici*, a cura del Giordani e del Pellegrini, e l'anno dopo dal quarto, a cura di Prospero Viani, con gli *Errori popolari*. Con spiegabile intervallo seguirono nel 1849, sempre a cura del Viani, gli ultimi due volumi dedicati all'Epistolario. Con questa edizione, compresa nella nuova Biblioteca Nazionale dell'editore Le Monnier, si concludeva in Italia, e di qui si riproponeva all'Europa, il riconoscimento dell'importanza letteraria del Leopardi. L'edizione stessa confermava e conferma, a chi l'esamini con occhio attento, che la battaglia era stata vinta, in Italia, a duro prezzo, non per colpa di quelli che al Leopardi erano irrimediabilmente ostili, ma per l'inevitabile

discordia di quelli che dell'eredità di lui volevano e dovevano servirsi a fini diversi nel presente e nel prossimo o prevedibile futuro. Già nel 1845 appariva chiaro che i primi due volumi delle *Opere* erano affatto indipendenti dal terzo, se anche autore e editore fossero gli stessi. I documenti in seguito pubblicati hanno consentito ai moderni studiosi di riconoscere, se non di apprezzare storicamente, il contrasto sottostante a quella vistosa indipendenza del Ranieri da un lato, del Giordani e della sua scuola dall'altro. Non è qui il caso di riconsiderare, neppur di sbieco, il ridicolo processo a suo tempo intentato contro il Ranieri o addirittura contro il Giordani. Basti, per il primo dei due, l'esempio di un benemerito e valente studioso, F. P. Luiso, il quale, pubblicando nel 1899 un importante saggio sull'edizione leopardiana del Ranieri, candidamente dichiarava di aver fondato il suo giudizio sul Ranieri, 'leggendo tutto ciò che s'è scritto intorno a lui'. Manco gli passava per il capo che tale lettura fosse facoltativa e in gran parte inutile, e che per contro indispensabile fosse, per giudicare di un'edizione allestita nel 1844–5, leggere quel che il Ranieri aveva scritto, non il senile e famigerato *Sodalizio*, ma le opere da lui scritte e pubblicate subito dopo la morte del Leopardi. Di lì soltanto si può ricavare un giudizio storico sul Ranieri, qual'era al momento dell'edizione, sull'impronta che il sodalizio col Leopardi aveva lasciato in lui, ancora fresca e ben segnata, e insomma sulle premesse e sui fini di quella sua edizione.

Con ciò si tocca il punto cui la vicenda sopra delineata sui soli dati bibliografici compresi fra il 1841 e il 1845 voleva giungere. È chiaro che di per sé quei dati servono a inquadrare la ricerca, ma non bastano a un quadro storico: danno giusto risalto a iniziative individuali, ma non spiegano i motivi, le circostanze e gli effetti di tali iniziative. In questione non è il culto leopardiano del Giordani, del De Sinner, del Ranieri, di pochi altri, ma il riconoscimento generale, comunque condizionato, della grandezza e importanza del Leopardi da parte della cultura italiana ed europea. Non sarà da prendere troppo alla lettera, ma neppure è trascurabile la testimonianza di E. (Villardi) de Montlaur nel suo saggio sul Leopardi, pubblicato a Moulins nel 1846: 'Il y a six ans, nous traversions l'Italie; à peine avait-on entendu parler de Leopardi, et nos questions sur lui restaient presque toujours sans réponse... Mais un grand changement s'est operé depuis un petit nombre d'années. À Florence, cet admirable sanctuaire de l'art et de la poésie, nous avons entendu, il y a quelques mois, louer Leopardi par tous, et comme poète, et comme penseur, et comme savant. A Naples... nous avons vu des jeunes écrivains s'agenouiller devant la modeste tombe'. Appena occorre rilevare qui il riscontro col 'pio pellegrinaggio' del giovane De Sanctis e della sua scuola alla tomba del poeta. Il Montlaur non aveva motivo di chiedersi perché fra il 1840 e il 1845 fosse di tanto cambiata la notorietà del Leopardi in Italia. Noi abbiamo buoni motivi per porci la questione. E anzi tutto dobbiamo guardare alla scena della letteratura italiana in quegli anni. Subito salta agli occhi che le due date estreme coincidono con la nuova edizione, tutta nuova linguisticamente ma immutata nella sostanza, dei *Promessi sposi*, e con la prima raccolta autentica delle *Opere varie* del Manzoni. Se da gran tempo ormai la rinuncia del Manzoni a produrre alcunché paragonabile alle sue opere giovanili era presupposta e accettata come probabile, ora bisognava prenderne atto, come di una rinuncia totale e irrevocabile, teoricamente giustificata, al di là del romanzo storico, per qualunque componimento misto di storia e d'invenzione. Al Manzoni vivo nessuno poteva negare il suo ossequio, ma era chiaro che la sua presidenza sulla letteratura italiana sarebbe stata indi innanzi onoraria: poteva servir di monito, non di guida. Di fatto la successione era aperta, e poiché nessuno fra i vivi poteva aspirare a succedergli, poiché il solo poeta autentico e nuovo, in quel momento [1844] apparso sulla scena, Giuseppe Giusti, per il carattere stesso della sua poesia era fuori questione, bisognava rivolgersi ai morti: per primo al Leopardi, da poco scomparso immaturamente, e che vivo si era opposto al Manzoni. Il richiamo era ovvio, ma non si sarebbe imposto né subito né largamente in Italia, se il successo strepitoso, nel 1843, del *Primato* del Gioberti, non avesse attribuito autorità di guida sulla discorde e disorientata cultura italiana a un amico e ammiratore del Leopardi. Il Gioberti era esule e si era interamente votato alla causa del risorgimento nazionale, ma anche era prete e filosofo, campione della Chiesa di Roma e di una filosofia ossequente all'ortodossia cattolica. Questi due titoli congiunti di prete e di filosofo certo non lo raccomandavano alla guida della cultura italiana, né parevano conciliabili con una rivendicazione del Leopardi. Prevedibile era piuttosto che il Gioberti si schierasse dalla parte del Manzoni. Dapprincipio infatti, nella *Teorica del sovrannaturale*, pubblicata nel 1838, si era schierato da quella parte, e a proposito del Leopardi, si era aperto la via a una coraggiosa ma insieme prudente rivendicazione, insinuando il sospetto che l'incredulità di lui fosse imputabile all'influsso che su di lui giovane aveva avuto il Giordani. Subito dopo, il Gioberti si era però reso conto che accanto al Manzoni il posto di ministro della filosofia era occupato dal Rosmini, prete anche lui e avversario implacabile, e che d'altra parte né il Manzoni né il Rosmini, secondo le rispettive loro competenze, erano disposti a concorrere in quel'impegno totale della letteratura e della filosofia, oltreché della religione, nell'impresa del risorgimento politico dell'Italia, che a lui Gioberti chiaramente, e alla maggioranza degli Italiani oscuramente,

pareva in quel momento avviata a sviluppi decisivi. L'impegno della
letteratura nell'impresa non era nuovo né faceva difficoltà: classicisti
e romantici erano tutti patrioti a parole, benché non finissero di
azzuffarsi, sempre a servizio della patria, sulla scelta e sull'uso delle
parole. Nuovo era in Italia l'impegno della filosofia, se anche fosse
stato proposto, già nel 1834, dall'esile voce del Mamiani. Il Gioberti
aveva la voce tonante e l'eloquenza torrenziale di un gran predica-
tore. Mai si era sentito in Italia predicare a quel modo. Inoltre, a
differenza del Mamiani, che veramente era quale subito, a fiuto, lo
aveva giudicato il cugino Leopardi, e quale egli stesso incidental-
mente si definì nel 1846 (*Dialoghi di scienza prima*, p. 123), 'un
Pesarese che dall'arte di vender parolette, anzi menzogne, è trapas-
sato oggi alle metafisiche contemplazioni', il Gioberti si era lunga-
mente preparato e da ultimo deciso a prendere la moderna filosofia
europea per le corna, affrontandosi direttamente, non soltanto
attraverso la mediazione francese del Cousin, a quell'idealismo
tedesco, che in gran parte d'Italia, dove già si rabbrividiva al solo
nome di Kant, appariva emblematico delle nebbie nordiche di un
altro mondo, vitando per motivi climatici prima che religiosi. Il
Gioberti non poteva accettare né questa filosofia idealistica tedesca
né quella opposta, pur così poco italiana, del Leopardi, ma dell'una
e dell'altra non si sbarazzava alla lesta, deridendo e compatendo,
secondo l'uso della sempre viva tradizione retorica italiana. Meglio
una filosofia inaccettabile, che l'ignoranza e il disdegno della
filosofia. Meglio in ispecie una letteratura appesantita da una
filosofia inaccettabile, che non vuota d'ogni preoccupazione filosofica. Da un pezzo in Italia tutti o quasi tutti erano d'accordo che
occorresse infondere nella letteratura un contenuto nuovo, e che non
bastassero più, comunque scelte e usate, le parole della più bella
lingua del mondo; ma in pratica, disponendo per grazia di Dio d'una
tale lingua, tutti anche erano d'accordo che non occorresse né
convenisse sforzarsi troppo nella ricerca del contenuto nuovo: storia
e politica di casa erano a portata di mano; in più, per gl'incontenta-
bili, una qualche invenzione romantica altrui, regalata di una veste
immancabilmente più bella che non fosse quella delle lingue
originali. Non era una disposizione propizia all'intelligenza dell'opera
leopardiana. Per la prima volta nella predicazione del Gioberti
l'opera del Leopardi insistentemente riappariva qual'era, aspra,
difficile, in parte inaccettabile, e però proprio per la sua difficoltà e
asprezza opera esemplare e sovrana all'estremo opposto di una
tradizione letteraria iniziata dal poeta-filosofo Dante. E anche
riappariva in quella predicazione, che era tutt'insieme filosofica e
politica, opera esemplare e augurale all'impresa di un risorgimento
dell'Italia. Tale appariva nel suo insieme, *Paralipomeni* inclusi, non

per il solo contributo esplicito delle canzoni giovanili. Su questo punto il Gioberti aveva buoni motivi per insistere. L'ostilità o freddezza dei cattolici di stretta osservanza nei confronti del Leopardi era in quel momento insuperabile e però aveva scarso peso in Italia e nessuno fuori. Per contro, e in Italia e sopra tutto fuori, fra gli esuli, pesava sul Leopardi la condanna del partito rivoluzionario, che in quella disperata filosofia di lui, nella sua stessa solitudine sdegnosa, vedeva negate la fede e la solidarietà necessarie all'impresa del risorgimento nazionale. Il capo di quel partito, Mazzini, fin dal 1837, proprio in una rivista inglese, discorrendo della letteratura italiana contemporanea, si era sbarazzato in breve del Leopardi poeta, spacciandolo come un anacronistico superstite della scuola classica. Il mazziniano Antonio Gallenga, che nel 1841 pubblicò a Londra, sotto il nome di Luigi Mariotti, due volumi sull'Italia, 'general views of its history and literature in reference to its present state', discorrendo dei contemporanei, fra Manzoni, Pellico, Guerrazzi, Grossi, D'Azeglio, Cantù, Rosini, Niccolini, Berchet, Giannone, Balbo, Troya, Capponi, non ricordava che fosse esistito un Leopardi. Affatto eccezionale resta, e però spiegabile per l'autentica, benché oscura, eccellenza intellettuale dell'uomo, l'edizione dell'*Inno ai patriarchi* con traduzione latina e note, pubblicata a Eton nel 1844 da Girolamo Picchioni.[1] Fra gli esuli italiani, anche e in ispecie fra quelli che avevano conosciuto il Leopardi, la memoria di lui soggiaceva a riserve politiche per lo più insuperabili. La predicazione del Gioberti, concorrendo nello stesso nazionalismo esasperato, ma insieme riaffermando la priorità di un risorgimento morale e civile dell'Italia nel quadro della civiltà europea, dell'Italia tutta al di sopra delle parti e al suo più alto livello, non poteva convincere il Mazzini né l'ala estrema del partito rivoluzionario, ma, convincendo la maggioranza, costrinse anche i dissenzienti a riconsiderare e giustificare le loro riserve sul Leopardi. Come per l'appunto si vede nella nuova edizione della citata opera del Gallenga, apparsa a Londra sotto altro titolo [*Italy, past and present*] nel 1848. Queste schermaglie italiane sul Leopardi non potevano certo colpire l'attenzione di un osservatore straniero, inglese per giunta. Ma gli eventi politici e militari del 1848–49 imposero all'Europa il riconoscimento che di fatto una questione italiana esisteva. Il Gladstone che in Italia era stato nell'estate del 1849, se ne rese conto tanto più chiaramente e volontieri, in quanto la questione italiana, che di per sé non lo aveva mai toccato davvicino, gli apparve inestricabilmente congiunta con quella, che da gran tempo gli stava a cuore e ora più che mai, della sopravvivenza o abolizione dello Stato pontificio e insomma dei rapporti fra la Chiesa Anglicana e la Chiesa di Roma. Si spiega che, ignaro delle non molte carte in cui era conchiusa la grandezza del Leopardi, si sobbarcasse all'inumana fatica di leggere il *Gesuita moderno* del Gioberti. Perché di lì, come il titolo stesso prometteva, avrebbe ricavato notizie e argomenti utili alla battaglia politica che in quel momento si apprestava a combattere. Per dieci anni, dal 1839 innanzi, aveva cercato di far argine alla sorprendente e travolgente rivalsa della Chiesa cattolica in Inghilterra. Ora sapeva di aver perduto la partita: non soltanto né tanto per la conversione clamorosa del Newman, quanto per quella imminente dei due amici sui quali, dal 1839 innanzi, aveva fatto maggiore assegnamento, Henry Manning e James Hope-Scott. Ma gli eventi aprivano a lui, uomo politico, la possibilità di rinnovare la battaglia e tentar la rivincita, non più sul fronte religioso interno, ma su quello dell'Italia sconquassata e ribelle e in essa della Chiesa di Roma. Nel libro del Gioberti il Gladstone ritrovava l'immagine non nuova, ma che in quel momento gl'importava osservare da vicino, dell'Italia gesuitica e borbonica, l'Italia insomma, non del Manzoni, ma di Monaldo Leopardi. Di contro inaspettatamente trovava una diversa Italia, che non era neppur questa del Manzoni, né dello stesso Gioberti col suo *Primato*, né tanto meno del rivoluzionario Mazzini: era, raccolta in sé, nobile e severa, alta e inflessibile, l'Italia di Giacomo Leopardi. Dieci anni prima, quando la nuova Italia s'identificava per lui col Manzoni, probabilmente il Gladstone non sarebbe riuscito a superare la repugnanza di una filosofia antitetica alla sua fede cristiana. Ma dieci anni non erano passati invano né per la fortuna del Leopardi né per lui Gladstone, che se fosse rimasto quale splendidamente lo aveva allora descritto e definito il Macaulay nella *Edinburgh Review* ('It would not be at all strange if Mr Gladstone were one of the most unpopular men in England') non sarebbe stato in procinto di diventare uno dei più autorevoli statisti inglesi dell'età sua. La sua fede cristiana era intatta, ma la sua intelligenza degli uomini e delle cose, che gli stavano intorno e contro, era mutata. Aveva capito che l'Italia umile e letterariamente tutta nuova dei *Promessi sposi* non sarebbe mai riuscita a prevalere sulla secolare e scaltrita Italia gesuitica e borbonica: occorreva all'impresa, dubbia ma necessaria, l'Italia poetica, insieme antica e nuova, del Leopardi.

London   CARLO DIONISOTTI

NOTE

1. Mi par di capire, ma non sono certo di aver capito, forse perché a tanto non giunge la mia conoscenza dell'onomastica italiana e del gergo furbesco, che su questo episodio della fortuna del Leopardi

si sia fatto un poco di spirito a buon mercato in *Italian Studies*, XXIV (1969), p. 139: 'an assistant master at Eton, Girolamo Picchioni (*nomina sunt consequentia rerum*)'. Sulla sola base dei due opuscoli pubblicati a Eton da quell'*assistant master* (oltre all'inno leopardiano, il programma di un *Cours général de sciences naturelles*) si potrebbe scrivere un buon articolo. Mi contenterò di precisare, per chi abbia una elementare conoscenza della filologia europea, che nelle note all'inno leopardiano sono citati Benfey, *Griechisches Wurzellexicon* e Bopp, *Vergleichende Grammatik*. Non sto a chiedermi se altri a Eton fosse allora in grado di maneggiare quei testi (ancora era lontana la chiamata di Max Müller a Oxford). Certo è che le dita di una mano saranno troppe per contare gli Italiani, dovunque fossero, in Italia o fuori, allora in grado di maneggiarli. Fra le rarissime testimonianze di una sia pur vaga consapevolezza in Italia della rivoluzione operata dalla nuova filologia tedesca, citerò il ricordo della 'preziosa grammatica di Jacopo Grimm' nella *Storia d'Italia dal quinto al nono secolo* del Ranieri, Brussels, 1841, p. 171. Il Picchioni sapeva commentare le parole dell'inno leopardiano, ma non si fermava a quelle. Valga il seguente commento conclusivo: 'Lectorem forsitan pigebit quod in hoc carmine, ut in aliis passim, naturae et innocentiae vel potius ignorantiae statum tam miris coloribus exornans, mala civilem cultum consequentia hic noster amplificet, et bonorum nullam habeat rationem. Sed reputandum non idem esse officium poeseos et philosophiae: philosophiae enim est proprium omnes simul rerum aspectus pariter contemplari, omnia semper aequa lance perpendere, et suum unicuique rei relativum pretium sive honoris gradum semper tribuere; poeseos contra, aliquam e variis singularium rerum faciebus acriter intueri, et idealem formam mente conceptam et consequentes affectus δεινῶς καὶ ἐναργῶς verbis exprimere. Licet non solum sed oportet philosophum semper esse *allseitig*; poeta, et praesertim lyricus poeta, est reipsa, saltem in singulis operibus suis, *einseitig*, ut Germanice dicam uno verbo quod magno verborum circuitu aegre possem Latine. Ceterum, ut et hoc de quo agitur et alia παράδοξα huic nostro condonemus, juvet meminisse quod Seneca jam scripsit: nullum est magnum ingenium sine mixtura dementiae'. Insomma non stupisce che chi nel 1844 commentava l'*Inno ai patriarchi* nella lettera e nello spirito a quel modo, meritasse nella sua vecchiaia di assumere la cattedra di lingua greca e la presidenza dell'Accademia scentifico-letteraria di Milano e, morendo nel 1873, di essere commemorato con alto elogio da un collega che si chiamava Graziadio Isaia Ascoli. Anche quando così s'incontrano, *nomina sunt consequentia rerum*.

Sculpture in The Nineteenth Century

Apropos of a statue in Professor J. H. Whitfield's Garden

There is a trait in J. H. Whitfield's taste which I find even more congenial than his love of Italian literature (excepting his interest in Pirandello's theatre, which I do not share): that trait surprised me when I saw standing out in the middle of the lawn behind his house in Edgbaston a neoclassical marble divinity braving the soot with his exposed white, slightly dilapidated, nudity.

Sculpture in the proper sense of the word is far from popular nowadays, and neoclassical sculpture in particular has been often dismissed by art critics as frigid and academic, and labelled monumental, i.e. sepulchral, by the man in the street. In fact, whereas there is no scarcity of critics dealing with paintings, competent critics of sculpture are rarely met with. Even Wilhelm von Bode's reputation is tarnished by his attribution to Leonardo of the wax bust of Flora (now destroyed), the work of the able modeller, Richard C. Lucas; and Leo Planiscig's work on the small bronzes of the Renaissance is far from flawless, as has been shown by Sir John Pope-Hennessy, who, a *rara avis* among art critics, is the only one to whom we owe whatever progress has been made in the philological side of sculpture criticism, which had remained, before his illuminating studies, at the stage at which the criticism of paintings was in the time of Cavalcaselle.

If fakes of sculptures are infinitely less common than those of paintings (although one of the most notorious fakers ever, Dossena, actually specialized in that branch of art), the reason is not solely to be found in the fact that a work of sculpture presents more difficulties than a painting, but chiefly in the limited market there is for it. A work of sculpture is heavy and cumbersome, unsuited to modern apartments which are anything but spacious; it moreover suffers from a limitation of subjects (I am speaking, needless to say, of sculpture proper, not of such things as Calder's mobiles): in the past it was concerned with sacred or mythological or allegorical themes, and with portraits; of the two subjects in painting most popular with the bourgeoisie, the landscape and the genre, the first one was out of question in sculpture, the second was seldom treated outside the field of popular art, and usually confined to terracotta (Pinelli for instance repeated in that medium, with great success, a number of the subjects of his engravings). It appears that the only collectors of sculpture existing at the present time are interested either in wood-carvings or else little bronzes. The very material which in the past was *par excellence* the medium of sculpture, marble, is seldom worked by modern artists, who prefer metal, even that of old automobiles (e.g. César's *Compressed Buick*). At an auction of our time an authentic work by Donatello would not fetch the price of a 'delightful' eighteenth-century painter like Zuccarelli, or even a fashionable painter of conversation pieces like Arthur Devis (witness the enormous sum reached at a Sotheby auction of 31st October, 1973 by this latter's 'A Family of Anglers').

True, Canova's statues have been sought after by American museums in recent years, and in one of them at least there was a Canova exhibition even before the 1972 London Neoclassical Exhibition allocated to Canova's marbles a whole room, which proved to be the most successful one of the whole show. In fact the group of the Graces (lent by the Duke of Bedford), which inspired Ugo Foscolo to write the poem included in the sumptuous 1822 folio of *Outline Engravings and Description of the Woburn Abbey Marbles*, figured on the cover of the catalogue of *The Age of Neoclassicism*, both as seen from the front and from the back, and this very back view that Thorvaldsen criticized on account of the 'agitated confusion of the arms', should open the eyes of worshippers of Henry Moore, because if one considers in isolation that harmonious arrangement of material in a plexus of flowing serpentine lines, would one not see in it an anticipation of the taste of the English sculptor whose work is so admired in our own time? To be sure, those lines belong to bodies which are modelled after nature, whereas in the case of Moore there are such anacolutha that for instance his *Recumbent Figure* (in the attitude of the *Ilyssos* in the Parthenon pediment) which attracts the attention of visitors to the Tate Gallery, may appear as an allusion to a phrase like: 'on an empty stomach' (facing it, Nahun Gabo's honeycombed *Head no. 2*, seems to complain, 'How muddle-headed am I!').

Some of the art critics, who until a few years ago were averse to Canova, have recanted since. Two commonplaces used to recur in all appreciations of Canova: that he is a master of the graceful who stands aloof from the political events of his time in order to dream of Graces and Muses; and that he had the temperament of an eighteenth-century artist, stuck and frozen in a superimposed style (the Neo-Classic), and therefore produced works which were not spontaneous and which thus really cannot be classified as art. The formula of a Canova who, in order to conform to the spirit of his time, 'had to stifle the aspirations of his youth and nearly always repudiated himself', was accepted not only by the common run of critics, but even by those of a bolder turn of mind who, owing to their impatience with commonplaces, and their impatience with each other, often surprised us with their sallies. Roberto Longhi's spiteful epitaph, at the close of his *Viatico per cinque secoli di pittura veneziana* (1946), 'Antonio Canova, the still-born sculptor, whose heart is at the Frari, whose hand is at the Accademia, and the rest I do not know where', summed up a widespread opinion which could be amply illustrated by quotations from Cesare Brandi (for him, as he wrote in 1949, '*Perseus*, sheathed in his pumice-polished body as in tights, is a trite and indecent nude: a naked person in a *tableau vivant*. He is neither alive nor true to life: nothing could be more frozen and lifeless...If the Gorgon he is brandishing had turned him into stone, no stone could be stonier than this....He stands thanks to the law of gravity, but plastically he collapses.'), and from Kenneth Clark ('Canova, a brilliant portraitist and master of contemporary chic, would produce ideal figures as ridiculous as the *Perseus* of the Vatican, in which a fashion-plate version of the *Apollo Belvedere* holds at arm's length a caricature of the *Rondanini Medusa*. Apollo, with all those beliefs which clustered round his name, had lost his place in the human imagination; and the husk of Apollo alone remained to provide a meaningless discipline in academies of art').

Now, as often happens with critical appraisals, the tide has turned. People have become aware that for Canova the mistake of the Romantics had been repeated who heard only a monotonous seesaw rhythm in Pope's heroic couplet, missing its infinite modulations, accustomed as they were to a prosody which, in its attempt to follow the flow of emotion, could only be untidy.

As Gérard Hubert has remarked, Sculpture resumed a role of primary importance in the neoclassical period;[1] it collaborated with architecture and laid down the law for painting, but, since the Renaissance, as another critic, Henry Hawley[2], has noticed, modern European sculpture had followed the examples of the ancients, therefore neoclassical style in sculpture was less revolutionary than in painting, and its manifestations are often difficult to ascertain. Its chief characteristics were, nevertheless, a giving up of contrasts, and a yearning for an elegance of outline created by the mass as seen in profile. Its origins in eighteenth-century rationalism are evident, witness, for instance, Johan Tobias Sergal's letters from Rome, where he resided between 1767 and 1778 (he was the first Swedish sculptor of European fame): 'On my arrival in Rome I saw that there were no other masters to follow but antiquity and nature. I began by saying: it is necessary to make a new start in my studies: anatomy, which is the basis of the knowledge of the human body, then to copy the ancients in order to acquire the capacity of appreciating the beauties of nature, to avoid the defects and imitate what perfection there is in nature, and learn that the antique has not what is commonly called mannerism, but on the contrary it stands for a selection of the most perfect sides of nature, and this is what we call style. The ancients, then, and nature have been my true masters, I have taken advice from them only, and I have studied and shall study under them throughout my life, as long as I may be called an artist'. Words which paraphrase some famous lines of the greatest poet of rationalism, Alexander Pope, in his *Essay on Criticism*:

> First follow Nature, and your judgment frame
> By her just standard, which is still the same:
> Unerring NATURE, still divinely bright,
> One clear, unchang'd, and universal light,
> Life, force, and beauty must to all impart,
> At once the source, and end, and test of Art.

And after Nature, the rules of the ancients, which are not artificial, but are 'Nature still, but Nature methodiz'd'. Rémy Saisselin aptly remarks that, based as it was on an aesthetic theory which was thoroughly rational, neoclassical style was eminently teachable. Hence its dangers: it was correct, but monotonous; it was universal, but so little individual that sometimes it is extremely difficult to distinguish the hand of the various artists. It is equally difficult for us moderns—the remark is Hubert's—to be aware of certain nuances which at the time caused actual controversies, and, while within the bounds of neoclassicism there arose two opposite schools, that of Canova more graceful and Alexandrian, and that of Thorvaldsen (who hated Canova) which followed the ancients more rigidly, with archaic aspirations, the modern man in the street applies to both these schools the general definition of 'academic frigidity'. In Italy Thorvaldsen's manner had many followers and proliferated in monumental sculpture; Canova, however, impressed the French artists, and both his grace and his strength were models for such sculptors as Chaudet, Bosio, and others, who, among much that is conventional, produced a few masterpieces which one begins to re-value today, e.g. Bosio's bust of the Marquise de la Carte, of such a purity and elegance that, were it not for the capricious head-dress which betrays its date, it might be ascribed to the Renaissance.

Neoclassical sculpture was more a sculpture of single figures than of groups, more of pose than of motion, with a single exception which is no less than Canova's masterpiece, the Tomb of Maria Christina of Austria in the Vienna Augustinerkirche. Compare Carlo Finelli's attempt at rendering the Dance of the Hours: instead of the traditional tranquil Graces, he presents three mannequins in the act of gingerly lifting their feet: whenever neoclassical sculptors ventured to compose groups they often came dangerously near what Cesare Brandi compared to frozen meat: Canova's *Hercules and Lichas*, and even less plausibly Bosio's *Hercules fighting Achelous*, or, worse still, compositions lacking unity, such as Thorvaldsen's *Tomb of Pius VII*, a colossal centre-piece for a funeral banquet, or else *ensembles* which turn out to be grotesque circus performances, such as certain groups contrived by Ceracchi, whose statues (intended for the funeral monument of Van der Capellen, the leader of the Dutch democratic party) are scattered about in the Giardino del Lago at the Villa Borghese in Rome. Giuseppe Ceracchi (1751–1801), a Roman whose frantic life ended on the scaffold, had planned for the United States a hundred feet high monument crowned by the goddess Liberty alighting from a quadriga, in the midst of clouds spanned by a rainbow: she was to shake a thunderbolt with her right hand, which, dispelling the mists of error, should flood the universe with light, while her left hand was to be stretched out in a gesture inviting the American people to listen to her voice. The base, three hundred feet in diameter, was intended to contain several allegorical statues. This project having failed in America, the sculptor offered a similar one to France, and was praised by no less a personality than David. Here too Freedom alighted from a chariot drawn by two swans which Zephyr was leading through the clouds; all round there were statues of Philosophy, of Nature, of republican Valour, and so on, about ten of them. The Berlin sculptor Christian Friedrich Tieck executed for Madame de Staël a bas-relief for the tomb of her parents: the pair, wrapped in flowing garments, soar in the air; Necker is stretching out his arms towards his daughter, who kneels before a funeral stele, while Madame Necker points out the sky to her husband: a combination of motions which reminds Hubert of a semaphore. The Vicenza sculptor G. B. Comolli executed a group of Dante and Beatrice (for Villa Melzi at Bellagio) which contemporaries judged a masterpiece. Beatrice, draped in a classical mantle and poised on a globe surrounded by clouds, representing the planet Jupiter, is pointing out the sky to Dante who is dressed like one of the trousered barbarians of the Roman triumphal arches: the whole on a Gothic pedestal. When the neoclassical sculptors tried to give a greater unity to their groups, they resorted to baroque patterns—just as Bosio did in his statue of Louis XVI assisted by an angel, for the Expiatory Chapel.

Among the sculptors who succeeded best in harmonizing realism and idealism Hubert singles out Bartolini, who under Elisa Baciocchi directed an academy at Carrara, striving 'to establish sure principles for true progress, because founded on the imitation of truth, and not on artistic rules which deceived the minds of men throughout so many centuries. However my efforts were unavailing, because the prejudices deep-rooted in the weak brains of the ignorant multitude are hard to conquer'. Words which sound like those of John Webster, the Jacobean dramatist, who inveighed against the 'uncapable multitude', but for the opposite reason: because it failed to appreciate the classical precepts of tragedy.

Hubert stresses the importance of Carrara in the production of statues in the Empire period. From there came endless replicas of busts of Napoleon and his family, inauthentically signed, which nowadays are offered as 'unique' to credulous collectors. Carrara, with Rome and Milan, was responsible for the high prestige of the Italian statuary art of the period, while Venice, Tuscany and Naples had little to their credit. What harmed Italian neoclassicism was its hybridization with Christian symbology, and its application to the decoration of cemeteries. Whoever visits the Certosa of Bologna, or Villa Carlotta on Lake Como, or Villa Torlonia in Via Nomentana, Rome—places where that style, outliving its moments of grace, has become stultified into limp and tiresome allegories—is apt to draw the most negative conclusions. 'Beneath the wrinkles of his old men', Chateaubriand said of Canova, 'one detects the smile of Hebe': a mixture no less repulsive than the one mentioned in a famous Shakespearian line: 'lilies that fester smell far worse than weeds'.

If allegory, as Quatremère de Quincy said, aimed at 'phenomenizing moral qualities into corporeal forms', we must admit that the clash of realism with symbology very often resulted in grotesque productions during the nineteenth century, during which the neo-classical influence lingered on until the last quarter. On the whole the sculptural art of this period has been little studied by critics, who, as I remarked earlier, were never much attracted by this branch of artistic production. Luigi Cicognara, who wrote in the early part of that century, admitted that he had been stimulated to write his *Storia della scultura* in order to make up for the deficiency of works on that subject. But in works on nineteenth-century art published in our time the sections concerned with sculpture are still deficient. Witness Fritz Novotny's *Painting and Sculpture in Europe 1780-1880* in the Pelican History of Art: only thirty pages are given over to a brief survey of sculpture as against two hundred to painting, and there are little more than twenty-five plates for the former as against the hundred and seventy for the latter. In this respect Rudolf Zeitler's volume on the nineteenth century in the *Propyläen Kunstgeschichte* is the only one which gives more information. Though the text of Maurice Rheims's *La Sculpture au XIXe* (Paris, Arts et Métiers graphiques, 1972) is not very relevant, the wealth of illustrations is such that one can really claim that a vast and little explored territory of art is for the first time brought before our eyes. The kind of interest which has inspired Rheims, a well-known revaluator of *Art nouveau*, has, however, a peculiar bias, the same as lies behind a Berlin show of 1968, *Le Salon imaginaire* (paintings of the official exhibitions in the second half of the nineteenth century), and of a Paris show of 1973, *Exposition équivoque* (Musée des Arts décoratifs): an interest in the curious, the bizarre, the surprising, in what was once derogatorily called *le style pompier*, which nowadays, in the huge *ébranlement* and upsetting of all criteria of evaluation, is being rediscovered from unexpected viewpoints. There is no doubt that to a slipshod age like ours the technical finish of those forgotten painters and sculptors of the nineteenth century appears next to astonishing, and it is no wonder that certain paintings by Tabar, a name which you may search for in vain in standard volumes on the art of the nineteenth century, have been attributed to no less names than Géricault and Delacroix, but it is not so much the technical skill which thrills the modern onlooker, as the type of subject and its treatment. In the case of Tabar, for instance, the *Exposition équivoque* showed the *Supplice de la reine Brunehault*: a beautiful naked lady tied to the tail of a rearing horse which a groom is on the point of launching on a wild race. But if you check up the dates, you will find that that sworn enemy of Frédégonde (a Merovingian story unknown to most) was eighty years old at the time of her punishment. This circumstance we find to be rather entertaining, almost camp.

A portion of Rheims's book is dedicated to *Kitsch*, another to the unusual. The notion of *Kitsch* is elastic; some people may find that the illustrations which document that chapter are less appropriate than other ones included in other sections where Rheims bestows only praise. Why, for instance, should John Gibson's *Psyche carried by Zephyrs*, past which visitors to the Corsini Gallery in Rome, and members of the Accademia dei Lincei walk every day without even the faintest shade of a smile, be considered typical *Kitsch* by Rheims? And the same question may be repeated for the bronze statuette of Maria Taglioni (by Auguste Barre) and for the marble Elisa Baciocchi as a child (by Lorenzo Bartolini), unless Rheims, in consequence of a prejudice which has become established since the beginning of our century, condemns as *Kitsch* any work that is suspected of sentimentalism. There are, however, other sculptures which are much better entitled to be classified in that entertaining category. Such are

Louis-Ernest Barrias's *Electricity* and Henry Chapu's *Steam*, which Rheims rescues, writing of the former: 'A curious piece of work, in which a certain sensuality combines rather successfully with the didactic morality fashionable at the beginning of the Third Republic', and of the latter: 'An astonishing work, in the sense that the sculptor succeeds in giving to his composition, liable to ridicule, an aspect of truth thanks to the realistic face of the model.' Only the reproductions can convey some idea of the grotesqueness of these two works intended, according to Quatremère de Quincy's already quoted definition of allegory, to 'phenomenize moral qualities in corporeal forms'. Suffice it to say that *Steam* shows a naked woman poised on a thick cloud of steam issuing from a cauldron, while one is not sure whether the naked athlete, with a leather apron, is on the point of embracing her or torturing her (like Saint Agatha) with the heavy tongs placed at his feet. Elsewhere Rheims takes seriously the monuments of the Staglieno Cemetery in Genoa (which evidently are coming back into fashion, witness Theodore Crombie's article in the May 1973 issue of the art magazine *Apollo*, in which they are appreciated for their extraordinary technical skill and their obsession with the horrible), because they make him think of Magritte and Delvaux.

There are effects, like the one just quoted of the steam-lady, which baroque sculptors knew how to achieve and those of other periods not only failed to equal, but decidedly rendered grotesque. A case in point is offered by Canova's early work *Eurydice*. As has been argued by Sergio Rossi in a contribution to a volume of *Studi canoviani* (Rome, Bulzoni, 1973), the legacy of the great theatrical baroque *Weltanschauung* continued to exert on Canova a weighty influence thanks to the intermediary practice of the eighteenth-century Venetian sculptors, to which Maria Grazia Messina (in another essay included in the same volume) has added the influence of the new plastic sensibility expressed in the paintings of Piazzetta and his school. Of baroque technical skill, however, Canova's statues of Orpheus and Eurydice offer a very poor example. *Eurydice*, Rossi remarks, is composed according to a dynamic Rococo pattern: her head leans backward, in a direction opposite to that of her bust, while her crossed legs form a new contraposition; the flame which sucks Eurydice back to the Lower World is 'deliberately scaly and curly just as much as the girl's body is smooth and glossy'. It seems evident to me that Canova derived inspiration from the Bernini group of *Apollo and Daphne*; Eurydice too has her mouth half open like Daphne, though her face is that of the peasant girl whom Canova obtained for his model with no little difficulty, but whereas the smooth limbs of Bernini's creature are being gradually invaded

by the rough bark of the tree into which she is being inimitably
metamorphosed, the big curl of a flame which creeps between
Eurydice's legs could be easily mistaken for pubic hair. Moreover
one of Orpheus' arms is outstretched, with an open hand, and he is
moving his legs with an uncouth mimicry which is almost a parody
of the juvenile rush of Bernini's Apollo. As for the other early work
of Canova which met with so much applause, the group of *Daedalus
and Icarus*, it has been said that its inspiration is of a pictorial kind,
Piazzetta-like, and also (in G. C. Argan's opinion) that it is closer to
baroque sculpture (and in particular to Bernini) than to classical
sculpture, but still there is a classical group, well-known in Canova's
time, which from the first (it had come to light about 1622) had been
in Cardinal Ludovisi's collection: a work of the Greek sculptor
Menelaus representing an adult woman who is laying her arms on
the shoulder and on one of the arms of a youth (by some believed to
be Elektra and Orestes). On the other hand the Canova group is even
closer to sculptures of the second half of the nineteenth century than
to eighteenth-century art: think of that taut string with which
Daedalus is fastening the wings on his son's shoulder, a heterogeneous
element like the metal foil whose pliant tip is being tested by A. J.
Moreau-Vauthier's *L'homme à l'épée* illustrated by Rheims in his
section: '*Les Matières précieuses*'.

This piece of realism in the career of a sculptor who later took a
quite different path (but one must remember that only Canova and
Quatremère de Quincy did not share the suspicious attitude of their
contemporaries when faced with the sense of nature evident in the
Elgin marbles, which the theorists of neoclassicism judged excessive
and unorthodox) illustrates a problem which frequently confronts us
when dating nineteenth-century marbles: the neoclassical tradition
lingers throughout the whole century; and very puzzled would the
student be who was challenged to date the five naked beauties lying
on a couch, which are shown on two pages of the neoclassical section
of Rheims's volume; it is very probable that he would place at the
same moment of time Canova's *Pauline* and Johan-Niklas Byström's
Juno and little Hercules (which are in fact separated by an interval of
twenty years), but he would never guess that a whole half century
had elapsed between Schadow's *Resting Girl* (1826) and Ion George-
scu's *Source* (1879), or between Byström's statue (1828) and Gustav
Crauk's *Youth and love*. Admittedly, there is a greater freedom of
movement, a greater facial animation in the later works, and the
introduction in them of slight dissonances in order to increase their
charm, but the pattern remains substantially the same. If we pass
on to the American female nudes executed by the mid-century
(Hiram Powers, *The Greek Slave*, 1843, *California*, 1858), then even

those criteria do not help, because the correctness of those statues is flawless (apart from the metal chains of the Greek slave, a weak echo of the latent sadism of the nineteenth century). The *Greek Slave* is placed side by side with James Pradier's *Nyssia* (1848), Edoardo Fantacchiotti's *Eve* (1884) and the other *Eve* by Ernest Hiolle (1883): the dates of these statues may surprise an onlooker who is not an expert. Indeed the nineteenth century is plethoric and chaotic; before the split caused by the advent of Rodin (anticipated by Daumier), the century is a criss-cross of currents, and the classification by motifs adopted by Rheims seems the only possible one.

I have just mentioned American sculpture; a closer view of it is of some interest, and Sylvia E. Crane's recent book on it[3] provides a good guide. We may be surprised to hear that until the early decades of the nineteenth century the majority of Americans had never seen a marble statue. This may explain a few facts, for instance that Horatio Greenough's vocation as a sculptor was awakened by the sight of a marble statue of the Athenian general Phocion, which stood as an ornament in his father's garden: he had no experience of other artistic models of the kind, and that marble must have appeared to him a prodigy; it accounts also for the reluctance of the Americans to accept the nude when they were confronted with the first statues, a reluctance not due only to novelty, but chiefly to Puritan abhorrence of any allusion whatever to sex. There were no museums then. When Charles Willson Peale, in association with Giuseppe Ceracchi, organized a drawing school at Philadelphia in 1791, being unable to find any live models, not even male ones, in desperation he stripped off his clothes and bared his own torso to the class for study. The school's only antique model was a plaster cast of the Medici Venus that had been tightly shut off from public view for reasons of propriety. A few factors contributed to educate taste: the habit of the Grand Tour for wealthy people and the sojourn in Italy, which was deemed indispensable for the training of artists; and the presence of Italian artists in America (Jefferson asked his neighbour Philip Mazzei, when this latter was in Italy in 1805, to procure him the services of good sculptors to collaborate in the decoration of the Capitol, and Giuseppe Franzone and Giovanni Andrei came over in response to this urgent request. Others followed: two of Canova's pupils in 1823, Enrico Causici and Antonio Capellano, and also Luigi Persico). Notwithstanding all this, James Fenimore Cooper, when he came back home in the mid-thirties, sadly remarked: 'New York, which is four times as large as Florence, and ten times as rich, does not possess a tithe of ancient art, or of noble palaces and churches and other historic monuments'.

It sounds almost a paradox, Mrs Crane remarks, that the first to

introduce the female nude in sculpture into America should have
been a scion of a Puritan family of New England, Horatio Greenough.
He espoused the aesthetic principles of neoclassicism which were
based on the beauty of the human body as it had issued from God's
hands. When Greenough came to Italy in 1825, three names were
paramount in the field of sculpture: Canova, Thorvaldsen and
Bartolini. So far, no American had ever produced a work of statuary:
why should Americans, Greenough asked himself, be obliged to
undertake the trip to Europe in order to gain aesthetic pleasures?
He thought of putting a remedy to this himself. He would vie with
the ancients and the moderns in the rendering of the female nude,
with a proviso, though, which reminds one of a similar intention of
Milton, who found that above the Latin poets, who occasionally
spoke 'unworthy things of themselves or unchaste of those names
which before they had extolled', he 'preferred the two famous re-
nowners of Beatrice and Laura, who never write but honour of them
to whom they devote their verse, displaying sublime and pure
thoughts, without transgression'. Greenough declared that in the
subject of the nude he would 'attempt to interest and charm the eye
and mind with a female form without appealing to the baser passions,
what has not been made in Italy for many years'. This is the constant
refrain of American neoclassical sculptors. Hiram Powers too intended to purge any lascivious overtone so as to render his subject
(*The Greek Slave*) pure. The nude had to be imbued with moral
respectability by illustrating a realistic story that would vindicate
the nude state. In the case of *The Greek Slave*, 'it was not her person
but her spirit that stood exposed': the spirit of oppressed innocence, of
the persecuted maiden. 'Naked, yet clothed with chastity, she stands',
said one critic, paraphrasing a line from Tennyson's *Godiva*. Thomas
Crawford also, the most realistic of these American sculptors, strove
to unite beauty with lovely innocence; his *Vesta* was praised for the
purity of her expression, and made a stir in the artistic milieu of
Rome in the forties. Now the nude, whatever neoclassicists may have
said in the wake of Winckelmann, had never been devoid of a
physical appeal, and quite rightly Kenneth Clark, confuting an
opinion of the philosopher S. Alexander ('If the nude is so treated
that it raises in the spectator ideas or desires appropriate to the
material subject, it is false art, and bad morals'), maintained on the
contrary that 'no nude, however abstract, should fail to arouse in
the spectator some vestige of erotic feeling, even although it be only
the faintest shadow—and if it does not do so, it is bad art and false
morals.'[4]

Nevertheless *The Greek Slave* caused a scandal, not so much at the
time of the Great Exhibition at the Crystal Palace (1851), where it

got somehow camouflaged in a forest of white statues, but when the Crystal Palace was moved in 1852–54 to the purer air of Sydenham. Contemporary moralists were troubled not because of her body, says Kenneth Clark,[5] 'which was a blameless pastiche of the Cnidian Venus, but because her wrists were handcuffed'.

The motives which inspired Powers were ostensibly entirely external: the subject of slavery was debated in America and was to culminate in the Civil War; the Greek war of independence was a popular one; the expression of the oppressed maiden was meant to convey 'what trust there could be still in a Divine Providence for a future state of existence'. The statue had therefore to appeal to Victorian feelings of admiration for a pure and innocent beauty and of compassion for her sad plight. The subject was then 'imbued with moral respectability', and, purged as it was supposed to be of lascivious thoughts, it could not fail to meet with general approval. But there was in that period an underground current which in a few years' time was to come to the surface in Swinburne's *Poems and Ballads* (1866); and was not the Greek Slave a twin sister of Juliette, the victim of the monstrous lust of the Marquis de Sade? Were not these handcuffed hands an anticipation of the *Scandales de Londres* revealed by the *Pall Mall Gazette?* 'Strapping girls down—'.

Anyhow, *The Greek Slave* made Hiram Powers famous: numberless copies were made of it; the handcuffed girl was for a time no less popular than the so-called *Beatrice Cenci* of the Barberini Gallery: it was the theme of beauty imperilled and contaminated which pierced the romantic sensibility to the quick. The statue inspired Elizabeth Barrett Browning to write a sonnet 'typical of the literary outpouring the statue evoked', says Mrs Crane:

They say ideal beauty cannot enter
The house of anguish. On the threshold stands
An alien image with enshackled hands
Called the Greek Slave! as if the artist meant her
(The passionless perfection which he lent her,
Shadowed not darkened where the sill expands)
To so confess man's crimes in different lands
With man's ideal sense. Pierce to the centre,
Art's fiery finger, and break up ere long
The serfdom of this world. Appeal fair stone,
From God's pure heights of beauty against man's wrong!
Catch up in thy divine face, not alone
East grief but west, and strike and shame the strong,
By thunders of white silence, overthrown.

A more obvious sensual appeal was not, however, absent, because the technical ability of Powers (more gifted with mechanical genius than with artistic talent, as many, among them Hawthorne, recognized; to such a degree, that his invention of contrivances to improve the processes of working on marble marked a remarkable technical progress) caused Edward Everett to remark that the instruments Powers used gave 'to the surface of the marble a delicate roughness...which absolutely counterfeits flesh and produces an illusion not merely beyond anything we have seen in the works of Donatello, Mino da Fiesole, or Gambarelli[6]...but beyond anything we have witnessed from the chisel of any other artist'. The nude, which the neoclassicists considered as the proper form to represent heroes, had not met with the approval of Napoleon, who, when Canova wanted to represent him in the nude, could be persuaded only with difficulty of the propriety of such a pose, and the statue, when executed, was not liked and was consigned to an obscure corner of the Louvre. But in America the male nude was disliked for a different reason; it was considered indecent by the average American. Fenimore Cooper advised Greenough to make the statue of Washington 'as servant and simple as possible', i.e. like that of a modest servant of the country, and to aim rather at the natural than at the classical, but the sculptor, in obedience to the classical convention, represented him with a nude torso, draped in a voluminous mantle, in a pose recalling Jupiter Tonans, pointing heavenward with his right hand, 'as a conductor between God and Man'. To the average American, though, the statue looked like a warrior 'with a huge napkin lying on his lap and covering his lower extremities...preparing to perform his ablutions in the act of consigning his sword to the care of the attendant'. Greenough, however, starting from the idea of neoclassical beauty, interpreted in the moral terms proper to New England transcendentalism, elaborated a personal ideal of functionalism, an aesthetic theory which to Mrs Crane seems to anticipate Sullivan's and Wright's principles. With him the perfection of the naked human body, considered as a reflection of God and the measure of the world by the Renaissance, assumed, through the ideas of Francesco Milizia, the paradigmatic meaning of 'unflinching adaptation of forms to functions', a consistency and harmony of parts. This was the fundamental law. He, foreshadowing Adolf Loos, disposed of embellishments as inorganic, nonfunctional encumbrances to harmony and rationality. He believed that the completeness and rational structure of nature showed the accord of truth and one God. Unadapted ornament Greenough considered sinful, again a concept which Loos was to stress at the beginning of our century. 'The advocate of independent beauty must necessarily believe in a God of evil, or the devil too, for unrelated embellishment is irrational, and refutes its being the work of a divine hand'. Greenough judged 'the flying hair and waving draperies of Bernini' as vagaries, no more admissible than 'the prolific silliness of Borromini'. He disapproved of the appropriation of the Greek temple form for indiscriminate modern commercial purposes. He stated that he would 'learn of the Greeks to be American'.

If Greenough was the Phidias of American sculptors, the later phases of Greek sculpture seem to be echoed by the other two American neoclassical sculptors, Powers and Crawford. Already in Powers, whom Thorvaldsen is supposed to have called 'the greatest sculptor since Michelangelo', realistic, idyllic, in a word, Alexandrian motifs are present: alongside works of impeccable, anonymous classical character (busts of *Genevra* and *Proserpine*), he produced realistic busts like that of Andrew Jackson, with wrinkles and sunken cheeks round a toothless mouth, and indulged in fashionable sentimentality in statues of children. Decidedly Hellenistic is the lively statue which gave fame to Thomas Crawford, *Orpheus and Eurydice*, with the Greek poet bending over the abyss of the nether world, out of which comes the wind that blows his cloak; no less typical are his *Dying Indian Princess*, modelled after the *Dying Amazon* of the Naples Museum, his treatment of anacreontic themes in the manner of Thorvaldsen, and his handling of Victorian sentimental subjects of children playing or else resting in an eternal sleep (*The Children in the Wood*, inspired by the pathetic story which was so popular because of the Dickensian theme of the death of children) ?; finally he dressed in modern clothes his statues of American heroes, like his Washington on horseback, a bronze equestrian statue of the type of Rauck's *Frederick II*. His bronze doors for the Senate were inspired by Ghiberti's for the Florence Baptistery.

On the whole the American neoclassical sculptors leave an impression of correctness, smoothness and insipidity, typical of the outgoing classicism of the 1840s even in Europe. They make me think of Agnes in *David Copperfield* (chapter IX): 'Ever pointing upward, Agnes; ever leading me to something better; ever directing me to higher things!' Cemeterial sculpture, maybe.

Rome   MARIO PRAZ

NOTES

1. *La Sculpture dans l'Italie napoléonienne*, Paris, Editions E. Boccard, 1964, p. 1.
2. *Neo-classicism, Style and Motif*, Cleveland Museum, 1964, together with an essay by Rémy G. Saisselin.

3.   *White Silence*, Greenough, Powers and Crawford, American Sculp-
     tors in Nineteenth-Century Italy, Clark Gables, University of
     Miami Press, 1972.
4.   Kenneth Clark, *The Nude*, London, Murray, 1956, p. 6.
5.   *Op cit.*, pp. 149, 379.
6.   i.e. Rossellino.
7.   This statue is reminiscent of Thomas Banks' Tomb of Penelope
     Boothby in Ashbourne church (Derbyshire).

Italo Svevo and Thomas Mann's
Buddenbrooks

In the brief preface to the first edition of *The World as Will and Representation*, Schopenhauer states what he expects of his reader in such a way as to deter all but the most persistent. The reader is not so much invited as commanded to read the substantial treatise twice. The suggestion, in the preface to the second edition, that the bulky *Supplements* be referred to only on the second reading, has all the air of being a concession to weaker mortals. Schopenhauer's earlier work, *On the Fourfold Root of the Principle of Sufficient Reason*, and his essay *On Vision and Colours* are also indicated as essential preliminary reading, a requirement which was, logically enough, extended still further when the philosopher wrote: 'In general, I make the demand that whoever wishes to make himself acquainted with my philosophy shall read every line of me'.[1] Nor was this all, for to the works of Schopenhauer were added those of Kant, while it would be all to the good, continued Schopenhauer, if in addition the reader were familiar with the works of Plato or, better still, the *Upanishads*. Schopenhauer's influence has been so great that one is tempted to believe that not all his readers satisfied the stringent conditions he laid down for access to his system of thought. Two who failed to do so figure as the central characters of the first novels of Italo Svevo and Thomas Mann.

The names of Svevo and Mann have from time to time been linked by the critics, usually in generic terms, indicating that both were influenced by Schopenhauer, Nietzsche and Freud, or that both responded to their vision of the world by adopting an ironic attitude which is not, as at least in the case of Svevo it might at first appear to be, totally negative and sceptical, but is on the contrary an assertion of the value of lucidity and honesty. And in the most important works of both men, irony is directed towards discovering the causes of what they regarded as the sickness undermining the society in which they lived. It would be interesting to compare the works and careers of the two novelists, who to a great extent drew their inspiration from common sources, but so far only one comparative study has been made. Lilian R. Furst, in a perceptive essay, has compared *La coscienza di Zeno* (1923) and *The Magic Mountain* (1924), both of which she sees as being shaped by the impact of the 1914–18 war, and both as dealing with the condition of modern man in terms of disease and health, although using very different narrative techniques.[2] G. Cattaneo, in an essay on Svevo and psychoanalysis, drew attention to the way in which Mann, like Svevo, had made use of Schopenhauer's philosophy in *Buddenbrooks*, which was published some nine years after *Una vita* (1892).[3] That *Una vita* is a discussion, in fictional terms, of Schopenhauerian ideas is by now a commonplace of Svevo criticism; but it is an over-simplification to suggest, as some critics do,[4] that the novel is primarily concerned with Schopenhauer's views on suicide, since Schopenhauerian ideas in fact permeate the whole work. In the main plot and in the sub-plots Svevo depicts life as a struggle which is capable of being interpreted on the biological level in Spencerian terms as the result of an impulse towards survival, and on the metaphysical level as the manifestation of the Will, blindly willing only its own life and warring against itself as it manifests itself in the separate, transient phenomena which men are and through which the Will expresses itself in time and space.

Alfonso at first understands nothing of this; unable to comprehend the motives which compel his colleagues at the bank to engage in what seems to him to be a worthless struggle, he wishes merely to return to the imagined tranquillity of his native village and to his mother's over-tender care—which has, in reality, made an emotional cripple of him. Little by little, however, he comes to understand that life is a struggle and even to think of his relationship with Annetta as a *lotta* in which he must win through to victory.[5] Thus the Will asserts itself even in a hero so un-heroic that Svevo's original title for the novel was *Un inetto*. And it is significant that the Will asserts itself most strongly in a seduction, an act of sexual aggression in which Alfonso is 'frettoloso e brutale':[6] for Schopenhauer had described the genitals as the 'focal point' of the 'dark impulse of willing' (I, 203).

Man in Schopenhauer's thought, and Alfonso in Svevo's novel, has a dual nature:

> man is simultaneously impetus and dark impulse of willing (indicated by the pole of the genitals at its focal point), and eternal, free, serene subject of pure knowing (indicated by the pole of the brain) (I, 203).

Nitti is a thoughtful young man and, limited though his culture is, it is superior to that of those around him. He makes resolutions which he is incapable of keeping—to dedicate himself to the study of philosophy, to teach Lucia Italian, to absent himself from Annetta's *salon*. This is Schopenhauerian man, imagining that 'he can at any moment enter upon a different way of life'. But as an individual, he is a mere phenomenon of the Will, and so his conduct is determined; '*a posteriori*, through experience, he finds to his astonishment that he is not free...that notwithstanding all his resolutions and reflexions he does not change his conduct...' (I, 113–14). Alfonso does not construct the new philosophical system which he had planned, his Italian lessons are a disaster, and before long he finds himself returning to Annetta's *salon*. He cannot abandon his ambitions for worldly success, and he aspires in vain to renunciation. Indeed, by means of a certain sophistry he manages to convince himself from time to time that he has achieved that state, as when, for example, he 'renounces' Annetta, and when he gives his inheritance from his mother as a dowry for Lucia. It is true that by leaving Trieste so soon after seducing Annetta he fails to follow up his initial victory, thus giving the Maller family time to arrange a socially more suitable match for her; but his departure has the air of a flight from danger, and rather than renouncing success he is avoiding a relationship which he has come to regard as a betrayal of his mother. And, significantly, he 'renounces' the wealth this marriage would bring him only after he learns that he has lost Annetta. He gives his inheritance as a dowry for Lucia, and Schopenhauer cites the giving away of money 'to persons in distress' as an example of nobility (I, 372), but he also points out that it is not enough to give solely in order to alleviate the wants of others: it must be done in order to mortify the Will (I, 381–2). Nitti, in effect, uses his money as a means of manipulating the Lanuccis, and expects to derive from his gesture rather more gratification than it in fact provides. There is in his actions a constant implied contrast between Schopenhauer's austere ideal of asceticism and the facile posturing which enables Alfonso to regard 'un piccolo sforzo' as 'una rinuncia' (II, i, 412). His mistake is that he looks always for 'una via aggradevole, facile e senza meta' (II, i, 392).

Nitti's suicide is equally un-Schopenhauerian. It has often been pointed out that Schopenhauer ruled out the possibility of suicide, since he regarded it as an affirmation of the Will to live.

> The suicide wills life, and is dissatisfied merely with the conditions on which it has come to him. Therefore he gives up by no means the will-to-live, but merely life, since he destroys the individual phenomenon.

Thus suicide is 'a quite futile and foolish act, for the thing-in-itself[7] remains unaffected by it, just as the rainbow remains unmoved, however rapidly the drops may change which sustain it for the moment' (I, 398–9). But Bouissy is only partly right to say that 'Le suicide d'Alfonso ne sera, à tout prendre, que la version caricaturale, provinciale, du renoncement schopenhauerien',[8] for there is more to it than has so far been suggested.

Alfonso sees that life is a struggle from which, in moments of dissatisfaction or pain, he would like to break free. This too is very Schopenhauerian.

> At times, in the hard experience of our own sufferings or in the vividly recognized suffering of others, knowledge of the vanity and bitterness of life comes close to us who are still enveloped in the veil of Maya. We would like to deprive desires of their sting, close the entry to all suffering, purify and sanctify ourselves by complete and final resignation. But the illusion of the phenomenon soon ensnares us again... ; we cannot tear ourselves free (I, 379).

What is striking in Alfonso's case, however, is not only the way in which his conduct exemplifies Schopenhauer's philosophy but also his failure to understand that this is the case. Is he not, after all, a budding philosopher? Consider the reasoning which leads him to decide to commit suicide. Firstly, he examines conventional arguments against suicide, which he dismisses as false. 'Non erano argomenti ma desiderî, il desiderio di vivere'. He then continues, in what is in effect a monologue in indirect free style;

> Egli si sentiva incapace alla vita. Qualche cosa, che di spesso aveva inutilmente cercato di comprendere, gliela rendeva dolorosa, insopportabile. L'abbandonava senza rimpianto. Era la via per divenire superiore ai sospetti e agli odii. Quella era la rinunzia che egli aveva sognata. Bisognava distruggere quell'organismo che non conosceva la pace; vivo avrebbe continuato a trascinarlo nella lotta perché era fatto a quello scopo (II, i, 425).

These final paragraphs of the novel imply that Alfonso, at least in his own estimation, was well read in philosophy and that he had read a certain amount of classical philosophy as well as the 'filosofi più moderni'. But clearly he has not read *The World as Will and Representation*, for there he would have found both Schopenhauer's argument against suicide and an explanation of the fallacy underlying the belief that 'bisognava distruggere quell'organismo'. Alfonso has failed completely to look beyond the surface of things, for

> the eyes of the uncultured individual are clouded, as the Indians say, by the veil of Maya. To him is revealed not the thing-in-itself, but only the

phenomenon in time and space, in the *principium individuationis*. In this form of his limited knowledge he sees not the inner nature of things, which is one, but its phenomena as separated, detached, innumerable, very different and indeed opposed (I, 352).

He regards pleasures and enjoyments on the one hand and pains and miseries on the other as different and opposed, failing to understand that they are merely different aspects of the Will-to-live. Nitti, then, is, in Schopenhauerian terms, an 'uncultured individual'—indeed Svevo seems constantly in the course of the novel to be hinting at the inadequacy of the culture of which Alfonso is so proud, as when he describes him as reading literary histories when he has not read a single Italian classic in its entirety and, with splendid irony, when he describes him as loftily despising the novel, 'avendo ancora sempre il disprezzo da ragazzo per la letteratura detta leggera' (II, i, 106).[9]

Nitti may however have read some Schopenhauer, even though he is the kind of reader who would have been deterred by the preface to *The World as Will and Representation*. There is no mistaking, in his dismissal of the traditional arguments against suicide, the echo of Schopenhauer's short essay *On Suicide* in *Parerga et Paralipomena*, in which the philosopher maintains that no-one—except, by implication, himself—has yet produced any valid philosophical argument against suicide. I doubt whether the implications of this essay could be understood without some knowledge of the ideas set out in *The World as Will and Representation*, since Schopenhauer merely states in the essay that suicide is a mistake because it substitutes a merely apparent release from this world of misery for a real one (that is, though this is not stated explicitly, through ascetic renunciation). And Schopenhauer goes on to say:

> Perhaps there is no one alive who would not already have put an end to his life if this end were not something purely negative, a sudden cessation of existence. But there is something positive in it as well: the destruction of the body. This is a deterrent because the body is the phenomenal form of the will to live.[10]

This is precisely why Nitti kills himself: a citizen of the post-Darwinian world, his view of life is narrowly materialistic. 'Bisognava distruggere quell'organismo che non conosceva la pace'. If, as seems possible, Alfonso has read at the most only part of *Parerga et Paralipomena*, then his incomplete reading is symbolic of his failure to achieve complete understanding of his predicament. And even if one considers that the partial parallelism of his thought with that of Schopenhauer on this point is presented by Svevo as fortuitous, showing how near and yet how far he is from complete understanding, the same symbolism holds good, with an incomplete intuitive coincidence of thought taking the place of an incomplete reading.

But to say this is to raise new questions. Why does Alfonso's understanding remain limited? What philosophy *has* he read? What kind of a philosopher does he aspire to become? It is not enough to say that he is an 'uncultured individual', although this is indeed true, or that he is psychologically handicapped. There are two reasons for his ignorance, and these reasons relate to important strands of thought in the novel. The first of these strands is Darwinism, or more precisely a combination of Darwinian theories of evolution and of 'social Darwinism' as propounded chiefly in the works of Herbert Spencer.[11] Macario introduces Alfonso to the notion of 'lotta' and describes the origin of the impulse to conflict in exclusively biological terms,[12] pointing out that the seagull, all wings and stomach, has evolved perfectly as a bird of prey without developing its brain. Alfonso, in his view, is unfit for the social struggle because his intelligence is too developed. The importance of Darwinism in Svevo's work needs no emphasizing here, but Macario's explanation of the phenomenon of conflict in exclusively biological terms is simplistic, a facile determinism, as Maxia points out,[13] which is comforting for the successful, although less so for the losers. Svevo, however, was never satisfied with a solely materialistic explanation and sought to fuse science, philosophy and psychology into a coherent whole.

The second of these strands of thought is represented by the philosopher whom Nitti has read and the kind of philosopher he aspires to be. He has read at least some of the 'filosofi più moderni'. We may take it that Schopenhauer (1778–1859) is not one of these. A clue to the identity of the philosopher whom Svevo has in mind is given in the narrator's account of Nitti's ambition to found 'la moderna filosofia italiana' with a projected work entitled *L'idea morale nel mondo moderno*, the aim of which is to show that the basis of conventional morality is 'un'impostazione necessaria per il vantaggio della collettività' (II, i, 199). At this point in the novel Alfonso has no idea how he will develop his theme since he has so far written only the title page and a preface, but one's initial impression is that this treatise could develop into a discussion of the relative rights of individualism against the demands of the community. 'Egoism' in this sense was discussed by Svevo in the essay *Un individualista*, in which he reviewed two novels by Joséphin Péladan (1858–1918) and condemned the author's extreme individualism as 'queste manifestazioni di un egoismo malaticcio' (III, 604).

Nitti's intentions become clearer when he describes to Annetta this projected 'lavoro sulla morale', which is now to be 'la negazione anzitutto della morale come tutti l'intendono fondata su una legge religiosa o sul bene individuale' (II, i, 230). The apparent confusion of thought behind the view that 'la morale come tutti l'intendono' has three bases—the demands of the community, religion, and individual well-being—disappears when one realizes that Svevo has in mind something more than Péladan's eccentricities. Nitti's intentions are destructive: the first part of his opus, the only part about which he has any clear ideas, is solely a 'negazione'. We learn very little about the superlatively intelligent being who would be required to practise Nitti's new morality. Moreover, Svevo specifically directs our attention to modern German philosophy, while Alfonso's surname is probably intended to put us in mind of Friedrich Nietzsche.

The action of *Una vita* takes place in the years around 1881,[14] thus coinciding in general terms with what Hollingdale has aptly described as Nietzsche's 'destructive period'[15] and, more specifically, with the publication in 1881 of *Morgenröte* (*Dawn: Thoughts on the Prejudices of Morality*). 'With this book I open my campaign against morality', Nietzsche later wrote of *Dawn*,[16] and the campaign is fought on several fronts, coinciding to a large extent with the three bases which Nitti seeks to undermine. The narrator's statement, in *Una vita*, that the basis of morality was 'un'impostazione necessaria per il vantaggio della collettività' is an echo of Nietzsche's scornful statement that 'only those actions which tend towards the common security and society's sense of security are to be accorded the predicate "good"!' (*Dawn*, 174). As for the notion that 'il bene individuale' was the source of morality, Nietzsche asked (rhetorically): 'Is the *origin of morality* not to be sought in such revoltingly petty conclusions as: "what harms *me* is *evil* (harmful in itself); what profits *me* is *good* (beneficent in itself)"?' (*Dawn*, 102). The religious basis of morality is destroyed by asserting the death of God: where once we looked towards the divine we now find, in the post-Darwinian world, only the ape. It follows from this that man's morality has evolved from man's animal state. In Nietzsche's philosophy the will to power is the only source of conduct, and if one links this with Nitti's megalomaniac day-dreams—of intellectual superiority, of social or sexual success, and of conveniently undefined forms of heroism—one can see that he is a provincial caricature of the superman. This is true even of his suicide, for what Nitti seeks in death is another means of asserting his imagined superiority, and an action which seems at first to have its roots in a quest for renunciation turns out to be a manifestation of the will to power. Indeed, how could it be otherwise? One of the problems which arise from the dualism inherent in Schopenhauer's thought is revealed when he requires his ascetic to overcome the will by means of the intellect; but how the

intellect can overcome will unless it, too, has will—which Schopenhauer denies—is not made clear. Nietzsche, on the other hand, avoids
this dualism by rejecting the notion of 'antithetical values'—'right'
and 'wrong', 'good' and 'bad'—and postulating instead a single
'scale of values' on which apparent opposites are in reality manifestations of the same will to power at different stages of sublimation.
One could appropriately say of *Una vita* what Thomas Mann wrote
of *Buddenbrooks*: 'These, indeed, were the thoughts of someone who
had read Nietzsche as well as Schopenhauer and carried the one
experience over into the other, setting up the most extraordinary
mixture between them'.[17]

Like *Una vita*, *Buddenbrooks* is its author's first novel. It gives an
account of the decline over four generations of an initially prosperous
family in which business acumen gives way to artistic sensibility. The
background of business life is common to both novels, and essential
to their meaning, for as Thomas Buddenbrook remarks, 'Life is
harsh'; and business, 'with its ruthless unsentimentality, [is] an
epitome of life', in which 'all better, gentler, and kindlier sentiments
creep away and hide themselves before the one raw, naked, dominating instinct of self-preservation'.[18] Since these are the reflections of
Thomas Buddenbrook in self-doubting mood, one could equally well
substitute for 'self-preservation' either 'power' or 'conquest', for
when Thomas is in confident mood, 'the thirst for action, for power
and success, the longing to force fortune to her knees [springs] up
quick and passionate in his eyes' (197).

Thomas is not the first of the Buddenbrooks in whom one can
detect signs that the will is weakening. In his grandfather, old
Johann, the will reigns supreme, not undermined by self-conscious-
ness or lack of confidence, for the elderly Consul distrusts what he
scornfully calls '*idées*'. His son, young Johann, who fails to take
adequate precautions to check the credentials of the confidence-
trickster Grünlich and who ages prematurely, is the member of the
family in whom the will shows the first, almost imperceptible, signs
of losing its grip on life. In Thomas's son Hanno, on the other hand,
the will has no sway whatever, and Hanno dies young because at the
height of his illness he abstains from willing to live. The account of
his death may be unconvincing from a medical point of view, but it
is nevertheless a perfect exemplification of the Schopenhauerian
abstention from willing which leads to a voluntary death which is
not suicide and therefore represents a true escape from the ceaseless
turmoil of life.

A comparison of the deaths of Nitti and Hanno reveals how un-
Schopenhauerian is the former's.

But if Hanno is the most Schopenhauerian character in Mann's

novel, Thomas is the complex character in whom the Schopenhauerian and the Nietzschean concepts of resignation and the will
clash. At an early age Thomas shows signs of a certain 'nervousness'
which bodes ill for his future: then, at the peak of his career—a
Senator, the owner of a sumptuous new house—he loses his 'firm
grip' on events, and at the age of forty-three he sees himself as 'an old,
worn-out man' (361), feeling 'revulsion and disgust at the hateful
and shameless harshness of life' (364). His youthful 'thirst for action,
for power and success' has disappeared, and it is while he is searching
vainly for something to replace it and give meaning to his life that he
chances to read part of *The World as Will and Representation* and is
deeply moved by the chapter on death and its relation to our personal immortality, which is one of the Supplements to the fourth
book and, as such, intended by Schopenhauer to be referred to only
at a second reading of the work as a whole. Thomas does not read
the volume in its entirety; still less does he understand it all, and
there is no indication that he ever refers to that chapter in the main
body of the work to which he reads the supplement: for there he
would have been reminded, in the final paragraph, of the need to
read the whole if he is to comprehend the separate sections (I, 285–6).
Consequently Thomas's subsequent reaction to what he reads is the
opposite of that which Schopenhauer had intended, for he welcomes
death as a release from the body, 'this heavy, hateful encumbrance,
which *prevented him from being something other and better*' (506). Just so
Alfonso had felt the need to 'distruggere quell'organismo che non
conosceva la pace'. Both men, blinded by the veil of Maya, draw
from their self-examination very un-Schopenhauerian conclusions
which then shade off into Nietzschean attitudes, for just as Nitti had
hoped in death to become 'superiore', so Thomas hopes to live on in
'all those who have ever, do ever, or ever shall say "I"—*especially,
however, in all those who say it most fully, potently, and gladly*' (507).
Thomas is even more explicitly Nietzschean at this point than his
Italian predecessor, who could still convince himself that he was
on the way to renunciation, but it is clear that both novelists are
setting up similar 'extraordinary mixtures' between the two philosophers.

In Nitti's case, the illusion is one which he dies with, and which
dies with him, for Svevo's novel ends with the impersonal letter from
the bank to his guardian which contains the bleak statement that
the reasons for his suicide are completely unknown. In the case of
Thomas Buddenbrook, the mood provoked by his reading does not
last; the Nietzschean flame flares up for the last time, then dies, and,
with his will exhausted of all energy, Thomas sinks into death with
only the dubious consolations of a religion which his conduct in life

has constantly belied. In Svevian terms, Thomas is a 'senile' character—not only in the sense that physically he ages prematurely, but
that psychologically he *feels* older than he is and he oscillates in his
latter years between ineffectual introspection and equally ineffectual
attempts to assert himself in action. And, like Nitti, he finds the
results of action distasteful.

What led two novelists, in many ways so different, to treat their
themes in such similar ways? Both set their plots in the middle-class
society of the flourishing sea-ports in which they lived, the banking
world of Trieste and the merchant society of Lübeck. Both were led
by temperament and culture to develop a penchant for irony; and,
more important, both had read the same philosophers and responded
in the same way to the possibilities for irony which they saw in their
reading. Schopenhauer repeatedly insisted on the need to read his
works in their entirety: Nitti knows at most only part of *Parerga et
Paralipomena*, and Thomas Buddenbrook reads only part of *The World
as Will and Representation*. A number of factors could have suggested
linking Schopenhauer and Nietzsche. The idea that the world sub-
sists on contradictions lies at the root of Hegelian dialectics, but the
more immediate sources of inspiration for the juxtaposition of two
such different philosophies are, firstly, that although Nietzsche later
rejected Schopenhauerianism as a symptom of Western man's
decadence he was in his youth strongly influenced by him, and in his
Rückblick auf meine zwei Leipziger Jahre he describes his reading of
The World as Will and Representation when in a mood of dejection in
terms which make it clear that the encounter was a decisive factor
in his intellectual development. Secondly, Nietzsche used the same
term as Schopenhauer—will—to describe a very different phenomenon. Finally, there is Nietzsche's paradoxical statement in the first
part of *Beyond Good and Evil*, entitled *On the prejudices of philosophers*,
that something can be born out of its opposite.[19] In his essay on
Schopenhauer, written in 1936, Mann takes up the hint and comments on the artist's capacity for creatively misreading his sources:

> But my point is the naïve misuse of a philosophy which precisely artists
> are 'guilty' of, and which I had in mind when I said that a philosophy is
> often influential less through its morality or its theory of knowledge, the
> intellectual bloom of its vitality, than by this vitality itself, its essential
> and personal character—more, in short, through its passion than its
> wisdom. In this way artists often become 'betrayers' of a philosophy, and
> thus was Schopenhauer 'understood' by Wagner, when he put his plays
> as it were under the protection of Schopenhauer's metaphysics...So
> artists go about to deal with philosophy—they 'understand' it in their own
> way, an emotional way...[20]

Making due allowance for the differences between Svevo's defensive, self-deprecating irony, and Mann's more solemn public manner, it is possible to see that Svevo had made a similar point about his creative misreading of Freud in the essay *Soggiorno londinese* of 1926.

Il destino vuole che l'artista venga ispirato dal filosofo ch'egli non perfettamente intende, e che il filosofo non intenda lo stesso artista ch'egli ispirò. È nota l'avventura del Wagner con lo Schopenhauer... Questo rapporto intimo fra filosofo e artista, rapporto che somiglia al matrimonio legale perché non s'intendono fra di loro proprio come il marito e la moglie e tuttavia come il marito e la moglie producono dei bellissimi figliuoli conquista all'artista un rinnovamento...' (III, 687).

No comparison of *Una vita* and *Buddenbrooks* should conceal that they are very different novels in spite of their similarities. Svevo, by means of plot and subplots, seeks to show that the struggle for life conditions human behaviour at all levels of society, and he is concerned with one central character only. Mann covers a more limited section of society—the Lübeck equivalent of the Mallers—but he describes their decline through four generations and sets off their decline by the rise of the acquisitive Hagenströms. He also discusses the relationship between decadence and the artistic temperament, exploiting for the purposes of this theme the sexual overtones of Wagnerian music, which Svevo is able to do only in *Senilità* (1898), in the episode in which Amalia lives out part of her fantasy-life while watching the first performance in Trieste of *Die Walküre*, identifying herself with Sieglinde. Nor has it been suggested that Svevo influenced Mann even though much of *Buddenbrooks* was written in Italy.

It is however possible that *Buddenbrooks* influenced Svevo. He certainly read the novel,[21] and I think that there were two aspects of *Buddenbrooks* which would have made a particularly strong impression on him in the light of his preoccupations when writing *La coscienza di Zeno*. The first of these is Mann's treatment of the theme of business morality (with the related theme of marriage as a financial contract); the second is the figure of Christian Buddenbrook.

Johann Buddenbrook sacrifices his daughter's happiness by manoeuvering her into marrying Grünlich, whom he deceives with regard to the traditional family dowry. He then appeals to Tony's loyalty to the family to persuade her to leave her bankrupt husband. Natural emotions are sacrificed to a morality which turns out to be no more than loyalty to the financial interests of the firm. The difference in these circles between morality and immorality is merely the difference between being successful and being detected, as the Weinschenk affair makes clear. Thomas comments:

The boundary line between usance and actual dishonesty is extremely
hard to draw. Well—if Weinschenk has done anything he shouldn't, he
has probably done no more than a good many of his colleagues who will
not get caught (406).

And when Kassbaum falsifies bills of exchange, 'No-one felt outraged
over the dishonesty: they spoke of it as an act of folly, laughed a bit
and shrugged their shoulders' (514). All this takes place against a
background of regular church-going, and the contrast between
gospel precept and the real conduct of life is heavily ironic.

Christian Buddenbrook, who suffers from a variety of psychosomatic illnesses and who tries unsuccessfully to be a business man,
was bound to appeal to Svevo's imagination, especially in the light
of his reading of Freud. The 'vague agony' in Christian's left side,
where 'all the nerves are too short' remind one irresistibly of one of
Zeno's symptoms, 'un formicolìo dei nervi come se avessero minac-
ciato di rattrappirsi' (II, ii, 710). Christian, like Zeno, is an able and
witty, not to say compulsive, raconteur, and the truth of the tales
they tell, and their appropriateness to the occasions on which they
tell them, is a matter of some doubt.[22] Thomas Buddenbrook's
explanation, that 'Christian busies himself too much with himself,
with what goes on in his own inside' (204), is too simple to be true.
But it is no more, and no less, simplistic than Zeno's claim that 'è
meno malato chi ha poco tempo per esserlo' (II, ii, 733). The
'unhealthy' Christian outlives his 'healthy' brother, just as Zeno outlives Guido Speier, Copler and Malfenti, albeit in very different
circumstances, for the last we hear of Christian is that he is confined
in an asylum while his wife continues her whoring, while Zeno is
hard at work, buying and selling whatever he can lay his hands on
in war-stricken Trieste.

Yet even this dénouement may owe something to Mann, for in
Christian Mann brings together in a most suggestive and disturbing
way the themes of psychosomatic illness, work, and morality. It is
Christian who remarks—in what he claims is a jest—that 'when one
really considers it, every business man is a swindler' (243), and the
sense of outrage which Thomas experiences when he hears of the
incident may be due in part to a feeling that the observation is not
entirely false: later, at all events, he recalls the remark and realizes
that in substance it was not so very different from what he had himself said to Tony when they discussed the Pöppenrade grain deal.
Svevo makes the same point, in more oblique fashion, when at the
end of *La coscienza di Zeno* the looting which marks Italy's entry into
the war prefigures and comments ironically on Zeno's activities as a
profiteer.

Christian, like Zeno, wants to become a business man; and when he joins the family firm and for a while experiences the effect of daily routine he claims that he has 'never felt so good before' (207). But he is not able to continue for long in permanent employment and soon reverts to his restless ways. As he does so, his condition deteriorates until—in the course, significantly enough, of a dispute about the division between them of their mother's property—the enraged Thomas cries:

> Don't you realize, you fool...that all these horrors are the consequence and effect of your vices, your idleness and your self-tormenting? Go to work! Stop petting your condition and talking about it! (446-7).

In this quarrel, and in Christian's attempts to find work, two different but related ideas are involved. The view that work could be some sort of cure for a sickness of the spirit had already found expression in *Werther*, in *Faust*, and in *Anna Karenina*, and this is at first sight what both brothers seem to have in mind. But since work provides Christian—like Nitti before him—only with temporary relief— and I have argued elsewhere that this is also the case with Zeno[23]— one must look to the later, 'decadent' version of the work-cure myth, which is that work is merely one of those drugs which enable man temporarily to forget the wretchedness of his plight. Mann was strongly influenced by the Goncourt brothers—his greatest literary debt in *Buddenbrooks* is to *Renée Mauperin*—and Svevo in 1887 reviewed the first volume of their memoirs.[24] He could hardly have failed to be impressed by the aphorism: 'L'horreur de l'homme pour la réalité lui a fait trouver ces trois échappatoires: l'ivresse, l'amour, le travail'.[25]

But if Christian and Zeno are both driven to attempt to work by a desire to forget their complaints, it is something very different that makes Thomas work and urge his brother to do likewise. Thomas admits to Christian:

> I have become what I am because I did not want to become what you are. If I have inwardly shrunk from you, it has been because I needed to guard myself—your being and your existence are a danger to me—that is the truth (447-8).

Thomas, by working, conforms to a socially acceptable norm and conceals the inner emptiness which threatens his life and which he can see revealed in Christian. Once again Mann is giving fictional form to an idea from Nietzsche's *Dawn:* 'In the glorification of "work"...I see a fear of everything individual. For at the sight of work—that is to say, severe toil from morning till night—we have the feeling that it is the best of police...that it holds everyone in check' (173, trans. Kennedy). This is also part of Nitti's attack on conventional morality. Work is the reductive discipline through which Thomas seeks to give meaning to his life and to which he wishes to subject Christian in order to make of him a pillar of society, while Christian represents essentially undirected individuality from which Thomas shrinks.

In the final chapter of *La coscienza di Zeno*, Svevo is also concerned to expose what he considers to be the falsity of the view of work as a moral discipline. Work ultimately fails to hold in check Thomas Buddenbrook's inner dissolution; and it fails also to control Zeno's individuality. If society is at war with itself, and if ruthless commerce is an epitome of society, then it follows that work, far from being a police force, is no more than the means by which individuals give fullest expression to their aggressive impulses (in Darwinian terms) or to the will to power (in Nietzschean terms). Zeno at work is expressing his will to power, and this is an important source of his new-found 'health'. Again, an aphorism from Nietzsche's *Dawn* makes the point: '*Field-dispensary of the soul.* What is the strongest remedy? Victory' (571). How easily the imagery of battle and victory springs to Zeno's mind at crucial points of the novel.

It is however at those points at which Svevo seems closest to Nietzsche that he is in reality farthest from him. In *La coscienza di Zeno*, and in the short stories which precede it, Svevo is concerned to demonstrate the will's capacity for destruction. Zeno is a war profiteer who takes advantage of a general catastrophe to prey upon society. It is not a sufficient answer to say that Nietzsche, too, was aware of the more brutish forms which the will to power could take. Nor did he *advocate* the will to power; he merely argued that it *was* the driving force behind all animate life forms. But his abandonment of traditional concepts of right and wrong made it impossible for him in the last analysis to *condemn* the lower forms in which the will to power expressed itself, although he did advocate that it should express itself in 'more spiritual' forms. Svevo constantly strives to show, however, that human nature is such that even in the apparently weak and maladjusted the will, undirected by morality, is destructive, and his condemnation of Zeno is based on moral grounds. He makes the point by once again juxtaposing the philosophies of Schopenhauer and Nietzsche.

Schopenhauer questioned the basis of morality by maintaining that 'right' was a negative concept and 'wrong' a positive one, in that wrong consisted in the extension of 'the affirmation of the will that appears in [one's] own body so far that it becomes the denial of the will that appears in the bodies of others' (I, 339). Right therefore consists merely in defending the extent of one's own will from invasion. Wrong is the invasion of another's area of freedom. It is thus not wrong, in Schopenhauerian terms, to refuse to help a man in dire distress, even calmly to contemplate his death from starvation—although even Schopenhauer has to admit that such a course would be 'cruel and diabolical'. Schopenhauer seems to be aware of the contradiction inherent in this position, for he goes on:

> It can, however, be said with complete certainty that whoever is capable of carrying uncharitableness and hardness to such lengths, will quite certainly commit any wrong the moment his desires demand it and no compulsion prevents it.

In these terms, Zeno Cosini commits no wrong against Guido Speier, whom he hates. He does not cause his ruin, bankruptcy and suicide; he merely refrains from helping him, by absenting himself at crucial moments and by not checking the firm's correspondence. Guido's incompetence does the rest, and Zeno, by leaving him free to ruin himself unaided, achieves the end he secretly desires. Having thus revealed himself to be cruel and inhuman, he commits positive wrong as soon as a suitable opportunity presents itself—firstly, after Guido's death, when by recouping the firm's losses he asserts his superiority over the dead man and ensures that he died, as Ada perceptively observes, 'proprio per una cosa che non ne valeva la pena' (II, ii, 922), and then in his profiteering activities, in which the will to power rampages unchecked. The implication of this is that Svevo is passing a moral judgement on the way in which the will to power expresses itself; here, as always in Svevo, there is the sense of an alternative, ethically more desirable, social order, and in the person of Zeno Cosini he rejects the individualistic morality which Nietzsche asserted and which had in the early decades of this century become, albeit often in debased form, such an important element in European culture.

University of Leeds BRIAN MOLONEY

NOTES

1. A. Schopenhauer, *The World as Will and Representation*, translated by E. F. J. Payne, New York, 1966, 2 vols. II, 461—henceforward referred to by volume and page number only.
2. L. R. Furst, 'Italo Svevo's *La coscienza di Zeno* and Thomas Mann's *Der Zauberberg*', *Contemporary Literature*, IX (1968), 4, 492–506.

3. G. Cattaneo, 'Svevo e la psicanalasi', *Belfagor*, XIV (1959), 4, 454–60, reprinted in *Esperienze intellettuali del primo Novecento*, Milan, 1968, pp. 119–137. Following Cattaneo, S. Maxia (*Lettura di Italo Svevo*, Padova, 1971, p. 45 n. 59) briefly compares Nitti's renunciation syndrome to 'la vicenda di Thomas, il protagonista dei *Buddenbrooks* . . .', but does not follow the point up.

4. E.g., P. N. Furbank, *Italo Svevo, the Man and the Writer*, London, 1966, p. 159. (N.B. Furbank refers to the version of Schopenhauer by Haldane and Kemp, whose use of *idea* to translate *Vorstellung* has inappropriate neo-Platonic overtones.)

5. For an analysis of human relationships in *Una vita* in terms of 'lotta', see B. Moloney, *Italo Svevo. A Critical Introduction*, Edinburgh, 1974, pp. 33–35.

6. I. Svevo, *Opera Omnia*, 4 vols. Milan, 1966–69, II, i, 294—henceforward referred to by volume and page number only.

7. i.e., the will.

8. A. Bouissy, 'Les fondements idéologiques de l'oeuvre d'Italo Svevo', *Revue des Études Italiannes*, XII (1966), iii, 209–45; 350–73; XIII (1967), i, 23–50; p. 212.

9. There is little evidence in the text for the view that Alfonso 'dispone di una buona cultura' (M. Ricciardi, 'Svevo, *Una vita*: sperimentazione del reale e fruizione onirica', *Sigma*, 20 (1968), pp. 21–41, p. 130.

10. A. Schopenhauer, *Essays and Aphorisms*. Selected and translated by R. J. Hollingdale (Penguin Classics ed.), 1970, p. 79.

11. For a good account of 'social Darwinism', see J. W. Burrow, *Evolution and Society. A Study in Victorian Social Theory*, Cambridge, 1966.

12. The exclusively biological basis of Macario's philosophy is revealed by his description of the brain as 'quantità da negligersi' and 'un essere inutile' (II, i, 207). In the essay *Del sentimento in arte* (1887) Svevo wrote of 'questo parassita dell'organismo, come chiamò Tiedemann il cervello' (III, 676). The reference, echoed in the novel, is to the studies in comparative anatomy of Friedrich Tiedemann, *Anatomie und Bildungsgeschichte des Gehirns im Foetus des Menschen nebst einer vergleichenden Darstellung des Hirnbaues in den Tieren*, Nürnberg, 1816. It is however possible that Svevo knew of Tiedemann's work only at second hand through his reading of *The World as Will and Representation*.

13. Cf. S. Maxia, *op. cit.*, p. 42.

14. The action is datable by reference to Annetta's projected visit to Paris, at which she will see the first performance of Sardou's *Odette* (II, i, 157).

15. R. J. Hollindale, *Nietzsche. The Man and his Philosophy*, London, 1966, p. 160.

16. Quoted by Hollindale, *op. cit.* p. 160. Nietzsche's aphorisms, referred to by number, are quoted where possible in Hollindale's version, otherwise in that of J. M. Kennedy (London, 1911).

17. Cf. T. Mann, *Essays of Three Decades*, New York, 1971, p. 396.

18. T. Mann, *Buddenbrooks. The Decline of a Family*. Translated . . . by H. T. Lowe-Porter (Penguin Classics ed.), 1971, p. 363—henceforward referred to by page number only.

19. F. Nietzsche, *Beyond Good and Evil*, translated . . . by R. J. Hollindale (Penguin Classics ed.), pp. 15–16.

20. T. Mann, *Essays of Three Decades cit.*, pp. 396–7.

21. I am indebted for this information to Svevo's daughter, Signora L. Svevo Fonda Savio, who catalogued her father's library.

22. Zeno's inability to tell any story twice in the same way is an important difference between them, however, which may derive from Gogol's Thoma Grigorovitch in the tale *St. John's Eve*.

23. Cf. B. Moloney, *Italo Svevo*, pp. 80–88.

24. For the text of this review, not in the *Opera Omnia* ed., see B. Moloney, 'Italo Svevo e *L'Indipendente*: sei articoli sconosciuti', *Lettere italiane*, XXV (1973), 4, pp. 536–556.

25. *Journal des Goncourt*, vol. I, Paris, 1912, 366 (not the best critical ed., but it reprints the abridged version of the text which Svevo knew).

Pound and Cavalcanti

Unlike *Homage to Sextus Propertius* (1917), which, as he kept insisting in the face of certain academic criticism,[1] is not a translation, Pound's translations of Cavalcanti are as nearly literally and textually faithful as anything he ever attempted. These translations as well as his observations on W. H. D. Rouse's translation of *Odyssey* and Laurence Binyon's translation of *Inferno* and *Purgatorio*—Pound himself never translated from the *Commedia*[2]—give us a clear notion as well as a concrete demonstration of what Pound thought a verse translation of Medieval poetry in modern English should be. He held translation in very high esteem—some of the best books in English are translation, he would say—and he regarded it as both an art and a critical function. Before examining Pound's views on Cavalcanti as well as his translations of him let us consider some of his ideas regarding the art and nature of translation—ideas that have a close bearing on his treatment of Cavalcanti.

'That part of your poetry', he tells us in *A Retrospect*, 'which strikes upon the imaginative *eye* of the reader will lose nothing by translation into a foreign tongue; that which appeals to the ear can reach only those who take it in the original'.[3] Thus while examining Browning's translation of Aeschylus's *Agamemnon* Pound lays his finger on Browning's weakness as a translator which lies

> where it essentially lay in all of his expression, it rests in the term 'ideas'. 'Thought' as Browning understood it—'ideas' as the term is current, are poor two-dimensional stuff, a scant, scratch covering. 'Damn ideas, anyhow'. An idea is only an imperfect induction from fact.[4]

Another thing that Browning did not realize is 'the patent fact that inversions of sentence order in an uninflected language like English are not, simply and utterly *are not* any sort of equivalent for inversions and perturbations of order in a language inflected as Greek and Latin are inflected'. As to the element of obscurity inherent in the text translated, and the way it is to be tackled, Pound offers some sensible advice which he himself almost invariably followed: 'Obscurities *not inherent in* the matter, obscurities due not to the thing but to the wording, are a botch, and are *not* worth preserving in a translation. The work lives not by them but despite them'.[5] In this respect D. G. Rossetti was sounder than Browning because he believed that the only thing worth bringing out is the beauty of the original; and by beauty Rossetti meant more or less what we mean by the 'emotional intensity' of the original.

Equally sound and fruitful is Pound's advice to W. H. D. Rouse, the English translator of Homer's *Odyssey*. 'I don't see', he observes,

> that one *translates* by leaving in unnecessary words; that is, words not necessary to the meaning of the *whole* passage. An author uses a certain number of *blank* words for the timing, the movement, etc., to make his work sound like natural speech. I believe one should check up all that verbiage as say 4% *blanks*, to be used where and when wanted in the translation, but perhaps never, or at any rate not usually where the original author has used them...tain't what a man sez, but wot he *means* that the traducer has got to bring over. The *implication* of the word.

A translator, therefore, while aiming at both real speech in the English version and fidelity to the original, both meaning and atmosphere, need not keep verbal literality for phrases 'which sing and run naturally in the original'.[6]

Similarly, in his comments on Binyon's translation of *Inferno*—which he reviewed in *The Criterion* (April 1934)—and of *Purgatorio* Pound touches upon certain fundamental issues regarding the diction and style of modern verse translation in English. He starts his review of Binyon's translation of *Inferno* by praising it as 'the most interesting English version of Dante that I have seen or expect to see', and this in spite of the fact that Binyon's 'sad youth...(was) poisoned in the cradle by the abominable dogbiscuit of Milton's rhetoric'. Another thing he notices in Binyon's translation is that he has carefully preserved all the faults of the original, whereas the 400 already existing translations of Dante carefully present the English reader 'with a set of faults alien to the original' which is of no possible use to the serious reader who wants to understand Dante. And yet Pound proposed to deal with Binyon's translation very severely. For although Binyon was, as he said, his elder in years, Pound claimed to be 'his senior in the struggle with early Italian verse' (which included not only his translations of Cavalcanti, but also of 'Prima canzone' of *Convivio*, the 'Cantico del Sole' of Saint Francis, the sonnets 'Vedut' ho la lucente stella diana' and 'Io vo del ver la mia donna lodare' of Guinizelli, a sonnet by Guido Orlandi, and a few fragments from the sonnets and canzoni by other poets of the *Dolce Stil Nuovo* school.) But while dealing severely with Binyon, he also pointed out characteristically that 'however drastically I hack at the present translation, I warn the rash novice that I can probably make a fool of any other critic who rushes in without similar preparation'.

Thus by virtue of his experience as a translator of medieval poetry, he could sympathise with Binyon's difficulty in translating Dante, the difficulty, that is, of deciding 'How you are to render work done with one set of criteria in a language *Now* subject to different criteria'. And although he was irritated by Binyon's inversions during the first 8 or 10 cantos, it nevertheless did not prevent him from being impressed by his 'courageous statement, and a sound one', namely that 'melodious smoothness is not the characteristic of Dante's verse', by his having got rid of 'pseudo-magniloquence, of puffed words', and by his 'having shown (let us hope once and for all) how little Dante needs NOTES'. It is only when Pound comes to the 'Minutia' of the translation, that we find him critical—critical, for instance, of Binyon's translating 'gaetta' into 'freckled' (Canto I), 'vermiglia' into 'crimson' (in the verse 'che balenò una luce vermiglia', Canto III) or 'D'ogni malizia, ch'odio in cielo acquista' (Canto XI) into 'Of all malice that finds in heaven a foe'. But on the whole, Pound's review was intelligently and sensitively appreciative and it concluded with the observation that the lines in Binyon's translation 'move to their end, that is, draw along the eye of the reader, instead of cradling him in a hammock. The main import is not sacrified to detail. Simple as this appears in bald statement, it takes time to learn how to achieve it'.[7] Moreover, Pound encouraged Binyon to go ahead and translate the other two Canticles as well. And when Binyon submitted his translation of *Purgatorio*, the general tenor of Pound's criticism, apart from the question of specific details, was summed up in his advice that Binyon should read his own translation himself and 'kick out every sentence that isn't as Jane Austen would have written in prose'.

Thus what Pound praises or criticises in Rouse's or Binyon's translations is something emerging from and at the same time dictated by his experience as a translator—and above all as a translator of Cavalcanti. For Pound's interest in medieval poetry in general and in that of Dante, Cavalcanti and the *Dolce Stil Nuovo* school in particular had started as early as—if not earlier than—his career as a poet. In fact in his earliest poetry—from *A lume spento* (1908) onwards—traces of his involvement in the poetry of that age manifested themselves in more than one form; i.e. as echoes, as imitations or translations, and as models on which Pound based his own metrical experiments. It was not for nothing, therefore, that in 'How to Read' (*Polite Essays*) Pound, while listing the kinds and degrees of writers, should have included Cavalcanti, together with Arnaut Daniel, in the category of 'the inventors'—discoverers, that, is, of 'a particular process or of more than one mode and process', and poets who not only introduce certain methods of rhyming, but also 'certain finenesses of perception'. And for the same reason he ranks Cavalcanti as a master, but not a poet like Donne. And in his essay on Cavalcanti, he observes how

> When the late T. E. Hulme was trying to be a philosopher in that milieu, and fussing about Sorel and Bergson and getting them translated into English, I spoke to him one day of the difference between Guido's precise interpretative metaphor, and the Petrarchan fustian and ornament, pointing out that Guido thought in accurate terms; that the phrases correspond to definite sensations undergone. . . .
>
> Hulme took some time over it in silence, and then finally said: 'That is very interesting'; and after a pause: 'That is more interesting than anything anyone ever said to me. It is more interesting than anything I ever read in a book'.

In the same essay (published in *Make It New*, 1935, and now included in *Literary Essays*, with Pound's note: 'The essay as a whole must be dated 1910–1931') he makes the comparison between Cavalcanti and Petrarch. The difference between Guido and Petrarch, Pound observes,

> is not a mere difference in degree, it is a difference in kind.
> There are certain things Petrarch does not know, cannot know. I am not postulating him as 'to blame' for anything, or even finding analogy for his tone in post-Peruginian painting.
> Leave all question of any art save poetry. In that art the gulf between Petrarch's capacity and Guido's is the great gulf, not of degree, but of kind. In Guido the 'figure', the strong metamorphic or 'picturesque' expression is there with purpose to convey or to interpret a definite meaning. In Petrarch it is ornament, the prettiest ornament he could find, but not an irreplaceable ornament, or one that he couldn't have used just about as well somewhere else. In fact he very often does use it, and them, somewhere, and nearly everywhere, else, all over the place.

Pound considered Cavalcanti not merely superior to Petrarch, but, in some respects, superior even to Dante. For one thing he regarded him as more modern than Dante 'qui était diablement dans les idées reçues'; for another, he found that while Dante was willing 'to take on any sort of holy and orthodox furniture', Cavalcanti was 'eclectic', swallowing 'none of his authors whole'. Moreover, 'Dante himself never wrote more poignantly, or with greater intensity than Cavalcanti'. And when in his earliest critical formulation apropos of Cavalcanti (in 'Lingua Toscana', *The Spirit of Romance*, 1910) Pound characterises him as

> A spirit more imperious and less subtle than Dante, more passionate, less likely to give ear to sophistries; his literary relation to Dante is not unlike Marlowe's to Shakespeare, though such comparisons are always unsafe—

he later on, in 1929, retracted the expression 'less subtle', though he said, 'The rest of the sentence stands'.

Hence the medieval Italian poets—and Cavalcanti more than anyone else—

> brought into poetry something which had not been or not been in any so marked and developed degree in the poetry of the troubadours. It is still more important for anyone wishing to have well-balanced critical appreciation of poetry in general to understand that this quality, or this assertion of value, has not been in poetry since; and that the English 'philosophical' and other 'philosophical' poets have not produced a comparable Ersatz.[8]

Pound's critical appreciation of Cavalcanti's poetry constituted both a fascination and a challenge for him as a translator and as a poet. And this appreciation was partly based on his conviction that 'no psychologist of the emotions is more keen in his understanding, more precise in his expression'[9] than Cavalcanti. His poetry, like that of the other Tuscan poets, does not tend toward 'erotic sentimentality'; nor does it tend towards or is affected by what are popularly regarded as the two maladies of the medieval age— asceticism (asceticism that is anti-flesh and that is anti-intelligence) and fanaticism. Together with Dante, Cavalcanti represents what Pound calls the 'medieval clean line' as distinct from 'medieval niggle' and that 'radiant world' which we appear to have lost and where 'one thought cuts through another with clean edge, a world of moving energies "mezzo oscuro rade", "risplende in sè perpetuale effecto", magnetisms that take form, that are seen, or that border on the visible, the matter of Dante's *Paradiso*'.[10] After quoting his translation of Cavalcanti's Canzone 'Donna mi prega', Pound offers what he calls the 'Partial Explanation' of its meaning and nature. 'The less we know,' he says, 'the longer our explanations', and his own amounts to five pages. He calls Cavalcanti a 'natural philosopher' as distinguished from a 'moral philosopher'. This makes Cavalcanti much less safe, not so much because of what he says in the 'Canzone' as because of the familiarity he shows with what was regarded in his times as dangerous thinking—i.e. dangerous 'to the peace of the medieval mind, if immobility may be considered as "peace"'—namely, 'natural demonstration and the proof by experience or (?) experiment'; and going along with this or ensuing from this 'the freedom of thought, the contempt, or at least a moderated respect, for stupid authority'.

To a significant degree Pound's encounter with Cavalcanti was not so much an encounter between two congenial spirits, as an innate and passionate predisposition on the part of one—in this case Pound—towards the work, spirit and personality of the other based on a complex of affinities—literary, temperamental and intellectual. This, of course, doesn't mean that Pound saw in Cavalcanti's poetry —or foisted upon it—what was not there. In fact, any notion, concept or belief he ascribes to or deduces from it is examined in terms of the citable text. In other words, Pound does not so much theorise about or interpret the poem in terms of any *a priori* ideas or concepts which he applies to the text of the poem, as adduce those ideas and concepts from his critical-analytical exegesis of the text. Thus Cavalcanti's phrase 'non razionale ma che si sente' is interpreted in terms of Cavalcanti's—and implicitly also Pound's—opposition to 'the tyranny of the syllogism, blinding and obscurantist', and not the other way round. Similarly when Cavalcanti talks of 'naturale dimostramento', he is not, Pound observes, contradicting the 'rationes naturales', nor is he 'jamming down a dogma unsupported by nature', but enunciating 'a truth for elect recipients, not a truth universally spreadable or acceptable'. All this Cavalcanti does 'with the suavity of a song, with the neatness of scalpel-cut'. There is no 'open "atheism"' in Cavalcanti, nor any direct attack on any church dogma, but there is probably, 'a sense of briskness; I mean it would not have been comforting to lovers of quiet'. However, in spite of a complete precision of technique in the use of philosophic terms, Pound finds the poem, on the whole, very obscure, and full of certain enigmas which the celebrated commentators have done nothing to solve. Thus we are still faced with the same difficulties with which Dino del Garbo was faced in 1302 or Di Giunta in 1527.

Coming to the technical and metrical aspects of 'Donna mi prega', Pound again makes some penetrating comments which show that his knowledge of Provençal and Tuscan poetry may not have been that of an academic scholar[11] or a literary historian, but it was of a poet or, to use Eliot's phrase, 'a practitioner of verse' as well as of an original critic. And consequently his comments on Dante's as well as Cavalcanti's metrical and structural forms are inextricably linked with his sense of their poetry, so that these forms are not something to be detached from it, analysed and classified in the light of pre-existing or at any rate conventional prosodic norms and patterns. In the sections of his Cavalcanti essay entitled 'The Other Dimension' and 'Hendecasyllables' Pound observes how a canzone composed entirely in hendecasyllabics runs the danger 'of going heavy'. In 'Donne ch'avete' Dante, for instance, avoids this danger without using inner rhymes, whereas in 'Donna mi prega' Cavalcanti has to employ them. Moreover, inasmuch as there are three kinds of melopoeia, that is to say, poems made to speak, to chant and to sing, a just appreciation of 'Donna mi prega', and of Cavalcanti's poetry as well as of medieval Provençal and Tuscan poetry in general, depends on one's awareness of the fact that they were all meant to be sung. Hence 'relative estimates of value inside these periods must take count of the cantabile values'. Pound therefore prints the canzone (copying it from the manuscript 'Ld', Laurenziano 46–40, folio 32 verso, with a few errors corrected and accents added from the Giuntine edition) in such a way that 'its articulations strike the eye without need of a rhyme table'. While indicating the differences between the strophe as used in 'Donna mi prega'—a strophe that consists of four parts and the second lobe of which is equal to the first and the fourth lobe equal to the third—and the sonnet, Pound notes how the strophe reverses the proportions of the sonnet. Hence by virtue of its structural complexity alone the Canzone is a more difficult form to translate into English than the sonnet and this because it is 'in intention a *Capolavoro*, a consummation of métier', whereas by A.D. 1290 the sonnet 'is already ceasing to be lyric, it is already the epistle without a tune, it is in a state of becoming, and tends already to oratorical *pronunciamento*'. But the relative dearth of the canzone form in English is not because 'there aren't rhymes in English; or enough rhymes or even enough two-syllable rhymes, but that the English two-syllable rhymes are of the wrong timbre and weight. They have extra consonants at the end, as in *flowing* and *going*; or they go squashy; or they fluff up as in *snowy* and *goeth*. They are not *rime agute*; they do not offer readily the qualities and contrasts that Dante has discussed so ably in *De Eloquio*'. But it is not the presence or absence of certain rhymes in English, or the operating of one rhyme-aesthetic rather than another that can 'ever do as much damage to English verse as that done by Latinization, in Milton's time and before'. In Pound's own translation of Cavalcanti's canzone the departures from the original text—or what he calls 'the atrocities of my translation'—have for the most part been intentionally committed—committed with a view to 'driving the reader's perception further into the original than it would without them have penetrated'.

In another section 'The Vocabulary' Pound deals with the technical philosophical terms used by Cavalcanti in 'Donna mi prega' and quotes certain passages from such sources as Averroes and Avicenna (*Metaphysics Compendium*), Del Garbo's exegesis of the canzone and Albertus Magnus's *Sex principiis* in order to elucidate certain concepts, words and phrases. Along with these sources, Pound also quotes from Boccaccio's portrait of Cavalcanti as well as from old and modern critics, editors and commentators such as Del Garbo, Rivalta, Di Giunta, Michele Barbi and Luigi Valli.

Lastly in the section of the essay entitled 'Guido's Relations' Pound comes to discuss what led him to undertake his translations of Cavalcanti into English and what he felt not merely towards Cavalcanti's poetry as such, but also vis-à-vis D. G. Rossetti's translations of Cavalcanti. Recalling his experience eighteen years after having translated Cavalcanti, Pound says that at that time he 'did *not* see Guido at all'. It was not that his perception was 'obfuscated by Guido's Italian, difficult as it then was for me to read it'; it was obfuscated by the Victorian language, which left its sediment in his own 'available vocabulary'. He also knew that Rossetti had already translated most of the best sonnets by Cavalcanti. But the difference between him and Rossetti was that when the latter translated Cavalcanti, he had already forged his own language, whereas Pound hadn't done so in 1910, when he undertook the translation. 'I don't mean a language to use, but even a language a think in'. At the same time he was aware of the value of what his predecessors had achieved in terms of 'lingual inventions'—Keats 'out of Elizabethans, Swinburne out of a larger set of Elizabethans and a mixed bag (Greeks, *und so weiter*), Rossetti out of Sheets, Kelly, and Co, plus early Italians (written and painted); and so forth, including *King Wenceslas*, ballads and carols'. Besides he knew—and he came to see it more vividly in retrospect—that Rossetti 'had made better English poems than he was likely to make by (in intention) sticking closer to the direction of the original'. And yet there was something in Cavalcanti that escaped Rossetti or that was, at any rate, absent from his translations. Pound calls it 'A *robustezza*, a masculinity. I had a great enthusiasm (perfectly justified), I did not clearly see exterior demarcations—Euclid inside his cube, with no premonition of Cartesian axes'.

Thus in retrospect Pound himself realized the limitations of his Cavalcanti versions—versions which he found 'bogged in Dante Gabriel and in Algernon', because he had been influenced by these two poets in his early education and, when he translated Cavalcanti, had not yet outgrown that influence. 'It takes six or eight years to get educated in one's art, and another ten to get rid of that education'. And with critical acumen as well as hindsight he analyses what was wrong not only with his own translations but also with Rossetti's.

Where both Rossetti and I went off the rails was in taking an English sonnet as the equivalent for a sonnet in Italian. I don't mean in over-looking the mild difference in the rhyme scheme. The mistake is 'quite natural', very few mistakes are 'unnatural'. Rime looks very important. Take the rimes off a good sonnet, and there is a vacuum. And besides the movement of *some* Italian sonnets *is* very like that in some sonnets in English. The feminine rhyme goes by the board...again for obvious reasons. It had gone by the board, quite often, in Provençal. The French made an ecclesiastical law about using it 50/50.

As a bad analogy, imagine a Giotto or Simone Martini fresco, 'translated' into oils by 'Sir Joshua', or Sir Frederick Leighton. Something is lost, something is somewhat denatured.

Suppose, however, we have a Cimabue done in oil, not by Holbein, but by some contemporary of Holbein who can't paint as well as Cimabue.

In other words as a translator of early Italian poetry Pound was dogged from the very outset—although on a critical plane he may have realized it fully only well after he had done the translations—by the difficulty of being able to preserve its cantabile quality, with-out losing another quality—'its specific weight'. The difficulty is analysed by Pound in terms of the distinction between 'poetic lyricism, the emotional force of the verbal movement' and 'melopoeic lyricism, the letting the words flow on a melodic current, realized or not, realizable or not, if the line is supposed to be sung on a sequence of notes of different pitch'. Such a distinction constitutes the 'root difference between early Italian, "The philosophic school coming out of Bologna", and the Elizabethan lyric', between the Italian sonnets and the English sonnets. For the 'cogency' and the 'sobriety' of the early Italian sonnets, like those of Cavalcanti, is one thing, and their uninterrupted flow of syllables, their perfect melody, 'care-less of exactitude of idea' is another. By following or trying to repro-duce the latter, at the almost inevitable expense of the former, what one gets is much more typical of the English seventeenth century song-books than of Cavalcanti. Pound's principal difficulty in trans-lating Cavalcanti was not merely the lack of a language to use or even a language to think in at the time when he translated him, but it was also his realization that there was 'no question of giving Guido an English contemporary to himself', and that if one reached back to pre-Elizabethan English, 'of a period when the writers were still intent on clarity and explicitness, still preferring them to magnilo-quence and the thundering phrase', the result, so far as Pound himself was concerned, couldn't be any better than, say, his own trans-lation—or the 'bungling version of twenty years back', as he calls it —of Cavalcanti's sonnet 'Chi è questa che ven, ch'ogn'om la mira'.

His own judgement on this translation is unmitigatedly severe—and, if we compare it with D. G. Rossetti's version of the same, with its typically Victorian poeticality, as well as polish and smoothness of surface, one is inclined to think that it is perhaps too severe. First of all he charges himself with having taken a serious poem and turned it into 'a mere exercise in quaintness', thereby perpetrating a 'misrepresentation', not of the poem's antiquity, but 'of the proportionate feel of that antiquity, by which I mean that Guido's thirteenth-century language is to twentieth-century Italian sense much less archaic than any fourteenth-, fifteenth-, or early sixteenth-century English for us'.

Before we discuss Pound's translations and compare them with those of D. G. Rossetti, with a view to assessing the validity and implications of his own judgement regarding them, let us see what Pound set out to do. In his 'Introduction' (dated 15th November, 1910) to *Cavalcanti Poems* (1912, revised 1920, 1931) he refers to 'the poetry of a far-off time or place' and the sort of translation it re-quires—'a translation not only of word and of spirit, but of "accompaniment"', so that the modern audience 'must in some measure be made aware of the mental content of the older audience, and of what these orders drew from certain fashions of thought and speech'. And this is all the more imperative in the case of a poet like Cavalcanti in view of the fact that 'six centuries of derivative convention and loose usage have obscured the exact significances of such phrases as: "The death of the heart", and "The departure of the soul"'. For Cavalcanti, both as a poet and as a psychologist of the emotions, does not indulge in rhetoric; instead he always offers us

> a true description, whether it be of pain itself, or of the apathy that comes when the emotions and possibilities of emotion are exhausted, or of that stranger state when the feeling by its intensity surpasses our powers of bearing and we seem to stand aside and watch it surging across some thing or being with whom we are no longer identified.

In translating such a poet, Pound soon realized, one needed a special kind of rhythm and style. And the sort of rhythm and style one needed was in a way revelatory of the translator as much as of the poet translated. 'I believe', Pound observes:

> in an ultimate and absolute rhythm as I believe in an absolute symbol or metaphor. The perception of the intellect is given in the word, that of the emotions in the cadence. It is only, then, in perfect rhythm joined to the perfect word that the two-fold vision can be recorded. I would liken Guido's cadence to nothing less powerful than line in Blake's drawing.

Thus it was not so such that in his translations of Cavalcanti Pound wanted to 'call new beauties forth from ev'ry line'[12] as that he wanted to bring over the qualities of Cavalcanti's rhythm, not indeed line by line, but by embodying 'some trace of that power which implies the man'.

Of course Pound knew of Rossetti's translations of some nineteen sonnets, six ballate and four canzoni, which are to be found in *The Early Italian Poets* and which Pound regarded as being among the best things Cavalcanti wrote. In fact his awareness of Rossetti's translations—which he duly praised at least so long as he was himself to some extent under Rossetti's influence—was in a way an incentive for him not merely to translate what Rossetti had not translated, but to retranslate in his own way as many as 18 sonnets, ballate and canzoni already translated by Rossetti. While acknowledging frankly his debt to Rossetti—'In the matter of these translations and of my knowledge of Tuscan poetry, Rossetti is my father and my mother'— Pound significantly adds: 'but no one man can see everything at once'. One of his ambitions, therefore, was to see and to bring out in his translations what Rossetti had missed in his. For one thing Pound intended to avoid in his translations what he calls "Rossetti's purple plush and molasses trimmings';[13] for another he did not so much want to substitute 'verse in one language for verse in another' as Rossetti did, as to offer translations which are exegetic, while embodying at the same time 'the qualities of Guido's rhythm'.

Let us now consider the divergences between Rossetti's and Pound's translations of the same sonnet by Cavalcanti 'Chi è questa che vien, ch'ogni uom la mira' in terms of verbal and rhythmic divergences. The text accompanying Pound's translation reads:

Chi è questa che vien, ch'ogni uom la mira,
Che fa di clarità l'aer tremare,
E mena seco Amor, sì che parlare
Null'uom ne puote, ma ciascun sospira?

Ahi, Dio, che sembra quando gli occhi gira?
Dicalo Amor, ch'io nol saprei contare:
Cotanto d'umiltà donna mi pare,
Che ciascun'altra in vêr di lei chiam'ira.

Non si potria contar la sua piacenza,
Ch'a lei s'inchina ogni gentil virtute,
E la beltate per sua Dea la mostra.

Non fu sì alta già la mente nostra,
E non si è posta in noi tanta salute,
Che propriamente n'abbiam conoscenza.

Rossetti's translation is as follows:

> Who is she coming, whom all gaze upon,
>   Who makes the air all tremulous with light,
> And at whose side is Love himself? that none
>   Dare speak, but each man's sighs are infinite.
> Ah me! how she looks round from left to right,
>   Let Love discourse: I may not speak thereon.
>   Lady she seems of such high benison
> As makes all others graceless in men's sight.
> The honour which is hers cannot be said;
>   To whom are subject all things virtuous,
>   While all things beauteous own her deity.
> Ne'er was the mind of man so nobly led
>   Nor yet was such redemption granted us
>   That we should ever know her perfectly.

And this is Pound's version:

> Who is she that comes, makyng turn every man's eye
> And makyng the air to tremble with a bright clearenesse
> That leadeth with her Love, in such nearness
> No man may proffer of speech more than a sigh?
>
> Ah God, what she is like when her owne eye turneth, is
> Fit for Amor to speake, for I can not at all;
> Such is her modesty, I would call
> Every woman else but an useless uneasiness.
>
> No one could ever tell all of her pleasauntness
> In that every high noble vertu leaneth to herward,
> So Beauty sheweth her forth as her Godhede;
>
> Never before was our mind so high led,
> Nor have we so much of heal as will afford
> That our thought may take her immediate in its embrace.

One can see at once that Rossetti's version has what one might call a Victorian blend of poeticality and mellifluous roundedness about it that Pound's version, in spite of its cultivated air of verbal and orthographic quaintness and archaicism, noticeably lacks. Moreover, while working within the equally tightly knit rhyme-pattern of a sonnet as Rossetti, Pound's version has, on the whole, a greater degree of literal fidelity to Cavalcanti's text than Rossetti's. And if a translator's task is, as Rossetti himself observed in his preface to *Early Italian Poets*, 'one of self-denial', so that 'often would some cadence serve him but for his author's structure—some structure but for his author's cadence: often the beautiful turn of a stanza must be weakened to adopt some rhyme which will tally', it is obvious that both in the interest of the tallying rhymes and the even larger interest of the elegance, decorum and melodiousness of Victorian (but chiefly Tennysonian) poetic diction, Rossetti in fact sacrifices more vital and more crucial things in translating Cavalcanti than does Pound. Take for instance the first two lines in Pound's version. They convey the sense of dramatic challenge and surprise ('Chi è questa che vien'), the inescapableness of the consequence ('ch'ogni uom la mira'), and the even more lyrically charged consequence of the consequence, so to speak, ('Che fa di clarità l'aer tremare') much more convincingly than do the corresponding lines in Rossetti. And this is largely because there is a greater degree of precision and concreteness of detail in Pound than in Rossetti—precision and concreteness of detail which is all the more enhanced by the break in the first phrase ('she that comes' instead of 'she coming'), and by the suggested dual status of the word 'che' (in the first and the second lines) both as a relative pronoun and as a causal conjunction. In fact Rossetti's chief aim seems to have been that of achieving something poetical in itself—substituting 'verse in one language for verse in another', as Pound says, but verse written in that diction which was not so much characterised as dominated by the Keats/Tennyson line—Tennyson whose ambition had been 'to bring English as near the Italian as possible'. Hence what Leavis says of Rossetti's poetry is, to a large extent, also true of his translations. In his essay on Hopkins, Leavis observes how

> Rossetti's shamelessly cheap evocation of a romantic and bogus Platonism —an evocation in which 'significance' is vagueness, and profundity an uninhibited proffer of large drafts on a merely nominal account ('Life', 'love', 'death', 'terror', 'mystery', 'Beauty'—it is a bankrupt's lavishness) —exemplifies in a gross form the consequences of that separation of feeling ('soul'—the source of 'genuine poetry') from thinking which the Victorian tradition, in its 'poetical' use of language, carries with it.[14]

Pound, on the other hand, even though, while translating Cavalcanti, he was still under the influence of Rossetti and Swinburne—'bogged in Dante Gabriel and Algernon', as he says—showed a certain impatience with and an audacious departure from that influence in his best Cavalcanti translations. In certain lines and parts of his translations he even managed to tap those linguistic resources which were going to form the life-blood of his own poetry later on. In other words, in the face of Rossetti's Victorian (or Keatsian–Tennysonian) poeticalities and conventions, Pound now and then struck a note that was later to characterise modern poetry—and especially

Pound's own poetry. For instance, take this example. In the sonnet
to Guido Orlandi ('La bella donna, dove Amor si mostra') Cavalcanti says: 'Tragge lo cor de la persona vostra'. Rossetti translates
it as: 'Hath ta'en the living heart out of thy breast', but in Pound's
hands it becomes: 'Tuggeth the heart out of thy masking-shell'.
Again in Rossetti's rendering of the lines 'Mercè le chiesi, sol che di
baciare, / E d'abbracciare—fosse 'l suo volere' (from the Ballata 'In
un boschetto trovai pastorella') we get: 'And so, in her sweet favour's
name, I sued / That she should kiss there and embrace with me',
where the words 'there' and 'with me' seem to be dragged in solely
for the sake of padding and rhyming, thereby weakening the effect
of the original. Moreover, the element of banality that Gianfranco
Contini notes in the phrase 'di baciare e d'abbracciare' is accentuated in the phrase 'kiss there and embrace'. Pound's translation, on
the other hand, ('Favour I asked her, but for kisses only, / And then
I felt her pleasant arms upon me'), not only eliminates that element
of banality, but also offers us something strikingly vital and creative.
It is not merely that the poet gets from the shepherdess more than he
had asked for, but the more was both implicitly present in the less
and a natural extension of it—something in the nature of 'a consummation devoutly to be wished' and at the same time something
coming with the surprise and suddenness of an unexpected favour.
Similarly the last stanza, where the encounter between the poet and
the shepherdess reaches its climax with such dramatic inevitability,
and where the lyric force and impulsiveness of events is matched with
the brisk movement of the verse—

Per man mi prese d'amorosa voglia,
E disse che donato m'avea 'l core:
Menommi sotto una freschetta foglia,
Là dov'io vidi fior d'ogni colore;
E tanto vi sentio gioi' e dolzore,
Che Dio d'Amore mi parve ivi vedere—

becomes in Rossetti's version an effete business—something of a
ritual that is both uninspired and uninspiring.

She took my hand to her with amorous will,
And answer'd that she gave me all her heart,
And drew me where the leaf is fresh and still,
Where spring the wood-flowers in the shade apart.
And on that day, by Joy's enchanted art,
There Love in very presence seem'd to be.

Pound's translation, on the other hand—

She held to me with a dear willfulness
Saying her heart had gone into my bosom,
She drew me on to a cool leafy place
Where I gat sight of every coloured blossom,
And there I drank in so much summer sweetness
Meseemed Love's god connived at its completeness—

aptly preserves the sense of the decisive turn that the narration takes
and the irresistible sequence of events through which it moves to its
climax—the verbs 'prese', 'disse' and 'menommi' conferring an
energetic vitality on the movement, while the choice of such explicitly meaningful phrases as 'held to me', 'a dear willfulness' and
'gone into my bosom' confirms the purposefully active role the
shepherdess plays in bringing about the climax in response to the
favour asked of her in the preceding stanza. The complete departure from the original text that one notes in Pound's translation
of the last line—'Meseemed Love's god connived at its completeness'
(for 'Che Dio d'Amore mi parve ivi vedere')—is a characteristic
example of Pound's trying to convey, in addition to the qualities of
Cavalcanti's rhythm, also what he calls apropos of Sigismundo 'a
state of mind, of sensibility, of all-roundness and awareness'. For
having indicated the limitlessness of joy and sweetness that the
ecstasy of love brought in its train—having i.e. drunk in 'so much
summer sweetness'—Pound not only makes the god of love (or Love)
appear in person; but he also makes him connive at what has been
so fully and so completely realized, instead of being jealous of it.

Apart from the sonnets, madrigals, ballate and canzoni (18 in all)
that Rossetti and Pound both translated, Pound also translated other
'rime' by Cavalcanti. The total number of poems translated by him
amount to 35 sonnets, 14 ballate, 1 madrigal and 1 canzone ('Donna
mi prega'). In fact with the exception of ten ballate, sonnets, canzoni
and motets, ('Fresca rosa novella', 'Io non pensava che lo cor giammai',
'Noi sian le triste penne isbigottite', 'Gianni, quel Guido salute',
Bernardo Da Bologna's sonnet to Cavalcanti 'A quella amorosetta
foresella', 'Da più a uno face un sollegismo', Guido Orlandi's sonnet—
or 'sonnetto rinterzato'—to Cavalcanti 'S'avessi detto, amico, di
Maria', Orlandi's reply to Cavalcanti 'A suon di trombe, anzi che di
corno', 'Di vil matera mi conven parlare', and Orlandi's sonnet to
Cavalcanti 'Amico, i' saccio ben che sa' limare') Pound has translated all the poems by Cavalcanti included in Contini's *Poeti del
Duecento* (Tomo II, Ricciardi, Milan). Moreover, he has also translated two sonnets ('Morte gentil, rimedio de' cattivi' and 'Amore, e

Mona Lagia, e Guido, ed io'), two ballate ('Io vidi donne con la donna mia' and 'Sol per pietà ti prego, giovinezza') and a madrigal ('O cieco mondo, di lusinghe pieno') that are not to be found in *Poeti del Duecento*.

In doing this Pound rendered an immense service to Cavalcanti on the one hand and to the English reader as well as to English poetry on the other. For all the quaintness of phrasing and certain verbal and rhythmic infelicities as well as certain cases of mistranslation or distortion of the text (whether deliberate or otherwise), Pound's translations and Rossetti's are the only ones available in English. Pound's essay on Cavalcanti too is the only comment in English on Cavalcanti's art and craft that contains the sort of critical insight and acumen that only a critic of the calibre of Pound who was also a poet—a poet who 'altered expression'[15]—could have shown. And one has to remember that Pound translated Cavalcanti and wrote on him (in his preface to his translations as well as in *The Spirit of Romance*) when even in Italian there weren't many critical editions of or comments on Cavalcanti's work by a modern poet or critic. If one reads, say, Sapegno's essay on Cavalcanti (in *Il Trecento*, 1933) or Contini's (in *Poeti del Duecento*, 1960) one would be hard put to discover any important aspect of Cavalcanti's art and personality discussed there that Pound, in his own way (sometimes maybe even in a provocatively unscholarly way) hadn't already discussed, while turning his critical attention to those very sources—Dante, Boccaccio, Villani, Dino Compagni, on the one hand, and Dino Del Garbo, Egidio Colonna, Di Giunta, Rivalta, Vossler, Arnone, Carducci and Michele Barbi on the other, to which subsequent Italian critics and scholars have themselves had to resort.

But the greatest impact of Pound's encounter with Medieval and Provençal poetry in general and with Cavalcanti's poetry in particular is to be assessed in terms of the influence that that poetry exercised on Pound's own career and development as a poet and on his efforts 'to resuscitate the dead art of poetry'. But to deal with this would, of course, require a separate essay.

The Queen's University of Belfast   G. SINGH

NOTES

1.   For instance by W. R. Hale, Professor of Latin in Chicago and J. W. MacKail. Pound wrote to A. R. Orage (April 1919) explaining that in *Homage to Sextus Propertius*, 'there was never any question of translation, let alone literal translation. My job was to bring a

dead man to life, to present a living figure' and that 'mask of
erudition is precisely what I have not assumed; it is precisely what
I have thrown on the dust heap'. And apropos of MacKail's
criticism Pound writes to Felix E. Schelling (July 1922) that Mac-
Kail 'hasn't apparently *any* inkling of the *way* in which *Propertius* is
using Latin. Doesn't see that S.P. is tying blue ribbon in the tails
of Virgil and Horace, or that sometime after his first 'book' S.P.
ceased to be the dupe of magniloquence and began to touch words
somewhat as Laforgue did'. (The Letters of Ezra Pound, 1907–1941,
ed. by D. D. Paige, Faber, London, 1951).

2. The only verse translation Pound made from Dante was of 'Canzone
Prima' from *Convivio* (included in *The Spirit of Romance*, 1910).

3. *A Retrospect* (*Literary Essays of Ezra Pound*, ed. by T. S. Eliot, Faber,
London, 1954).

4. See 'Translators of Greek: Early Translators of Homer' (*Literary
Essays*).

5. Ibid.

6. See Pound's letters to W. H. D. Rouse (*The Letters of Ezra Pound*).

7. See Pound's review of Binyon's translation of *Inferno* (now in
Literary Essays) and his letters to Binyon discussing the latter's
translation of *Purgatorio* (in *The Letters of Ezra Pound*).

8. 'Cavalcanti', *Literary Essays*.

9. See Pound's Introduction (November 15, 1910) to his *Cavalcanti
Poems*. Cf. also what he wrote to Felix E. Schelling (July 9, 1922):
'Provençal "poetry romantic"—that doesn't so much interest me.
The fact that Arnaut and Guido were psychological, almost
physiological, diagnosticians does interest me' (*The Letters of Ezra
Pound*).

10. 'Cavalcanti', *Literary Essays*.

11. And yet it is Eliot, himself a learned poet, who calls Pound 'one
of the most learned of poets' and quotes the *Daily News* review of
Pound's *Canzoni* as saying that Pound 'seems to us rather a scholar
than a poet, and we should like to see him giving his unusual talent
more to direct translation from the Provençal' (*Ezra Pound: His
Metric and Poetry* originally published in 1917, New York; now in
To Criticize the Critic, Faber, London, 1964, pp. 166, 172). See
also Stuart Y. McDougal's book *Ezra Pound and the Troubadour
Tradition* (Princeton University Press, 1972) and my review of it in
Agenda (Vol. 11, No. 4—Vol. 12, No. 1, Winter-Spring, 1974)
London.

12. Alexander Pope, *An Essay on Criticism, III.*

13. In his essay on 'Early Translators of Homer', *Literary Essays*.

14. *The Common Pursuit* (London, 1952).

15. Sensibility, said Eliot, alters from generation to generation; but
expression is altered only by a man of genius.

LIST OF SUBSCRIBERS

R. N. L. Absalom, Esq.
Mrs G. Ackerley
Sir Robert Aitken
Miss R. Al-Sabah
Prof. G. Aquilecchia
C. M. Ardito, Esq.
P. G. Armour, Esq.
Dr R. Beccarelli
Dr A. Beghé
Prof. T. G. Bergin
Dr J. W. Binns
Prof. T. Bolelli
Dr R. R. Bolgar
Mrs C. Bowe-Soave
Dr P. Boyde
Prof. C. P. Brand
Mrs L. Bromhead
Miss R. I. Brookes
G. A. Bull, Esq.
Prof. E. Byrne Costigan
Dr C. S. Cairns
Dr P. Calì
Mrs A. Callaghan
Dr M. M. Callander
Dr G. Carsaniga
Prof. S. B. Chandler
Mrs E. A. Cheshire
Prof. F. Chiappelli
Sir Ashley Clarke,
  G.C.M.G., G.C.V.O.
Mrs K. E. Clay
Dr C. H. Clough
Miss K. Connell
Prof. B. Corrigan
R. H. Cosford, Esq.,
C. D. N. Costa, Esq.
Miss A. M. Cotten
Dr J. A. Cremona
Dr C. Dall'Olio
Mrs J. A. Davies
Prof. J. G. Davies

H. C. Davis, Esq.
Prof. R. H. C. Davis
Mrs C. De Joannon
Prof. A. P. d'Entrèves
Prof. C. Dionisotti
Prof. F. Donini
Prof. D. S. Duncan
Prof. P. W. Edwards
H. B. Evans, Esq.
E. P. Ewart, Esq.
Prof. C. F. Fahy
Dr R. G. Faithfull
Prof. L. Firpo
Prof. L. W. Forster
Prof. E. Forti
The Rev. K. Foster
Prof. E. B. Fryde
Dr K. J. Garlick
J. C. Gatiss Esq.
Prof. M. Gigante
Prof. M. P. Gilmore
P. Girolami, Esq.
Prof. V. R. Giustiniani
Mrs. E. M. Greenwood
D. B. Gregor, Esq.
Prof. T. G. Griffith
C. E. J. Griffiths, Esq.
Prof. J. R. Hale
C. G. Hardie, Esq.
Miss A. E. Harvey Wood
Mrs E. Haswell
J. M. Hatwell, Esq.
Prof. D. Hay
Mrs. D. M. Henwood
Prof. I. Hijmans-Tromp
Dr B. Hill
Prof. R. H. Hilton
Mrs A. M. Hitchens
P. R. Horne, Esq.
Dr K. W. Humphreys
Prof. F. J. Jones

Miss M. E. King
Prof. R. C. Knight
Mrs A. M. Kornfeld
J. R. Lamb, Esq.
Miss M. E. Le Maître
Mrs D. Lennie
Mrs A. L. Lepschy
Prof. U. Limentani
J. M. A. Lindon, Esq.
Prof. D. W. Lomax
Mrs C. S. Lonergan
J. Garcia Lora, Esq.
Miss J. A. Lorch
Prof. M. de P. Lorch
Miss A. L. Lucas
Mrs A. McConnell
Prof. P. M. J. McNair
Prof. G. H. McWilliam
Miss A. Makin
H. E. Signor R. Manzini, G.C.V.O.
Prof. F. Marenco
Prof. C. Margueron
Prof. H. Martin
L. V. M. Martin, Esq.
†Prof. M. F. M. Meiklejohn
Prof. L. Meneghello
Prof. H. A. D. Miles
Mrs B. M. Miller
J. M. Milner, Esq.
Dr B. Moloney
Prof. M. Montuori
G. A. P. Morby, Esq.
P. Morgan, Esq.
Dr E. Nissim
Prof. T. Nurmela
C. O'Cuilleanain, Esq.
T. O'Neill, Esq.
Marchesa Iris Origo
N. G. Painting, Esq.
Miss S. Pantazzi
Mrs M. M. Parry
Mr & Mrs J. M. Pask-Hughes
Miss J. E. Perry
Prof. O. Hood Phillips
Miss R. H. Pitt
J. M. Potter, Esq.
R. Price, Esq.
Dr M. Puccini
Prof. O. Ragusa
Mrs J. A. Rawson
D. G. Rees, Esq.
Dr L. J. Rees
Miss J. E. Reeve
T. E. Richards, Esq.

B. F. N. Richardson, Esq.
Dr P. T. Ricketts
Miss M. M. Rigby
Dr E. C. M. Roaf
J. B. W. Robertson, Esq., O.B.E.
Dr D. D. Ronco
P. L. Rossi, Esq.
Prof. N. Rubinstein
Prof. E. M. Ruffini
Miss J. M. Salmons
Prof. A. Scaglione
H. M. Scott, Esq.
J. A. Scott, Esq.
Prof. M. A. Screech
Miss R. I. K. Sennitt
Miss J. E. Seymour
Dr R. Shackleton
Prof. G. Singh
G. W. Slowey, Esq.
G. N. G. Smith, Esq., O.B.E.
H. W. Smith, Esq.
Prof. R. E. F. Smith
Prof. A. Soria Ortega
Dr K. Speight
Professor R. Spongano
Mrs N. Stainton
Miss V. Steiner
Dr S. Stewart
N. A. Stiles, Esq.
Dom Paul Stonham
F. S. Stych, Esq.
A. M. Sutton, Esq.
S. J. Tobin, Esq.
F. B. Turner, Esq.
Miss M. A. Tyler
Miss M. A. Valgimigli
Prof. A. Vallone
Conte Lodovico di Valmarana
Prof. P. Van Bever
F. C. Vegnuti, Esq.
Prof. V. Vettori
Prof. E. R. Vincent, C.B.E.
Dr F. St. Clair Vivian
S. T. Walker, Esq.
Prof. D. M. White
L. N. Wild, Esq.
Prof. J. J. Wilkes
A. Wilkin, Esq.
Prof. R. F. Willetts
Prof. E. M. Wilson
Prof. R. Wis
Dr J. R. Woodhouse
Mrs A. Young
Miss L. A. Zaina

Donations have been received from the following:

Miss R. Al-Sabah
Dr D. Bressan
Mrs L. Bromhead
G. A. Bull, Esq.
Miss M. N. Clements
Prof. H. A. Cronne
C. E. Ellis, Esq.
Prof. L. W. Forster
Dr N. C. Fortune
Dr K. J. Garlick
Prof. J. A. S. Grenville
Miss M. K. Grindrod
H. A. Howes, Esq.
Dr E. W. Ives

J. H. Keegan, Esq.
R. J. Knecht, Esq.
Prof. R. C. Knight
J. Garcia Lora, Esq.
Prof. B. Mayo
Marchesa Iris Origo
Prof. R. Pascal
B. D. Phillips, Esq.
Prof. B. R. Rees
I. A. Shapiro Esq.
P. Styles, Esq.
Prof. A. V. Subiotto
Prof. D. P. & Mrs. P. Waley
Dr D. Zancani

A donation was also received from a group of members of the Society for Italian Studies.

LIBRARIES AND INSTITUTIONS SUBSCRIBING

Associazione Internazionale per gli Studi di Lingua e Letteratura Italiana

Aarhus:	State and University Library
Aberystwyth:	University College Library
Amsterdam:	University Library
Bangor:	University College Library
Bari:	Facoltà di Lettere, Filosofia e Magistero
Bath:	University Library
Belfast:	The Queen's University Library
	Belfast Public Libraries
Bergamo:	Biblioteca Civica A. Mai
Berlin:	Freie Universität, Universitätsbibliothek Staatsbibliothek
	der Stiftung Preussischer Kulturbesitz
Berne:	University of Berne, Seminario Italiano
Birmingham:	University Library
	Shakespeare Institute Library
	University Italian Department Library
	University Italian Society
	Birmingham Public Libraries
	Dante Alighieri Society Library
Bologna:	British Council Library
Bonn:	University of Bonn, Romanisches Seminar
Brescia:	Università Cattolica Sacro Cuore
Brighton:	University of Sussex Library
Bristol:	University Library
Buffalo, N.Y.:	Buffalo and Erie County Library
Cambridge:	University Library
	Christ's College Library
	Girton College Library
	Modern and Medieval Languages Libraries
	St Catherine's College Library
	Trinity Hall Library
Cambridge, Mass.:	Harvard College Library
Canberra:	National Library of Australia
Canterbury:	University of Kent Library
Cardiff:	University College Library
Chapel Hill:	University of North Carolina Library
Cologne:	Petrarca-Institut
Copenhagen:	University of Copenhagen, Romansk Bibliotek
Dijon:	Faculté de Langues et Civilisations Étrangères
Downsview, Ontario:	York University Library
Dublin:	University College Library

Dundee:	University Library
Durham:	University Library
Durham, N. Carolina:	Duke University Library
Edmonton:	University of Alberta Library
Edinburgh:	University Library
	College of Commerce Library
	Edinburgh Central Library
Erlangen:	University Library
Eugene:	University of Oregon Library
Florence:	Accademia della Crusca
	Facoltà di Lettere, Istituto di Lingue e Letterature Neolatine
	Gonzaga-in-Florence Library
	Società Dantesca Italiana
Frankfurt/M:	Deutsch-Italienische Vereinigung
Freiburg:	University Library
Fribourg:	Bibliothéque Cantonale et Universitaire
Galway:	University College Library
Gardone Riviera:	Biblioteca Dannunziana, Vittoriale degli Italiani
Genoa:	Facoltà di Lettere, Istituto di Letteratura Italiana
	Facoltà di Magistero
Glasgow:	University Library
Göteburg:	University Library
Halifax, Nova Scotia:	Dalhousie University Library
Hamburg:	University of Hamburg, Romanisches Seminar
	Staats- und Universitätsbibliothek
Hanover, New Hampshire:	Dartmouth College, Baker Library
Hayward:	California State College, Hayward Library
Heidelberg:	University of Heidelberg, Romanisches Seminar
Helsinki:	University Library
Hull:	University of Hull, Brynmor Jones Library
Lausanne:	University of Lausanne, Faculté des Lettres
Lecce:	Istituto di Filologia Moderna—Filologia Romanza
Leeds:	University of Leeds, Brotherton Library
Leicester:	University Library
Liverpool:	City Library
	University Library
London:	Italian Institute
	University of London Library
	Bedford College Library
	Birkbeck College Library
	King's College Library
	Royal Holloway College Library
	University College Library
	Warburg Institute Library
	Westfield College Library
	The London Library
	Polytechnic of Central London Library
	Borough of Merton Libraries
	Westminster Central Reference Library
Lund:	University Library
Mainz:	University of Mainz, Romanisches Seminar
Malta:	Royal University of Malta Library

Manchester:	John Rylands University Library
Milan:	British Council Library
	The Oxford Institutes italiani
Milwaukee:	University of Wisconsin, Milwaukee Library
Naples:	British Council Library
	Università di Napoli, Istituto di Filologia Moderna
Nedlands:	University of Western Australia Library
New Brunswick N.J.:	Rutgers University Library
New York:	Columbia University Library
	New York Public Library
Normal:	Illinois State University, Milner Library
Northfield, Vermont:	Norwich University Library
Ottawa:	University Library
Oxford:	Taylor Institution Library
	Magdalen College Library
	St Hilda's College Library
	Somerville College Library
	Worcester College Library
	Oxford and Cambridge Schools Examination Board
Padua:	Biblioteca Universitaria
	Biblioteca del Museo Civico
Paris:	Bibliothèque Universitaire du Grand Palais
Parma:	Biblioteca Palatina
Philadelphia:	Temple University Library
	University of Pennsylvania Library
Pisa:	Istituto di Filologia Romanza
Pistoia:	Biblioteca Comunale Forteguerriana
Portsmouth:	Polytechnic Library
Prague:	Italian Institute
Princeton, N.J.:	University Library
Reading:	University Library
Rome:	Società Dante Alighieri
	British Council Library
	British School at Rome
	Biblioteca Apostolica Vaticana
	Facoltà di Magistero, Istituto di Lingua e Letteratura Italiana
	Biblioteca Nazionale Centrale Vittorio Emanuele II
Saarbrücken:	University Library
St Catharines, Ontario:	Brock University Library
Salford:	University Library
San Francisco:	California State University Library
Seattle:	University of Washington Libraries
Sheffield:	Sheffield City Libraries
	University Library
Siena:	Biblioteca Comunale degli Intronati
Southampton:	University Library
Stanford, California:	Stanford University Libraries
Stuttgart:	Italian Istitute Library
	Württembergische Landesbibliothek
Swansea:	University College Library
Sydney:	University of Sydney, Fisher Library
Trieste:	Università di Trieste, Istituto di Filologia Moderna
Turin:	Biblioteca Nazionale Universitaria

Uppsala:	University Library
Venice:	Fondazione Giorgio Cini
Verona:	Biblioteca Civica
Vicenza:	Biblioteca Civica Bertoliana
Victoria, B.C.:	McPherson Library, University of Victoria
Vienna:	University of Vienna, Institut für Romanische Philologie
Waterloo, Ontario:	St. Jerome's College Library
Warwick:	University Library
Washington, D.C.:	The Folger Shakespeare Library